Fodor's

MUNICH & BAVARIA

1st Edition

Where to Stay and Eat for All Budgets

Must-See Sights and Local Secrets

Ratings You Can Trust

Excerpted from Fodor's Germany and Fodor's Austria
Fodor's Travel Publications   New York, Toronto, London, Sydney, Auckland
www.fodors.com

FODOR'S MUNICH & BAVARIA

Editors: Linda Cabasin, Matthew Lombardi

Editorial Production: Evangelos Vasilakis
Editorial Contributors: Uli Ehrhardt, Christina Knight, Marton Radkai, Horst E. Reischenböck, Kevin White
Maps & Illustrations: David Lindroth, *cartographer;* Bob Blake and Rebecca Baer, *map editors*
Design: Fabrizio LaRocca, *creative director;* Guido Caroti, Siobhan O'Hare, *art directors;* Tina Malaney, Chie Ushio, Ann McBride, *designers;* Melanie Marin, *senior picture editor;* Moon Sun Kim, *cover designer*
Cover Photo (Antiquarium in the Residenzmuseum, Munich): Jens Wolf/dpa/Corbis
Production/Manufacturing: Angela L. McLean

1st Edition

ISBN 978–1–4000–1923–6

ISSN 1939–991X

SPECIAL SALES

This book is available at special discounts for bulk purchases for sales promotions or premiums. Special editions, including personalized covers, excerpts of existing books, and corporate imprints, can be created in large quantities for special needs. For more information, write to Special Markets/Premium Sales, 1745 Broadway, MD 6-2, New York, New York 10019, or e-mail specialmarkets@randomhouse.com.

AN IMPORTANT TIP & AN INVITATION

Although all prices, opening times, and other details in this book are based on information supplied to us at press time, changes occur all the time in the travel world, and Fodor's cannot accept responsibility for facts that become outdated or for inadvertent errors or omissions. So **always confirm information when it matters,** especially if you're making a detour to visit a specific place. Your experiences—positive and negative—matter to us. If we have missed or misstated something, **please write to us.** We follow up on all suggestions. Contact the Munich & Bavaria editor at editors@fodors.com or c/o Fodor's at 1745 Broadway, New York, NY 10019.

PRINTED IN THE UNITED STATES OF AMERICA

10 9 8 7 6 5 4 3 2 1

Be a Fodor's Correspondent

Your opinion matters. It matters to us. It matters to your fellow Fodor's travelers, too. And we'd like to hear it. In fact, we need to hear it.

When you share your experiences and opinions, you become an active member of the Fodor's community. That means we'll not only use your feedback to make our books better, but we'll publish your names and comments whenever possible. Throughout our guides, look for "Word of Mouth," excerpts of your unvarnished feedback.

Here's how you can help improve Fodor's for all of us.

Tell us when we're right. We rely on local writers to give you an insider's perspective. But our writers and staff editors—who are the best in the business—depend on you. Your positive feedback is a vote to renew our recommendations for the next edition.

Tell us when we're wrong. We're proud that we update most of our guides every year. But we're not perfect. Things change. Hotels cut services. Museums change hours. Charming cafés lose charm. If our writer didn't quite capture the essence of a place, tell us how you'd do it differently. If any of our descriptions are inaccurate or inadequate, we'll incorporate your changes in the next edition and will correct factual errors at fodors.com immediately.

Tell us what to include. You probably have had fantastic travel experiences that aren't yet in Fodor's. Why not share them with a community of like-minded travelers? Maybe you chanced upon a beach or bistro or B&B that you don't want to keep to yourself. Tell us why we should include it. And share your discoveries and experiences with everyone directly at fodors.com. Your input may lead us to add a new listing or highlight a place we cover with a "Highly Recommended" star or with our highest rating, "Fodor's Choice."

Give us your opinion instantly at our feedback center at www.fodors.com/feedback. You may also e-mail editors@fodors.com with the subject line "Munich & Bavaria Editor." Or send your nominations, comments, and complaints by mail to Munich & Bavaria Editor, Fodor's, 1745 Broadway, New York, NY 10019.

You and travelers like you are the heart of the Fodor's community. Make our community richer by sharing your experiences. Be a Fodor's correspondent.

Happy Traveling!

Tim Jarrell, Publisher

CONTENTS

ABOUT THIS BOOK

Our Ratings

Sometimes you find terrific travel experiences and sometimes they just find you. But usually the burden is on you to select the right combination of experiences. That's where our ratings come in.

As travelers we've all discovered a place so wonderful that its worthiness is obvious. And sometimes that place is so experiential that superlatives don't do it justice: you just have to be there to know. These sights, properties, and experiences get our highest rating, **Fodor's Choice,** indicated by orange stars throughout this book.

Black stars highlight sights and properties we deem **Highly Recommended,** places that our writers, editors, and readers praise again and again for consistency and excellence.

By default, there's another category: any place we include in this book is by definition worth your time, unless we say otherwise. And we will.

Disagree with any of our choices? Care to nominate a place or suggest that we rate one more highly? Visit our feedback center at www.fodors.com/feedback.

Budget Well

Hotel and restaurant price categories from ¢ to $$$$ are defined in the opening pages of each chapter. For attractions, we always give standard adult admission fees; reductions are usually available for children, students, and senior citizens. Want to pay with plastic? **AE, D, DC, MC, V** following restaurant and hotel listings indicate if American Express, Discover, Diners Club, MasterCard, and Visa are accepted.

Restaurants

Unless we state otherwise, restaurants are open for lunch and dinner daily. We mention dress only when there's a specific requirement and reservations only when they're essential or not accepted—it's always best to book ahead.

Hotels

Hotels have private bath, phone, TV, and air-conditioning and operate on the European Plan (a.k.a. EP, meaning without meals), unless we specify that they use the Continental Plan (CP, with a continental breakfast), Breakfast Plan (BP, with a full breakfast), or Modified American Plan (MAP, with breakfast and dinner) or are all-inclusive (including all meals and most activi-

ties). We always list facilities but not whether you'll be charged an extra fee to use them, so when pricing accommodations, find out what's included.

Many Listings

★   Fodor's Choice
★   Highly recommended
✉   Physical address
✛   Directions
🕮   Mailing address
☎   Telephone
🖷   Fax
⊕   On the Web
✉   E-mail
🎫   Admission fee
☉   Open/closed times
Ⓜ   Metro stations
▭   Credit cards

Hotels & Restaurants

🏨   Hotel
🛏   Number of rooms
♨   Facilities
🍽   Meal plans
✗   Restaurant
⟁   Reservations
〽   Smoking
🍷   BYOB
✗🏨   Hotel with restaurant that warrants a visit

Outdoors

⛳   Golf
⛺   Camping

Other

☕   Family-friendly
⇨   See also
✉   Branch address
☞   Take note

WHAT'S WHERE

MUNICH 	If Germany has a second capital, it must be Munich. The southern capital of the Free State of Bavaria is a stubborn and proud adversary of Berlin and likes to top the federal capital in culture, sports, entertainment, society, and even politics. Despite being one of Germany's top tourist destinations, even for Germans, Munich never feels overwhelmed by tour-bus groups like cities such as Heidelberg can. The historic part of the city is large enough to maintain its own identity even during the busiest seasons. The city has a wonderful opera, great theater, many historic museums, and precious churches, but the main appeal is the laid-back, almost Mediterranean flair found in the many parks, cafés, and beer gardens. Thanks to the mild Föhn winds blowing across the Bavarian Alps, the weather is usually very amicable, with a mild spring, cold winter, and picture-perfect summers.
THE BAVARIAN ALPS 	Majestic peaks, lush green pastures, and frescoed houses brightened by window boxes of flowers make for Germany's most photogenic region. Quaint little towns like Mittenwald, Garmisch-Partenkirchen, Oberammergau, and Berchtesgaden have preserved their charming historic architecture. There's not much in the way of nightlife here; in summer and winter alike, the landscape provides the chief form of entertainment. You can find the country's finest skiing in Garmisch-Partenkirchen and take countless scenic hikes above mountain lakes such as Tegernsee, Schliersee, or the pristine Königsee.
THE ROMANTIC ROAD	Picturesque beyond words, the Romantische Strasse (Romantic Road) is more than 355 km (220 mi) of soaring castles, medieval villages, half-timber houses, and imposing churches all set in a pastoral backdrop of hills and greenery. Best explored by bicycle or train (though certainly accessible by car), the route winds its way from Würzburg to Füssen crossing a few top destinations such as Rothenburg-ob-der-Tauber and Schloss Neuschwanstein, King Ludwig II's fantastical castle, along the way. This area can get very busy during the summer, so if you're allergic to crowds, beware. You may prefer to visit in the fall when the grapes ripen on the vines around Würzburg, or in December when the Christmas markets bring a more authentic bustle to the town squares.

FRANCONIA & THE GERMAN DANUBE 	An immensely affluent area, thanks to the centuries-old success of craftsmanship and trade, Franconia is a proud, independent-minded region in northern Bavaria. Dominated by the Fränkische Schweiz (Franconian Switzerland), an appealing, hilly, and rural triangle between Nürnberg, Bamberg, and Bayreuth, Franconia offers plenty of outdoor diversions including skiing, golfing, hiking, and cycling. If you prefer urban adventures, you will certainly like Nürnberg, the region's unofficial capital and an odd mix of high-tech industry and one of Europe's most enticing medieval settings. Nightlife, entertainment, and culture follow more traditional paths here, but the Christkindlmarkt in December is a once-in-a-lifetime experience (and the stands with mulled wine make up for the conservative nightlife).
SALZBURG	Depending on who is describing this elegant city filled with gilded salons, palatial mansions, and Italianate churches, Salzburg is alternately known as the "Golden City of the High Baroque," the "Austrian Rome," or, thanks to its position astride the River Salzach, the "Florence of the North." What you choose to call this beloved city will depend on what brings you here. It may well be music, of course, as Mozart was born here in 1756. His operas and symphonies ripple through the city constantly, most particularly during its acclaimed, celebrity-packed, summer music festival. Art lovers, on the other hand, will pounce on the city's heritage of baroque churches, cloistered abbeys, and rococo palaces, and, inevitably, climb the hill to Hohensalzburg, the brooding medieval fortress whose lavish state rooms are belied by its grim exterior. Many come here to follow in the footsteps of the Trapp family, or, at least, their Hollywood counterparts, as many of the city's most celebrated sights were used as ageless backdrops for that beloved Oscar-winner, *The Sound of Music*. Music may top the bill for some, but everyone will enjoy the stupendous panoply of churches and museums, old-fashioned cafés, narrow medieval streets, and glorious fountains.

WHEN TO GO

The tourist season in most of Bavaria runs from April through October. In the mountains, things pick up again for the winter season from December to around February or even March, depending on the snow. Prices are generally higher in summer, so **consider visiting during the off-season to save money** (but be aware that the weather is often cold and many attractions are closed or have shorter hours in winter). Most resorts offer between-season (*Zwischensaison*) and edge-of-season (*Nebensaison*) rates, and tourist offices can provide lists of hotels that offer low-price inclusive weekly packages (*Pauschalangebote*). It's wise to **avoid cities at times of major trade fairs,** when attendees commandeer all hotel rooms and prices soar. You can check trade fair schedules with the German National Tourist Office.

Climate

Bavaria's climate is temperate, although cold spells can drop temperatures well below freezing, particularly in the Alps and the higher regions of northern Franconia. Summers are usually warm, though you should **be prepared for a few rainy days,** especially in the north. As you get nearer to the Alps, the summers get shorter, with warm weather often not beginning until the end of May. Fall can be spectacular in the south. Germans measure temperature in Celsius.

Forecasts Weather.com ⊕*www.weather com.*

The adjacent charts show average daily maximum and minimum temperatures for Munich and Salzburg.

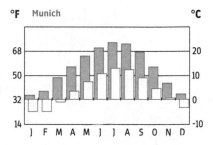

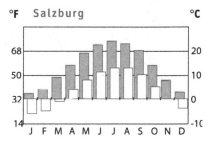

QUINTESSENTIAL MUNICH & BAVARIA

Meeting at the Market

The tradition of market shopping still thrives in Germany, especially in cities. On market day, often Saturday and/or midweek, a square or small street is closed to traffic and vendors—from butchers to beekeepers—set up stands. Grandmothers rub elbows with fashionable thirty-somethings, selecting from seven kinds of bread from the baker, organic (Bio) vegetables from the hippie farmer, and less-expensive ones from the Turkish seller.

Come Christmas, everything you need to celebrate the holiday is sold at the *Weihnachtsmarkt* (Christmas markets): handmade wooden ornaments from the Erzgebirge (Erz Mountains), *Stollen* (fruit cake) from Dresden, and *Lebkuchen* (gingerbread) from Nürnberg. Artists and artisans set up stands decorated with green boughs and lights to sell their wares; there may be a chill in the

air, but it makes Christmas shopping an enjoyable fresh-air experience.

More Beer, Bitte

Bavaria is the epitome of German beer brewing. It was here that the famous "Purity Law" was instituted in 1516, stating that beer is to be made of barley, hops, and water. It's astonishing that these three ingredients can generate such a variety of drink, from the light *Helles* lager to the smoky black beers found in Bamberg (among other places). In between there are vigorous pilsners and the refreshing *Weizenbier* (wheat beer, sometimes taken with a slice of lemon). Lenten season brings the extra-strength *Doppelbock* beers, with names ending in "or," such as Salvator or Kulminator (considered the strongest). Their extra richness is said to compensate for calories lost in fasting.

The drinking age for beer and wine in Germany is 16, and drinking in public is

If you want to get a sense of contemporary Bavarian culture, and indulge in some of its pleasures, start by familiarizing yourself with the rituals of daily life.

permitted. Beer's fixture within the culture seems to abate its abuse. Beer gardens are popular with families, who often bring their own food. You sit at long tables, buy beer, wine, or soft drinks, enjoy the sun, and chat with your neighbors. The greatest expression of Bavaria's beery culture is Oktoberfest, of course, often referred to as the Wiesn.

Churchgoing

Bavarians take their religion—primarily Catholicism—seriously. You can sense it from the moment they greet you: they're likely to say "Grüss Gott" (God's greetings), a phrase used nowhere else in Germany.

Christianity came early to the region and it left its mark in myriad superb churches, chapels, and monasteries. These houses of worship continue to play a central role in day-to-day life, to a degree you don't see elsewhere in the country. Among the most famous is the Frauenkirche (Church

of Our Lady) in Munich, a city landmark. Religious fervor is also visible in numerous votive churches and chapels. The 18th-century Wieskirche attracts pilgrims from all over. The simple St. Zeno in Bad Reichenhall was built long ago by salt miners seeking divine protection. And in Rothenburg-ob-der-Tauber, the St. Wolfgang, the shepherd's church, is incorporated into the city's old wall.

When you're looking to get a sense of the soul of Bavaria, you can hardly go wrong by beginning with the nearest church. If you have time, join a tour or speak to the local parish priest, who might have a secret or two to share.

IF YOU LIKE

Being Outdoors

Bavaria has been blessed with some of Germany's most beautiful real estate. The countryside is crisscrossed with paved bike paths, and large stretches of land have been designated as natural parks. The cities, including Munich, are of humane dimension and motorized traffic has generally been channeled so as not to be a nuisance to pedestrians. In places such as **Würzburg,** you can set off along the river and reach pristine countryside within 30 minutes.

The Bavarian Alps are naturally famous. The Winter Olympics town **Garmisch-Partenkirchen** offers cable cars ascending Germany's highest mountain. This is one of the country's best spots for skiing in the winter and hiking in the summer. Another spectacular spot for winter or summer sports is the region around **Berchtesgaden,** near Salzburg.

The southern part of Bavaria is especially known for its lakes, which have exceptional water quality. Most famous are the **Chiemsee,** the **Starnbergersee** and the **Ammersee.** These lakes are ideal for both hikers and bikers, and boat rentals are possible, though you'll need a German-recognized license.

Medieval Towns

The trail of walled towns and half-timber houses known as the **Romantic Road** is a route long marketed by German tourism, and therefore the road more traveled. It essentially connects the Swabian and Franconian regions of Bavaria. The towns here are lovely, and a far cry from the typical "Alpine" towns of Upper and Lower Bavaria. **Würzburg** at the northern tip of the Romantic Road, is a former royal residence that has a big name in wine. Having been spared a massive bombardment, **Rothenburg-ob-der-Tauber** maintained its medieval look, much to the delight of millions of visitors. If you'd prefer fewer group tours spilling into your photographs, venture eastward to the regions of Franconia around **Coburg** and **Kronach.** This area of thick forests was once flush with East Germany and hence off the beaten track. It's still far from overcrowded.

Options for exploring closer to Munich include **Regensburg** and **Nürnberg.** The former is a beautiful medieval city, relatively unknown even to Germans, and has a soaring French Gothic cathedral that can hold 6,000 people. Nürnberg dates to 1050 and is among the most historic cities in the country. Not only emperors but artists convened here, including the Renaissance genius Albrecht Dürer.

The crowning glory of Bavarian medieval towns is across the Austrian border: the old town of **Salzburg** is a maze of narrow streets and passages interspersed with airy, elegant plazas from later periods.

Music

Thanks in great part to the wise and cultivated reigns of the Wittelsbach dynasty, Bavaria has developed into a veritable hub of culture. At its center is **Munich**, with a number of world famous orchestras, including the Munich Philharmonic and the Bavarian Radio Orchestra, and the venues to go with them.

In summer, many orchestras and opera houses shut down for the season and outdoor music festivals spring to life. In Bayreuth, the **Wagner Festival** is an important indoor exception. For four days each May, churches and other important monuments in **Regensburg** are used for recitals of ancient music. And composers are often honored with special "days" in their hometowns: Richard Strauss, for instance, in Garmisch-Partenkirchen, and Carl Orff in Andechs Monastery.

Salzburg, the city of Mozart, attracts international crowds for its two-month festival featuring the top names in the music business. It's the perfect backdrop for society-conscious Austrians who gather in their most opulent evening attire to admire each other (and to hear good music, too). If you can't find tickets to the "Festspielhaus" venue, there are many others places to hear music, such as Mirabell Palace, where Mozart once played as a little boy, or any of the churches.

Castles & Palaces

Watching over nearly any town that ends in "-burg" is a medieval fortress or Renaissance palace, often now serving as a museum, restaurant, or hotel. Grand 18th- and 19th-century palaces are the pride of almost every *Residenzstadt,* a city that was once a king's, duke's, or bishop's seat.

Munich was the main seat of the Bavarian rulers, and it has its share of special residences. Topping the list is the phenomenal Residenz in the center of town. The summer castle of the Wittelsbachs at Nymphenburg is also quite spectacular, with its huge, wild park. Just to the north of town, off the beaten track, is Schloss Schleissheim, a baroque masterpiece that's used for concerts. The *Residenz* in **Würzburg** dates to the prince-bishops of the town, whose tremendous wealth permitted construction of a grand, airy palace with a magnificent Tiepolo fresco on the ceiling of the main hall.

Louis XIV's Versailles inspired Germany's greatest castle-builder, the Bavarian King Ludwig II, to construct the opulent **Schloss Herrenchiemsee.** One of Ludwig's palaces in turn inspired a latter-day visionary— his **Schloss Neuschwanstein** is the model for Walt Disney's Sleeping Beauty castle. **Schloss Linderhof,** also in the Bavarian Alps, was Ludwig's favorite retreat, and the only one of the royal residences completed during his lifetime.

Across the border in **Salzburg,** the formidable Fortress Hohensalzburg towers over the city, and the Residenz and the Mirabell Palace are the height of baroque opulence.

GREAT ITINERARY

Day 1: Arrival Munich

You will need some time to settle into the city, especially if you have just flown in. Though a wealthy city with Wittelsbach palaces, great art collections, and a technology museum holding trains, planes, and even an imitation coal mine, what really distinguishes Munich from other state capitals are its beer halls, beer gardens, and proud identity: even designer-conscious Müncheners wear traditional dirndls and hunter-green jackets for special occasions. On Day 1, stroll the streets of the Altstadt (Old City), visit the Frauenkirche, the Peterskirche, Marienplatz (11 AM is the Glockenspiel) and the Viktualienmarkt (the central food market) for a quick bite to eat; try a *Weisswurst* (white sausage), a mild, boiled sausage normally eaten before noon with sweet mustard. Then head to the Deutsches Museum for deep insights into science and technology, and find a café for a pick-me-up. Save the Hofbräu-haus or any other teeming brew house for last. ⇨ *See Chapter 1, Munich*

Logistics: Good for couples or families is the €18 Partner Day Ticket for the 40-minute suburban rail trip from the airport into the city. Before boarding the train, stop by the airport's tourist office to begin getting your bearings. Most flights from North America to Bavaria's capital land before 10 AM; no matter how tired you may feel, try to stay on your feet to adjust to the new time zone.

Day 2: Munich

After a solid breakfast at your hotel, return to the Altstadt for a visit to the Residenz, from where the Wittelsbacher once ruled. Make your way to the north on foot, weather permitting, for a stroll through the Englischer Garten. You might want to have lunch at the famous Chinese Tower beer garden or in the Schwabing district. The afternoon should be devoted to visiting the three Pinakothek art museums. Dinner might be either in the student quarter around the museums, or in the Old City.

Logistics: A transit day ticket (€5) might well be worth the money, especially if your hotel isn't in the center of town. Make sure you purchase the ticket for the inner zone (*Innenraum*), unless you are intending to head out to Starnberg or one of the palaces outside the city.

Day 3: Neuschwanstein

From Munich, it's an easy day trip to Germany's fairy-tale castle in Schwangau. Though the 19th-century castle's fantastic silhouette has made it famous, this creation of King Ludwig II is more opera set than piece of history—the interior was never even completed. A tour reveals why the romantic king earned the nickname "Mad King Ludwig." Across the narrow wooded valley from Schloss Neuschwanstein is the ancient castle of the Bavarian Wittelsbach dynasty, Schloss Hohenschwangau, also open for tours. ⇨ *See Chapter 3, The Romantic Road*

Logistics: You can join an all-day bus trip or even a bike tour from Munich, or make the 2½-hour journey on your own by rail (the best connection goes direct to Füssen and includes a bus transfer to the castle's village, Hohenschwangau). Call ahead (08362/930–830) to book your timed ticket entrance to the castles.

Day 4: Munich to Würzburg via Rothenburg-ob-der-Tauber

Millions of people visit Rothenburg every year to see its old medieval town, the most spectacular in Germany. Mar-

ket square is the place to start; to get an overview, climb the 60-meter tower on the Renaissance Town Hall. A must in Rothenburg is Jakobs-Kirche (Church of St. James) with an altar by the great woodcarver Tilamn Riemenschneider. While strolling, make sure you see the garden of the former castle (Burggarten) at the western edge of town and the so-called Plönlein—just a fork in the road, but what a fork. Lunch should be light, since you will be continuing onto Würzburg, where a solid dinner of Franconian specialties, including wine from the famed *Bocksbeutel* bottles, awaits. A consitutional through Würzburg's old town closes the day, or an open-air concert at the Residenz if you're there during the annual Mozart festival. ⇨ *See Chapter 3, The Romantic Road*

Logistics: Using the train is most probably the most pleasant way to travel, as well as the fastest. Trains are frequent between Munich and Rothenburg, though not direct. The ride lasts between two-and-a-half and three hours depending on the connections.

Day 5: Würzburg to Nürnberg

The morning should be spent at the Residenz and the Cathedral of St. Killian. If time allows, stop at the Marienkappelle (Chapel of Mary) for a look at more works by Tilman Riemenschneider and for a remarkable interpretation of the Immaculate Conception over the northern entrance. Have a quick lunch in one of the cozy establishments of the inner city before crossing the picturesque old Main Bridge and visiting the Marienburg Castle on a hill overlooking the city. Then catch the train to Nürnberg, where you can stroll the old streets and enjoy a rich *Schäufele* with a dumpling before turning in. ⇨ *See Chapter 3, The Romantic Road, and* ⇨ *Chapter 4, Franconia & the German Danube*

Logistics: The train ride from Würzburg to Nürnberg takes about one hour and gives you a good view of the Franconian landscape.

Day 6: Nürnberg to Munich

The most important sights of Nürnberg are all located within the perimeter of the Old Town. Begin at the fortress and make your way down to the Dürer house, the Toy Museum, and the market square with the "Beautiful Fountain" and the Church of Our Lady. After sampling some authentic bratwurst, head to the Germanisches Museum, which documents more than 30,000 years of the history of the German-speaking peoples. In the evening return to Munich, in anticipation of your trip across the border to Salzburg the next day. While in Munich you can relax at the Müllerbad (spa) followed by a jazz or world-music concert at the Muffathalle. ⇨ *See Chapter 4, Franconia & the German Danube, and* ⇨*Chapter 1, Munich*

Logistics: Nürnberg is one hour by train from Munich.

Day 7: Salzburg

Wake up bright and early in Munich and take the 90-minute train ride through the breathtaking landscape at the foot of the Alps. In Salzburg, head straight for the Old Town. Mozart's birthplace on Get-reidegasse is a must, as are the old castle on the promontory over the town and Schloss Mirabell. Fine eateries abound. You can enjoy the city until about 9 PM, when the last express train leaves for Munich. ⇨ *See Chapter 5, Salzburg*

ON THE CALENDAR

	Bavaria's top seasonal events include Karneval festivities in January and February, spring festivals around Easter and Pentecost, Bayreuth's Richard Wagner Festival in August, wine festivals in late summer and fall, the Oktoberfest in Munich in late September and early October, and December's Christmas markets. For event listings, see the German National Tourist Office's Web site (⊕ *www.germany-tourism.de*).
WINTER December	**Christmas Markets,** with outdoor festivals of light, choral and trumpet music, handcrafted gift items, and mulled wine (*Glühwein*), are held in just about every city and town in Bavaria. Nürnberg's is the most famous.
	New Year's Eve is a noisy, colorful event in Munich with fireworks set off from nearly every neighborhood street.
February	The Rhineland is Germany's capital of **Karneval** events, but there's also plenty of activity in Munich and southern Germany. Festivities always run through February, finishing on Fasching Dienstag (Shrove or Fat Tuesday).
March	**Strong Beer Season** in Munich brings out the bands and merrymaking in all the beer halls.
SPRING May	By downing a huge tankard of wine in one gulp, a 17th-century mayor of Rothenburg-ob-der-Tauber saved the town from sacking. At the **Medieval Festival** on Pentecost weekend, his Meistertrunk is reenacted. **Religious processions,** featuring hundreds of horses, giant candles, and elaborate statues, are particularly spectacular in Catholic eastern Bavaria during Pentecost weekend. The best ones are at Bogen, Sankt Englmar, and Bad Kötzting.
SUMMER July	**Kinderzeche** is Dinkelsbühl's medieval pageant and festival. It reenacts an incident from the Thirty Years' War in which the children stood at the gate and pleaded with the conquerors to spare their homes.
	The **Richard Wagner Festival** unfolds the Wagner operas in Bayreuth in July and August. Reserve well in advance; the waiting list for tickets is epic.
August	**Kulmbach Beer Festival** takes place in Franconia.

AUTUMN	
September	**Oktoberfest** ⊕*www.muenchen-tourist.de*) in Munich (late September–early October) draws millions of visitors to cavernous beer tents and fairgrounds
	Toward the end of September (the date is never fixed, but it's after St. Michael's) **cattle are driven** down from the high Alpine fields. The animals are decorated with flowers and ribbons. Near Berchtesgaden, they are even carried across the Obersee Lake by boat.
November	Many towns and villages in southern Bavaria celebrate "the farmer's god" St. Leonard around the saint's feast day, November 6. The **Leonhardiritt** involves elaborate processions with decorated horses; it's a great occasion to see lots of folklore and traditional costumes.
	St. Martin's Festival, on or around November 11, includes children's lantern processions and is celebrated throughout Bavaria.

Munich

WORD OF MOUTH

"The market near the Marienplatz is wonderful. I had a great time stopping at one booth for an apple, another for cheese, yet a third for a beer, and a fourth for bread to assemble a fun lunch!"
—bluecheesegirl

"I always seem to have the most fun with the Bavarians."
—mikemo

"The Schatzkammer [at the Residenz] left me enchanted, especially the dazzling and fascinating Renaissance gold statue of St. George slaying the dragon—thousands of diamonds, rubies, emeralds, sapphires, and semiprecious stones."
—Mary_Fran

Updated by
Kevin White

IN THE RELAXED AND SUNNIER southern part of Germany, Munich (München) is the proud capital of the state of Bavaria. Even Germans come here to vacation, mixing the city's pleasures with the inviting and accessible natural surroundings—on clear days it's even possible to see the Alps from downtown. The city bills itself *"Die Weltstadt mit Herz"* ("the cosmopolitan city with heart"), but in rare bouts of self-depre-catory humor, friendly Bavarians will remind you that it isn't much more than a country town with a million people. It's the overall feeling of *Gemütlichkeit*—loosely translated as conviviality—that makes the place so special, with open-air markets, numerous parks, the lovely Isar River, and loads of beer halls.

Founded in the 12th century as a market town on the "salt road" between mighty Salzburg and Augsburg, Munich is now the city of "laptops and lederhosen." Ravishing baroque styling and smoky beer cellars offset grand 19th-century architecture and sleek steel-and-glass office buildings. Millionaires and farmers rub shoulders at the outdoor markets. A host of media companies have settled here, from publishing houses and top-notch digital postproduction companies to world-class film studios. The concentration of electronics and computer firms—Sie-mens, Microsoft, and SAP, for example—makes the area a sort of Sili-con Valley of Europe.

For all its modernity, Munich also represents what the rest of the world sees as "typical German" with its world-famous Oktoberfest, tradi-tional*lederhosen* (leather pants), busty Bavarian waitresses in *dirndls* (traditional dresses), beer steins, and sausages. Indeed, you would be crazy not to indulge in the local brew, either in one of the larger beer halls or a smaller *Kneipe*, a bar where all types of people get together for meals and some drinks. And when the first rays of spring sun begin warming the air, join Müncheners and tourists alike as they flock to the beloved beer gardens to enjoy the relaxed atmosphere under the shade of massive chestnut trees.

However, the *other* Munich is absolutely chock full of activities, such as wandering on foot through beautiful neighborhoods, biking through parks and along the river, browsing in shops, or enjoying outdoor cafés. It is on the cutting edge of hip with its fashionable boutiques, upscale restaurants, dynamic music scene, and DJ bars, but it also has the relaxed pace of the Mediterranean. Some even call it the northernmost city in Italy.

The cultural attractions are also legion. "All-nighter" events through-out the year celebrate museum-going, literature, and musical perfor-mances. The city's appreciation of the arts began under the kings and dukes of the Wittelsbach Dynasty, which ruled Bavaria for more than 750 years until 1918. The Wittelsbach legacy is alive and well in the city's fabulous museums, the Opera House, the Philharmonic, and of course, the Residenz, the city's royal palace.

Munich's cleanliness, safety, and comfortable pace give it an ever so slightly rustic feeling. The broad sidewalks, endless shops and eateries, views of the Alps, a sizeable river running through town, and a huge

TOP REASONS TO GO

Views from the Frauenkirche: This 14th-century church tower gives you a panorama of downtown Munich that cannot be beat. There are 86 steps in a circular shaft to get to the elevator, but it's worth it.

Deutsches Museum: The museum has a world-renowned collection of science and technology exhibits, and its location on the lovely Isar River is perfect for a relaxing afternoon stroll.

Street food: The Viktualienmarkt is a unique farmers'-market-style culinary shopping experience with fresh produce, Turkish finger food, and Argentine wine. Grab a snack, sit in the beer garden, and watch the world go by.

A lazy afternoon in Gärtnerplatz: Gärtnerplatz, 200 yards from Viktualienmarkt, is a relaxing roundabout with a few cafés where you can sit, have lunch, and enjoy Munich's hippest neighborhood before checking out the numerous trendy boutiques.

Englischer Garten: With expansive greens, picturesque lakes, a handful of beer gardens, and creeks running through it, the English Garden is a great place for a bike ride or a long walk. Enjoy a mug of cold beer at the Chinese Tower, take in the scenery, and snack on some local grub.

green park that easily gives Central Park a run for its money make Munich one of Germany's most enjoyable cities.

EXPLORING MUNICH

Munich is a wealthy city—and it shows. At times this affluence may come across as conservatism. But what makes Munich so unique is that it's a new city superimposed on the old. Hip neighborhoods are riddled with traditional locales, and flashy materialism thrives together with a love of the outdoors.

THE CITY CENTER

Munich's Old Town has been rebuilt so often over the centuries that it no longer has the homogeneous look of so many other German towns. World War II leveled a good portion of the center, but an amazing job has been done to restore a bit of the fairy-tale feel that once prevailed here.

TIMING Set aside at least a whole day for the Old Town, hitting Marienplatz when the glockenspiel plays at 11 AM or noon before a crowd of spectators. The pedestrian zone can get maddeningly full between noon and 2, when everyone in town seems to be taking a quick shopping break.

Numbers in the margin correspond to numbers on the Munich map.

MAIN ATTRACTIONS

⓱ **Deutsches Museum** *(German Museum).* Aircraft, vehicles, locomotives, and FodorśChoice machinery fill a monumental building on an island in the Isar River. The ★ immense collection is spread out over 19 km (12 mi) of corridors, six ☺ floors of exhibits, and 30 departments. Children now have their own

GREAT ITINERARIES

IF YOU HAVE 3 DAYS

Visit the tourist information office at the **Hauptbahnhof** ❶ (main train station) and then head for one of the cafés at the pedestrian shopping zone to get your bearings. Plan an eastward course across (or rather under) **Karlsplatz** ❷ and into Neuhauserstrasse and Kaufingerstrasse, plunging into the bustling shopping area. Escape the crowds inside one of the three churches that punctuate the route: the Bürgersaal, the **Michaelskirche** ❸, or the **Frauenkirche** ❺, a soaring Gothic cathedral. Try to arrive in the city's central square, **Marienplatz** ❻, in time for the 11 AM performance of the glockenspiel in the tower of the **Neues Rathaus** ❼ (New Town Hall). Proceed to the city market, the **Viktualienmarkt** ❾, for lunch, and then head a few blocks north for an afternoon visit to the **Residenz** ㉒, the rambling palace of the Wittelsbach rulers. End your first day with coffee at Munich's oldest café, the Tambosi, on Odeonsplatz.

On your second day, go on one of the guided bicycle tours. They're very educational, giving you a better feel for some highlights you may want to go back to for a closer look. You'll be shown things like the **Englischer Garten** ㉛ (where you stop for a beer), the Maximilianeum, the Peace Angel, and the **Haus der Kunst** ㉜. After the tour is over you

can meander over the river at Isartor to the **Deutsches Museum** ⑰, an incredible collection of science and technology. On the third day take a closer look at some of the world-class museums. Walk north to **Königsplatz** ㊳, wandering past the Grecian-style pavilions there on your way to the **Alte Pinakothek** ㊷ and **Neue Pinakothek** ㊸ museums and the **Pinakothek der Moderne** ㊹. You may not be able to see all of them in one day. After the museums, you can walk east to Ludwigstrasse and make your way south back toward Odeonsplatz and Marienplatz.

IF YOU HAVE 5 DAYS

For the first three days follow the itinerary described above. On the fourth day venture out to suburban Nymphenburg for a visit to Schloss Nymphenburg, the Wittelsbachs' summer residence. Allow a whole day to view the palace's buildings and its museums and to stroll through its lovely park. On the fifth day, tour the Olympiapark in the morning. Ride to the top of the Olympic Tower for the best view of Munich and the surrounding countryside. Then either take a walk along the quiet city banks of the Isar River or visit one of the two villa-museums, the **Museum Villa Stuck** ㊱ or the **Städtische Galerie im Lenbachhaus** ㊶. The latter is huge and has a popular café.

area, the **Kinderreich,** where they can learn about modern technology and science through numerous interactive displays (parents must accompany their child). The most technically advanced planetarium in Europe has up to six shows daily and includes a Laser Magic display. The Internet café on the third floor is open daily 9–3. ■TIP➜ To arrange for a two-hour tour in English, call at least two weeks in advance. The Verkehrszentrum (Center for Transportation), on the former trade fair grounds at the Theresienhöhe (where Oktoberfest is held), has been completely renovated and houses an amazing collection of the museum's transportation exhibits. It is open until 8 PM on Thursdays. ✉*Museumsinsel 1, City Center* ☎*089/21791, 089/217–9252 for tour* ⊕*www.deutsches-museum.de* ✉*Museum €8.50, Center for Transportation €2.50 (€10 with museum plus shuttle)* ⊙*Daily 9–5* Ⓜ *Isartor (S-bahn).*

❺ Frauenkirche *(Church of Our Lady).* Munich's *Dom* (cathedral) is a dis-
★ tinctive late-Gothic brick structure with two towers. Each is more than 300 feet high, and both are capped by onion-shaped domes. The towers are an indelible feature of the skyline and a Munich trademark—some say because they look like overflowing beer mugs.

The main body of the cathedral was completed in 20 years (1468–88)—a record time in those days. The onion domes on the towers were added, almost as an afterthought, in 1524–25. Jörg von Halspach, the Frauenkirche's original architect, apparently dropped dead after laying the last brick and is buried here. The building suffered severe damage during Allied bombing and was restored between 1947 and 1957. Inside, the church combines most of von Halspach's original features with a stark, clean modernity and simplicity of line, emphasized by slender, white octagonal pillars that sweep up through the nave to the tracery ceiling. As you enter the church, look on the stone floor for the dark imprint of a large foot—the *Teufelstritt* (Devil's Footprint). According to lore, the devil challenged von Halspach to build a nave without windows. The architect accepted the challenge. When he completed the job, he led the devil to the one spot in the bright church from which the 66-foot-high windows could not be seen. The devil stomped his foot in rage and left the Teufelstritt. The cathedral houses an elaborate 15th-century black-marble tomb guarded by four 16th-century armored knights. It's the final resting place of Duke Ludwig IV (1302–47), who became Holy Roman Emperor Ludwig the Bavarian in 1328. The Frauenkirche's great treasure, however, is the collection of 24 wooden busts of the apostles, saints, and prophets above the choir, carved by the 15th-century Munich sculptor Erasmus Grasser.

The observation platform high up in one of the towers offers a splendid view of the city. But beware—you must climb 86 steps to reach the tower elevator. ✉*Frauenpl., City Center* ☎*089/290–0820* ✉*Cathedral free, tower €2* ⊙*Tower elevator Apr.–Oct., Mon.–Sat. 10–5* Ⓜ *Marienplatz (U-bahn and S-bahn).*

❻ Marienplatz. Bordered by the Neues Rathaus, shops, and cafés, this
★ square is named after the gilded statue of the Virgin Mary that has watched over it for more than three centuries. It was erected in 1638 at the behest of Elector Maximilian I as an act of thanksgiving for the city's survival of the Thirty Years' War, the cataclysmic religious struggle that devastated vast regions of Germany. When the statue was taken down from its marble column for cleaning in 1960, workmen found a small casket in the base containing a splinter of wood said to be from the cross of Christ. ■**TIP➔On the fifth floor of a building facing the**

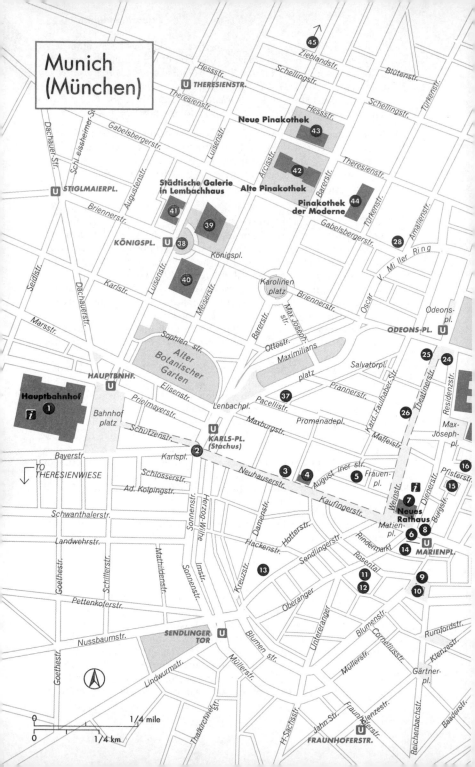

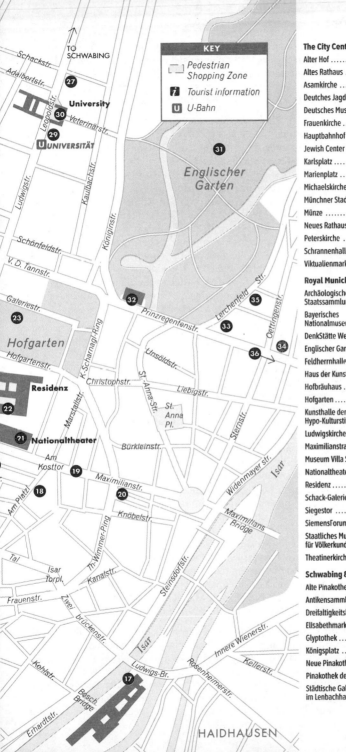

Neues Rathaus is the Café Glockenspiel. It overlooks the entire Platz and provides a perfect view of the glockenspiel from the front and St. Peter's Church from the back terrace. Entrance is around the back. ⊠*Bounded by Kaufingerstr., Rosenstr., Weinstr., and Dienerstr., City Center* Ⓜ *Marienplatz (U-bahn and S-bahn).*

❸ **Michaelskirche** *(St. Michael's Church).* A curious story explains why this sturdy Renaissance church has no tower. Seven years after the start of construction the main tower collapsed. Its patron, pious Duke Wilhelm V, regarded the disaster as a heavenly sign that the church wasn't big enough, so he ordered a change in the plans—this time without a tower. Completed seven years later, the barrel vaulting of Michaelskirche is second in size only to that of St. Peter's in Rome. The duke is buried in the crypt, along with 40 other Wittelsbach family members, including the eccentric King Ludwig II. A severe neoclassical monument in the north transept contains the tomb of Napoléon's stepson, Eugene de Beauharnais, who married one of the daughters of King Maximilian I and died in Munich in 1824. The church is the venue for free performances of church music. A poster to the right of the front portal gives the dates. ⊠*Neuhauserstr. 52, City Center* ☎*089/231–7060* 🎫*€1* ⊗*Daily 8–7, except during services* Ⓜ *Karlsplatz (U-bahn and S-bahn).*

❼ **Neues Rathaus** *(New Town Hall).* Munich's present town hall was built between 1867 and 1908 in the fussy, turreted, neo-Gothic style so beloved by King Ludwig II. Architectural historians are divided over its merits, though its dramatic scale and lavish detailing are impressive. Perhaps the most serious criticism is that the Dutch and Flemish styles of the building seem out of place amid the baroque and rococo styles of so much of the rest of the city. The tower's 1904 **glockenspiel** (a chiming clock with mechanical figures) plays daily at 11 AM, noon, and 9 PM, with an additional performance at 5 PM June–October. As chimes peal out over the square, the clock's doors flip open and brightly colored dancers and jousting knights act out two events from Munich's past: a tournament held in Marienplatz in 1568 and the *Schäfflertanz* (Dance of the Coopers), which commemorated the end of the plague of 1517. When Munich was in ruins after World War II, an American soldier contributed some paint to restore the battered figures, and he was rewarded with a ride on one of the jousters' horses, high above the cheering crowds. ■TIP→ You, too, can travel up there, by elevator, to an observation point near the top of one of the towers. On a clear day the view is spectacular. ⊠*Marienpl., City Center* 🎫*Tower €2* ⊗*Nov.– Apr., Mon.–Thurs. 9–4, Fri. 9–1; May–Oct., weekdays 9–7, weekends 10–7* Ⓜ *Marienplatz (U-bahn and S-bahn).*

⓮ **Peterskirche** *(St. Peter's Church).* Munich's oldest and smallest parish church traces its origins to the 11th century and has been restored in various architectural styles. The rich baroque interior has a magnificent late-Gothic high altar and aisle pillars decorated with exquisite 18th-century figures of the apostles. In clear weather it's well worth the long climb up the 300-foot tower—the view includes glimpses of the Alps on a clear day. The Peterskirche has a Scottish priest who is glad to show English-speaking visitors around. ✉*Rindermarkt, City Center* ☎*089/260–4828* ⛲*Tower €1.50* ⊙*Mon.–Sat. 9–6, Sun. 10–6* Ⓜ *Marienplatz (U-bahn and S-bahn).*

❾ **Viktualienmarkt** *(Victuals Market).*
★ The city's open-air market really is the beating heart of downtown Munich. It has just about every fresh fruit or vegetable you can imagine, as well as German and international specialties. All kinds of people come here for a quick bite, from well-heeled business-people and casual tourists to mor-

tar- and paint-covered workers. It's also the realm of the garrulous, sturdy market women who run the stalls with dictatorial authority. ■**TIP**➔ Whether here, or at a bakery, *do not* try to select your pickings by hand. Ask for it first and let the owner bring it to you. Try Poseidon's for quality fish treats, Mercado Latino on the south side of the market for an empanada and fine wines from South America, or Freisinger for Mediterranean delights. There's also a great beer garden (open pretty much whenever the sun is shining), where you can enjoy your snacks with some cold local beer. A sign above the counter tells you which beer is on tap. The choice rotates throughout the year among the six major Munich breweries, which are displayed on the May Pole. These are also the only six breweries officially allowed to serve their wares at the Oktoberfest, because they all brew within the city limits. Ⓜ *Marienplatz (U-bahn and S-bahn).*

ALSO WORTH SEEING

⓯ **Alter Hof** *(Old Palace).* This palace was the original medieval residence of the Wittelsbachs, the ruling dynasty established in 1180. The palace now serves as local government offices. Don't pass through without turning to admire the oriel (bay window) that hides on the south wall, just around the corner as you enter the courtyard. The west wing is home to the **Vinorant Alter Hof,** a fine restaurant and wine cellar with decent prices. ✉*Burgstr., City Center* Ⓜ *Marienplatz (U-bahn and S-bahn).*

❽ **Altes Rathaus** *(Old Town Hall).* Munich's first town hall was built in ☪ 1474. Its great hall—destroyed in 1944 but now fully restored—was the work of architect Jörg von Halspach. It's used for official receptions and is not normally open to the public. The tower provides a fairy-tale-like setting for the **Spielzeugmuseum** (Toy Museum), accessible via a winding staircase. Its toys and dolls are on display, with a collection of Barbies from the United States. ✉*Marienpl., City Center* ☎*089/294–001* ⛲*Museum €3* ⊙*Daily 10–5:30* Ⓜ *Marienplatz (U-bahn and S-bahn).*

⓭ **Asamkirche** *(Asam Church)*. Munich's most unusual church has a suit-
★ ably extraordinary entrance, framed by raw rock foundations. The
insignificant door, crammed between its craggy shoulders, gives little
idea of the opulence and lavish detailing within the small 18th-century
church (there are only 12 rows of pews). Above the doorway St. Nepomuk, a 14th-century Bohemian monk who drowned in the Danube, is
being led by angels from a rocky riverbank to heaven. The church's
official name is Church of St. Johann Nepomuk, but it's known as the
Asamkirche for its architects, the brothers Cosmas Damian and Egid
Quirin Asam, who lived next door. The interior of the church is a prime
example of true southern German late-baroque architecture. Frescoes
by Cosmas Damian Asam and rosy marble cover the walls. The sheer
wealth of statues and gilding is stunning—there's even a gilt skeleton
at the sanctuary's portal. ⊠*Sendlingerstr., City Center* ⊙*Daily 9–5:30*
Ⓜ *Sendlingertor (U-bahn)*.

❹ **Deutsches Jagd- und Fischereimuseum** *(German Museum of Hunting and
Fishing)*. This quirky museum contains the world's largest collection of
fishhooks, some 500 stuffed animals (including a 6½-foot-tall North
American grizzly bear), a 12,000-year-old skeleton of a deer found
in Ireland, and a valuable collection of hunting weapons. You'll even
find the elusive *Wolpertinger,* the Bavarian equivalent of the jackalope.
The museum also sells fine hunting equipment, from knives and rifles
to sturdy clothing. ⊠*Neuhauserstr. 2, City Center* ☎*089/220–522*
⊠€*3.50* ⊙*Fri.–Sun., Tues., and Wed. 9:30–5, Thurs. 9:30–9* Ⓜ *Karlsplatz (U-bahn and S-bahn)*.

**OFF THE
BEATEN
PATH**

**Franziskanerklosterkirche St. Anna (Franciscan Monastery Church of St.
Anne).** This striking example of the two Asam brothers' work in the Lehel
district impresses visitors with its sense of movement and heroic scale. The
ceiling fresco by Cosmas Damian Asam glows in all its original glory. The
ornate altar was also designed by the Asam brothers. Towering over the
delicate little church, on the opposite side of the street, is the neo-Roman-
esque bulk of the 19th-century church of St. Anne. ⊠*St.-Anna-Str., Lehel*
☎*089/212–1820* Ⓜ *Lehel (U-bahn)*.

❶ **Hauptbahnhof** *(Central Station)*. Obviously not a cultural site, but it is
a particularly handy spot. The city tourist office here has maps and
helpful information on events around town. On the underground level
are all sorts of shops that remain open even on Sundays and holidays.
There are also a number of places to get a late-night snack in and
around the station. ⊠*Bahnhofpl., Hauptbahnhof* ☎*089/2333–0256
or 089/2333–0257* Ⓜ *Hauptbahnhof (U-bahn and S-bahn)*.

⓬ **Jewish Center Munich.** The striking new Jewish Center Munich has transformed the formerly sleepy Jakobsplatz into quite an elegant square. The
Center includes a museum focusing on Jewish history in Munich, a formidable new synagogue with rough marble slabs imported from Israel,
and a community center with kosher restaurant (☎ 089/202–400333)
that is open seven days a week from 11 to 11. ⊠*St.-Jakobspl. 16, City*

Center ☎089/233–96096 ⊕www.juedisches-museum-muenchen.de
⊠Free ⊙Tues.–Sun. 10–6 Ⓜ Marienplatz (U-bahn and S-bahn).

❷ **Karlsplatz.** In 1755 Eustachius Föderl opened an inn and beer garden here, which became known as the Stachus. The beer garden is long gone, but the name has remained—locals still refer to this busy intersection as the Stachus. One of Munich's most popular fountains is here—it acts as a magnet on hot summer days when city shoppers and office workers seek a cool place to relax. ■TIP➡ **In winter it makes way for an ice-skating rink.** It's a bustling meeting point. Ⓜ Karlsplatz (U-bahn and S-bahn).

⓫ **Münchner Stadtmuseum** (City Museum). Wedged in by Oberanger, Rosental, and the newly-renovated St.-Jakobsplatz, this museum is as eclectic inside as the architecture is outside. The original building facing St.-Jakobsplatz dates to 1491. Inside are instrument collections, international cultural exhibits, a film museum showing rarely screened movies, notably German silents, a photo and fashion museum, a puppet theater, and a very lively café. ⊠St.-Jakobspl. 1, City Center ☎089/2332–2370 ⊕www.stadtmuseum-online.de ⊠€2.50, free Sun.; special exhibitions €4 ⊙Tues.–Sun. 10–6 Ⓜ Marienplatz (U-bahn and S-bahn).

⓰ **Münze** (Mint). Originally royal stables, the Münze was created by court architect Wilhelm Egkl between 1563 and 1567 and now serves as an office building. A stern neoclassical facade emblazoned with gold was added in 1809. The interior courtyard with Renaissance-style arches is worth a look. ⊠Pfisterstr. 4, City Center ⊠Free ⊙Mon.–Thurs. 8–4, Fri. 8–2 Ⓜ Marienplatz (U-bahn and S-bahn).

⓾ **Schrannenhalle.** On the south side of the Viktualienmarkt, behind Pschorr tavern, is the Schrannenhalle. A former grain depot from the mid-1850s until just after the turn of the 20th century, the hall now houses numerous shops, bars, and restaurants serving Asian cuisine, sushi, traditional Bavarian food, and more. One vendor even serves champagne with German-style "Currywurst" (sausage with curry ketchup and curry powder). Events range from swing jazz to rock-and-roll concerts. ■TIP➡ **One unusual and welcome feature of the Schrannenhalle for this somewhat sleepy city is the opening times: 24 hours a day, seven days a week there is always something open here, be it a coffee shop or the late-night Weisswurst (Bavarian white sausages) stand.** Ⓜ Marienplatz (U-bahn and S-bahn).

ROYAL MUNICH

From the modest palace of the Alter Hof, the Wittelsbachs expanded their quarters northward, away from the jumble of narrow streets in the old quarter. Three splendid avenues radiated outward from their new palace and garden grounds, and fine homes arose along them. One of them—Prinzregentenstrasse—marks the southern edge of Munich's huge public park, the Englischer Garten, which was also created by a Wittelsbach. Lehel, an upmarket residential neighborhood that straddles the Prinzregentenstrasse, plays host to one of

Munich's most famous museums, the Haus der Kunst, as well as to some lesser-known but architecturally stunning museums.

MAIN ATTRACTIONS

③① **Englischer Garten** *(English Garden).*
★ This virtually endless park, which melds into the open countryside at Munich's northern city limits, was designed for the Bavarian prince Karl Theodor by Benjamin Thompson, later Count Rumford, from Massachusetts, who fled America after having taken the wrong side during the War of Independence. Five kilometers (3 mi) long and 1½ km (about 1 mi) wide, it's Germany's largest city park. The open, informal nature of the park—reminiscent of the rolling parklands with which English aristocrats of the 18th century liked to surround their country homes—gave the park its name. It has a boating lake, four beer gardens, and a series of curious decorative and monumental constructions, including the Monopteros, a Greek temple designed by Leo von Klenze for King Ludwig I and built on an artificial hill in the southern section of the park. There are great sunset views of Munich from the Monopteros hill. In the center of the park's most popular beer garden is a Chinese pagoda erected in 1789. It was destroyed during the war and then reconstructed. ■TIP→ **The Chinese Tower beer garden is world famous, but the park has prettier places for sipping a beer: the Aumeister, for example, along the northern perimeter. The Aumeister's restaurant is in an early-19th-century hunting lodge.** At the Seehaus, on the shore of the Kleinhesseloher *See* (lake), choose between a smart restaurant or a cozy *Bierstube* (beer tavern) in addition to the beer garden right on the lake.

The Englischer Garten is a paradise for joggers, cyclists, musicians, soccer players, sunbathers, dog owners, and, in winter, cross-country skiers. The park has designated areas for nude sunbathing—the Germans have a positively pagan attitude toward the sun—so don't be surprised to see naked bodies bordering the flower beds and paths. ⊠ *Main entrances at Prinzregentenstr. and Königinstr., Schwabing and Lehel.*

②④ **Feldherrnhalle** *(Generals' Hall).* This open-sided pavilion was modeled after the 14th-century Loggia dei Lanzi in Florence and honors three centuries of Bavarian generals. Two huge Bavarian lions are flanked by the larger-than-life statues of Count Johann Tserclaes Tilly, who led Catholic forces in the Thirty Years' War, and Prince Karl Philipp Wrede, hero of the 19th-century Napoleonic Wars. The imposing structure was turned into a militaristic shrine in the 1930s and '40s by the Nazis, who found it significant because it marked the site of Hitler's

TOURING TIPS

Breakfast: Start with a Bavarian breakfast of Weisswurst, pretzels, and Weissbier at the Weisses Bräuhaus on Tal Street between Marienplatz and Isartor or at the Wirtshaus Isarthor just across the road from the Isartor itself.

Scenic Spot: Head to Odeonsplatz and take a peek at the Hofgarten—the former palace grounds.

Snacks: Grab a bite at one of the many laid-back cafés on Schellingstrasse.

1

abortive coup, or putsch, in 1923. All who passed it had to give the Nazi salute. Viscardigasse, a tiny alley behind the Feldherrnhalle linking Residenzstrasse and Theatinerstrasse and now lined with exclusive boutiques, was used by those who wanted to dodge the tedious routine, hence its nickname Heil Hitler Street. ⊠*South end of Odeonspl., City Center* Ⓜ *Odeonsplatz (U-bahn).*

㉜ **Haus der Kunst** *(House of Art).* This colonnaded, classical-style building is one of Munich's few remaining examples of Hitler-era architecture and was officially opened by the Führer himself. In the Hitler years it showed only work deemed to reflect the Nazi aesthetic. One of its most successful postwar exhibitions was devoted to works banned by the Nazis. It hosts exhibitions of art, photography, and sculpture, as well as theatrical and musical happenings. The survival-of-the-chicest disco, P1, is in the building's west wing. ⊠*Prinzregentenstr. 1, Lehel* ☎*089/2112–7113* ⊕*www.hausderkunst.de* ⊠*Varies; generally €7* ⊙*Mon.–Wed. and Fri.–Sun. 10–8, Thurs. 10–10* Ⓜ *Odeonsplatz (U-bahn).*

⑱ **Hofbräuhaus.** Duke Wilhelm V founded Munich's most famous brewery in 1589. Hofbräu means "court brewery," and the golden beer is poured in pitcher-sized liter mugs. If the cavernous ground-floor hall is too noisy for you, there is a quieter restaurant upstairs. In this legendary establishment Americans, Australians, and Italians far outnumber Germans, and the brass band that performs here most days adds modern pop and American folk music to the traditional German numbers. ⊠*Am Platzl 9, City Center* ☎*089/290–136* ⊙*Daily 11–11* Ⓜ *Marienplatz (U-bahn and S-bahn).*

㉓ **Hofgarten** *(Royal Garden).* The formal garden was once part of the royal palace grounds. It's bordered on two sides by arcades designed in the 19th century by court architect, Leo von Klenze. On the east side of the garden is the state chancellery, built around the ruins of the 19th-century Army Museum and incorporating the remains of a Renaissance arcade. Its most prominent feature is a large copper dome. Bombed during World War II air raids, the museum stood untouched for almost 40 years as a grim reminder of the war. It's now known as Palazzo Prozzi, an untranslatable joke referring to the huge sums that went into rebuilding it and its ostentatious look.

In front of the chancellery stands one of Europe's most unusual—some say most effective—war memorials. Instead of looking up at a monument, you are led down to a **sunken crypt** covered by a massive granite block. In the crypt lies a German soldier from World War I. The crypt is a stark contrast to the **memorial** that stands unobtrusively in front of the northern wing of the chancellery: a simple cube of black marble bearing facsimiles of handwritten wartime manifestos by anti-Nazi leaders, including members of the White Rose movement. ⊠*Hofgartenstr., north of Residenz, City Center* Ⓜ *Odeonsplatz (U-bahn).*

㉒ ★ **Residenz** *(Royal Palace).* One of the city's true treasures, Munich's royal palace began as a small castle in the 14th century. The Wittelsbach dukes moved here when the tenements of an expanding Munich encroached upon their Alter Hof. In succeeding centuries the royal residence developed according to the importance, requirements, and interests of its occupants. It came to include the Königsbau (on Max-Joseph-Platz) and then (clockwise) the Alte Residenz; the Festsaal (Banquet Hall); the Altes Residenztheater/Cuvilliés-Theater (at this writing, closed for renovations until sometime in 2008); the newly restored Allerheiligenhofkirche (All Saints' Church), a venue for cultural events; the Residenztheater; and the Nationaltheater.

Building began in 1385 with the **Neuveste** (New Fortress), which comprised the northeast section. Most of it burned to the ground in 1750, but one of its finest rooms survived: the 16th-century **Antiquarium,** which was built for Duke Albrecht V's collection of antique statues (today it's used chiefly for state receptions). The throne room of King Ludwig I, the **Neuer Herkulessaal,** is now a concert hall. The accumulated Wittelsbach treasures are on view in several palace museums. The **Schatzkammer** (*Treasury* €6, *combined ticket with Residenzmuseum €9* *Apr.–Oct. 15, daily 9–6; Oct. 16–Mar., daily 10–4*) has a rather rich centerpiece—a small Renaissance statue of St. George studded with 2,291 diamonds, 209 pearls, and 406 rubies. Paintings, tapestries, furniture, and porcelain are housed in the **Residenzmuseum** (*€4* *Apr.–Oct. 15, daily 9–6; Oct. 16–Mar., daily 10–4*). Antique coins glint in the **Staatliche Münzsammlung** (*€2, free Sun.* *Wed.–Sun. 10–5*). Egyptian works of art make up the **Staatliche Sammlung Ägyptischer Kunst** (*Hofgarten entrance* *089/298–546* *€5, Sun. €1* *Tues. 9–5 and 7–9* PM, *Wed.–Fri. 9–5, weekends 10–5*). ■ TIP→ All the different halls and galleries of the Residenz can be visited with a combination ticket that costs €9. *Max-Joseph-Pl. 3, entrance through archway at Residenzstr. 1, City Center* *089/290–671* *Closed a few days in early Jan.* Odeonsplatz (U-bahn).

㉕ **Theatinerkirche** *(Theatine Church).* This glorious baroque church owes its Italian appearance to its founder, Princess Henriette Adelaide, who commissioned it in gratitude for the birth of her son and heir, Max Emanuel, in 1663. A native of Turin, the princess distrusted Bavarian architects and builders and thus summoned a master builder from Bologna, Agostino Barelli, to construct her church. Barelli worked on the building for 11 years but was dismissed before the project was completed. It was another 100 years before the building was finished. Its lofty towers frame a restrained facade capped by a massive dome. The superb stuccowork on the inside has a remarkably light feeling owing to its brilliant white color. ■ TIP→ The expansive square before the Feldherrnhalle and Theatinerkirche is often used for outdoor stage events. *Theatinerstr. 22, City Center* Odeonsplatz (U-bahn).

■ NEED A BREAK?   Munich's oldest café, **Tambosi** (*Odeonspl., Maxvorstadt* *089/224–768*), borders the street across from the Theatinerkirche. Watch the hustle and bustle from an outdoor table, or retreat through a gate in the Hofgarten's western wall to the café's tree-shaded beer garden. If the weather is cool or rainy, find a corner in the cozy, eclectically furnished interior.

ALSO WORTH SEEING

35 Archäologische Staatssammlung *(State Archaeological Collection).* This is Bavaria's fascinating record of its prehistoric, Roman, and Celtic past. The perfectly preserved body of a ritually sacrificed young girl, recovered from a Bavarian peat moor, is among the more spine-chilling exhibits. Head down to the basement to see the fine Roman mosaic floor. At this writing, the Early Middle Ages and Roman exhibits were closed for renovation, due to open some time in 2008. ⊠ *Lerchenfeldstr. 2, Lehel* ☎ *089/211–2402* ⊕ *www.archaeologie-bayern.de* ⌖ *€3, €1 on Sun.* ⊙ *Tues.–Sun. 9–5* Ⓜ *Lehel (U-bahn).*

33 Bayerisches Nationalmuseum *(Bavarian National Museum).* Although the museum places emphasis on Bavarian cultural history, it has art and artifacts of international importance and regular exhibitions that attract worldwide attention. The museum is a journey through time, from the Middle Ages to the 20th century, with medieval and Renaissance wood carvings, works by the great Renaissance sculptor Tilman Riemenschneider, tapestries, arms and armor, a unique collection of Christmas crèches (the *Krippenschau*), and Bavarian and German folk art. ⊠ *Prinzregentenstr. 3, Lehel* ☎ *089/211–2401* ⊕ *www.bayerisches-nationalmuseum.de* ⌖ *€5 recommended combined ticket for museum and Bollert collection, €1 Sun.* ⊙ *Tues.–Sun. 10–5, Thurs. 10–8* Ⓜ *Lehel (U-bahn).*

30 DenkStätte Weisse Rose *(Memorial to the Weisse Rose Resistance Group).* Siblings Hans and Sophie Scholl, fellow students Alexander Schmorell and Christian Probst, and Kurt Huber, professor of philosophy, founded the short-lived resistance movement against the Nazis in 1942–43 known as the Weisse Rose (White Rose). All were executed. A small exhibition about their work is in the inner quad of the university, where the Scholls were caught distributing leaflets and denounced by the janitor. ⊠ *Geschwister-Scholl-Pl. 1, Maxvorstadt* ☎ *089/2180–3053* ⌖ *Free* ⊙ *Mon.–Thurs. 10–4, Fri. 10–3* Ⓜ *Universität (U-bahn).*

26 Kunsthalle der Hypo-Kulturstiftung *(Hall of the Hypobank's Cultural Foundation).* Chagall, Giacometti, Picasso, and Gauguin were among the artists featured in the past at this exhibition hall in the midst of the commercial pedestrian zone. The foundation's success over the years has led to its expansion, designed by the Swiss architect team Herzog and de Meuron, who also designed London's Tate Modern. ■ TIP→ The gallery is in the upscale Fünf Höfe shopping mall. ⊠ *Theatinerstr. 8, City Center* ☎ *089/224–412* ⊕ *www.hypo-kunsthalle.de* ⌖ *€8* ⊙ *Daily 10–8* Ⓜ *Odeonsplatz (U-bahn).*

29 Ludwigskirche *(Ludwig's Church).* Planted halfway along the stark, neoclassically styled Ludwigstrasse is this curious neo-Byzantine–early-Renaissance church, built at the behest of Ludwig I to provide his newly completed suburb with a parish church. It's worth a stop to see the fresco of the *Last Judgment* in the choir. At 60 feet by 37 feet, it's one of the world's largest. ⊠ *Ludwigstr. 22, Maxvorstadt* ☎ *089/287–7990* ⊙ *Daily 7–7* Ⓜ *Universität (U-bahn).*

NEED A BREAK?

For lunch, wander across Ludwig-strasse to the heart of the student quarter, where there are a wide variety of inexpensive but good restaurants. Light vegetarian food with a definite Asian touch is served to those on the fly at **S.M. Vegetarisch** (✉ *Amalienstr. 45* ☎ *089/281–882*). ■TIP➔ The prices are perfect for those on a budget.

⑲ **Maximilianstrasse.** Munich's sophisticated shopping street was named after King Maximilian II, who wanted to break away from the Greek-influenced classical architecture favored by his father, Ludwig I. He thus created this broad boulevard lined with majestic buildings culminating on a rise above the Isar River at the stately **Maximilianeum,**

LEOPOLDSTRASSE

Leopoldstrasse throbs with life from spring to fall, with cafés, wine terraces, and the occasional artist stall. Formerly Munich's bohemian quarters, Schwabing has unfortunately become a bit monotonous in its present-day form, but you can explore the side streets of old Schwabing around Wedekindplatz near Münchener Freiheit or enjoy the shops and cafés in the student quarter to the west of Leopoldstrasse (the intersection of Turkenstrasse and Schellingstrasse is always buzzing).

---

a lavish 19th-century palace built for Maximilian II and now home to the Bavarian state parliament. Only the terrace can be visited.

㊱ **Museum Villa Stuck.** This beautiful neoclassical villa is the former home of one of Munich's leading turn-of-the-20th-century artists, Franz von Stuck (1863–1928). His work, at times haunting, at times erotic, and occasionally humorous, covers the walls of the ground-floor rooms. The museum also features the artist's former quarters, which were renovated in 2005, as well as special exhibits. There are now guided tours in English. ✉ *Prinzregentenstr. 60, Haidhausen* ☎ *089/455–5510* ⊕ *www.villastuck.de* 🎫 *€8* 🕐 *Wed.–Sun. 11–6* Ⓜ *Prinzregentenplatz (U-bahn).*

㉑ **Nationaltheater** *(National Theater).* Built in the late 19th century as a royal opera house with a pillared portico, this large theater was bombed during the war but is now restored to its original splendor and has some of the world's most advanced stage technology. It is home to the Bavarian State Opera Company. ✉ *Max-Joseph-Pl. 2, City Center* ☎ *089/2185–1920 for tickets* Ⓜ *Odeonsplatz (U-bahn).*

㉞ **Schack-Galerie.** Florid and romantic 19th-century German paintings (some now obscure) make up the collections of the Schack-Galerie, originally the private collection of Count Schack. ✉ *Prinzregentenstr. 9, Lehel* ☎ *089/2380–5224* 🎫 *€3, €1 Sun.* 🕐 *Wed.–Mon. 10–5* Ⓜ *Lehel (U-bahn).*

㉗ **Siegestor** *(Victory Arch).* Marking the beginning of Leopoldstrasse, the Siegestor has Italian origins—it was modeled after the Arch of Constantine in Rome—and was built to honor the achievements of the Bavarian army during the Wars of Liberation (1813–15). The inscription on the side facing the inner city reads: DEDICATED TO VICTORY, DESTROYED

BY WAR, ADMONISHING PEACE. ✉ *Leopoldstr., Schwabing* Ⓜ *Unversität (U-bahn).*

❷⑧ **SiemensForum.** Siemens has been one of Germany's major employers and technological innovators for more than 150 years. This surprisingly entertaining company museum, housed in a spaceship-like building, shows visitors the many areas in which Siemens has been active, from old-fashioned telegraph systems to hypermodern dentist chairs and fuel cells. Hands-on displays such as video telephones spice up the experience. ✉ *Oskar-von-Miller-Ring, Maxvorstadt* ☎ *089/6363–3210* ⊕ *www.siemensforum.de* 🎟 *Free* ⊙ *Sun.–Fri. 9–5, 1st Tues. in month 9–9* Ⓜ *Odeonsplatz (U-bahn).*

❷⓿ **Staatliches Museum für Völkerkunde** (*State Museum of Ethnology*). Arts and crafts from around the world are displayed in this extensive museum. There are also regular special exhibits. ✉ *Maximilianstr. 42, Lehel* ☎ *089/2101–3610* ⊕ *www.voelkerkundemuseum-muenchen.de* 🎟 *€3.50, €1 Sun.* ⊙ *Tues.–Sun. 9:30–5:15* Ⓜ *Lehel (U-bahn).*

LUDWIGSTRASSE ARCHITECTURE

The stretch of buildings designed by royal architect Leo von Klenze gives Ludwigstrasse a grandiose air. Klenze swept aside the small dwellings and alleys that once stood here and replaced them with severe neoclassical structures such as the Universität (University) and the peculiarly Byzantine Ludwigskirche. Müncheners tend to either love or hate Klenze's formal buildings, which end at the Siegestor (Victory Arch). Another leading architect, Friedrich von Gärtner, took over from here, adding more delicate structures that are a pleasant backdrop to the busy street life of Schwabing.

SCHWABING & MAXVORSTADT: ART MUSEUMS & GALLERIES

Most of the city's leading art galleries are located in lower Schwabing and Maxvorstadt, making this area the primary museum quarter. Schwabing, the former artists' neighborhood, is no longer quite the bohemian area where such diverse residents as Lenin and Kandinsky were once neighbors, but the cultural foundations of Maxvorstadt are immutable. Where the two areas meet, in the streets behind the university, life hums with a creative vibrancy that is difficult to detect elsewhere in Munich. The difficult part is having time to see it all.

TIMING This area could take an entire day, depending on how long you linger at any of the major museums found here. Avoid the museum crowds by visiting as early in the day as possible. All Munich seems to discover an interest in art on Sunday, when admission to most municipal and state-funded museums is free; you might want to take this day off from culture and join the late-breakfast and brunch crowd at the Elisabethmarkt, a beer garden, or at any of the many bars and *Gaststätten* (taverns). Some have Sunday-morning jazz concerts. Many Schwabing bars have happy hours between 6 and 8—a relaxing way to end your day.

MAIN ATTRACTIONS

42 Alte Pinakothek *(Old Picture Gal-*
Fodor'sChoice *lery)*. The long, massive brick Alte
★ Pinakothek was constructed by Leo
von Klenze between 1826 and 1836
to exhibit the collection of old masters begun by Duke Wilhelm IV in
the 16th century. By all accounts
it is one of the world's great picture galleries. Among the European
masterpieces here from the 14th to
the 18th centuries are paintings by
Dürer, Titian, Rembrandt, Rubens
(the museum has one of the world's largest collections of works by
Rubens), and two celebrated Murillos. Not to be missed. ⊠ *Barerstr. 27, Maxvorstadt* ☎ *089/2380–5216* ⊕ *www.alte-pinakothek.de*
☑ *€5.50, €1 Sun.; combined day ticket with Neue Pinakothek and
Pinakothek der Moderne €11* ☉ *Daily 10–6, Tues. 10–8,* Ⓜ *Königsplatz (U-bahn)*.

38 Königsplatz *(King's Square)*. This elegant and expansive square is lined
on three sides with the monumental Grecian-style buildings designed
by Leo von Klenze that gave Munich the nickname Athens on the Isar.
The two templelike structures opposite each other are now the Antikensammlungen and the Glyptothek museums. Although a busy road
passes through it, the square has maintained the dignified appearance
intended by Ludwig I thanks to the broad green lawns sprawling in
front of the museums. In summertime, concerts and outdoor cinema
take place on this grand square. Ⓜ *Königsplatz (U-bahn)*.

43 Neue Pinakothek *(New Picture Gallery)*. This fabulous museum opened
in 1981 to house the royal collection of modern art left homeless and
scattered after its building was destroyed in the war. The exterior of the
modern building mimics an older one with Italianate influences. The
interior offers a magnificent environment for picture gazing, at least
partly owing to the natural light flooding in from skylights. French
impressionists—Monet, Degas, Manet—are all well represented. The
19th-century German and Scandinavian paintings—misty landscapes
predominate—are only now coming to be recognized as admirable
products of their time. Another must see. ⊠ *Barerstr. 29, Maxvorstadt*
☎ *089/2380–5195* ⊕ *www.neue-pinakothek.de* ☑ *€5.50, €1 Sun.*
☉ *Daily 10–6, Wed. 10–8* Ⓜ *Königsplatz (U-bahn)*.

44 Pinakothek der Moderne. Munich's latest cultural addition is also Germany's largest museum for modern art, architecture, and design. The
striking glass-and-concrete complex holds four outstanding art and
architectural collections, including modern art, industrial and graphic
design, the Bavarian State collection of graphic art, and the Technical University's architectural museum. Exhibitions rotate every several
months. This one is another must in the museum quarter. ⊠ *Barerstr.
40, Maxvorstadt* ☎ *089/2380–5360* ⊕ *www.pinakothek-der-moderne.
de* ☑ *€9.50, €1 Sun.; combined day ticket with Neue Pinakothek and*

CLOSE UP

Bavaria: A Country Within a Country

1

For most visitors, Bavaria, with its traditional Gemütlichkeit, beer gardens, quaint little villages, and culturally rich cities, is often seen as the quintessence of Germany. In fact, nothing could be further from the truth. Of the 16 German Länder, as the German federal states are called, none is more fiercely independent than Bavaria. In fact, it was an autonomous dukedom and later kingdom until 1871, when it was incorporated into the German empire.

For Bavarians, anything beyond the state's borders remains foreign territory. The state has its own anthem and its own flag, part of which, the blue-and-white lozenges in the center, has virtually become a regional trademark symbolizing quality and tradition. Bavarian politicians discussing the issue of Europe in speeches will often refer to Bavaria almost as if it were a national state. And they

will inevitably call it by its full official name: Freistaat Bayern, or simply der Freistaat, meaning "the Free State." The term was coined by Kurt Eisner, Minister President of the Socialist government that rid the land of the Wittelsbach dynasty in 1918. It is simply a German way of saying republic—a land governed by the people. And it has an honorable place in the first line of the separate Bavarian constitution that was signed under the aegis of the American occupational forces in 1946.

Bavaria is not the only Freistaat in Germany, a fact not too many Germans are aware of. Thuringia and Saxony also boast of that title. But the Bavarians are the only ones who make such a public point of it. As they say, clocks in Bavaria run differently. Now you know why...

—Marton Radkai

Pinakothek der Moderne €11 ⊙ *Tues., Wed., and weekends 10–5, Thurs. and Fri. 10–8* Ⓜ *Königsplatz (U-bahn).*

NEED A BREAK?

Ideal for a quick lunch with German, French, or Italian flair is the ever popular **Brasserie Tresznjewski** (⊠ *Theresienstr. 72, at Barerstr., Maxvorstadt* ☎ *089/282–349*). It's a good spot especially if you are visiting the neighboring Pinakotheks, and it serves food well into the wee hours.

④ **Städtische Galerie im Lenbachhaus** *(Municipal Gallery).* This exquisite late-19th-century Florentine-style villa is the former home and studio of the artist Franz von Lenbach (1836–1904). If for no other reason, this museum is worth a visit for the awe-inspiring assemblage of art from the early-20th-century Der *Blaue Reiter* (Blue Rider) group: Kandinsky, Klee, Jawlensky, Macke, Marc, and Münter. But there are also vivid pieces from the New Objectivity movement, and a variety of local Munich artists are represented here. Rotating exhibits round off this eclectic and stylish museum. Lenbach's former chambers are on display as well. The adjoining **Kunstbau** (art building), a former subway platform of the Königsplatz station, hosts changing exhibitions of modern art. ⊠ *Luisenstr. 33, Maxvorstadt* ☎ *089/233–32000* ⊕ *www.lenbachhaus.de* 🎫 *€6* ⊙ *Tues.–Sun. 10–6* Ⓜ *Königsplatz (U-bahn).*

ALSO WORTH SEEING

40 **Antikensammlungen** *(Antiquities Collection)*. This museum has a beautiful collection of small sculptures, Etruscan art, Greek vases, gold, and glass. ⊠*Königspl. 1, Maxvorstadt* ☎*089/5998–8830* ⊕*www.antike-am-koenigsplatz.mwn.de* ⊠€3.50 €1 Sun.; combined ticket to Antikensammlungen and Glyptothek €5.50 ⊙Tues. and Thurs.–Sun. 10–5, Wed. 10–8 Ⓜ Königsplatz (U-bahn).

37 **Dreifaltigkeitskirche** *(Church of the Holy Trinity)*. Take a quick look at this fanciful church near Maximiliansplatz. After a local woman prophesied doom for the city unless a new church was erected, its striking baroque exterior was promptly built between 1711 and 1718. It has frescoes by Cosmas Damian Asam depicting various heroic scenes. ⊠*Pacellistr. 10, City Center* ☎*089/290–0820* ⊙*Daily 7–7, except during services* Ⓜ *Karlsplatz (U-bahn and S-bahn)*.

45 **Elisabethmarkt** *(Elisabeth Market)*. Schwabing's permanent outdoor market is smaller than the popular Viktualienmarkt, but hardly less colorful. It has a pocket-size beer garden, where a jazz band performs on Saturdays in summer. ⊠*Arcistr. and Elisabethstr., Schwabing* Ⓜ *Giselastrasse (U-bahn)*.

39 **Glyptothek.** This amazing collection of Greek and Roman sculptures is
★ among the finest exhibits in Munich. ■**TIP**➔ **The small café that expands into the quiet courtyard is a favorite for visitors, which include budding artists practicing their drawing skills.** ⊠*Königspl. 3, Maxvorstadt* ☎*089/286–100* ⊕*www.antike-am-koenigsplatz.mwn.de* ⊠€3.50 €1 Sun.; combined ticket to Glyptothek and Antikensammlungen €5.50 ⊙Tues., Wed., and Fri.–Sun. 10–5, Thurs. 10–8 Ⓜ Königsplatz (U-bahn).

OUTSIDE THE CENTER

MAIN ATTRACTIONS

Oktoberfest Grounds at Theresienwiese. The site of Munich's notorious Oktoberfest and the seasonal Tollwood markets is only a 10-minute walk from Hauptbahnhof, or one stop on the subway (U-4 or U-5). The enormous exhibition ground is named after Princess Therese von Sachsen-Hildburghausen, who celebrated her marriage to the Bavarian crown prince Ludwig I here in 1810. The fair was such a success that it became an annual event that has now morphed into a 16-day international beer bonanza attracting more than 6 million people each year (it is the *Oktober* fest because it always ends on the first Sunday in October).

Overlooking the Theresienwiese is a 19th-century hall of fame (Ruhmeshalle) featuring busts of numerous popular figures of the time—one of the last works of Ludwig I—and a monumental bronze statue of the maiden **Bavaria,** more than 60 feet high. The statue is hollow, and 130 steps take you up into the braided head for a view of Munich through Bavaria's eyes. ⊠€3 ⊙Apr.–Nov., daily 9–6. Ⓜ *Theresienhöhe (U-bahn)*.

OKTOBERFEST

1

Not even the wildest Bavarians can be held wholly responsible for the staggering consumption of beer and food at the annual Oktoberfest, which starts at the end of September and ends in early October. On average, around 1,183,000 gallons of beer along with 750,000 roasted chickens and 650,000 sausages are put away by revelers from around the world. To partake, book lodging by April, and if you're traveling with a group, also reserve bench space within one of the 14 tents. See Munich's Web site, ⊕ *www.* *muenchen-tourist.de*, for beer-tent contacts. The best time to arrive at the grounds is lunchtime, when it's easier to find a seat—by 4 PM it's packed and they'll close the doors. Take advantage of an hour or two of sobriety to tour the fairground rides, which are an integral part of Oktoberfest. Under no circumstances attempt any rides—all of which claim to be the world's most dangerous— after a couple of pints. The disgrace of throwing up on the figure eight is truly Germanic in scale.

⟳ **Olympiapark** *(Olympic Park)*. On the northern edge of Schwabing, undulating circus-tent-like roofs cover the stadiums built for the 1972 Olympic Games. The roofs are made of translucent tiles that glisten in the sun and act as amplifiers for the rock concerts held here. ■ **TIP→ For €30 you can climb the roofs with rubber-sole shoes in good weather, and for an extra €10 you can rappel down from the roof.** Tours of the park are conducted on a Disneyland-style train throughout the day. An elevator will speed you up the 960-foot **Olympia Tower** (€4) for a view of the city and the Alps (on a clear day). There's also a revolving restaurant near the top. ☏ *089/3067–2414, 089/3066–8585 restaurant* ⊕ *www. olympiapark-muenchen.de* ▦ *Adventure tour €7, stadium tour €5, tower €4* ⊗ *Tour schedules vary; call ahead for departure times* Ⓜ *Olympiazentrum (U-bahn 3).*

★ **Schloss Nymphenburg.** This glorious baroque and rococo palace is the largest of its kind in Germany, stretching more than 1 km (½ mi) from one wing to the other. The palace grew in size and scope over a period of more than 200 years, beginning as a summer residence built on land given by Prince Ferdinand Maria to his beloved wife, Henriette Adelaide, on the occasion of the birth of their son and heir, Max Emanuel, in 1663. The princess hired the Italian architect Agostino Barelli to build both the Theatinerkirche and the palace, which was completed in 1675 by his successor, Enrico Zuccalli. Within the original building, now the central axis of the palace complex, is a magnificent hall, the **Steinerner Saal**, extending over two floors and richly decorated with stucco and grandiose frescoes. In summer, chamber-music concerts are given here. One of the surrounding royal chambers houses the famous **Schönheitsgalerie** (Gallery of Beauties). The walls are hung from floor to ceiling with portraits of women who caught the roving eye of Ludwig I, among them a butcher's daughter and an English duchess. The most famous portrait is of Lola Montez, a sultry beauty and high-class courtesan who, after a time as the mistress of Franz Liszt and later

Alexandre Dumas, so enchanted King Ludwig I that he almost bankrupted the state for her sake and was ultimately forced to abdicate.

The palace is in a park laid out in formal French style, with low hedges and gravel walks extending into woodland. Among the ancient tree stands are three fascinating structures. The **Amalienburg** hunting lodge is a rococo gem built by François Cuvilliés. The silver-and-blue stucco of the little Amalienburg creates an atmosphere of courtly high life, making clear that the pleasures of the chase did not always take place outdoors. Of the lodges, only Amalienburg is open in winter. In the lavishly appointed kennels you'll see that even the dogs lived in luxury. The **Pagodenburg** was built for royal tea parties. Its elegant French exterior disguises a suitably Asian interior in which exotic teas from India and China were served. Swimming parties were held in the **Badenburg,** Europe's first post-Roman heated pool.

Nymphenburg contains so much of interest that a day hardly provides enough time. Don't leave without visiting the former royal stables, now the **Marstallmuseum** (*Museum of Royal Carriages* €2.50). It houses a fleet of vehicles, including an elaborately decorated sleigh in which King Ludwig II once glided through the Bavarian twilight, postilion torches lighting the way. On the walls hang portraits of the royal horses. Also exhibited are examples of Nymphenburg porcelain, produced here between 1747 and the 1920s. A popular museum in the north wing of the palace has nothing to do with the Wittelsbachs but is one of Nymphenburg's major attractions. The **Museum Mensch und Natur** (*Museum of Man and Nature* ☎089/179–5890 €2.50, €1 Sun. ⊘ Tues.–Sun. 9–5) concentrates on three areas of interest: the variety of life on Earth, the history of humankind, and our place in the environment. Main exhibits include a huge representation of the human brain and a chunk of Alpine crystal weighing half a ton. Take Tram 17 or Bus 41 from the city center to the Schloss Nymphenburg stop. ✉Notburgastr. at bridge crossing Nymphenburg Canal, Nymphenburg ☎089/179–080 ⊕www.schloesser.bayern.de ✉Schloss Nymphenburg complex, combined ticket including Marstallmuseum but not Museum Mensch und Natur, €10, €8 in winter, when parts of complex are closed ⊘Apr.– Oct. 15, daily 9–6; Oct. 16–Mar., daily 10–4.

ALSO WORTH SEEING

Bavaria Filmstadt. For real movie buffs, Munich has its own Hollywood-like neighborhood, Geiselgasteig, on the southern outskirts of the city. Films like *Das Boot* (*The Boat*) and *Die Unendliche Geschichte* (*The Neverending Story*) were made here. There are a number of tours and shows ranging in price from €4 to a combined €19 ticket. Check the Web site or call for more information. ☎089/64990 ⊕www.film-stadt.de.

BMW Museum. Munich is the home of the famous BMW car company. Its museum, a circular tower that looks as if it served as a set for *Star Wars,* is unfortunately closed until mid-2008. No exact date has been set for its reopening. However, the exhibition has been moved across the street to a building next to the Olympia tower. It contains not only

1

a dazzling collection of BMWs old and new but also items and exhibitions relating to the company's social history and its technical developments. It's a great thing to do if you're at the Olympia Park already. ⊕*www.bmw-welt.de* ☞*€2* ⊗*Daily 10–8* Ⓜ *Petuelring (U-bahn).* The **BMW factory** (✉*Petuelring 130, Milbertshofen* ☎*089/3895–3308* ⊕*www.bmw-plant-munich.com* ⊗*Tours Mon.–Fri. at 6* PM) is also nearby and can be toured on weekdays. However, registration for plant tours is *only* possible in advance using the electronic registration form, which is only in German. There is no longer a phone number to call for reservations.■TIP→ **Reserve weeks in advance if you want to get a slot during your trip.**

Botanischer Garten *(Botanical Garden).* Located on the eastern edge of Schloss Nymphenburg, this collection of 14,000 plants, including orchids, cacti, cycads, Alpine flowers, and rhododendrons, makes up one of the most extensive botanical gardens in Europe. Take Tram 17 or Bus 41 from the city center. ✉*Menzingerstr. 67, Nymphenburg* ☎*089/1786–1316* ☞*€3* ⊗*Garden Oct.–Mar., daily 9–4:30; Apr., Sept., daily 9–6; May, Aug., daily 9–7. Hothouses close 30 min. earlier and during lunch from 11:45 to 1 in summer.*

Deutsches Museum–"Flugwerft Schleissheim." Connoisseurs of airplanes and flying machines will appreciate this magnificent offshoot of the Deutsches Museum, some 20 km (12 mi) north of the city center. It's an ideal complement to a visit to Schloss Schleissheim. ■TIP→ **There is a combination ticket with the Deutsches Museum, too.** ✉*Effnerstr. 7, Oberschleissheim* ☎*089/315–7140* ⊕*www.deutsches-museum.de* ☞*€5, combined ticket with the Deutsches Museum €10* ⊗*Daily 9–5* Ⓜ *Oberschleissheim (S-bahn 1) and 15-min. walk or bus 292 (no weekend service).*

↻ **Hellabrunn Zoo.** Set right down on the Isar a bit upstream from town, this attractive zoo has many park-like enclosures but a minimum of cages. Some of the older buildings are in typical art-nouveau style. Care has been taken to group animals according to their natural and geographical habitats. The **Urwaldhaus** (Rain-Forest House) offers guided tours at night (call ahead of time). The 170 acres include restaurants and children's areas. Take Bus 52 from Marienplatz or U-bahn 3 to Thalkirchen, at the southern edge of the city. ✉*Tierparkstr. 30, Thalkirchen* ☎*089/625–080* ⊕*www.zoo-munich.de* ☞*€9* ⊗*Apr.–Sept., daily 8–6; Oct.–Mar., daily 9–5* Ⓜ *Thalkirchen (U-bahn).*

Schloss Schleissheim *(Schleissheim Palace).* In 1597 Duke Wilhelm V decided to look for a peaceful retreat outside Munich, and found what he wanted at this palace. Prince Max Emanuel later added two more palaces. One, the **Lustheim,** houses Germany's largest collection of Meissen porcelain. Take the S-bahn 1 line to Oberschleissheim station and then walk about 15 minutes or take bus 292 (no weekend service). ✉*Maximilianshof 1, Oberschleissheim* ☎*089/315–8720* ☞*Combined ticket for 3 palaces €6* ⊗*Apr.–Oct. 15, Tues.–Sun. 9–6; Oct. 16–Mar., Tues.–Sun. 10–4.*

WHERE TO EAT

Munich claims to be Germany's gourmet capital. It certainly has an inordinate number of very fine restaurants, but you won't have trouble finding a vast range of options in both price and style. For connoisseurs, wining and dining at Tantris, widely regarded as Munich's best restaurant, or the Königshof could well turn into the equivalent of a religious experience. Alternatively, the high-quality traditional fare at more modest establishments will get you into the Bavarian swing of things. Either way, epicureans are convinced that one can dine as well in Munich as in any other city on the continent.

Some Munich restaurants serve sophisticated cuisine and expect their patrons to dress for the occasion. Unfortunately, folks in Munich have a tendency to look down their noses at the sartorially unprepared. Most restaurants, however, will serve you regardless of what you wear.

WHAT IT COSTS IN EUROS					
	¢	$	$$	$$$	$$$$
AT DINNER	under €9	€9–€15	€16–€20	€21–€25	over €25

Restaurant prices are per person for a main course at dinner.

CITY CENTER

$$$$ ✕**Königshof.** They say this reliable old hotel restaurant is second only to Tantris. The unfortunate concrete slab exterior of the building with its advertising signs belies an elegant restaurant and outstanding French- and Japanese-influenced menus created by chef Martin Fauster, former sous-chef at Tantris. If you book a window table you'll have a wonderful view of Munich's busiest square, the Stachus, an incandescent experience at night. Fantastic wine selection. ⊠ *Karlspl. 25, City Center, D–80335* ☎*089/5513–6142* ⚑*Reservations essential.* Jacket and tie ⊟*AE, DC, MC, V* ⊘*Closed Sun. No lunch in Aug.* Ⓜ *Karlsplatz (U-bahn and S-bahn).*

$$–$$$ ✕**Halali.** With nearly 100 years of history to its credit, the Halali is an old-style Munich restaurant with polished wood paneling and antlers on the walls, and it is *the* place to try traditional dishes of venison and other game. Save room for the homemade vanilla ice cream. ⊠*Schönfeldstr. 22, City Center, D–80539* ☎*089/285–909* Jacket and tie recommended ⊟*AE, MC, V* ⊘*Closed Sun. No lunch Sat.* Ⓜ *Odeonsplatz (U-bahn and S-bahn).*

$$–$$$ ✕**Hunsinger's Pacific.** Werner Hunsinger, one of Munich's top restaurateurs, has created a reasonably priced restaurant serving eclectic cuisine that borrows from the Pacific Rim. The menu, which is constantly in flux but always seductive, focuses on seafood. Try the tuna carpaccio or one of the many "small dishes," which will give you a good panoramic taste of the place. At lunch, two-course meals cost around €12. ⊠*Maximilianspl. 5 (entrance around corner on Max-Josef Str.), City Center, D–80333* ☎*089/5502–9741* ⊟*AE, DC, MC, V* ⊘*No lunch weekends* Ⓜ *Karlsplatz (U-bahn and S-bahn).*

$$–$$$ ✗**Seven Fish.** A couple hundred yards from Viktualienmarkt on Gärt-
★   nerplatz is the upmarket but not uptight Seven Fish restaurant. With
decor reminiscent of New York, the place has a delightful array of fish
dishes and a nice wine selection. The list of fish and seafood dishes
changes daily, based on the freshest catch. You can either go for a lovely
multi-course meal or choose the Japanese-influenced appetizers at the
tiny bar. Sit outside if the weather is nice and watch the people go by
on Gärtnerplatz. Reservations recommended. ⊠ *Gärtnerplatz 6, City
Center, D–80469* ☎ *089/2300–0219* ⊟ *AE, MC, V* Ⓜ *Marienplatz
(U-bahn).*

$$–$$$ ✗**Buffet Kull.** This simple yet comfortable international bistro delivers
★   a high-quality dining experience accompanied by a wonderful variety
of wines and friendly service. Dishes range from Bohemian pheasant
soup to venison medallions and excellent steaks. The daily specials
are creative, portions are generous, and the prices are good value for
the quality. Reservations are recommended, or at least get there early
(dinner service starts at 6 PM). ⊠ *Marienstr. 4, City Center, D–80331*
☎ *089/221–509* ⊟ *No credit cards* Ⓜ *Marienplatz (U-bahn and
S-bahn).*

$$–$$$ ✗**Dukatz.** A mixed crowd frequents this stylish gallery, bistro, and res-
★   taurant in the Literaturhaus, a converted city mansion. Fare includes
German nouvelle cuisine and Mediterranean flavors, but there's a strong
Gallic touch with dishes such as veal marengo and leg of venison. Note
the verbal art, some of it by New York artist Jennifer Holzer, such as
the statement at the bottom of your cup saying: MORE EROTICISM, GEN-
TLEMEN! ⊠ *Salvatorplatz 1, City Center, D–80333* ☎ *089/291–9600*
⊟ *No credit cards* Ⓜ *Odeonsplatz (U-bahn).*

$$–$$$ ✗**Weinhaus Neuner.** Munich's oldest wine tavern serves good food as
well as superior wines in its three nooks: the wood-panel restaurant,
the Weinstube, and the small bistro. The choice of food is remarkable, from roast duck to fish to traditional Bavarian. Specialties include
home-smoked beef and salmon. ⊠ *Herzogspitalstr. 8, City Center, D–
80333* ☎ *089/260–3954* ⊟ *AE, MC, V* ☾ *Closed Sun.* Ⓜ *Marienplatz
(U-bahn and S-bahn).*

$$–$$ ✗**Monaco.** This Italian place makes its guests feel at home right away,
ensuring a loyal clientele. The decor is simple and unpretentious. Excellent wines on the menu are backed by a nice selection of homestyle
pasta dishes, pizza, and salads. They have nicely priced lunch specials
as well. Ask your waiter for recommendations. Just a few minutes from
Viktualienmarkt heading toward Gärtnerplatz. ⊠ *Reichenbachstr. 10,
City Center, D–80469* ☎ *089/268–141* ⊟ *MC, V* Ⓜ *Marienplatz (U-
bahn and S-bahn).*

$$–$$ ✗**Nürnberger Bratwurst Glöckl am Dom.** Munich's most original beer tavern is dedicated to the delicious *Nürnberger Bratwürste* (finger-size
sausages), a specialty from the rival city of Nürnberg. They're served by
a busy team of friendly waitresses dressed in Bavarian dirndls who flit
between the crowded tables with remarkable agility. In summer, tables
are placed outside under a large awning and in the shade of the nearby
Frauenkirche. In winter the mellow dark-panel dining rooms provide
relief from the cold. ■ TIP➔ **For a quick beer you can check the side door**

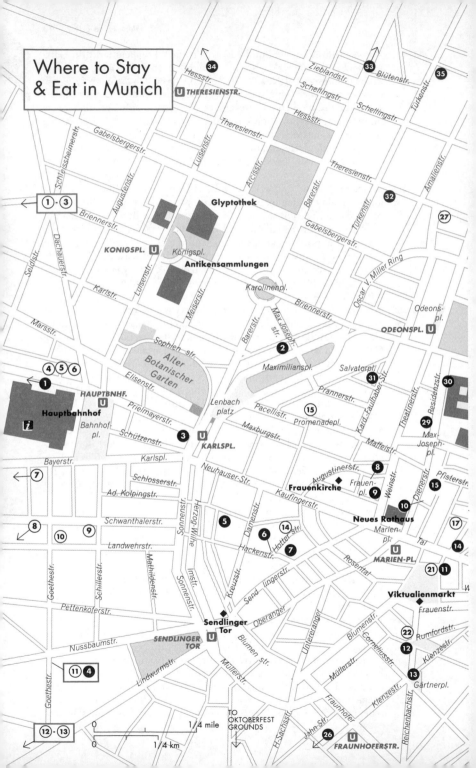

Where to Stay & Eat in Munich

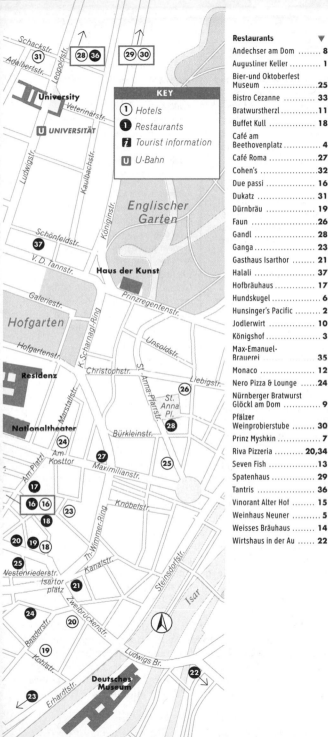

KEY

- ① *Hotels*
- ❶ *Restaurants*
- 🛈 *Tourist information*
- Ⓤ *U-Bahn*

SNACKS

It seems that Munich loves to snack, and a tempting array of food is available almost anytime. The generic term for snacks is *Imbiss,* and thanks to growing international-ism you'll find all types of them, from the generic *Wiener* (hot dogs) to the Turkish *Döner Kebap* sand-wich (pressed and roasted lamb, beef, or chicken). Almost all butcher shops and bakeries offer some sort of *Brotzeit* snack, which can range from a modest sandwich to a steam-ing plate of goulash with potatoes and salad.

Some edibles come with social eti-quette attached. The *Weisswurst,* a tender minced-veal sausage—made fresh daily, steamed, and served with sweet mustard and a crisp roll or a pretzel—is a Munich institution and is served before noon with a *Weissbier* (wheat beer), suppos-edly to counteract the effects of a hangover. Legend has it that this white sausage was invented in 1857 by a butcher who *had* a hangover and mixed the wrong ingredients. A plaque on a wall on Marienplatz marks where the "mistake" was made. Some people use a knife and fork to remove the edible part from the skin; the rougher crowd might indulge in *auszuzeln,* sucking the sausage out of the Weisswurst.

Another favorite Bavarian specialty is *Leberkäs*—literally "liver cheese," although neither liver nor cheese is among its ingredients. It's a sort of meat loaf baked to a crusty turn each morning and served in suc-culent slabs throughout the day. A *Leberkäs Semmel*—a wedge of the meat loaf between two halves of a crispy bread roll slathered with a slightly spicy mustard—is the favorite Munich on-the-go snack.

For late-night snacks, previously almost unobtainable in this sleepy town, go to the Schrannenhalle next to the Viktualienmarkt.

where, just inside, there is a little window serving fresh Augustiner from a wooden barrel. You can stand there with some of the regulars or enjoy the small courtyard if the weather is nice. ⊠ *Frauenpl. 9, City Center, D–80333* ☎ *089/220–385* ☐ *DC, MC, V* Ⓜ *Marienplatz (U-bahn and S-bahn).*

¢–$$ ✕ **Andechser am Dom.** At this Munich mainstay for both locals and visi-tors, the vaulted, frescoed ceiling and the old stone floor recall the Andechs monastery. The boldly Bavarian food—blood sausage with potatoes, Weisswurst in champagne—and fine selection of delectable Andechs beers will quickly put you at ease. The covered terrace with a view of the Frauenkirche is a favorite meeting place, rain or shine, for shoppers, local businesspeople, and even the occasional VIP. ⊠ *Weinstr. 7a, City Center, D–80333* ☎ *089/298–481* ☐ *AE, MC, V* Ⓜ *Marien-platz (U-bahn and S-bahn).*

¢–$$ ✕ **Café Roma.** At the opposite end of Maximilianstrasse from the Opera
★ is the spacious and popular Café Roma. With a massive outdoor seating area, a wide selection of excellent dishes, and perhaps the best coffee in town, Roma suits as a lunch break while window-shopping on Maxi-milianstrasse or a nicely priced dinner before hitting the town. Dishes range from salads and sandwiches to Asian and fish or pasta. They

also have a great cocktail selection. ⊠*Maximilianstr. 31, City Center, D–80539* ☎*089/227435* ▤*AE, MC, V* Ⓜ *Tram 19 Kammerspiele.*

¢–$$ ✗**Dürnbräu.** A fountain plays outside this picturesque old Bavarian inn. Inside, it's crowded and noisy, and you should expect to share a table (the 21-foot table in the middle of the place is a favorite). At this true Munich classic in the old town your fellow diners will range from businesspeople to students. The food is resolutely traditional—try the cream of spinach soup and the boiled beef. ⊠*Dürnbräug. 2, City Center, D–80331* ☎*089/222–195* ▤*AE, DC, MC, V* Ⓜ *Marienplatz (U-bahn and S-bahn).*

¢–$$ ✗**Hundskugel.** This is Munich's oldest tavern, and also one of the city's
★ smallest. You'll be asked to squeeze together and make room for late-comers looking for a spot at one of the few tables clustered in the handkerchief-size dining room. The tavern dates from 1440, and in many ways doesn't appear to have changed much over the centuries. Even the menu is medievally basic and a bit hit-or-miss, although any combination of pork and potatoes or sauerkraut can be recommended. ⊠*Hotterstr. 18, City Center, D–80331* ☎*089/264–272* ▤*No credit cards* Ⓜ *Marienplatz (U-bahn and S-bahn).*

¢–$$ ✗**Jodlerwirt.** This cozy little Alpine lodge-styled restaurant is a splendid treat for those craving an old-world tavern combined with a bit of live entertainment. As its name suggests, yodelers perform nightly, telling jokes and poking fun at their adoring guests in unintelligible Bavarian slang. The food is traditional, including *Käsespätzle* (a hearty German version of macaroni and cheese), goulash, and meal-size salads. The tasty beer is from the Ayinger brewery. The place is small and fills up fast. ⊠*Altenhof 4, City Center, D–80331* ☎*089/221–249* ▤*No credit cards* ⊙*Closed Sun. No lunch* Ⓜ *Marienplatz (U-bahn and S-bahn).*

¢–$$ ✗**Prinz Myshkin.** For those looking to break away from the meaty Bavar-
Fodor's Choice ian diet, this sophisticated vegetarian restaurant spices up predictable
★ cuisine by mixing Italian and Asian influences. You have a choice of antipasti, homemade gnocchi, tofu, stir-fried dishes, and excellent wines. If you're not very hungry, you can request half portions. The airy room has a majestically vaulted ceiling, and there's always some art exhibited to feed the eye and mind. ⊠*Hackenstr. 2, City Center* ☎*089/265–596* ▤*MC, V* Ⓜ *Sendlinger Tor (U-bahn).*

¢–$$ ✗**Riva Pizzeria.** This stylish but casual Italian joint serves brick-oven pizzas, a variety of pastas, and the city's best beer, Augustiner. Its chic status is reflected in slightly higher prices, the food is quite tasty, and the lively staff makes it an enjoyable experience. Get here early, as it fills up fast after 7 PM. Due to their huge success downtown, these guys have now opened another restaurant in the Feilitzschstrasse in München-ner Freiheit, Schwabing. ⊠*Tal 44, City Center, D–80331* ☎*089/220–240* Ⓜ *Marienpl. (U-bahn and S-bahn)* ⊠*Feilitzschstr. 4, Schwabing, D–80802* ☎*089/3090–51808* Ⓜ *Münchener Freiheit (U-bahn)* ▤*No credit cards.*

$ ✗**Vinorant Alter Hof.** If you don't make it to Franconia, then you can at least get a taste of the region's food and wine in this simply dec-orated restaurant nestled in the old vaulted cellar and first floor of

Munich's castle. The wine bar in the cellar serves hearty Franconian snacks along with Franconian wines, which can be ordered in small amounts, allowing you to let your taste buds travel among Franconia's vineyards. ■TIP→ **It's the perfect place to recover after a concert at the nearby National Theater or the Residenz.** ✉*Alter Hof 3, City Center, D–80331* ☎*089/2424–3733* ⊟*AE, DC, V* ⊙*Closed Sun.* Ⓜ *Marienplatz (U-bahn and S-bahn).*

¢–$ ✕**Bier- und Oktoberfest Museum.** The non-profit foundation that now controls the Augustiner brewery has done an amazing job with this project. In one of the oldest buildings in Munich, dating to 1327, the museum is an imaginative look at the history of this popular elixir, the monasteries that produced it, the Purity Laws that govern it, and Munich's own long tradition with it. After making your way through the exhibit, grab a fresh brew and dig into some hearty Bavarian snacks. ■TIP→ **The *Museumteller* (museum plate) is free with museum admission and includes *Obatzda* (a tangy Camembert-based Bavarian specialty), *Leberwurst,* and *Schmalz* (lard spread) to go with the freshly baked bread—and of course a beer. Without museum admission it's still a great deal at €4.** Hot meals are not served until 6 PM when they begin serving traditional dishes such as Schnitzel and Schweinebraten. The restaurant is open until midnight. ✉*Sterneckstr. 2, City Center, D–80331* ☎*089/2423–1607* ⊕*www. bier-und-oktoberfestmuseum.de* 🖃*€4* ⊙*Tue.–Sat., 1–5* Ⓜ *Isartor (U-bahn and S-bahn).*

¢–$ ✕**Bratwurstherzl.** Tucked into a quaint little square off the Viktualienmarkt, this low-key Bratwurst joint cooks up their specialty sausages right there in the main room over an open grill. For those looking for a bit less meat, there is also a hearty farmer's salad with turkey strips and tasty oyster mushrooms. They have outdoor seating, perfect for people-watching when the weather is good. ✉*Dreifaltigkeitspl. 1, City Center, D–80331* ☎*089/295–113* ⊟*AE, MC, V* Ⓜ *Marienplatz (U-bahn and S-bahn).*

¢–$ ✕**Due passi.** This former dairy shop, now an Italian specialty shop, offers excellent Italian meals for a quick, stand-up lunch. There's a small but fine selection of fresh antipasti, pasta, and desserts such as the white chocolate mousse. You can eat at the high marble tables and counters, or take your food to go. Menus change daily. ✉*Ledererstr. 11, City Center, D–80331* ☎*089/224–271* ⊟*No credit cards* ⊙*Closed Sun. No dinner Sat.* Ⓜ *Isartor (S-bahn).*

¢–$ ✕**Faun.** Not quite City Center, but still central to the action, the beloved
 ★   Faun is off Klenzestrasse, past Gärtnerplatz. It's a happy combination of Munich tavern and international bistro, with great outdoor seating. Their Thai curries are wonderful, and their juicy Schweinebraten will satisfy any meat cravings you may still have in the course of a trip to Bavaria. The beer is Augustiner, so you can't go wrong there. Build up your appetite by browsing your way through the neighborhood shops and boutiques, or walk off your meal along the river back toward the Isartor. ✉*Hans-Sachs-Str. 17, Isarvorstadt, D–80469* ☎*089/263–798* ⊟*AE, MC, V.*

¢–$ ✕**Ganga.** The upholstery is wearing thin at the Ganga, but this, and the friendly service, only contributes to the warm atmosphere. So do

A REAL MEAL

Typical, more substantial dishes in Munich include *Tellerfleisch*, boiled beef with freshly grated horseradish and boiled potatoes on the side, served on wooden plates (there is a similar dish called *Tafelspitz*). Among roasts, sauerbraten (beef) and *Schweinebraten* (roast pork) are accompanied by dumplings and sauerkraut. *Hax'n* (ham hocks) are roasted until they're crisp on the outside and juicy on the inside. They are served with sauerkraut and potato puree. Game in season (venison or boar, for instance) and duck are served with potato dumplings and red cabbage. As for fish, the region has not only excellent trout, served either smoked as an hors d'oeuvre or fried or boiled as an entrée, but also the perch-like *Rencke* from Lake Starnberg.

You'll also find soups, salads, casseroles, hearty stews, and what may well be the greatest variety and the highest quality of baked goods in Europe, including pretzels. And for dessert, indulge in a bowl of Bavarian cream, apple strudel, or *Dampfnudel*, a fluffy leavened-dough dumpling usually served with vanilla sauce.

the curry and tandoori dishes, which are among the best in Munich, and the price is right. Remember that what is mild for an Indian may send you through the roof. But if you're daring, you can ask them to really spice it up for you. ✉ *Baaderstr. 11, Isarvorstadt, D–80469* ☎ *089/201–6465* 🚍 *AE, MC, V* 🕐 *No lunch weekends* Ⓜ *Isartor (U-bahn).*

¢–$ ✕ **Hofbräuhaus.** A classic. The pounding oompah band draws the curious into this father of all beer halls, where singing and shouting drinkers contribute to the earsplitting din. This is no place for the fainthearted, although a trip to Munich would be incomplete without at least having a look. Upstairs is a quieter restaurant if that suits, but let's face it: the food isn't why you come here. In March, May, and September ask for one of the special, extra-strong seasonal beers (Starkbier, Maibock, Märzen), which complement the traditional Bavarian fare. ✉ *Am Platzl 9, City Center, D–80331* ☎ *089/221–676 or 089/290–1360* 🗲 *Reservations not accepted* 🚍 *V* Ⓜ *Marienplatz (U-bahn and S-bahn).*

¢–$ ✕ **Nero Pizza & Lounge.** This pizza joint is a definite rival to Riva Pizzeria
★ as far as the quality of the pie, and the prices are in the same range. Try their Diavolo, with spicy Neopolitan salami. On a side street between Gärtnerplatz and Isartor, Nero's has high ceilings that give it a very open feel; you can sit upstairs in the lounge for a cozier experience. ✉ *Rumfordstr. 34, City Center, D–80469* ☎ *089/2101–9060* 🚍 *AE, MC, V* Ⓜ *Marienplatz (U-bahn).*

¢–$ ✕ **Pfälzer Weinprobierstube.** A maze of stone-vaulted rooms, wooden tables, flickering candles, dirndl-clad waitresses, and a long list of wines add up to a storybook image of a timeless Germany. The wines are mostly from the *Pfalz* (Palatinate), as are many of the specialties on the limited menu. You'll find former chancellor Kohl's favorite dish, *Saumagen* (meat loaf, spiced with herbs and cooked in a pig's stomach). Beer drinkers, take note—beer is not served here. ✉ *Residenzstr. 1,*

City Center, D–80333 ☎089/225–628 ⚠Reservations not accepted 🖃No credit cards Ⓜ Odeonsplatz (U-bahn).

¢–$ ✕**Weisses Bräuhaus.** If you have developed a taste for Weissbier, this institution in downtown Munich is the place to indulge it. The flavorful brew (from Schneider) is served with hearty Bavarian dishes, mostly variations of pork and dumplings or cabbage. The waitresses here are famous in Munich for purposely making life difficult for customers, but if you are good-natured, the whole thing can be quite funny. The art-nouveau styling of the restaurant was beautifully restored, and when the weather is good it's a great place to sit outside. ✉Tal 7, City Center, D–80331 ☎089/299–875 🖃No credit cards Ⓜ Isartor (S-bahn).

> **GOOD HOME COOKING**
>
> Old Munich inns feature solid regional specialties and *gutbürgerliche Küche,* loosely translated as good home cooking. The settings for such victuals include boisterous brewery restaurants, beer halls, beer gardens, rustic cellars, and *Kneipen,* restaurant-pubs serving any manner of food depending on the owner's fancy. The crowd here is generally a mix of students, white-collar workers, and chic artist types.

LEHEL

$–$$ ✕**Gandl.** This Italian specialty shop, where you can buy various staples from vinegar to coffee, doubles as a comfortable, relaxed restaurant. Seating is a little crowded inside, but the excellent service will make you feel right at home. For lunch it's just the place for a quick pastry or excellent antipasto misto before proceeding with the day's adventures. In the evenings the cuisine is Mediterranean-influenced and just plain good; there are changing two- and three-course meals for under €20. They also have breakfast. ✉St.-Anna-Pl. 1, Lehel, D–80538 ☎089/2916–2525 🖃V ⊘Closed Sun. No dinner Ⓜ Lehel (U-bahn).

¢–$ ✕**Gasthaus Isarthor.** This old-fashioned *Wirtshaus,* where the innkeeper keeps a close eye on the entire scene from behind the bar, is one of the few places that serves Augustiner beer exclusively from wooden kegs, freshly-tapped on a daily basis. It simply doesn't get any better than this. Traditional Bavarian fare, and it's all good. Add the unusual social mix at the simple wooden tables to the recipe and you've got the secret of this solid establishment—actors, government officials, apprentice craftspersons, journalists, and retirees all sit side by side. Cash only. ✉Kanalstr. 2, Lehel, D–80538 ☎089/227–753 🖃No credit cards Ⓜ Isartor (S-bahn).

MAXVORSTADT

$ ✕**Cohen's.** Reviving the old Jewish Central European tradition of good, healthy cooking together with hospitality and good cheer seems to be the underlying principle at Cohen's. Dig into a few hearty latkes, a steaming plate of Chulend stew, or a standard gefilte fish doused with excellent Golan wine from Israel. The kitchen is open from 12:30 PM to about 10:30 PM, and if the atmosphere is good, patrons may hang out chattering until the wee hours. ■TIP→ **Klezmer singers perform on Friday evenings.** ✉ *Theresienstr. 31, Maxvorstadt, D–80333* ☎ *089/280–9545* ▤ *AE, MC, V* Ⓜ *Theresienstrasse (U-bahn).*

SCHWABING

$$$$ ✕ **Tantris.** Chef Hans Haas has kept his restaurant at the top of the
★ critics' charts in Munich. You, too, will be impressed by the exotic nouvelle cuisine on the menu, including such specialties as shellfish and creamed-potato soup or roasted wood pigeon with scented rice. But you may wish to ignore the bare concrete surroundings and the garish orange-and-yellow decor. ✉ *Johann-Fichte-Str. 7, Schwabing, D–80805* ☎ *089/361–9590* ⚘ *Reservations essential.* Jacket and tie ▤ *AE, DC, MC, V* ⊘ *Closed Sun.* Ⓜ *Münchener Freiheit (U-bahn).*

$–$$ ✕ **Cézanne.** You're in for Provençal dining at this truly Gallic bistro-restaurant in the heart of Munich's former bohemian quarter. Owner-chef Patrick Geay learned his craft from some of Europe's best teachers. His regularly changing blackboard menu offers the freshest market products, with vegetables prepared as only the French can do. Among the fish dishes, the scallops melt in the mouth, while the coq au vin will conquer the greatest hungers. Reservations recommended. ✉ *Konradstr. 1, Schwabing, D–80801* ☎ *089/391–805* ▤ *No credit cards* ⊘ *No lunch. Closed Mon.* Ⓜ *Giselastrasse (U-bahn).*

¢–$ ✕ **Max-Emanuel-Brauerei.** This historic old brewery tavern is a great value, with Bavarian dishes rarely costing more than €10. The main dining room has a stage, and there's often a cabaret or jazz concert during dinner. They even have salsa lessons in the evenings. The best part about this place, however, is the cozy, secluded little beer garden tucked in the back amid the apartment blocks. ✉ *Adalbertstr. 33, Schwabing, D–80799* ☎ *089/271–5158* ▤ *AE, MC* Ⓜ *Josephsplatz (U-bahn).*

LUDWIGVORSTADT

¢–$ ✕ **Augustiner Keller.** This 19th-century establishment is the flagship beer restaurant of one of Munich's oldest breweries. It is also the location of the absolutely unbeatable Augustiner beer garden, which you have to experience once in your life. The menu changes daily and offers Bavarian specialties, but try to order *Tellerfleisch* (boiled beef with horseradish), served on a big wooden board. Follow that with a *Dampfnudel* (yeast dumpling served with custard), and you probably won't feel hungry again for the next 24 hours. ✉ *Arnulfstr. 52, Leopoldvorstadt, D–80335* ☎ *089/594–393* ▤ *AE, MC* Ⓜ *Hauptbahnhof (U-bahn and S-bahn).*

¢–$ ✕ **Café am Beethovenplatz.** Live music accompanies excellent fare every evening. An international breakfast menu is served daily (on Sunday with live classical music), followed by suitably creative lunch and dinner menus. The pork is supplied by a farm where the free-range pigs are fed only the best natural fodder—so the *Schweinsbraten* (roast pig) is recommended. Reservations are advised, as a young and intellectual crowd fills the tables quickly. They have a hotel in the building as well. ✉ *Goethestr. 51 (at Beethovenpl.), Leopoldvorstadt, D–80336* ☎ *089/5440–4348* ✉ *AE, MC, V* Ⓜ *Goetheplatz (U-bahn).*

HAIDHAUSEN & AU

¢–$$ ✕ **Wirtshaus in der Au.** One of the oldest taverns in Munich, this Wirt-
★ shaus has an excellent combination of fantastic service and outstanding local dishes. It serves everything from *Hofente* (roast duck) to *Schweinsbraten* (roast pork), but the real specialty is *Knödels* (dumplings), which, in addition to traditional *Semmel* (bread) and *Kartoffel* (potato) varieties, come in spinach, cheese, and even red-beet flavors. They're delectable. It's only a five-minute walk from the bridge at the Deutsches Museum. ✉ *Lilienstr. 51, Haidhausen, D–80669* ☎ *089/448–1400* ✉ *V* Ⓜ *Isartor (S-bahn and Tram).*

WHERE TO STAY

Though Munich has a vast number of hotels in all price ranges, booking one can be a challenge, as this is a major trade-show city as well as a prime tourist destination. If you're visiting during any of the major trade fairs such as the ispo (sports, fashion) in February or the IHM (crafts) in mid-March, or during Oktoberfest at the end of September, try to make reservations at least a few months in advance. It is acceptable practice in Europe to request to see a room before committing to it, so feel free to ask the concierge.

Some of the large, upscale hotels that cater to expense-account business travelers have very attractive weekend discount rates—sometimes as much as 50% below normal prices. Conversely, hotels openly and shamelessly raise their regular rates by at least 30% during big trade fairs and Oktoberfest. Online booking sites often have prices well below the hotel's published prices (i.e. price ranges in this book) in slow periods and on short notice. Look for the names we suggest here and search online for potential deals.

■ **TIP→** Munich's two tourist information offices can help you with hotel bookings if you haven't reserved in advance. One is at the central station and the other is on Marienplatz, in the Rathaus. Your best bet is to visit in person.

A technical note: many hotels in Munich have chosen of late to farm out their wireless Internet services to third parties—meaning that you can get online with their Wi-Fi hotspot, but you log in with a credit card and pay with a separate service provider. Convenient but not very personal.

WHAT IT COSTS IN EUROS					1
	¢	$	$$	$$$	$$$$
FOR 2 PEOPLE	under €50	€51–€100	€101–€175	€176–€225	over €225

Hotel prices are for two people in a standard double room, including tax and service.

CITY CENTER

$$$$ ⊞ **Bayerischer Hof.** Still one of Germany's most respected family-owned hotels, the Bayerischer Hof began its rich history by hosting Ludwig I's guests. To this day it still plays host to VIPs and international political confabs. Public rooms are grandly laid out with marble, antiques, and oil paintings. Laura Ashley–inspired rooms look out to the city's skyline of towers. Nightlife is built into the hotel, with Trader Vic's bar and dancing at the Night Club. ⊠ *Promenadepl. 2–6, City Center, D–80333* ☎ *089/21200* 🖷 *089/212–0906* ⊕ *www.bayerischerhof.de* 🛏 *395 rooms, 58 suites* 🔧 *In-room: ethernet, dial-up, Wi-Fi. In-hotel: 3 restaurants, bars, pool, spa, public Wi-Fi, parking (fee), no-smoking rooms, some pets allowed (fee)* 🖃 *AE, DC, MC, V* |◯|*BP* Ⓜ *Karlsplatz (U-bahn and S-bahn) or Marienplatz (U-bahn and S-bahn).*

$$$$ ⊞ **Kempinski Hotel Vier Jahreszeiten München.** The Kempinski has been
★ playing host to the world's wealthy and titled for more than a century. It has an unbeatable location on Maximilianstrasse, Munich's premier shopping street, and is only a few minutes' walk from the heart of the city. Elegance and luxury set the tone throughout; many rooms have handsome antique pieces. The Vier Jahreszeiten Eck restaurant is on the main floor. The afternoon tea in the poshly decorated foyer is a special treat. ■ TIP➡ **Keep an eye open for their special packages, which can be very good deals.** ⊠ *Maximilianstr. 17, City Center, D–80539* ☎ *089/21250, 516/794–2670 Kempinski Reservation Service* 🖷 *089/2125–2000* ⊕ *www.Kempinski-Vierjahreszeiten.de* 🛏 *268 rooms, 48 suites* 🔧 *In-room: ethernet, dial-up, Wi-Fi. In-hotel: restaurant, bar, pool, gym, public Internet, parking (fee), no-smoking rooms, some pets allowed (fee)* 🖃 *AE, DC, MC, V* |◯|*BP* Ⓜ *Tram 19 Kammerspiele (Tram).*

$$$–$$$$ ⊞ **Torbräu.** Munich's oldest hotel, the Torbräu, has been run by the
★ same family for more than a century. It is next to one of the ancient city gates—the 14th-century Isartor—and the location is perfect for this walkable downtown, as it's midway between the Marienplatz and the Deutsches Museum (and around the corner from the Hofbräuhaus). Comfortable rooms are decorated in a plush and ornate Italian style. Its Italian restaurant, La Famiglia, is one of the best in town. ⊠ *Tal 41, City Center, D–80331* ☎ *089/242–340* 🖷 *089/2423–4235* ⊕ *www.torbraeu.de* 🛏 *89 rooms, 3 suites* 🔧 *In-room: ethernet, dial-up, Wi-Fi. In-hotel: restaurant, public Internet, no-smoking rooms, some pets allowed (fee)* 🖃 *AE, MC, V* |◯|*BP* Ⓜ *Isartor (S-bahn).*

$$–$$$$ ⊞ **Mercure.** This straightforward, comfortable hotel is a great deal for its location. Set just between Marienplatz and Sendlingertor, it is within walking distance of the entire city center. An extra €13 buys breakfast in the hotel. It's better than any breakfast you'll get at a restaurant, and they have a fresh-orange-juice machine so you can tank up on the good stuff. Suites are available but not for families. ⊠*Hotterstr. 4, City Center, D–80331* ☎*089/232–590* 🖷*089/232–59127* ⊕*www. mercure.com* ⇖*75 rooms* ⌂*In-room: a/c, dial-up, Wi-Fi. In-hotel: public Internet, no-smoking rooms* ⊟*AE, MC, V* ⦿l*BP* Ⓜ *Marienplatz (U-bahn and S-bahn).*

\$\$–\$\$\$\$ 🖭 **Platzl.** The privately-owned Platzl has won awards and wide recognition for its ecologically aware management, which uses heat recyclers in the kitchen, environmentally friendly detergents, recyclable materials, waste separation, and other ecofriendly practices. It stands in the historic heart of Munich, near the famous Hofbräuhaus beer hall and a couple of minutes' walk from Marienplatz and many other landmarks. Its Pfistermühle restaurant, with 16th-century vaulting, is one of the area's oldest and most historic establishments. ⊠*Sparkassenstr. 10, City Center, D–80331* ☎*089/237–030, 800/448–8355 in U.S.* 🖷*089/2370–3800* ⊕*www.platzl.de* ⇖*167 rooms* ⌂*In-room: no a/c (some), ethernet, dial-up, Wi-Fi (some). In-hotel: restaurant, bar, gym, parking (fee), no-smoking rooms, some pets allowed (fee)* ⊟*AE, DC, MC, V* ⦿l*BP* Ⓜ *Marienplatz (U-bahn and S-bahn).*

\$\$\$ 🖭**Cortiina.** One of Munich's designer hotels, Cortiina follows the minimalist gospel. The reception is done in sleek gray stone with a high-tech gas fireplace along one wall. For guests, the emphasis is on subtle luxury—fresh flowers, mattresses made from natural rubber, sheets made of untreated cotton. The rooms are paneled in dark moor oak and come with all the amenities. The hotel has no fitness center, but the Elixir, 15 minutes on foot to Lenbachplatz, gives special discounts for hotel guests. ⊠*Ledererstr. 8, City Center, D–80331* ☎*089/242–2490* 🖷*089/2422–49100* ⊕*www.cortiina.com* ⇖*54 rooms* ⌂*In-room: ethernet, dial-up, Wi-Fi. In-hotel: bar, public Wi-Fi, parking (fee), no-smoking rooms, some pets allowed (fee)* ⊟*AE, DC, MC, V* ⦿l*BP* Ⓜ *Marienplatz (U-bahn and S-bahn).*

\$\$ 🖭**Hotel am Markt.** You can literally stumble out the door of this hotel
★   onto the Viktualienmarkt. Perfect location, fair prices, simple rooms. At this writing, this beautiful building was undergoing interior renovations, so call ahead to check the status. There were also plans to turn the breakfast room into a full-blown café. Wi-Fi Internet access is available for free in the hotel's public spaces. ⊠*Heiliggeiststr. 6, City Center, D–80331* ☎*089/225–014* 🖷*089/224–0173* ⊕*www.hotel-am-markt.eu* ⇖*22 rooms* ⌂*In-room: no a/c. In-hotel: public Wi-Fi* ⊟*No credit cards* ⦿l*CP* Ⓜ *Marienplatz (U-bahn and S-bahn).*

HAUPTBAHNHOF

\$\$–\$\$\$\$ 🖭**Creatif Hotel Elephant.** Tucked away on a quiet street near the train station and a 10-minute walk from the city center, this hotel appeals to a wide range of travelers, from businesspeople on the fly to tourists on a budget. The rooms are simple, clean, and quiet. A bright color scheme in the reception and breakfast room creates a cheery atmosphere. Note that prices skyrocket during Oktoberfest. Wi-Fi is free in the building. ■**TIP→Check out the hotel's online booking deals for dramatically-reduced rates.** ⊠*Lämmerstr. 6, Leopoldvorstadt, D–80335* ☎*089/555–785* 🖷*089/550–1746* ⊕*www.creatifelephanthotel.com* 🛏*40 rooms* ⟡*In-room: no a/c, dial-up, free Wi-Fi. In-hotel: public Wi-Fi, some pets allowed* ⊟*AE, MC, V* |⊙|*BP* Ⓜ *Hauptbahnhof (U-bahn and S-bahn).*

$$–$$$$ 🏨**Eden-Hotel Wolff.** Chandeliers and dark-wood paneling in the public rooms contribute to the old-fashioned elegance of this downtown favorite. It's directly across the street from the train station and near the Theresienwiese fairgrounds. The rooms are well furnished with large, comfortable beds, and the colors are relaxing pastels. You can dine on excellent Bavarian specialties in the intimate wood-panel Zirbelstube restaurant. ⊠*Arnulfstr. 4, Hauptbahnhof, D–80335* ☎*089/551–150* 🖷*089/5511–5555* ⊕*www.ehw.de* 🛏*209 rooms, 7 suites* ⟡*In-room: ethernet, dial-up, Wi-Fi. In-hotel: restaurant, bar, gym, public Wi-Fi, parking (fee), some pets allowed (fee)* ⊟*AE, DC, MC, V* |⊙|*BP* Ⓜ *Hauptbahnhof (U-bahn and S-bahn).*

$$–$$$ 🏨**Hotel Amba.** The Amba, which is right next to the train station, has clean, bright rooms, good service, no expensive frills, and everything you need to plug and play. The lobby, with a small bar, invites you to relax in a Mediterranean atmosphere of wicker sofas with bright-color upholstery. No sooner have you enjoyed a solid breakfast at the buffet (with sparkling wine) on the first floor overlooking the station than you'll be out on the town visiting the nearby sights on foot. Budget travelers should ask for rooms without bathrooms. There are also occasional special deals on weekends. ⊠*Arnulfstr. 20, Hauptbahnhof, D–80335* ☎*089/545–140* 🖷*089/5451–1555* ⊕*www.hotel-amba.de* 🛏*86 rooms* ⟡*In-room: no a/c, Wi-Fi. In-hotel: public Wi-Fi, no-smoking rooms, some pets allowed (fee)* ⊟*AE, DC, MC, V* |⊙|*BP* Ⓜ *Hauptbahnhof (U-bahn and S-bahn).*

$–$$ 🏨**Hotel Mirabell.** This family-run hotel is used to American tourists
★ who appreciate the friendly service, central location (between the main railway station and the Oktoberfest fairgrounds), and reasonable room rates. Three apartments are for small groups or families. Rooms are furnished in modern light woods and bright prints. Breakfast buffet is included, and snacks can be ordered at the bar. Prices are much higher during trade fairs and Oktoberfest. ⊠*Landwehrstr. 42, entrance on Goethestr., Hauptbahnhof, D–80336* ☎*089/549–1740* 🖷*089/550–3701* ⊕*www.hotelmirabell.de* 🛏*65 rooms, 3 apartments* ⟡*In-room: dial-up. In-hotel: bar, public Wi-Fi, no-smoking rooms, some pets allowed (fee)* ⊟*AE, MC, V* |⊙|*BP* Ⓜ *Hauptbahnhof (U-bahn and S-bahn).*

LEHEL

$$$–$$$$ 🏨**Opera.** In the quiet residential district of Lehel (St.-Anna-Strasse is
Fodor'sChoice a cul-de-sac accessed through the neo-Renaissance arcades of the Eth-
★ nographic Museum), the Opera offers rooms decorated in an elegant style—lots of Empire, some art deco. Some rooms have glassed-in balconies. The service is perhaps the best in Munich. There are no mini-

bars, but guests can order room service round the clock. Enjoy summer breakfast in the back courtyard decorated with orange and lemon trees. ⊠ *St.-Anna-Str. 10, Lehel, D–80331* ☎ *089/210–4940* 🖷 *089/2104– 9477* ⊕ *www.hotel-opera.de* 🖙 *25 rooms* △ *In-room: no a/c, dial- up, Wi-Fi. In-hotel: bar, public Wi-Fi, no-smoking rooms, some pets allowed* ⊟ *AE, DC, MC, V* |❍| *BP* Ⓜ *Lehel (U-bahn).*

$$–$$$ 🏨 **Adria.** This modern, comfortable hotel is ideally located near a num- ber of great museums and the English Garden. Rooms are large and tastefully decorated, with old prints on the pale-pink walls, Oriental rugs on the floors, and flowers beside the double beds. A spectacular breakfast buffet (including a glass of sparkling wine) is included in the room rate. There's no hotel restaurant, but there's free coffee and tea in the lobby and the area is rich in good restaurants, bistros, and bars. Wi-Fi Internet access is free in the lobby but there is a fee for it in the rooms. ⊠ *Liebigstr. 8a, Lehel, D–80538* ☎ *089/242–1170* 🖷 *089/2421–17999* ⊕ *www.adria-muenchen.de* 🖙 *43 rooms* △ *In- room: no a/c, dial-up, Wi-Fi. In-hotel: public Wi-Fi, no-smoking rooms, some pets allowed (fee)* ⊟ *AE, MC, V* |❍| *BP* Ⓜ *Lehel (U-bahn).*

$$ 🏨 **Hotel Concorde.** The privately owned Concorde is right in the middle of Munich and yet very peaceful owing to its location on a narrow side street. The nearest S-bahn station (Isartor) is only a two-minute walk away. Rooms in one tract are done in pastel tones and light woods; in the other tract they tend to be somewhat darker and more rustic. Fresh flowers and bright prints add a colorful touch. A large breakfast buffet is served in a stylish, mirrored dining room. ⊠ *Herrnstr. 38, Lehel, D–80539* ☎ *089/224–515* 🖷 *089/228–3282* ⊕ *www.concorde- muenchen.de* 🖙 *67 rooms, 4 suites* △ *In-room: no a/c, dial-up, Wi-Fi. In-hotel: public Wi-Fi, parking (fee), no-smoking rooms, some pets allowed (fee)* ⊟ *AE, DC, MC, V* |❍| *BP* Ⓜ *Isartor (S-bahn).*

ISARVORSTADT

$$–$$$$ 🏨 **Admiral.** The small, privately owned Admiral enjoys a quiet side- street location and its own garden, close to the Isar River and Deutsches Museum. Many of the simply furnished and warmly decorated bed- rooms have a balcony overlooking the garden. Bowls of fresh fruit are part of the friendly welcome awaiting guests. The breakfast buffet is a dream, complete with homemade jams, fresh bread, and Italian and French delicacies. Minibar is included in the price. Wi-Fi Inter- net access is free in the building. ⊠ *Kohlstr. 9, Isarvorstadt, D–80469* ☎ *089/216–350* 🖷 *089/293–674* ⊕ *www.hotel-admiral.de* 🖙 *33 rooms* △ *In-room: no a/c, ethernet, Wi-Fi. In-hotel: bar, public Wi-Fi, parking (fee), no-smoking rooms, some pets allowed* ⊟ *AE, DC, MC, V* |❍| *BP* Ⓜ *Isartor (S-bahn).*

$$–$$$$ 🏨 **Advokat.** If you value the clean lines of modern taste over plush **Fodor's Choice** luxury, this is the hotel for you. It's within a residential neighborhood ★   that's an easy walk from the Marienplatz and a shorter one from the subway. Between outings you can snack on the fruit plate that welcomes you upon arrival. Breakfast buffet and minibar included. ⊠ *Baaderstr. 1, Isarvorstadt, D–80469* ☎ *089/216–310* 🖷 *089/216–3190* ⊕ *www.*

hotel-advokat.de ➪*50 rooms* &*In-room: no a/c, ethernet, Wi-Fi. In-hotel: public Wi-Fi, parking (fee), no-smoking rooms, some pets allowed* ☰*AE, DC, MC, V* ◎*|BP* Ⓜ *Isartor (S-bahn).*

$ ▥**Pension Seibel.** If you're looking for a very affordable and charming

Fodor'sChoice little European-style "pension" just a stone's throw from the Viktu-

★ alienmarkt, this is the place. You can't get any closer than this for the price. It's family-run and has a fantastic breakfast buffet. The rooms are not fancy, but they are furnished with cute antique dressers and tables. Ask for the maisonette on the top floor for a split-level double room with a spectacular view for the same price as a normal double. There are also three suites for 4 to 6 people. The Seibel family owns two other hotels, one very near the Oktoberfest grounds. ✉*Reichenbachstr. 8, Isarvorstadt, D–80469* ☏*089/99520* ⊟*089/995299* ⊕*www.seibel-hotels-munich.de* ➪*22 rooms, 3 suites* &*In-hotel: no elevator* ☰*AE, MC, V* ◎*|BP* Ⓜ *Marienplatz (U-bahn and S-bahn).*

MAXVORSTADT

$-$$ ▣**Renner Hotels–Carlton.** The Carlton is one of three little hotels—all

★ within a block of each other—that form a privately-owned chain in the heart of the museum quarter and a hop-skip from the English Garden and Schwabing. The location is also really close to downtown, just north of City Center. The Carlton has a bit more flair than the other two (Antare and Savoy), but if the Carlton is booked up you have a good chance of getting something at the others. All three are clean and simple, have generous breakfast buffets, and are very fairly priced (keep an eye on www.hrs.com for the prices at this operation). The Indian restaurant below the Carlton offers a 10% discount to guests. The Last Supper (☏089/288–0809) restaurant in the same street has fantastic three-course meals for around €27 and is a really funky dining experience. ✉*Fürstenstr. 12, Maxvorstadt, D–80333* ☏*089/282–061* ⊟*089/287–871705* ⊕*www.carlton-garni.de* ➪*32 doubles* &*In-room: no a/c, phone, TV. In-hotel: public Wi-Fi* ☰*MC, AE, V* ◎*|CP* Ⓜ *Between Universität and Odeonsplatz (U-bahn).*

$ ▣**Hotel Pension Am Siegestor.** This pension takes up three floors of a fin-

★ de-siècle mansion between the Siegestor monument, on Leopoldstrasse, and the university. An ancient elevator with a glass door brings you to the fourth-floor reception desk. Most of the simply furnished rooms face the impressive Arts Academy across the street. Rooms on the fifth floor are particularly cozy, tucked up under the eaves. Modest but very appealing, this is a great deal in a fairly expensive city. ✉*Akademiestr. 5, Maxvorstadt, D–80799* ☏*089/399–550 or 089/399–551* ⊟*089/343–050* ⊕*www.siegestor.com* ➪*20 rooms* &*In-room: no a/c, no phone, no TV (some). In-hotel: public Internet* ☰*No credit cards* ◎*|CP* Ⓜ *Universität (U-bahn).*

SCHWABING

$$–$$$$ ⊡ **Biederstein.** This hotel is not the prettiest from the outside—a modern, uninspired block—but it seems to want to fit into its old Schwabing surroundings. At the edge of the English Garden, the Biederstein has many advantages: peace and quiet; excellent service; and comfortable, well-appointed rooms that were carefully renovated. Guests are requested to smoke on the balconies, not inside. The breakfast buffet costs €9.50 extra but is worth it. ⊠ *Keferstr. 18, Schwabing, D–80335* ☎ *089/389–9970* ☐ *089/3899–97389* ⊕ *www.hotelbiederstein.de* ⌁ *34 rooms, 7 suites* ⌂ *In-room: no a/c. In-hotel: bar, bicycles, public Internet, parking (no fee), some pets allowed (fee)* ⊟*AE, DC, MC, V* Ⓜ *Münchner Freiheit (U-bahn).*

$–$$$ ⊡ **Gästehaus am Englischen Garten.** Reserve well in advance for a room
★ at this popular converted water mill, more than 300 years old, adjoining the English Garden. The hotel is only a five-minute walk from the bars, shops, and restaurants of Schwabing. Be sure to ask for one of the 12 nostalgically old-fashioned rooms in the main building, which has a garden on an island in the old millrace; a modern annex down the road has 13 apartments, all with cooking facilities. In summer, breakfast is served on the terrace of the main house. There is free Internet access at their partner hotel, the Biederstein. ⊠ *Liebergesellstr. 8, Schwabing, D–80802* ☎ *089/383–9410* ☐ *089/3839–4133* ⊕ *www.hotelenglischergarten.de* ⌁ *12 rooms, 6 with bath or shower; 13 apartments* ⌂ *In-room: no a/c. In-hotel: bicycles, parking (no fee), no elevator, some pets allowed (fee)* ⊟*AE, DC, MC, V* ⦿|*BP* Ⓜ *Münchner Freiheit (U-bahn).*

LUDWIGVORSTADT

$–$$ ⊡ **Brack.** Under new management since late 2006, this hotel has retained its simple charm. Oktoberfest revelers value the Brack's proximity to the beer-festival grounds, and its location—on a busy, tree-lined thoroughfare just south of the city center—is handy for city attractions. The rooms are furnished in light, friendly veneers and are soundproof (a useful feature during Oktoberfest) and have amenities such as hair dryers. The buffet breakfast, which lasts until noon, will prepare you for the day. ⊠ *Lindwurmstr. 153, Ludwigvorstadt, D–80337* ☎ *089/747–2550* ☐ *089/7472–5599* ⊕ *www.hotel-brack. de* ⌁ *50 rooms* ⌂ *In-room: no a/c, ethernet, dial-up. In-hotel: public Wi-Fi, parking (no fee), some pets allowed* ⊟*AE, DC, MC, V* ⦿|*BP* Ⓜ *Poccistrasse (U-bahn).*

$–$$ ⊡ **Hotel-Pension Mariandl.** The American armed forces commandeered this turn-of-the-20th-century neo-Gothic mansion in May 1945 and established Munich's first postwar nightclub, the Femina, on the ground floor (now the charming Café am Beethovenplatz, which also has free Wi-Fi Internet access). Most rooms are mansion-size, with high ceilings and large windows overlooking a leafy avenue. The Oktoberfest grounds and the main railway station are both a 10-minute walk away. Prices during Oktoberfest increase by 50%. ⊠ *Goethestr. 51, Ludwigvorstadt, D–80336* ☎ *089/534–108* ☐ *089/5440–4396* ⊕ *www.*

1

hotelmariandl.com 📞*28 rooms* 🔑*In-room: no a/c, no phone, no TV, Wi-Fi (some). In-hotel: restaurant, public Internet, public Wi-Fi, no elevator, some pets allowed* ▤*AE, DC, MC, V* ❘○❘*BP* Ⓜ *Hauptbahnhof (U-bahn and S-bahn).*

$ 🎫**Hotel-Pension Schmellergarten.** Popular with young budget travelers,
★   this genuine family business will make you feel right at home. It's a little place on a quiet street off Lindwurmstrasse, a few minutes' walk from the Theresienwiese (Oktoberfest grounds). The Poccistrasse subway station is around the corner to take you into the center of town. Wi-Fi Internet access is free, and they have a computer for guests to go online. ✉*Schmellerstr. 20, Ludwigvorstadt, D–80337* ☎*089/773–157* 📠*089/725–6886* ✉*milankuhn@web.de* 📞*14 rooms* 🔑*In-room: no a/c, no TV. In-hotel: public Internet, public Wi-Fi, no elevator, some pets allowed* ▤*No credit cards* ❘○❘*CP* Ⓜ *Poccistrasse (U-bahn).*

THERESIENHÖHE

$$–$$$$ 🎫**Park-Hotel Theresienhöhe.** The Park-Hotel claims that none of its rooms is less than 400 square feet. Suites are larger than many luxury apartments, and some of them come with small kitchens. The sleek, modern rooms are mostly decorated with light woods and pastel-color fabrics and carpeting; larger rooms and suites get a lot of light, thanks to the floor-to-ceiling windows. Families are particularly welcome, and a babysitting service is provided. There's no in-house restaurant, but you can order in. ✉*Parkstr. 31, Theresienhöhe, D–80339* ☎*089/519 950* 📠*089/5199–5420* 🌐*www.parkhoteltheresienhoehe. de* 📞*35 rooms* 🔑*In-room: no a/c, dial-up (some), Wi-Fi. In-hotel: bar, no-smoking rooms, some pets allowed* ▤*AE, DC, MC, V* ❘○❘*BP* Ⓜ *Theresienwiese (U-bahn).*

$ 🎫**Kurpfalz.** Visitors have praised the friendly welcome and service they receive at this well-maintained and affordable lodging above the Oktoberfest grounds. Rooms are comfortable, if furnished in a manner only slightly better than functional, and all are equipped with satellite TV. The main train station and Oktoberfest grounds are both within a 10-minute walk, and the area is rich in restaurants, bars, and movie theaters. There is free Wi-Fi Internet access in the building. ■**TIP**➜**Prices can vary radically depending on the season.** ✉*Schwantalerstr. 121, Theresienhöhe, D–80339* ☎*089/540–9860* 📠*089/5409– 8811* 🌐*www.kurpfalz-hotel.de* 📞*44 rooms* 🔑*In-room: no a/c, ethernet, dial-up. In-hotel: public Wi-Fi, bar, no-smoking rooms, some pets allowed* ▤*AE, MC, V* ❘○❘*BP* Ⓜ *Hackerbrücke (S-bahn).*

NYMPHENBURG

$$–$$$ 🎫**Erzgiesserei Europe.** Though this hotel is in a residential section of the city, the nearby subway whisks you in five minutes to Karlsplatz, convenient to the pedestrian shopping area and the main railway station. Rooms in this attractive, modern hotel are particularly bright, decorated in soft pastels with good reproductions on the walls. The cobblestone garden café is quiet and relaxing. Rates vary greatly, even on their own

Web site. The English Cinema is around the corner if you're hankering for a film. ⊠*Erzgiessereistr. 15, Nymphenburg, D–80335* ☎*089/126–820* 🖷*089/123–6198* ⊕*www.topinternational.com* ⋚*105 rooms, 1 suite* ⚒*In-room: no a/c, dial-up, Wi-Fi. In-hotel: restaurant, bar, Wi-Fi, parking (fee), no-smoking rooms, some pets allowed (fee)* ⊟*AE, DC, MC, V* ⎇*BP* Ⓜ *Stiglmaierplatz (U-bahn).*

$$-$$$ 🏨**Rotkreuzplatz.** This small, family-run business on lively Rotkreuzplatz is five minutes by subway (U-1 and U-7) from the main train station. Breakfast in the neighboring café is included in the price. There are no grand amenities, but a pleasant stay is guaranteed. The café and many rooms look out over one of Munich's most original squares, Rotkreuzplatz, where people from all walks of life meet around a modern fountain. ⊠*Rotkreuzpl. 2, Neuhausen, D–80634* ☎*089/139–9080* 🖷*089/166–469* ⊕*www.hotel-rotkreuzplatz.de* ⋚*56 rooms* ⚒*In-room: no a/c, ethernet, dial-up, Wi-Fi. In-hotel: parking (no fee), no-smoking rooms, some pets allowed* ⊟*AE, DC, MC, V* ⎇*BP* Ⓜ *Rotkreuzplatz (U-bahn).*

$–$$ 🏨**Kriemhild.** This welcoming, family-run pension is in a quiet west-
ↄ   ern suburb. ■**TIP→If you're traveling with children, you'll appreciate that it's a 10-minute walk from Schloss Nymphenburg and around the corner from the Hirschgarten Park.** The tram ride (No. 16 or 17 to Kriemhildenstrasse stop) from the train station is 10 minutes. Wi-Fi Internet access is free in the building. ⊠*Guntherstr. 16, Nymphenburg, D–80639* ☎*089/171–1170* 🖷*089/1711–1755* ⊕*www.kriemhild.de* ⋚*18 rooms* ⚒*In-room: no a/c, dial-up. In-hotel: public Wi-Fi, bar, free parking, some pets allowed, no elevator* ⊟*AE, MC, V* ⎇*BP* Ⓜ *Kriemhildstrasse (Tram-bahn 16/17).*

OUTSIDE THE CENTER

$$–$$$$ 🏨**Arabella Sheraton Grand Hotel.** The building itself may raise a few eyebrows. It stands on a slight elevation and is not the most shapely on the Munich skyline. What goes on inside, however, is sheer five-star luxury. Guests are greeted with a glass of champagne, and snacks and drinks are available round the clock in the Towers Lounge. The excellent restaurant Ente vom Lehel has come to roost here as well. And if you'd like to add a special Bavarian flavor to your stay, book one of the 60 "Bavarian rooms" with antique wood furniture and a country feel. ⊠*Arabellastr. 5, Bogenhausen, D–81925* ☎*089/92640* 🖷*089/9264–8699* ⊕*www.arabellasheraton.de* ⋚*644 rooms, 31 suites* ⚒*In-room: dial-up, Wi-Fi (some). In-hotel: 2 restaurants, bars, pool, public Internet, public Wi-Fi, parking (no fee), no-smoking rooms, some pets allowed (fee)* ⊟*AE, DC, MC, V* ⎇*BP* Ⓜ *Richard-Strauss-Strasse (U-bahn).*

$–$$ 🏨**Jagdschloss.** This century-old hunting lodge in Munich's leafy Obermenzing suburb is a delightful hotel. The rustic look has been retained with lots of original woodwork and white stucco. Many of the comfortable pastel-tone bedrooms have wooden balconies with flower boxes bursting with color. In the beamed restaurant or sheltered beer garden you'll be served Bavarian specialties by a staff dressed in traditional lederhosen (shorts in summer, breeches in winter). ⊠*Alte Allee 21, D–81245 München-Obermenzing* ☎*089/820–820* 🖶*089/8208–2100* ⊕*www.jagd-schloss.com* 🖾*22 rooms, 1 suite* ⚒*In-room: no a/c, ethernet. In-hotel: restaurant, bar, parking (no fee), some pets allowed, no elevator* ⊟*MC, V* ◎|*BP.*

NIGHTLIFE & THE ARTS

THE ARTS

Bavaria's capital has an enviable reputation as an artistic hot spot. Details of concerts and theater performances are listed in *Vorschau* and *Monatsprogramm*, booklets available at most hotel reception desks, newsstands, and tourist offices. The English-language magazine *Munich Found* also has some information. Otherwise, just keep your eye open for advertising pillars and posters, especially on church walls. Tickets for performances at the Bavarian State Theater–New Residence Theater, Nationaltheater, Prinzregententheater, and Staatstheater am Gärtnerplatz are sold at the **central box office** (⊠*Marstallpl. 5, City Center* ☎*089/2185–1920*). It's open weekdays 10–7, Saturday 10–1, and one hour before curtain time. One ticket agency, **München Ticket** (☎*0180/5481–8181, 0.14 cents a minute* ⊕*www.muenchenticket. de*), has a German-language Web site where tickets for most Munich theaters can be booked. Two **Zentraler Kartenverkauf** (⊠*City Center* ☎*089/264–620*) ticket kiosks are in the underground concourse at Marienplatz.

CONCERTS

Munich and music go together. The city has two world-renowned orchestras. The Philharmonic is now directed by Christian Thielemann, formerly of the Deutsche Oper in Berlin; the Bavarian State Opera Company is managed by Japanese-American director Kent Nagano. The leading choral ensembles are the Munich Bach Choir, the Munich Motettenchor, and Musica Viva, the last specializing in contemporary music. The choirs perform mostly in city churches.

The Bavarian Radio Symphony Orchestra sometimes performs at the **Bayerischer Rundfunk** (⊠*Rundfunkpl. 1, Hauptbahnhof* ☎*089/558–080* ⊕*www.br-online.de*) and other city venues like Gasteig. The box office is open Monday–Thursday 9–noon and 2–4, Friday 9–noon.

Munich's world-class concert hall, the **Gasteig Culture Center** (⊠*Rosenheimerstr. 5, Haidhausen* ☎*089/480–980* ⊕*www.muenchenticket. de*), is a lavish brick complex standing high above the Isar River, east of downtown. Its Philharmonic Hall is the permanent home of the Munich Philharmonic Orchestra and the largest concert hall in Munich. Gasteig also hosts the occasional English-language work. Ⓜ *Rosenheimerplatz (S-bahn).*

Herkulessaal in der Residenz (⊠*Hofgarten, City Center* ☎*089/2906–7263*) is a leading orchestral and recital venue in the former throne room of King Ludwig I. Free concerts featuring conservatory students are given at the **Hochschule für Musik** (✉ *Arcisstr. 12, Maxvorstadt* ☎ *089/289–03*).

The Bavarian State Orchestra is based at the **Nationaltheater** (*also called the Bayerische Staatsoper* ✉ *Opernplatz, City Center* ☎ *089/2185–01* ⊕ *www.staatsorchester.de*). Munich's major pop-rock concert venue is the **Olympiahalle** (✉ *U-3 Olympiazentrum stop, Georg-Brauchle-Ring* ☎ *089/3061–3577* ⊕ *www.olympiapark-muenchen.de*). The box office, at the ice stadium, is open weekdays 10–6 and Saturday 10–3. You can also book by calling **München Ticket** (☎ *089/5481–8181*). The romantic art-nouveau **Staatstheater am Gärtnerplatz** has a variety of performances including operas, ballet, and musicals. (✉ *Gärtnerpl. 3, Isarvorstadt* ☎ *089/2185–1960*).

FESTIVALS In early May the **Long Night of Music** (☎ *089/3061–0041* 🎟 *€10*) is devoted to live performances through the night by untold numbers of groups, from heavy-metal bands to medieval choirs, at more than 100 locations throughout the city. One ticket covers everything, including transportation on special buses between locations.

OPERA, BALLET & MUSICALS

Munich's Bavarian State Opera Company and its ballet ensemble perform at the **Nationaltheater** (✉ *Opernpl., City Center* ☎ *089/2185–1920*). The **Staatstheater am Gärtnerplatz** (✉ *Gärtnerpl. 3, Isarvorstadt* ☎ *089/2185–1960* ⊕ *www.staatstheater-am-gaertnerplatz.de*) presents a less ambitious but nevertheless high-quality program of opera, ballet, operetta, and musicals.

THEATER

Munich has scores of theaters and variety-show venues, although most productions will be largely impenetrable if your German is shaky. Listed here are all the better-known theaters, as well as some of the smaller and more progressive spots. Note that most theaters are closed during July and August.

Amerika Haus (*America House* ✉ *Karolinenpl. 3, Maxvorstadt* ☎ *089/552–5370* ⊕ *www.amerikahaus.de*) is the venue for the very active American Drama Group Europe, which presents regular English-language productions here.

Bayerisches Staatsschauspiel/Neues Residenztheater (*Bavarian State Theater–New Residence Theater* ✉ *Max-Joseph-Pl., City Center* ☎ *089/2185–2160* ⊕ *www.bayerischesstaatsschauspiel.de*) is Munich's leading stage for classic playwrights such as Goethe, Schiller, Lessing, Shakespeare, and Chekhov.

Musicals, revues, balls, and big-band shows take place at **Deutsches Theater** (✉ *Schwanthalerstr. 13, Leopoldvorstadt* ☎ *089/5523–4444* ⊕ *www.deutsches-theater.de*). The box office is open weekdays noon–6 and Saturday 10–1:30.

With the Substanz Live Club & Bar, the **English Comedy Club** (✉ *Rupertstr. 28, Leopoldvorstadt* ☎ *089/721–2749* ⊕ *www.englishcomedyclub.*

All About German Beer

However many fingers you want to hold up, just remember the easy-to-pronounce *Bier* (beer) *Bit-te* (please) when ordering a beer. The tricky part is, Germans don't just produce *one* beverage called beer; they brew more than 5,000 varieties. Germany has about 1,300 breweries, 40% of the world's total. The hallmark of the country's dedication to beer is the Purity Law, *das Reinheitsgebot,* unchanged since Duke Wilhelm IV introduced it in Bavaria in 1516. The law decrees that only malted barley, hops, yeast, and water may be used to make beer, except for specialty Weiss- or Weizenbier (wheat beers, which are a carbonated, somewhat spicy, and sour brew, often with floating yeast particles).

Most taverns have several drafts in addition to bottled beers. The type available depends upon the region you're in, and perhaps on the time of year. The alcohol content of German beers also varies. At the weaker end of the scale is the light Munich Helles (a lager, from 3.7% to 4.8% alcohol by volume); stronger brews are the bitter-flavored Pilsner (around 5%) and the dark Doppelbock (more than 7%).

In Munich you'll find the most famous breweries, the largest beer halls and beer gardens, the biggest and most indulgent beer festival, and the widest selection of brews. Even the beer glasses are bigger: a *Mass* is a 1-liter (almost 2-pint) serving; a *Halbe* is half liter and the standard size. The Hofbräuhaus is Munich's best-known beer hall, but its oompah band's selections are geared more to Americans and Australians than to your average Münchener. You'll find locals in one of the English Garden's four beer gardens or in the local *Wirtshaus* (tavern).

—Robert Tilley

de) has gotten rave reviews. Entry for this evening on the first Sunday of each month is €14.

A city-funded rival to the nearby state-backed Staatliches Schauspiel, **Münchner Kammerspiele-Schauspielhaus** (⊠*Maximilianstr. 26, City Center* ☎*089/233–96600* ⊕*www.muenchner-kammerspiele.de*) presents the classics as well as new works by contemporary playwrights.

NIGHTLIFE

Munich has a lively nocturnal scene ranging from beer halls to bars to chic, see-and-be-seen clubs. The fun neighborhoods for a night out are City Center, Isarvorstadt (around Gärtnerplatz), and Schwabing around Schellingstrasse and Münchener Freiheit. Regardless of their size or style, many bars, especially around Gärtnerplatz, have DJs spinning either mellow background sounds or funky beats. The city's eclectic taste in music is quite commendable.

In summer, last call at the beer gardens is around 11 PM; ask your table neighbors where they are heading afterward—it's the best way to find out what's happening on the ground. Most of the traditional Bavarian joints stay open until 1 AM or so and are great for a couple hours of wining and dining before heading out on the town. Most bars stay open until at least 3 AM on weekends; some don't close until 5 or 6 AM. The easiest way to find what you like is to just ask people at your table.

Be warned that the bouncers at clubs and discos in Munich can make it frustratingly difficult to get into often not-so-special establishments. They can be rude, and have achieved dubious notoriety throughout Germany. They are in charge of picking who is "in" and who is "out," and there's no use trying to warm up to them.

BARS

CITY CENTER Around the corner from the Hofbräuhaus, **Bar Centrale** (⊠ *Ledererstr. 23, City Center* ☎*089/223–762*) is very Italian—the waiters don't seem to speak any other language. The coffee is excellent; small fine meals are served as well. They have a retro-looking back room with leather sofas. Also near the Hofbräuhaus is the **Atomic Café** (⊠ *Neutrumstr. 5, City Center* ☎*089/2283–053*). This club/lounge has excellent DJs nightly, playing everything from 60s Brit pop to 60s/70s funk and soul. Atomic also has great live acts on a regular basis. Cover charge is typically €7. Just behind the Frauenkirche, **Kilian's Irish Pub and Ned Kelly's Australian Bar** (⊠ *Frauenpl.11, City Center* ☎*089/2421–9899*) offers an escape from the German tavern scene. Naturally, they have Guinness and Foster's, but they also serve Munich's best lager, Augustiner, and regularly televise international soccer, rugby, and sports in general.

At **Schumann's** (⊠ *Odeonspl. 6–7, City Center* ☎*089/229–060*) the bartenders are busy shaking cocktails after the curtain comes down at the nearby opera house. Keep an eye out for Boris Becker and other local celebs lurking in the shadows. Exotic cocktails are the specialty at **Trader Vic's** (⊠ *Promenadenpl. 4, City Center* ☎*089/226–192*), a smart cellar bar in the Hotel Bayerischer Hof that's popular among out-of-town visitors. The Bayerischer Hof's **Night Club** (⊠ *Promenadepl. 2–6, City Center* ☎*089/212–00*) has live music, from jazz to reggae to hip-hop; a small dance floor; and a very lively bar.

Eisbach (⊠ *Marstallplatz 3, City Center* ☎*089/2280–1680*) occupies a corner of the Max Planck Institute building opposite the Bavarian Parliament. The bar is among Munich's biggest and is overlooked by a mezzanine restaurant area where you can choose from a limited but ambitious menu. Outdoor tables nestle in the expansive shade of huge parasols. The nearby Eisbach brook, which gives the bar its name, tinkles away like ice in a glass.

The **Kempinski Vier Jahreszeiten** (⊠ *Maximilianstr. 17, City Center* ☎*089/21250*) offers piano music until 9 PM and then dancing to recorded music or a small combo. At the English, nautical-style **Pusser's New York Bar** (⊠ *Falkenturmstr. 9, City Center* ☎*089/220–500*), great cocktails and Irish-German black and tans (Guinness and strong German beer) are made to the sounds of live jazz. Try the "Pain Killer," a specialty of the house. The pricey sandwiches are about the only "New York" in Pusser's.

1

ISARVORSTADT Around Gärtnerplatz are a number of cool bars and clubs for a somewhat younger, hipper crowd. Take a seat on Grandma's retro couches at **Trachtenvogel** (⊠ *Reichenbachstr. 47, Isarvorstadt* ☎*089/215–160*). DJs spin on most weekend nights, playing everything from reggae to hip-hop and soul. Trachtenvogel serves good toasties and Tegernseer beer, a favorite in Munich. For a New York City–corner-bar type experience, check out **Holy Home** (⊠ *Reichenbachstr. 21, Isarvorstadt* ☎*089/2014–546*). A hip local crowd frequents this smoky hole-in-the-wall that books great low-key DJs.

If you're looking for a bit more action, check out the **Café am Hochhaus** (⊠ *Blumenstr. 29, Isarvorstadt* ☎*089/8905–8152*). The glass-front former coffee shop is now a scene bar with funky DJs playing music to shake a leg (if it's not too crowded).

SCHWABING Media types drink Guinness and Kilkenny at the square bar at **Alter Simpl** (⊠ *Turkenstr. 57, Schwabing* ☎*089/272–3083*). Over one hundred years old, this establishment serves German pub food throughout the day and night. Across the street is the **Türkenhof** (⊠ *Turkenstr. 78, Schwabing* ☎*089/2800–235*), another solid local joint that serves Augustiner and good food. Up on Schellingstrasse is **Schall und Rauch** (⊠ *Schellingstr. 22, Schwabing* ☎*089/2880–9577*). This legendary student hangout, whose name literally means "Noise and Smoke," has great music and food. Another absolute cornerstone in the neighborhood is the **Schelling Salon** (⊠ *Schellingstr. 54, Schwabing* ☎*089/2720–788*). On the corner of Barerstrasse, the bar has several pool tables and even a secret Ping-Pong room in the basement with an intercom for placing beer orders.

BEER GARDENS
Everybody in Munich has at least one favorite beer garden, so you're usually in good hands if you ask someone to point you in the right direction. You do not need to reserve. No need to phone either: if the weather says yes, then go. Most—but not all—allow you to bring your own food, but if you do, don't defile this hallowed territory with something so foreign as pizza or a burger from McDonald's. Note that Munich has very strict noise laws, so beer gardens tend to close around 11.

CITY CENTER The only true beer garden in the city center, and therefore the easiest to find, is the one at the **Viktualienmarkt** (☎*089/2916–5993*). The beer on tap rotates every six weeks among the six Munich breweries to keep everyone happy throughout the year. The rest of the beer gardens are a bit further afield and can be reached handily by bike or S- and U-bahn.

AROUND TOWN The famous **Biergarten am Chinesischen Turm** (⊠ *Englischer Garten 3* ☎*089/383–8730*) is at the five-story Chinese Tower in the Englischer Garten. Enjoy your beer to the strains of oompah music played by traditionally dressed musicians. The Englischer Garten's smaller beer garden, **Hirschau** (⊠ *Gysslingstr. 15* ☎*089/322–1080*), has minigolf to test your skills after a few beers. It's about 10 minutes north of the Kleinhesselohersee. The **Seehaus im Englischen Garten** (⊠ *Kleinhessel-*

ohe 3 ☎*089/381–6130*) is on the banks of the artificial lake Kleinhesselohersee, where all of Munich converges on hot summer days (bus line 44, exit at Osterwaldstrasse; you can't miss it).

The **Augustiner Beer Garden** (✉*Arnulfstr. 52, Hauptbahnhof* ☎*089/594–393*) is one of the more authentic of the beer gardens, with excellent food, beautiful chestnut shade trees, a mixed local crowd, and Munich's legendary Augustiner beer. From the north exit of the main train station, go left on Arnulfstrasse and walk about 10 minutes. It's on the right.

Surprisingly large and green for a place so centrally located is the **Hofbräukeller** (✉*Innere Wiener Str. 19, tramway 18 to Wiener-Pl. or U-bahn 4 or 5 to Max-Weber-Pl., Haidhausen* ☎*089/459–9250*), which is a beer relative of the Hofbräuhaus. Some evenings you can move into the spacious cellar for live jazz and cheap food deals (everything €5). Out in the district of Laim is the huge **Königlicher Hirschgarten** (✉*Hirschgarten 1* ☎*089/172–591*), where the crowd is somewhat more blue-collar and foreign. To get there, take any S-bahn toward Pasing, exit at Laim, walk down Wotanstrasse, and take a right on Winifriedstrasse and then a left onto De-la-Paz-Strasse.

The crowd at the **Taxisgarten** (✉*Taxisstr. 12* ☎*089/156–827*) in the Gern district (U-bahn Gern, Line 1 toward "Westfriedhof") is more white-collar and tame, hence less chance of communicating with the natives, but the food is excellent, and while parents refresh themselves, children exhaust themselves on the playground.

If you want to get out of town either on a bike or with the S-bahn, the **Waldwirtschaft Grosshesselohe** (*also known as the "Wawi"* ✉*Georg-Kalb-Str. 3, Grosshesselohe* ☎*089/795–088*) is a fantastic beer garden a few miles south of town. It's a superb location—on a cliff overlooking the Isar—and if it's a nice day the excursion is well worth it. They've got a great jazz band. Take the S-bahn 7 to Grosshesselohe. From there it's about a 10-minute walk. Or by bike you can cruise the path along the west side of the Isar until you see a small sign saying Waldwirtschaft pointing up a steep hill. Ask someone if you can't find it.

UNDER THE CHESTNUT TREES

Munich has more than 100 beer gardens, ranging from huge establishments that seat several hundred to small terraces tucked behind neighborhood pubs and taverns. Beer gardens are such an integral part of Munich life that a council proposal to cut down their hours provoked a storm of protest in 1995, culminating in one of the largest mass demonstrations in the city's history. They open whenever the thermometer creeps above 10°C (50°F) and the sun filters through the chestnut trees that are a necessary part of beer-garden scenery.

DANCE CLUBS
There are a few dance clubs in town worth mentioning, but be warned: the larger the venue the more questionable the music tends to be and the more difficult the entry. In general, big nightclubs are giving way to

smaller, more laid-back lounge types of places scattered all over town. If you're really hankering for a big club, go to Optimolwerke in the Ostbahnhof section. Otherwise, enjoy the handful of places around the city center.

CITY CENTER, LEHEL & ISARVORSTADT

At Maximiliansplatz there is a cluster of clubs including **Rote Sonne, Pascha,** and **089** (⊠*Maximianspl. 5, City Center* Ⓜ *Karlsplatz [U-bahn and S-bahn]*). They each have something a bit different: hard electro, dance house music, and '80s music, respectively. Ask the bouncers what kind of music is planned when you get there. Rote Sonne sometimes has live bands as well.

Bordering the Englischer Garten, **P1** (⊠*Prinzregentenstr., on the west side of Haus der Kunst, Lehel* ☎*089/294–252*) is definitely one of the most popular clubs in town for the see-and-be-seen crowd. It is chockablock with the rich and the wanna-be rich but can be fun if you're in the mood. Good luck getting past the bouncer. If you don't get in, head across the street to **Edmoses** at Prinzregentenstrasse 2. **Erste Liga** (⊠*Hochbrückenstr. 3, right near Sendlinger Tor, Isarvorstadt* ☎*089/1893–2788*) is a popular club with a variety of music styles and the occasional surprise live performance by hip-hop bands or well-known DJs. The neighborhood is also very lively, and has lots of other options if you don't get in.

HAIDHAUSEN/ OSTBAHNHOF

A former factory premises hosts the city's largest late-night party scene: the **Optimolwerke** (⊠*Friedenstr. 10, Ostbahnhof* Ⓜ *Ostbahnhof [S-bahn]* ☎*089/4900–9070*) has no fewer than 13 clubs including a Latin dance club, the (in)famous Temple Bar, and more snack trucks than you can shake a currywurst at. **Muffathalle** (⊠*Rosenheimerstr. 1, behind the Müllersche Volksbad near the river, Haidhausen* ☎*089/4587–5010*) usually posts orange-and-purple schedules on advertising pillars. It has a wide range of concerts, and the crowd is refreshingly unpretentious. The café-bar here has different DJs just about every night of the week and can be really fun. Great bar staff.

The **Backstage** (⊠*Friedenheimerbrücke 7, Laim* Ⓜ *Friedenheimerbrücke [S-bahn]* ☎*089/126–6100*) is out past the Hauptbahnhof and is mostly a live-music venue for alternative music of all kinds, but they have a chilled-out club as well with a beer garden.

GAY & LESBIAN BARS

Munich's well-established gay scene stretches between Sendlingertorplatz and Isartorplatz in the Glockenbach neighborhood. For an overview check ⊕*www.munich-cruising.de.*

The laid-back **Selig** (⊠*Hans-Sachs-Str. 3, Isarvorstadt* ☎*089/2388–8878*) has a bit of outdoor seating, diverse cuisine, and good breakfasts. Right across the street from Selig, **Nil** (⊠*Hans-Sachs-Str. 2, Isarvorstadt* ☎*089/265–545*) is famous for its decent prices and its schnitzel. The upscale **Morizz** (⊠*Klenzestr. 43, Isarvorstadt* ☎*089/201–6776*) fills with a somewhat moneyed crowd.

The **Ochsengarten** (⊠*Müllerstr. 47, Isarvorstadt* ☎*089/266–446*) is Munich's leather bar. **Old Mrs. Henderson** (⊠*Rumfordstr. 2, Isarvorstadt*

☎*089/263–469*) puts on the city's best transvestite cabaret for a mixed crowd and has various other events. You can dance here too.

JAZZ

Munich has a decent jazz scene, and some beer gardens have even taken to replacing their brass oompah bands with funky combos. Jazz musicians sometimes accompany Sunday brunch, too.

The **Jazzbar Vogler** (✉*Rumfordstr. 17, City Center/Isarvorstadt* ☎*089/294–662*) is a nice bar with jam sessions on Monday nights and regular jazz concerts. At tiny **Alfonso's** (✉*Franzstr. 5, Schwabing* ☎*089/338–835*) the nightly live music redefines the concept of intimacy. **Coccodrillo** (✉*Hohenzollernstr. 11, Schwabing* ☎*089/336–639*) is in a smoky basement accessed through the Caffè Florian (where you can eat as well). From September to May the old brick vaulting resounds to the sounds of live jazz and rock three times a week. The tiny **Mr. B's** (✉*Herzog-Heinrich-Str. 38, Ludwigvorstadt* ☎*089/534– 901*) is a treat. It's run by New Yorker Alex Best, who also mixes great cocktails and, unlike so many other barkeeps, usually wears a welcoming smile.

The **Unterfahrt** (✉*Einsteinstr. 42, Haidhausen* ☎*089/448–2794*) is the place for the serious jazzologist, though hip-hop is making heavy inroads into the scene. The **Jazz Cantina** (✉*Steinstr. 83, Haidhausen* ☎*089/489–99808*) is a cozy little place with live music and Mexican food. Outdoor seating in summer.

The **Big Easy** (✉*Frundsbergstr. 46, Nymphenburg* ☎*089/158–90253*) is a classy restaurant with jazz-accompanied Sunday brunch for €17.50, not including drinks. Pricey but good. Sunday is set aside for jazz at **Waldwirtschaft Grosshesselohe** as well (*also known as the "Wawi"* ✉*Georg-Kalb-Str. 3, Grosshesselohe* ☎*089/795–088; see Beer Gardens section*), a lovely beer garden in a southern suburb. If it's a nice day, the excursion is worth it.

SPORTS & THE OUTDOORS

The **Olympiapark** (Ⓜ *Olympiazentrum [U-bahn]*), built for the 1972 Olympics, is one of the largest sports and recreation centers in Europe. The Olympic-size pool is open to visitors if you're dying for a swim. For general information about sports in and around Munich contact the sports emporium **Sport Scheck** (✉*Sendlingerstr. 6, City Center* ☎*089/21660*). The big store not only sells every kind of equipment but is very handy with advice.

BICYCLING

A bike is hands-down the best way to experience this flat, pedal-friendly city. There are loads of bike lanes and paths that wind through its parks and along the Isar River. The rental shop will give you maps and tips, or you can get a map at any city tourist office.

Weather permitting, here is a route to try: Go through Isartor to the river and head north to the Englischer Garten. Ride around the park and have lunch at a beer garden. Exit the park and go across Leopoldstrasse into Schwabing, making your way back down toward the museum quarter via the adorable Elisabethmarkt. Check out one or two of the galleries then head back to town passing Königsplatz.

You can also take your bike on the S-bahns (except during rush hours from 6 AM to 9 AM and from 4 PM to 6 PM), which take you out to the many lakes and attractions outside town. Bicycles on public transportation cost either one strip on a multiple ticket or €2.50 for a day ticket, €0.90 for a single ticket.

TOURS There is really no better way to see this beautiful city than by bike, and two very good bike-tour operators can show you around. **Mike's Bike Tours** (☎089/2554–3988 ⊕*www.mikesbiketours.com*) is the oldest operation, but there is a newcomer in the field for entertaining, informative, non-strenuous tours, and he's a veteran guide from Mike's. Mike's tours last 3½ hours, with a 45-minute break at a beer garden, and cover approximately four miles. Tours start daily at the Altes Rathaus at the end of Marienplatz at 11:30 and 4:00 (from Apr. 15–Aug. 31) and at 12:30 (Mar. 1–Apr. 15 and Sep. 1–Nov. 10). There are tours at 12:30 on Saturdays in November and February if weather permits. The cost is €24, including the bike. No reservations required. Bus Bavaria (part of Mike's Bikes) also offers a more active daytrip to Neuschwanstein castle. You travel to the area via coach in high season (€49), via train in the shoulder season (€39). **Insomniac Bike & Bar Tours** (✉*Herrenstr. 11, City Center* ☎*0176/64280392* ⊕*www.insomniacbiketours.com*), run by former Mike's guide, Frankie, combines the expectedly hilarious and informative bike ride that made Mike's famous with the bonus of exploring the social scene. The tour is an hour longer than Mike's and takes you to places Mike's doesn't. You may even go for a swim if the weather permits, and you get a free beer after the tour. They're looking to make you feel like a local during your short visit here, and it works. The bike tour is €15; bar tour is €15; combined is €24. Meeting point is at the Isartor, and times are: 12:30 PM (Mar. 15–Apr. 15); 11:30 and 4 (Apr. 16–Aug. 15); and 12:30 PM (Aug. 16–Oct. 15). No need to reserve—just show up at Isartor. The bar tour starts at 8:30 PM

RENTALS **Mike's Bike Tours** (✉*Bräuhausstr. 10, City Center* ☎*089/2554–3988* ⊕*www.mikesbiketours.com*) also rents bikes, as does **Insomniac** (from the A&O Hostel, (✉*Arnulfstr. 102, Hauptbahnhof* ☎*089/4523–590* ⊕*www.aohostels.com*). Mike's is around the corner from the rear entrance of the Hofbräuhaus, and A&O is near the train station. Day rental is €12 for the first day, €9 for subsequent days. Return time is 8 PM from May–August, earlier in other seasons.

Based at the central station, one other company worth mentioning for bike rentals is **Radius Bike Rental** (✉*opposite platform 32, Hauptbahnhof* ☎*089/596–113*). A 3-gear bike costs €14 per day. A 21-gear bike costs €18. Hourly rates are €3 and €4, respectively.

ICE-SKATING

Global warming permitting, there's outdoor skating on the lake in the Englischer Garten and on the Nymphenburger Canal in winter. Watch out for signs reading GEFAHR (danger), warning you of thin ice. In winter the fountain on **Karlsplatz** is turned into a public rink with music and an outdoor bar.

JOGGING

The best place to jog is the **Englischer Garten,** which is 11 km (7 mi) around and has dirt and asphalt paths throughout. The banks of the **Isar River** are a favorite route as well. You can also jog through **Olympiapark** if you're in the area. The 500-acre park of **Schloss Nymphenburg** (⊠ *Tramway 12 to Romanplatz*) is also ideal for running.

SWIMMING

Munich set itself a goal of making the Isar River drinkable by 2005, and nearly did it. Either way, the river is most definitely clean enough to wade in or dunk your head in on a hot summer day. Hundreds of people sunbathe on the banks upriver from the Deutsches Museum and take the occasional dip. If you prefer stiller waters, you can try swimming outdoors in the Isar River at the Maria-Einsiedel public pool complex. However, because the water comes from the Alps, it's frigid even in summer. Warmer lakes near Munich are the **Ammersee** and the **Starnbergersee.**

SHOPPING

Munich has three of Germany's most exclusive shopping streets. At the other end of the scale, it has flea markets to rival those of any other European city. In between are department stores, where acute German-style competition assures reasonable prices and often produces outstanding bargains. Artisans and artists bring their wares of beauty and originality to the Christmas markets. Collect their business cards—in summer you're sure to want to order another of those little gold baubles that were on sale in December.

SHOPPING DISTRICTS

Munich has an immense central shopping area, a 2-km (1-mi) *Fussgängerzone* (pedestrian zone) stretching from the train station to Marienplatz and then north to Odeonsplatz. The two main streets here are Neuhauserstrasse and Kaufingerstrasse, the sites of most major department stores. For upscale shopping, Maximilianstrasse, Residenzstrasse, and Theatinerstrasse are unbeatable and contain classy and tempting stores that are some of the best in Europe. Schwabing, north of the university, has more offbeat shopping streets—Schellingstrasse and Hohenzollernstrasse are two to try. ■ TIP→ The neighborhood around Gärtnerplatz also has a slew of new boutiques to check out.

DEPARTMENT STORES & MALLS

1

The main pedestrian area has two mall-type locations. The aptly named **Arcade** (✉*Neuhauserstr. 5, City Center*) is where the young find the best designer jeans and accessories. **Kaufinger Tor** (✉*Kaufingerstr. 117, City Center*) has several floors of boutiques and cafés packed neatly together under a high glass roof. For a more upscale shopping experience, visit the many stores, boutiques, galleries, and cafés of the **Fünf Höfe,** a modern arcade carved into the block of houses between Theatinerstrasse and Kardinal-Faulhaber-Strasse. The architecture of the passages and courtyards is cool and elegant, in sharp contrast to the facades of the buildings. There's a great Thai restaurant in there as well.

Apartment 20 (✉*Hohenzollernstr. 20, Schwabing* ☎*089/391–519*) is in the midst of a ton of boutiques on this bustling street. This stylish shop sells a selected assortment of brand-name gear and urban styles. For a classic selection of German clothing, including some with a folk touch, and a large collection of hats, try Munich's traditional family-run **Breiter** (✉*Kaufingerstr. 23, City Center* ☎*089/599–8840* ✉*Stachus underground mall, City Center* ☎*089/599–8840* ✉*Schützenstr. 14, Maxvorstadt* ☎*089/599–8840* ✉*Zweibrückenstr. 5–7, Isarvorstadt* ☎*089/599–8840*).

★ **Hertie** (✉*Bahnhofpl. 7, City Center* ☎*089/55120* ✉*Leopoldstr. 82, Schwabing* ☎*089/381–060*), commanding an entire city block between the train station and Karlsplatz, is the largest and, some claim, the best department store in the city. Hertie's Schwabing branch was renamed Karstadt and is a high-gloss steel-and-glass building that dominates the main corner at Münchener Freiheit.

Hirmer (✉*Kaufingerstr. 28, City Center* ☎*089/236–830*) has Munich's most comprehensive collection of German-made men's clothes, with a markedly friendly and knowledgeable staff. **Karstadt** (✉*Neuhauserstr. 18, City Center* ☎*089/290–230* ✉*Schleissheimerstr. 93, Schwabing* ☎*089/13020*), in the 100-year-old Haus Oberpollinger, at the start of the Kaufingerstrasse shopping mall, is another upscale department store, with Bavarian arts and crafts.

Kaufhof (✉*Karlspl. 21–24, City Center* ☎*089/51250* ✉*Kaufingerstr. and Marienpl., City Center* ☎*089/231–851*) offers goods in the middle price range. ■**TIP→ The end-of-season sales are bargains. Ludwig Beck** (✉*Marienpl. 11, City Center* ☎*089/236–910*) is considered a step above other department stores by Müncheners. It's packed from top to bottom with highly original wares and satisfies even the pickiest of shoppers.

Pool (✉*Maximilianstr. 11, City Center* ☎*089/266–035*) is an überhip shop on the upscale Maximilianstrasse, with fashion, music, and accessories for house and home. A shopping experience for the senses. **Slips** (✉*Gärtnerplatz. 2, Isarvorstadt* ☎*089/2022–500*), a beautiful shop on Gärtnerplatz, has a wide range of dresses, jeans, shoes, and accessories. Prices are a bit outrageous, but it's a successful store so they must be doing something right.

GIFT IDEAS

Munich is a city of beer, and items related to its consumption are obvious choices for souvenirs and gifts. Munich is also the home of the famous Nymphenburg Porcelain factory. Between Karlsplatz and the Viktualienmarkt there are loads of shops for memorabilia and trinkets.

CRAFTS

Bavarian craftspeople have a showplace of their own, the **Bayerischer Kunstgewerbe–Verein** (⊠*Pacellistr. 6–8, City Center* ☎*089/290–1470*); here you'll find every kind of handicraft, from glass and pottery to textiles. If you've been to the Black Forest and forgot to equip yourself with a clock, or if you need a good Bavarian souvenir, try **Max Krug** (⊠*Neuhauserstr. 2, City Center* ☎*089/224–501*) in the pedestrian zone. All sorts of lighters, little statues, fine Bavarian snuff boxes, and many other quality gifts to bring home are available at the **Münchner Feuerzeugzentrale** (⊠*Karlspl. 3, City Center* ☎*089/591–885*).

Otto Kellnberger's Holzhandlung (⊠*Heiliggeiststr. 7–8, City Center* ☎*089/226–479*) specializes in wooden crafts.

FOOD & BEER

Dallmayr (⊠*Dienerstr. 014–15, City Center* ☎*089/21350*) is an elegant gourmet food store, with delights ranging from the most exotic fruits to English jams, served by efficient Munich matrons in smart blue-and-white-linen costumes. The store's famous specialty is coffee, with more than 50 varieties to blend as you wish. There's also an enormous number of breads and a temperature-controlled cigar room.

Götterspeise (⊠*Jahnstr. 30, Isarvorstadt* ☎*089/2388–7374*) is across the street from the restaurant Faun. The name of this delectable choco-late shop means "ambrosia," a fitting name for their gifts, delights, and hot drinks. **Chocolate & More** (⊠ *Westenriederstr. 15, City Center* ☎*089/255–44905*) also specializes in all things chocolate. Difficult shops to leave, these two.

Ludwig Mory (⊠*Marienpl. 8, City Center* ☎*089/224–542*) has every-thing relating to beer, from mugs of all shapes and sizes and in all sorts of materials to warmers for those who don't like their beer too cold.

PORCELAIN

Porzelan Nymphenburg (⊠*Odeonspl. 1, City Center* ☎*089/282–428*) resembles a drawing room of the Munich palace of the same name and has delicate, expensive porcelain safely locked away in bowfront cabinets. You can buy directly from the factory on the grounds of **Schloss Nymphenburg** (⊠*Nördliches Schlossrondell 8, Nymphenburg* ☎*089/1791–9710*).

For Dresden and Meissen wares, go to **Kunstring** (⊠*Briennerstr. 4, City Center* ☎*089/281–532*) near Odeonsplatz.

MISCELLANEOUS

In an arcade of the Neues Rathaus is tiny **Johanna Daimer Filze aller Art** (⊠*Dienerstr., City Center* ☏*089/776–984*), a shop selling every kind and color of felt imaginable. **Lehmkuhl** (⊠*Leopoldstr. 45, Schwabing* ☏*089/3801–5013*), one of Munich's finest bookshops, also sells beautiful cards.

Obletter's (⊠*Karlspl. 11–12, City Center* ☏*089/5508–9510*) has two extensive floors of toys, many of them handmade playthings of great charm and quality. Check out **Sebastian Wesely** (⊠*Rindermarkt 1, at Peterspl., City Center* ☏*089/264–519*) for beer-related vessels and schnapps glasses (*Stampferl*), walking sticks, scarves, and napkins with the famous Bavarian blue-and-white lozenges.

SPECIALTY STORES

ANTIQUES

A few small shops around the Viktualienmarkt sell Bavarian antiques, though their numbers are dwindling under the pressure of high rental rates. Also try the area north of the university—Türkenstrasse, Theresienstrasse, and Barerstrasse are all filled with antiques stores.

Strictly for window shopping—unless you're looking for something really rare and special and money's no object—are the exclusive shops lining Prannerstrasse, at the rear of the Hotel Bayerischer Hof. Interesting and inexpensive antiques and assorted junk from all over Eastern Europe are laid out at the weekend flea markets beneath the Donnersberger railway bridge on Arnulfstrasse (along the northern side of the Hauptbahnhof).

In **Antike Uhren Eder** (⊠*Hotel Bayerischer Hof, Prannerstr. 4, City Center* ☏*089/220–305*), the silence is broken only by the ticking of dozens of highly valuable German antique clocks and by discreet negotiation over the high prices. Nautical items and antiquated sports equipment fill the curious **Captain's Saloon** (⊠*Westenriederstr. 31, City Center* ☏*089/221–015*). For Munich's largest selection of dolls and marionettes, head to **Die Puppenstube** (⊠*Luisenstr. 68, Maxvorstadt* ☏*089/272–3267*). Antique German silver and porcelain are the specialty of **Roman Odesser** (⊠*Westenriederstr. 16, City Center* ☏*089/226–388*). Old, beautiful beer steins are the specialty of **Ulrich Schneider** (⊠*Am Radlsteg 2, City Center* ☏*089/292–477*).

BOOKSTORES

The monthly English-language magazine *Munich Found* is sold at most newspaper stands and in many hotels. It contains excellent listings and reviews of restaurants and shows and generally gives an idea of life in the city.

Hugendubel (⊠*Marienpl. 22, 2nd fl., City Center* ☏*089/23890* or *01803/484–484* ⊠*Karlspl. 3, City Center* ☏*089/552–2530*) has a good selection of novels in English. The **Internationale Presse** (☏*089/13080*) in the main train station has magazines and novels.

FOLK COSTUMES

If you want to deck yourself out in lederhosen or a dirndl, or acquire a green loden coat and little pointed hat with feathers, you have a wide choice in the Bavarian capital. ■TIP➜ There are a couple of other shops along Tal "street" that have new and used lederhosen and dirndls at very good prices in case you want to spontaneously get into the spirit of the 'Fest.

Much of the fine loden clothing on sale at **Lodenfrey** (⊠ *Maffeistr. 7–9, City Center* ☎ *089/210–390*) is made at the company's own factory, on the edge of the Englischer Garten. The tiny **Lederhosen Wagner** (⊠ *Tal 2, City Center* ☎ *089/225–697*), right up against the Heiliggeist Church, carries lederhosen, woolen sweaters called *Walk* (not loden), and children's clothing. For a more affordable option, try the department store **C&A** (⊠ *Kaufingerstr. 13, City Center* ☎ *089/231930*), in the pedestrian zone.

MARKETS

Munich's **Viktualienmarkt** is *the* place to shop and to eat. Just south of Marienplatz, it's home to an array of colorful stands that sell everything from cheese to sausages, from flowers to wine. A visit here is more than just an opportunity to find picnic makings; it's a key part of understanding the Müncheners' easy-come-easy-go nature. If you're in the Schwabing area, the daily market at **Elisabethplatz** is worth a visit—it's much, much smaller than the Viktualienmarkt, but the range and quality of produce are comparable. ■TIP➜ There are also fruit stands scattered all over the city with prices that invariably beat the grocery stores.

From the end of November until December 24, the open-air stalls of the **Christkindlmarkt** (⊠ *Marienpl., City Center*) are a great place to find gifts and warm up with mulled wine. Two other perennial Christmas-market favorites are those in Schwabing (Münchner-Freiheit Square) and at the Chinese Tower, in the middle of the Englischer Garten.

SIDE TRIPS FROM MUNICH

Munich's excellent suburban railway network, the S-bahn, brings several quaint towns and attractive rural areas within easy reach for a day's excursion. The two nearest lakes, the Starnbergersee and the Ammersee, are popular year-round. Dachau attracts overseas visitors, mostly because of its concentration-camp memorial site, but it's a picturesque and historic town in its own right. Landshut, north of Munich, is way off the tourist track, but if it were the same distance south of Munich, this jewel of a Bavarian market town would be overrun. All these destinations have a wide selection of restaurants and hotels, and you can bring a bike on any S-bahn train. German Railways, DB, often has weekend specials that allow a family or group of five to travel for as little as €17.50 during certain times. (Inquire at the main train station for the *Wochenendticket,* or Weekend Ticket. Look for a *Tageskarte,* or Day Ticket, in the ticket machines in the subway stations.)

■ TIP→ Keep in mind that there are quite a few options for day trips to the famous castles built by King Ludwig, which are only a couple of hours away. Mike's Bike Tours organizes trips, or ask at your hotel for bus tour excursions. A train out to Schloss Neuschwanstein in Schwangau takes 2½ hours. *For more information on this fairy-tale castle and others, see Chapter 3, The Romantic Road.*

STARNBERGERSEE

20 km (12 mi) southwest of Munich.

The Starnbergersee was one of Europe's first pleasure grounds. Royal coaches were already trundling out from Munich to the lake's wooded shores in the 17th century. In 1663 Elector Ferdinand Maria threw a shipboard party at which 500 guests wined and dined as 100 oarsmen propelled them around the lake. Today pleasure steamers provide a taste of such luxury for the masses. The lake is still lined with the small baroque palaces of Bavaria's aristocracy, but their owners now share the lakeside with public parks, beaches, and boatyards. The Starnbergersee is one of Bavaria's largest lakes—20 km (12 mi) long, 5 km (3 mi) wide, and 406 feet at its deepest point—so there's plenty of room for swimmers, sailors, and windsurfers. The water is of drinking quality (like most Bavarian lakes), a testimony to stringent environmental laws and the very limited number of motorboats allowed.

The Starnbergersee is named after its chief resort, **Starnberg**, the largest town on the lake and the nearest to Munich. Pleasure boats set off from the jetty for trips around the lake. The resort has a tree-lined lakeside promenade and some fine turn-of-the-20th-century villas, some of which are now hotels. There are abundant restaurants, taverns, and chestnut-tree-shaded beer gardens both along the shore and in town.

On the lake's eastern shore, at the village of Berg, you'll find the **König Ludwig II Votivkapelle Berg** *(King Ludwig II Memorial Chapel)*. A well-marked path leads through thick woods to the chapel, built near the point in the lake where the drowned king's body was found on June 13, 1886. He had been confined in nearby Berg Castle after the Bavarian government took action against his withdrawal from reality and his bankrupting castle-building fantasies. A cross in the lake marks the point where his body was recovered.

The castle of **Possenhofen,** home of Ludwig's favorite cousin, Sissi, stands on the western shore, practically opposite Berg. Local lore says they used to send affectionate messages across the lake to each other. Sissi married the Austrian emperor Franz Joseph I, but spent more than 20 summers in the lakeside castle. The inside of the castle cannot be visited, but there is a nice park around it. ⊠ *Tutzingerstr. 2–6, Feldafing* ☎ *08157/93090* ⊕ *www.kaiserin-elisabeth.de.*

The **Buchheim Museum,** on the western shore of the lake, has one of the finest private collections of German expressionist art in the form of paintings, drawings, watercolors, and prints. Among the artists represented are Otto Dix, Max Beckmann, Ernst Ludwig Kirchner, Karl

Schmitt-Rotluff, and other painters of the so-called Brücke movement (1905–13). The museum is housed in an impressive modern building on the lakeside. Some areas of the museum are reserved for African cultic items and Bavarian folk art. The nicest way to get to the museum from Starnberg is by ship. ⊠*Am Hirschgarten 1* ☎*08158/99700* ⊕*www. buchheimmuseum.de* ☷€*8.50* ☉*Apr.–Oct., Tues.–Sun. 10–6; Nov.– Mar., Tues.–Sun. 10–5.*

Just offshore is the tiny **Roseninsel** *(Rose Island)* , where King Maximilian II built a summer villa. You can swim to its tree-fringed shores or sail across in a dinghy or on a Windsurfer (rentals are available at Possenhofen's boatyard and at many other rental points along the lake). There is a little ferry service for €4. It runs twice a day at 11 and 6 in May and at the end of September, and at 10 and 6 from June to mid-September.

WHERE TO STAY & EAT

¢–$$$ ✗**Seerestaurant Undosa.** This restaurant is only a short walk from the Starnberg railroad station and boat pier. Most tables command a view of the lake, which provides some of the best fish specials on the international menu. This is the place to try the mild-tasting *Renke,* a perch-type fish. The Undosa also has jazz evenings and a large café, the Oberdeck, also overlooking the lake. ⊠*Seepromenade 1* ☎*08151/998–930* ⌂*Reservations not accepted* ☰*AE, MC, V* ☉*Closed 2 wks in Feb. Call to confirm hrs.*

¢–$$ ✗**Ristorante bei Rosario.** The decor at this modest Italian restaurant might not be all that one might choose, but they more than compensate with friendly service, quality food, and reasonable prices. They make their own pasta, and the mussels are popular. Lunch menus are a real bargain at this find located just a block or two from the train station. ⊠*Ludwigstr. 3, Starnberg* ☎*08151/746–280* ☰*MC, V.*

¢–$ ✗**Königswasser.** A large, airy atrium welcomes you to this comfortable spot. You can enjoy coffee and cakes or a meal ranging from fresh salad to an Argentinean steak drowned in pepper sauce. The Königswasser has a shelf full of photography books and travel guides that invite you to just sit, relax, and enjoy some time off your feet. It's open past midnight from Wednesday through Saturday and until 6 PM the rest of the week. ⊠*Maximilianstr. 2b, Starnberg* ☎*08151/444–088* ☰*MC, V.*

$–$$$ ✗⌂**Hotel Schloss Berg.** King Ludwig II spent his final days in the small castle of Berg, from which this comfortable hotel gets its name. It's on the edge of the castle park where Ludwig liked to walk and a stone's throw from where he drowned. The century-old main hotel building is on the lakeside, and a modern annex overlooks the lake from the woods. All rooms are spacious and elegantly furnished. The restaurant ($–$$$$) and waterside beer garden are favorite haunts of locals and weekenders. The menu in the restaurant changes monthly, and there are four-course meals for €30–€40. ⊠*Seestr. 17, D–82335 Berg* ☎*08151/9630* ☷*08151/96352* ⊕*www.hotelschlossberg.de* ⇆*60 rooms* ⌂*In-room: no a/c, ethernet, Wi-Fi. In-hotel: restaurant, bar, bicycles, public Internet, no elevator in main building, some pets allowed (fee)* ☰*AE, MC, V* ☉◎*BP.*

1

$$ ✕🖾 **Forsthaus am See.** The handsome, geranium-covered Forsthaus faces the lake, and so do most of the large, pinewood-furnished rooms. The excellent restaurant ($$–$$$$) has a daily changing international menu, with lake fish a specialty. The hotel has its own lake access and boat pier, with a chestnut-shaded beer garden nearby. ⊠*Am See 1, D–82343 Possenhofen* ☎*08157/93010* 🖷*08157/4292* ⊕*www. forsthaus-am-see.de* ⇌*21 rooms, 1 suite* ⌂*In-room: no a/c. In-hotel: restaurant, bar, some pets allowed (fee), no elevator* ⊟*AE, MC, V* ⦿*BP.*

$$ ✕🖾 **Hotel Seehof.** This small hotel right next to the train station has several rooms with a view of the lake. Rooms are simply done, with light colors and flower prints hanging on the walls. The Italian restaurant attached, Al Gallo Nero (¢–$$$), has dishes ranging from low-price pizzas to high-price fish items that will satisfy any palate. ⊠*Bahnhofpl. 6, D–82319 Starnberg* ☎*08151/908–500* 🖷*08151/28136* ⊕*www. hotel-seehof-starnberg.de* ⇌*38 rooms* ⌂*In-room: no a/c, Wi-Fi, minibar. In-hotel: restaurant, public Wi-Fi, some pets allowed (fee)* ⊟*AE, DC, MC, V* ⦿*BP.*

STARNBERGERSEE ESSENTIALS

TRANSPORTATION

Starnberg and the north end of the lake are a 25-minute drive from Munich on the A–95 autobahn. Follow the signs to Garmisch and take the Starnberg exit. Country roads then skirt the west and east shores of the lake, but many are closed to the public.

The S-bahn 6 suburban line runs from Munich's central Marienplatz to Starnberg and three other towns on the lake's west shore: Possenhofen, Feldafing, and Tutzing. The journey from Marienplatz to Starnberg takes 35 minutes. The east shore of the lake can be reached by bus from the town of Wolfratshausen, the end of the S-bahn 7 suburban line. A wonderful way to spend a summer day is to rent bicycles in Munich, take the S-bahn to Starnberg and ride along the eastern shore and back. Another appealing option is to take the train to Tutzing and ride up the western shore back to Starnberg.

CONTACTS & RESOURCES

The quickest way to visit the Starnbergersee area is by ship. On Saturday evenings the good ship *Seeshaupt* has dancing and dinner.

Information Seeshaupt (☎*08151/12023*).

Visitor Information Tourismusverband Starnberger Fünf-Seen-Land (⊠*Wittelsbacher Str. 2c, D–82319 Starnberg* ☎*08151/90600* 🖷*08151/906–090* ⊕*www.sta5.de*).

AMMERSEE

40 km (25 mi) southwest of Munich.

The Ammersee, or the Peasant Lake, is the country cousin of the better-known, more cosmopolitan Starnbergersee (the Prince Lake), and, accordingly, many Bavarians (and tourists, too) like it all the more.

Munich cosmopolites of centuries past thought it too distant for an excursion, not to mention too rustic, so the shores remained relatively free of villas and parks. Though some upscale holiday homes claim some stretches of the eastern shore, the Ammersee still offers more open areas for bathing and boating than the larger lake to the east. Bicyclists circle the 19-km-long (12-mi-long) lake (it's nearly 6 km [4 mi] across at its widest point) on a path that rarely loses sight of the water. Hikers can spread out the tour for two or three days, staying overnight in any of the comfortable inns along the way. Dinghy sailors and windsurfers zip across in minutes with the help of the Alpine winds that swoop down from the mountains. A ferry cruises the lake at regular intervals during summer, stopping at several piers. Board it at Herrsching.

Herrsching has a delightful promenade, part of which winds through the resort's park. The 100-year-old villa that sits so comfortably there seems as if it were built by Ludwig II; such is the romantic and fanciful mixture of medieval turrets and Renaissance-style facades. It was actually built for the artist Ludwig Scheuermann in the late 19th century, and became a favorite meeting place for Munich and Bavarian artists. It's now a municipal cultural center and the setting for chamber-music concerts on some summer weekends.

The Benedictine monastery **Andechs,** one of southern Bavaria's most famous pilgrimage sites, lies 5 km (3 mi) south of Herrsching. You can reach it on Bus 951 from the S-bahn station (the bus also connects Ammersee and Starnbergersee). This extraordinary ensemble, surmounted by an octagonal tower and onion dome with a pointed helmet, has a busy history going back more than 1,000 years. The church, originally built in the 15th century, was entirely redone in baroque style in the early 18th century. The **Heilige Kapelle** contains the remains of the old treasure of the Benedictines in Andechs, including Charlemagne's "Victory Cross" and a monstrance containing the three sacred hosts brought back from the crusades by the original rulers of the area, the Counts of Diessen-Andechs. One of the attached chapels contains the remains of composer Carl Orff, and one of the buildings on the grounds has been refurbished as a concert stage for the performance of his works.

Admittedly, however, the crowds of pilgrims are drawn not just by the beauty of the hilltop monastery but primarily by the beer brewed here (600,000 liters [159,000 gallons] annually) and the stunning views. The monastery makes its own cheese as well, and serves organic Bavarian food, an excellent accompaniment to the rich, almost black beer. You can enjoy both at large wooden tables in the monastery tavern or on the terrace outside. ☎ *08152/376–167* ⊕ *www.andechs.de* ⊙ *Daily 7–7.*

The little town of **Diessen** at the southwest corner of the lake has one of the most magnificent religious buildings of the whole region: the **Augustine abbey church of St. Mary.** No lesser figure than the great Munich architect Johann Michael Fischer designed this airy, early rococo structure. François Cuvillié the Elder, whose work can be seen all over Munich, did the sumptuous gilt-and-marble high altar. Visit in late afternoon, when the light falls sharply on its crisp gray, white, and gold facade, etching the pencil-like tower and spire against the darkening sky over the lake. Don't leave without at least peeping into neighboring St. Stephen's courtyard, its cloisters smothered in wild roses. But Diessen is not all church. It has attracted artists and craftspeople since the early 20th century. Among the most famous who made their home here was the composer Carl Orff, author of numerous works inspired by medieval material, including the famous *Carmina Burana*. His life and work—notably the pedagogical Schulwerk instruments—are exhibited in the **Carl-Orff-Museum** (✉ *Hofmark 3, Diessen* 📞*08807/91981* ☉ *Weekends 2–5*).

WHERE TO STAY & EAT

$$–$$$ ✕🍴 **Ammersee Hotel.** This very comfortable, modern resort hotel has views from an unrivaled position on the lakeside promenade. Rooms overlooking the lake are more expensive and in demand. The Artis restaurant ($–$$) has an international menu with an emphasis on fish. You can enjoy a spicy bouillabaisse or catfish from the Danube. Free Wi-Fi Internet access is available in the building. ✉*Summerstr. 32, D–82211, Herrsching* 📞*08152/96870, 08152/399–440 restaurant* 🖨*08152/5374* ⊕*www.ammersee-hotel.de* ↪*40 rooms* ⌂*In-room: no a/c, ethernet, Wi-Fi. In-hotel: restaurant, gym, some pets allowed (fee)* ▤*AE, DC, MC, V* ⭘⎮*BP.*

$–$$ 🍴 **Hotel Garni Zur Post.** Families feel particularly at home here, where ☺ children can amuse themselves at the playground and small deer park. Rooms are Bavarian country style, with solid-pine furnishings, and are clean and functional. A delicious breakfast buffet will prepare you for a long day of touring. ✉*Starnberger Str. 2, D–82346 Andechs* 📞*08152/91820* 🖨*08152/2303* ⊕*www.hotelzurpost-andechs.de* ↪*17 rooms* ⌂*In-room: no a/c, dial-up. In-hotel: some pets allowed (fee), no elevator* ▤*MC* ⭘⎮*CP.*

AMMERSEE ESSENTIALS

TRANSPORTATION

Take A–96, follow the signs to Lindau, and 20 km (12 mi) west of Munich take the exit for Herrsching, the lake's principal town.

Herrsching is also the end of the S-bahn 5 suburban line, a 47-minute ride from Munich's Marienplatz. From the Herrsching train station, Bus 952 runs north along the lake, and Bus 951 runs south and continues on to Starnberg in a 40-minute journey.

Getting around on a boat is the best way to visit. Each town on the lake has an *Anlegestelle* (pier).

CONTACTS & RESOURCES

Visitor Information Verkehrsbüro (✉ *Bahnhofspl. 2, Herrsching* 📞*08152/5227* ☉ *May–Oct., weekdays 9–1 and 2–6, Sat. 9–1; Nov.–Apr., weekdays 10–5*).

DACHAU

20 km (12 mi) northwest of Munich.

Dachau predates Munich, with records going back to the time of Charlemagne. It's a handsome town, too, built on a hilltop with views of Munich and the Alps. A guided tour of the town, including the castle and church, leaves from the Rathaus on Saturday at 10:30, from May through mid-October. Dachau is infamous worldwide as the site of the first Nazi concentration camp, which was built just outside it. Dachau preserves the memory of the camp and the horrors perpetrated there with deep contrition while trying, with commendable discretion, to signal that the town has other points of interest.

To get a history of the town, drop in on the **Bezirksmuseum,** the district museum, which displays historical artifacts, furniture, and traditional costumes from Dachau and its surroundings. ✉ *Augsburgerstr. 3* ☎ *08131/567–50* 🖃 *€3.50* ⊘ *Tues.–Fri. 11–5, weekends 1–5.*

The site of the infamous camp, now the **KZ-Gedenkstätte Dachau** *(Dachau Concentration Camp Memorial)*, is just outside town. Photographs, contemporary documents, the few remaining cell blocks, and the grim crematorium create a somber and moving picture of the camp, where more than 30,000 of the 200,000-plus prisoners lost their lives. A documentary film in English is shown daily at 11:30 and 3:30. The former camp has become more than just a grisly memorial: it's now a place where people of all nations meet to reflect upon the past and on the present. Several religious shrines and memorials have been built to honor the dead, who came from Germany and all occupied nations. To reach the memorial by car, leave the center of the town along Schleissheimerstrasse and turn left onto Alte Römerstrasse; the site is on the left. By public transport take Bus 724 or 726 from the Dachau S-bahn train station or the town center. Both stop within a two-minute walk from the site (ask the driver to let you out there). If you are driving from Munich, turn right on the first country road (marked B) before entering Dachau and follow the signs. ✉ *Alte Römerstr. 75* ☎ *08131/669–970* ⊕ *www.kz-gedenkstaette-dachau.de* 🖃 *Free, guided tour €3* ⊘ *Tues.–Sun. 9–5. Tours May–Oct., Tues.–Fri. at 1:30, weekends at noon and 1:30; Nov.–Apr., Thurs. and weekends at 1:30.*

Schloss Dachau, the hilltop castle, dominates the town. What you'll see is the one remaining wing of a palace built by the Munich architect Josef Effner for the Wittelsbach ruler Max Emanuel in 1715. During the Napoleonic Wars the palace served as a field hospital and then was partially destroyed. King Max Joseph lacked the money to rebuild it, so all that's left is a handsome cream-and-white building, with an elegant pillared and lantern-hung café on the ground floor and a former ballroom above. About once a month the grand Renaissance hall, with a richly decorated and carved ceiling, covered with painted panels depicting figures from ancient mythology, is used for chamber concerts. The east terrace affords panoramic views of Munich and, on fine days, the distant Alps. There's also a 250-year-old *Schlossbrauerei* (castle brewery), which hosts the town's beer and music festival each year in the first two weeks of August. ⊠*Schlosspl.* 🕾*08131/87923* 🎫*€1, tour €2* ⊙*Apr.–Sept., Tues.–Sun. 9–6; Oct.–Mar., Tues.–Sun. 10–4; tour of town and Schloss May–mid-Oct., Sat. at 10:30.*

St. Jacob, Dachau's parish church, was built in the early 16th century in late-Renaissance style on the foundations of a 14th-century Gothic structure. Baroque features and a characteristic onion dome were added in the late 17th century. On the south wall you can admire a very fine 17th-century sundial. A visit to the church is included in the guided tour of the town. ⊠*Konrad-Adenauer-Str. 7* ⊙*Daily 7–7.*

An artists' colony formed here during the 19th century, and the tradition lives on. Picturesque houses line Hermann-Stockmann-Strasse and part of Münchner Strasse, and many of them are still the homes of successful artists. The **Gemäldegalerie** displays the works of many of the town's 19th-century artists. ⊠*Konrad-Adenauer-Str. 3* 🕾*08131/567–516* 🎫*€3.50* ⊙*Tues.–Fri. 11–5, weekends 1–5.*

WHERE TO EAT

¢–$$

Fodor'sChoice

★

✕**Weilachmühle.** You have to drive a ways for this absolute gem of a restaurant–cum–beer garden–cum–stage and exhibition room in the little village of Thalhausen. It's in a farmhouse that was restored the way it should be, the old dark wooden door opening onto a generous dining area paneled in simple light pine. The food is faultless, beginning with the benchmark Schweinsbraten. Live bands play in the beer garden. To get to the Weilachmühle, drive 26 km (16 mi) north of Dachau toward Aichach; when you reach the village of Wollomoos, take a right toward Thalhausen. (Thalhausen is 2 km [1 mi] from Wollomoos.) ⊠*Am Mühlberg 5, D–85250 Thalhausen* 🕾*08254/1711* 🖃*No credit cards* ⊙*Closed Mon.–Thurs.*

¢–$

✕**Gasthof drei Rosen.** In a 19th-century building at the foot of Dachau's old town, this little inn caters primarily to locals. Among the inexpensive and filling Bavarian specialties on the menu is *Hendl à la Parkvilla,* chicken marinated in milk and deep fried. You can order it to go as well. ⊠*Schlossstr. 8* 🕾*08131/84363* ⊕*www.gasthaus-3rosen.de* 🖃*No credit cards* ⊙*Closed Mon. and Tues.*

¢–$

✕**Zieglerbräu.** Dachau's leading beer tavern, once a 17th-century brewer's home, is a warren of cozy wood-panel rooms where you'll probably share a table with a party of locals on a boys' night out. The food consists of pork, potato, and sausages prepared in various ways. ∎TIP➔In summer the tables spill out onto the street for a very Italian feeling. The restaurant runs the neighboring nightclub and a hotel. ⊠*Konrad-Adenauer-Str. 8* 🕾*08131/454–396* 🖃*No credit cards.*

DACHAU ESSENTIALS

TRANSPORTATION
Take the B–12 country road or the Stuttgart autobahn to the Dachau exit from Munich. Dachau is also on the S-bahn 2 suburban line, a 20-minute ride from Munich's Marienplatz.

CONTACTS & RESOURCES
Visitor Information **Verkehrsverein Dachau** (✉ *Konrad-Adenauer-Str. 1*
☎ *08131/75286* 🖨 *08131/84529* ⊕ *www.dachau.info*).

LANDSHUT

64 km (40 mi) north of Munich.

If fortune had placed Landshut south of Munich, in the protective folds of the Alpine foothills, instead of the same distance north, in the subdued flatlands of Lower Bavaria—of which it is the capital—the historic town would be teeming with tourists. Landshut's geographical misfortune is the discerning visitor's good luck, for the town is never overcrowded, with the possible exception of the three summer weeks when the *Landshuter Hochzeit* (Landshut Wedding) is celebrated (it takes place every four years, the next occasion being in 2009). The festival commemorates the marriage in 1475 of Prince George of Bavaria-Landshut, son of the expressively named Ludwig the Rich, to Princess Hedwig, daughter of the king of Poland. Within its ancient walls the entire town is swept away in a colorful reconstruction of the event. The wedding procession, with the "bride" and "groom" on horseback accompanied by pipes and drums and the hurly-burly of a medieval pageant, is held on three consecutive weekends while a medieval-style fair fills the central streets throughout the three weeks.

Landshut has two magnificent cobblestone market streets. The one in **Altstadt** (Old Town) is one of the most beautiful city streets in Germany; the other is in **Neustadt** (New Town). The two streets run parallel to each other, tracing a course between the Isar River and the heights overlooking the town.

A steep path from the Altstadt takes you up to **Burg Trausnitz.** This castle was begun in 1204 and accommodated the Wittelsbach dukes of Bavaria-Landshut until 1503. ☎*0871/924–110* ⊕*www.burgtrausnitz. de* 🎫*€4, including guided tour* ⊗*Apr.–Sept., daily 9–6; Oct.–Mar., daily 9–5:30.*

The **Stadtresidenz** in Altstadt was the first Italian Renaissance building of its kind north of the Alps. It was built from 1536 to 1537 but was given a baroque facade at the end of the 19th century. The Wittelsbachs lived here during the 16th century. The facade of the palace forms an almost modest part of the architectural splendor and integrity of the Altstadt, where even the ubiquitous McDonald's has to serve its hamburgers behind a baroque exterior. The Stadtresidenz includes exhibitions on the history of Landshut. ✉*Altstadt 79* ☎*0871/924–110* 🎫*€3* ⊗ *Apr.–Sept., Tues.–Sun. 9–6; Oct.–Mar., Tues.–Sun. 10–4.*

The **Rathaus** *(Town Hall),* which stands opposite the Stadtresidenz, is an elegant, light-color building with a typical neo-Gothic roof design. It was originally a set of 13th-century burghers' houses, taken over by the town in the late 1300s. The famous bride and groom allegedly danced in the grand ceremonial hall during their much-celebrated wedding in 1475. The frescoes here date to 1880, however. The tourist information bureau is on the ground floor. ⊠*Altstadt 315* ☎*0871/881–215* ⮢*Free* ⊘ *Weekdays 2–3, and on official tours.*

The **Martinskirche** *(St. Martin's Church),* with the tallest brick church tower (436 feet) in the world, soars above the other buildings. The church, which was elevated to the rank of *basilica minor* in 2002, contains some magnificent late-Gothic stone and wood carvings, notably a 1518 Madonna by the artist Martin Leinberger. It's surely the only church in the world to contain an image of Hitler, albeit in a devilish pose. The Führer and other Nazi leaders are portrayed as executioners in a 1946 stained-glass window showing the martyrdom of St. Kastulus. In the nave of the church is a clear and helpful description of its history and treasures in English. Every first Sunday of the month a tour is conducted between 11:30 and 12:30 that will take you up the tower and to the **Schatzkammer,** the church's treasure chamber. ⊠*Altstadt and Kirchg.* ☎*0871/922–1780* ⊘ *Apr.–Sept., Tues.–Thurs. and weekends 7–6:30; Oct.–Mar., Tues.–Thurs. and weekends 7–5.*

Built into a steep slope of the hill crowned by Burg Trausnitz is an unusual art museum, the **Skulpturenmuseum im Hofberg,** containing the entire collection of the Landshut sculptor Fritz Koenig. His own work forms the permanent central section of the labyrinthine gallery. ⊠*Kolpingstr. 481* ☎*0871/89021* ⮢*€3.50* ⊘ *Tues.–Sun. 10:30–1 and 2–5.*

OFF THE BEATEN PATH

Freising. This ancient episcopal seat, 35 km (22 mi) southwest of Landshut, houses a cathedral and old town well worth visiting. The town is also accessible from Munich (at the end of the S-bahn 1 line, a 45-minute ride from central Munich).

WHERE TO STAY & EAT
There are several attractive Bavarian-style restaurants in Altstadt and Neustadt, most of them with beer gardens. Although Landshut brews a fine beer, look for a Gaststätte offering a *Weihenstephaner,* from the world's oldest brewery, in Freising. Helles (light) is the most popular beer variety.

$$ ✕▣**Hotel Goldene Sonne.** The steeply gabled Renaissance exterior of the "Golden Sun" fronts a hotel of great charm and comfort. It stands in the center of town, near all the sights. Its dining options are a paneled, beamed restaurant (¢–$); a vaulted cellar; and a courtyard beer garden, where the service is friendly and helpful. The menu follows the seasons and toes the "quintessential Bavarian" line, with pork roast, steamed or smoked trout with horseradish, asparagus in the spring (usually accompanied by potatoes or ham), and venison in the fall. Free Wi-Fi Internet access is available in the building. ⊠*Neustadt 520, D–84028* ☎*0871/92530* 🖷*0871/925–30* ⊕*www.goldenesonne.de* ⮢*60 rooms* ⮢*In-room: no a/c, dial-up, free Wi-Fi. In-hotel: restaurant, bar, public Wi-Fi, no-smoking rooms, no elevator, some pets allowed (fee), minibar* ▤*AE, DC, MC, V* ⋈*BP.*

$$ ✕▣**Romantik Hotel Fürstenhof.** This handsome Landshut city mansion, located a few minutes on foot from the center of town, had no difficulty qualifying for inclusion in the Romantik group of hotels—it just breathes romance, from its plush gourmet restaurant ($$–$$$),

covered in wood paneling, to the cozy bedrooms. A vine-covered terrace shadowed by a chestnut tree adds charm. Price includes breakfast buffet and sauna use. Free Wi-Fi Internet access is available in the building. ⊠*Stethaimerstr. 3, D–84034* ☎*0871/92550* 🖷*0871/925–544* ⊕*www.fuerstenhof.la* ⮑*24 rooms* ⚿*In-room: no a/c (some), Wi-Fi. In-hotel: restaurant, public Wi-Fi, no-smoking rooms, no elevator* ▤*AE, DC, MC, V* ⊘*Restaurant closed Sun.* ⦿*BP.*

$–$$ ✕⌨**Schloss Schönbrunn.** This country mansion is now a luxurious hotel, with many of its original features intact. Rooms in the most historic part of the building are particularly attractive, with huge double beds, and represent excellent value. The handsome house stands in the Schönbrunn district of Landshut, about 2 km (1 mi) from the center. The journey is worthwhile even for the excellent restaurant ($–$$), where the menu includes fish from the hotel's own pond, or for a romantic evening at the beer garden. ⊠*Schönbrunn 1, D–84036* ☎*0871/95220* 🖷*0871/952–20* ⊕*www.hotel-schoenbrunn.de* ⮑*33 rooms* ⚿*In-room: no a/c, dial-up, Wi-Fi. In-hotel: restaurant, bar, public Wi-Fi, no-smoking rooms, some pets allowed (fee)* ▤*AE, DC, MC, V* ⦿*BP.*

LANDSHUT ESSENTIALS

TRANSPORTATION

Landshut is a 45-minute drive northwest of Munich on either the A–92 autobahn—follow the signs to Deggendorf—or the B–11 highway. The Plattling–Regensburg–Passau train line brings you from Munich in about 50 minutes. A round-trip costs about €20.

CONTACTS & RESOURCES

Visitor Information Verkehrsverein (⊠*Altstadt 315* ☎*0871/922–050* ⊕*www.landshut.de*).

MUNICH ESSENTIALS

TRANSPORTATION

BY AIR

Munich's International Airport is 28 km (17 mi) northeast of the city center, between the small towns of Freising and Erding. When departing from Munich for home, you can claim your V.A.T. refund (for purchases made during your stay) at a counter either between areas B and C or between C and D.

Information Flughafen München (☎*089/97500* ⊕*www.munich-airport.de*).

AIRPORT TRANSFERS An excellent train service links the airport with Munich's main train station. The S-1 and S-8 lines operate from a terminal directly beneath the airport's arrival and departure halls. Trains leave every 10 minutes, and the journey takes around 40 minutes. Several intermediate stops are made, including the Ostbahnhof (convenient for lodgings east of the Isar River) and such city-center stations as Marienplatz. A one-way ticket costs €8, or €7.20 if you purchase a multiple-use "strip" ticket (you will have two strips left at the end). A family of up to five (two adults and three children under 15) can make the trip for €15 by buying a *Tageskarte* (which allows travel until 6 AM the next morning). The bus service is slower than the S-bahn link (€9 one-way, €14.50 round-trip). A taxi from the airport costs around €50. During rush hours (7 AM–10 AM and 4 PM–7 PM), allow up to an hour of traveling time. If you're driving from the airport to the city, take route A–9 and follow the signs for MÜNCHEN STADTMITTE (downtown). If you're driving from the city center, head north through Schwabing, join the A–9 autobahn at the Frankfurter Ring intersection, and follow the signs for the airport (FLUGHAFEN).

BY LONG-DISTANCE BUS

Long-distance buses arrive at and depart from an area to the west of the main train station. The actual office of the bus company, Touring GmbH, is in the northern section of the train station itself, an area referred to as the Starnberger Bahnhof.

Information Zentraler Busbahnhof (✉ *Arnulfstr., Leopoldvorstadt* ☎ *089/545–8700*).

BY CAR

From the north (Nürnberg or Frankfurt), leave the autobahn at the Schwabing exit. From Stuttgart and the west, the autobahn ends at Obermenzing, Munich's most westerly suburb. The autobahns from Salzburg and the east, Garmisch and the south, and Lindau and the southwest all join the Mittlerer Ring (city beltway). When leaving any autobahn, follow the signs reading STADTMITTE for downtown Munich.

PARKING Parking in Munich is nerve-racking and not cheap. There are several parking garages throughout the center, but your best bet is to use public transportation, which is exemplary.

BY PUBLIC TRANSIT

Munich has an efficient and well-integrated public-transportation system, consisting of the U-bahn (subway), the S-bahn (suburban railway), the Strassenbahn (streetcars), and buses. Marienplatz forms the heart of the U-bahn and S-bahn network, which operates from around 5 AM to 1 AM. An all-night tram and bus service operates on main routes within the city. For a clear explanation in English of how the system works, pick up a copy of *Rendezvous mit München,* free at all tourist offices.

Fares are uniform for the entire system. As long as you are traveling in the same direction, you can transfer from one mode of transportation to another on the same ticket. You can also interrupt your journey as often as you like, and time-punched tickets are valid for up to four hours, depending on the number of zones you travel through. Fares are constantly creeping upward, but a basic *Einzelfahrkarte* (one-way ticket) costs €2.20 for a ride in the inner zone and €1.10 for a short journey of up to four stops. If you're taking a number of trips around the city, save money by buying a *Mehrfahrtenkarte,* or multiple-strip ticket. Red-strip tickets are valid for children under 15 only. Blue strips cover adults—€10.50 buys a 10-strip ticket. All but the shortest inner-area journeys (up to four stops) cost two strips (one for young people between 15 and 21), which must be validated at one of the many time-punching machines at stations or on buses and trams. For two to five people on a short stay the best option is the *Partner-Tageskarte,* which provides unlimited travel for one day (maximum of two adults, plus three children under 15). It's valid anytime except 6 AM to 9 AM on weekdays. The costs are €9 for an innerzone ticket and €18 for the entire network. The day card comes in a single version for €5 for the inner city, €10 for the whole network. A three-day card is also available, costing €12.30 for a single and €21 in the partner version.

■ TIP→ The *Welcome Card* covers transport within the city boundaries and includes up to 50% reductions in admission to many museums and attractions in Munich and in Bavaria (including lifts to the Zugspitze in Garmisch-Partenkirchen). The card, obtainable from visitor information offices, costs €7.50 for one day and €17.50 for three days. A three-day card for two people costs €25.50. You can also get a partner card that includes airport transport fare for €48.

All tickets are sold at the blue dispensers at U- and S-bahn stations and at some bus and streetcar stops. Bus drivers have single tickets (the most expensive kind). There are ticket-vending machines in trams, but they don't offer the strip cards. Otherwise tourist offices and Mehrfahrtenkarten booths (which display a white κ on a green background) also sell tickets. Spot checks are common and carry an automatic fine of €40 if you're caught without a valid ticket. ■ TIP→ Holders of a Eurail-Pass, a Youth Pass, or an Inter-Rail card can travel free on all suburban railway trains (S-bahn).

BY TAXI
Munich's cream-color taxis are numerous. Hail them in the street or phone for one (there's an extra charge of €1 if you call). Rates start at €2.40. Expect to pay €8–€10 for a short trip within the city. There's a €0.50 charge for each piece of luggage.

Information Taxi (☎ *089/21610 or 089/19410*).

BY TRAIN
All long-distance rail services arrive at and depart from the Hauptbahnhof; trains to and from some destinations in Bavaria use the adjoining Starnbergerbahnhof, which is under the same roof. The high-speed InterCity Express (ICE) trains connect Munich, Augsburg, Frankfurt, and Hamburg on one line, Munich, Nürnberg, Würzburg, and Hamburg on another. Regensburg can be reached from Munich on Regio trains. For tickets and travel information at the main train station, go to the DB counters or the EurAide office at Track 11 that serves English-speaking train travelers. You can also try the ABR-DER travel agency, right by the station on Bahnhofplatz.

Information ABR-DER (✉ *Bahnhofpl., Leopoldvorstadt* ☎ *089/5514–0200*).

Hauptbahnhof (⊠ *Bahnhofpl., Leopoldvorstadt* ☎ *089/2333–0256, 089/2333–0257, 01805/996–633 train schedules*).

CONTACTS & RESOURCES

TOUR OPTIONS
■**TIP→** For the cheapest sightseeing tour of the city center on wheels, board Streetcar 19 outside the Hauptbahnhof on Bahnhofplatz and make the 15-minute journey to Max Weber Platz. Explore the streets around the square, part of the old bohemian residential area of Haidhausen (with some of the city's best bars and restaurants, many on the village-like Kirchenstrasse), and then return by a different route on Streetcar 18 to Karlsplatz. A novel way of seeing the city is to hop on one of the bike-rickshaws. The bike-powered two-seater cabs operate between Marienplatz and the Chinesischer Turm in the Englischer Garten. Just hail one—or book ahead by calling Rikscha-Mobil. Cost is €37 per hour.

The tourist office offers individual guided tours for fees ranging between €100 and €250. Bookings must be made at least 10 days in advance. Taxi tours with specially trained drivers are offered by Isar-Funk Taxizentrale GmbH. These are a good alternative for groups of up to four people. Cost is €68 per trip for the first hour and €18 for each subsequent half hour. ⇨ *See Sports & the Outdoors for information on bike tours.*

Information IsarFunk Taxizentrale GmbH (☎ *089/450–540*). **Munich Tourist Office** (☎ *089/2333–0234*). **Rikscha-Mobil** (☎ *089/129–4808*).

BUS TOURS Bus excursions to the Alps, to Austria, to the royal palaces and castles of Bavaria, or along the Romantic Road can be booked through DER. Panorama Tours next to the central station operates numerous trips, including the Royal Castles Tour (Schlösserfahrt) of "Mad" King Ludwig's dream palaces; the cost is €49, excluding entrance fees to the palaces. Bookings for both companies can also be made at most hotels in the city. The tours depart from the front of the Hauptbahnhof outside the Hertie department store. Mike's Bikes also does a bus/bike tour to Neuschwanstein.

Panorama Tours also has one-hour tours of Munich highlights that depart every 20 minutes and cost €13. Other options include a trip to Bavaria Film Studios, Munich by Night, and an FC Bayern Munich soccer team tour.

Yellow Cab Stadtrundfahrten has a fleet of yellow double-decker buses, in which tours are offered simultaneously in eight languages. They leave hourly between 10 AM and 4 PM from the front of the Elisenhof shopping complex on Bahnhofplatz. Tours cost €9.

Information DER (⊠ *Hauptbahnhofpl. 2, in main train-station bldg., Leopoldvorstadt* ☎ *089/5514–0100*). **Panorama Tours** (⊠ *Arnulfstr. 8, Leopoldvorstadt* ☎ *089/5490–7560*). **Yellow Cab Stadtrundfahrten** (⊠ *Sendlinger-Tor-Pl. 2, Isarvorstadt* ☎ *089/303–631*).

WALKING   Downtown Munich is only a mile square and is easily explored on foot.
TOURS   Almost all the major attractions in the city center are on the interlink-
ing web of pedestrian streets that run from Karlsplatz, by the main
train station, to Marienplatz and the Viktualienmarkt and extend north
around the Frauenkirche and up to Odeonsplatz. The two tourist information offices issue a free map with suggested walking tours.

Two-hour tours of the Old City center are given daily in summer
(March–October) and on Friday and Saturday in winter (November–
February). Tours organized by the visitor center start at 10:30 and 1 in
the center of Marienplatz. The cost is €8. The theme walks of Radius
Tours & Bikes include Munich highlights, Third Reich Munich, Jewish
Munich, and the Dachau concentration camp. The cost is €10 (€19 for
the Dachau tour). Tours depart daily from the Hauptbahnhof, outside
the EurAide office by Track 11, and also meet 15 minutes later at the
New Town Hall's glockenspiel on Marienplatz.

Information Radius Tours & Bikes (☎ *089/5502–9374* ⊕ *www.radiusmunich.
com*).

VISITOR INFORMATION
The Hauptbahnhof tourist office is open Monday–Saturday 9–8 and
Sunday 10–6; the Info-Service in the Rathaus is open weekdays 10–8
and Saturday 10–4.

For information on the Bavarian mountain region south of Munich,
contact the Tourismusverband München-Oberbayern.

Information Hauptbahnhof (⊠ *Bahnhofpl. 2, next to DER travel agency, Leopoldvorstadt* ☎ *089/2333–0123* ⊕ *www.munich-tourist.de*). **Info-Service** (⊠ *Marienpl.,
City Center* ☎ *089/2332–8242*). **Tourismusverband München-Oberbayern**
(*Upper Bavarian Regional Tourist Office* ⊠ *Bodenseestr. 113, D–81243 Pasing*
☎ *089/829–2180*).

The Bavarian Alps

WORD OF MOUTH

"The best way to see this part of Germany is by car. Most of the truly quaint, charming, inexpensive, and authentic Bavarian lodgings will be found off the beaten path."

—Zeus

"Mittenwald is indeed a charming village. But don't discount Garmisch-Partenkirchen. There is an attractive pedestrian zone with shops and restaurants, all of which will be decorated for Christmas. And the setting of the town is stunning—surrounded by high peaks."

—enzian

Updated by
Marton Radkai

THE BAVARIAN ALPS, A REGION of fir-clad mountains, comes closest to what most of us envision as "Germany." Quaint towns full of half-timber houses—fronted by flowers in summer and snowdrifts in winter—pop up among the mountain peaks, as do the creations of "Mad" King Ludwig II. Shimmering Alpine lakes abound, and the whole area has sporting opportunities galore.

This part of Bavaria fans south from Munich to the Austrian border, and as you follow this direction, you'll soon find yourself on a gently rolling plain leading to lakes surrounded by ancient forests. In time the plain merges into foothills, which suddenly give way to jagged Alpine peaks. In places such as Königsee, near Berchtesgaden, snowcapped mountains rise straight up from the gemlike lakes.

Continuing south, you'll encounter cheerful villages with richly painted houses, churches and monasteries filled with the especially voluble and sensuous Bavarian baroque and rococo styles, and several spas where you can "take the waters" and tune up your system. Sports possibilities are legion: downhill and cross-country skiing, snowboarding, and ice-skating in winter; tennis, swimming, sailing, golf, and, above all (sometimes literally), hiking, paragliding, and ballooning in summer.

EXPLORING THE BAVARIAN ALPS

The Bavarian Alps compose a fairly small region. You can easily stay in one spot and make day trips to specific sights. The A–8 autobahn is the region's great traffic artery, though things can slow down there at the beginning and end of holidays.

ABOUT THE RESTAURANTS

You can still find many old *Gasthöfe* with geraniums gushing off balconies and a wood-panel dining area with simple tables and benches or beer gardens in the region. The mood at these spots is casual; you may even be asked to share a table with strangers. The more upscale places also try to maintain a feeling of familiarity, although you may feel more comfortable at the truly gourmet restaurants if you dress up a bit. Note that many restaurants take a break between 2:30 PM and 6 PM. If you want to eat during these hours, look for the magic words *Durchgehend warme Küche,* meaning warm food served throughout the day, possibly snacks during the off-hours.

ABOUT THE HOTELS

With few exceptions, a hotel or *Gasthof* in the Bavarian Alps and lower Alpine regions has high standards and is traditionally styled, with balconies, pine woodwork, and gently angled roofs upon which the snow sits and insulates. Many in the larger resort towns offer special packages online, so be sure to check them out. Private homes all through the region offer Germany's own version of bed-and-breakfasts, indicated by signs reading ZIMMER FREI (rooms available). Their rates may be less than €25 per person. As a general rule, the farther from the popular and sophisticated Alpine resorts you go, the lower the rates. Note, too, that many places offer a small discount if you stay more than one night.

TOP REASONS TO GO

Great nature: Whether it be the crystalline lakes, the grandiose mountains with endless views, the fresh air, the powdery snow, the deep caves, or the magical forests, the Bavarian Alps seem to have everything the nature lover needs.

Herrenchiemsee: Take the old steam-driven ferry to the island on Chiemsee to visit the last and most glorious castle of Mad King Ludwig. This imitation of Versailles broke the bank, but it has been attracting tourists for over a century.

Rejuvenation in Reichenhall: The new Rupertus spa in Bad Reichenhall has the applications you need to turn back your body's clock, from salt water baths to mysterious mudpacks.

Religious brewings: Enjoy the monkish life in Tegernsee, where the garden of the ancient monastery catches the first and last rays of the sun. In the hours between, the worthy institution serves its own full-bodied beer with an assortment of hearty dishes.

Meditating in Ettal Basilica: If it isn't the sheer complexity of the Baroque ornamentation and the riot of frescoes, then it might be the fluid sound of the ancient organ that puts you in a deep, relaxing trance.

By the same token, some places frown on staying only one night, especially during the high seasons, in summer, at Christmas, and on winter weekends. In spas and many mountain resorts a "spa tax" is added to the hotel bill. It amounts to no more than €3 per person per day and allows free use of spa facilities, entry to local attractions and concerts, and use of local transportation at times.

WHAT IT COSTS IN EUROS					
	¢	$	$$	$$$	$$$$
RESTAURANTS	under €9	€9–€15	€16–€20	€21–€25	over €25
HOTELS	under €50	€50–€100	€101–€175	€176–€225	Over €225

Restaurant prices are per person for a main course at dinner. Hotel prices are for two people in a standard double room, including tax and service.

TIMING

This mountainous region is a year-round holiday destination. Snow is promised by most resorts from December through March, although there's year-round skiing on the glacier slopes at the top of the Zugspitze. Spring and autumn are ideal times for leisurely hikes on the many mountain trails. November is a between-seasons time, when many hotels and restaurants close down or attend to renovations. Note, too, that many locals take a vacation after January 6, and businesses may be closed for anywhere up to a month.

GREAT ITINERARIES

Numbers in the text correspond to numbers in the margin and on the Bavarian Alps map.

IF YOU HAVE 3 DAYS

Consider basing yourself in one spot and exploring the immediate area—you'll still experience just about everything the Bavarian Alps have to offer. Choose between the western (Garmisch-Partenkirchen) area and the eastern (Berchtesgaden) corner. If busy little ⛄ **Garmisch-Parten-kirchen ❶** is your base, devote a couple of days to exploring the magnificent countryside. Wait for good weather to take the cable car or cog railway to the summit of Germany's highest mountain, the Zugspitze. A comfortable day trip takes in the monastery at ⛄ **Ettal ❷** and **Schloss Linderhof ❸**. Also worth a visit is **Oberammergau ❹**, where villagers stage the famous Passion Play every 10 years (the next performance is in 2010). Allow a third day to visit **Mittenwald ❺** and its violin museum, taking in the village of Klais (with Germany's highest-altitude railroad station) on the way. If you devote your three days to ⛄ **Berchtesgaden ❶**, allow one of them for **Obersalzberg ❶**, site of Hitler's retreat, called Eagle's Nest, and a second for a boat outing on Königsee, deep in the mountains' embrace. On the third day choose between a trip down into Berchtesgaden's salt mine, the Salzbergwerk, or a cross-border run into the Austrian city of Salzburg.

IF YOU HAVE 7 DAYS

Begin with a day or two based in ⛄ **Garmisch-Partenkirchen ❶** for excursions to **Schloss Linderhof ❸** and **Oberammergau ❹**. Next, strike out east along the

well-signposted Deutsche Alpenstrasse. Leave the route after 20 km (12 mi), at Wallgau, to relax for an hour or two on the southern shore of picturesque Walchensee. Then dodge in and out of Austria on a highland road that snakes through the tree-lined Aachen Pass to ⛄ **Tegernsee ❼**, where hills dip from all sides into the lake. Book two or three nights at one of the nearby, moderately priced Gasthöfe, or spoil yourself at one of the luxurious hotels in upscale Rottach-Egern. A day's walk (or a 20-minute drive) takes you to Tegernsee's neighboring lake, the shimmering **Schliersee ❽**. From there the road becomes a switchback (one stretch is a privately maintained toll road), climbing from narrow valleys to mountain ski resorts and finally plunging to the Inn River valley. Consider leaving the Alpine route here for a stay on the shores of the ⛄ **Chiemsee ❶**, where King Ludwig's Schloss Herrenchiemsee stands on one of the three islands. Back on the Alpine route, you'll inevitably head back into the mountains, dropping down again into elegant ⛄ **Bad Reichenhall ❶**, another overnight stop. From here it's only 20 km (13 mi) to ⛄ **Berchtesgaden ❶**, where you conclude your stay in the Alps viewing the town, its castle museum, Hitler's mountaintop retreat, and the beautiful Königsee in the **Berchtesgaden National Park ❶**.

THE BAVARIAN ALPS

GARMISCH-PARTENKIRCHEN

① *90 km (55 mi) southwest of Munich.*

Garmisch, as it's more commonly known, is a bustling, year-round resort and spa town and is the undisputed capital of Alpine Bavaria. Once two separate communities, Garmisch and Partenkirchen fused in 1936 to accommodate the Winter Olympics. Today, with a population of 28,000, the area is large enough to offer every facility expected from a major Alpine resort without being overwhelming. Garmisch is walkable but spread out, and the narrow streets and buildings of smaller Partenkirchen hold snugly together. In both parts of town pastel frescoes of biblical and bucolic scenes decorate facades.

Winter sports rank high on the agenda here. There are more than 99 km (62 mi) of downhill ski runs, 40 ski lifts and cable cars, and 180 km (112 mi) of *Loipen* (cross-country ski trails). One of the principal stops on the international winter-sports circuit, the area hosts a week of races every January. You can usually count on good skiing from December through April (and into May on the Zugspitze).

The number one attraction in Garmisch is the **Zugspitze,** the highest mountain (9,731 feet) in Germany. There are two ways up the mountain: a leisurely 75-minute ride on a cog railway from the train station in the town center, combined with a cable-car ride up the last stretch; or a 10-minute hoist by cable car, which begins its giddy ascent from the Eibsee, 10 km (6 mi) outside town on the road to Austria. There are two restaurants with sunny terraces at the summit and another at the top of the cog railway. ■ TIP→ A round-trip combination ticket allows you to mix your modes of travel up and down the mountain. Prices are lower in winter than in summer, even though winter rates include use of all the ski lifts on the mountain. You can rent skis at the top.

There are also a number of other peaks in the area with gondolas, but the views from the Zugspitze are the best. A four-seat cable car goes to the top of one of the lesser peaks: the **Wank** or the **Alpspitze,** some 2,000 feet lower than the Zugspitze. You can tackle both mountains on foot, provided you're properly shod and physically fit. ✉ *Zugspitze: Cog railway leaves from Olympiastr. 27* ☎ *08821/7970* ⊕ *www.zugspitze.de* ✆ *Funicular or cable car €45 in summer, €37 in winter, round-trip; parking €3.*

Garmisch-Partenkirchen isn't all sporty, however. In Garmisch, beautiful examples of Upper Bavarian houses line Frühlingstrasse, and a pedestrian zone begins at Richard-Strauss-Platz. Off Marienplatz, at one end of the car-free zone, is the 18th-century parish church of **St. Martin.** It contains some significant stuccowork by the Wessobrunn artists Schmutzer, Schmidt, and Bader. The chancel is by another fine 18th-century artist from Austria, Franz Hosp.

The Bavarian Alps

München

Ebersburg

Stegen
Inning
Pullach
Unterhaching
Ottobrunn
Kirchseeon
Grafing

Grünwald
Taufkirchen
Hohenbrunn

Starnberg
Oberhaching

Herrsching
Berg

Andechs
Feldkirchen

Diessen
Wolfratshausen
Westerham
Bruckmühl

Tutzing
Geretsried
Holzkirchen
Bad Aibling

Miesbach

Bad Tölz **6**
Gmund
Schliersee **8**

Blomberg
Tegernsee

Tegernsee **7**
Rottach-
Egern

Benediktbeuern
Bad Wiessee

Murnau
Wallberg
9

Staffelsee
Lenggries
Spitzingsee

Kochelsee
Kochel

4 **Oberammergau**
Walchensee
*Sylvenstein
Stausee*

**Schloss
Linderhof**
3 **2**

Ettal
Vorderiss

**Garmisch-
Partenkirchen**

Grainau
1

Zugspitze
Jenbach

Klais

Schwaz

5 **Mittenwald**

Ammersee

Starnberger See

Isar

KEY

— Deutsche
Alpenstrasse

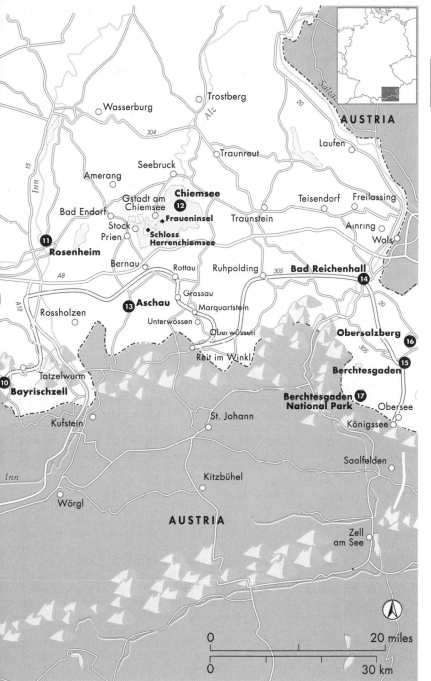

Across the Loisach River, on Pfarrerhausweg, stands another **St. Martin** church, dating from 1280, whose Gothic wall paintings include a larger-than-life-size figure of St. Christopher.

Objects and exhibitions on the region's history can be found in the excellent **Werdenfelser Museum,** which is itself housed in a building dating back to around 1200. The museum is spread over five floors and explores every aspect of life in the Werdenfels region, which was an independent county for more than 700 years (until 1802). ⊠*Ludwigstr. 47, Partenkirchen* ☎*08821/2134* 🖾*€2.50* ☾*Tues.–Sun. 10–5.*

On the eastern edge of Garmisch, at the end of Zöppritzstrasse, stands the **villa of composer Richard Strauss,** who lived here until his death in 1949. It's the center of activity during the *Richard-Strauss-Tage,* an annual music festival held in mid-June that features concerts and lectures on the town's most famous son. Displays are audiovisual, and each day at 10, 12, 2, and 4 samples of Strauss's works are played in the concert hall.

WHERE TO STAY & EAT
For information about accommodation packages with ski passes, call the **Zugspitze** (☎*08821/7970* 🖾*08821/797–901* ⊕*www.zugspitze.de*) or get in touch with the tourist office in Garmisch.

¢–$$$ ✕ **See-Hotel Riessersee.** On the shore of a small, green, tranquil lake—a 3-km (2-mi) walk from town—this café-restaurant is an ideal spot for lunch or afternoon tea (on summer weekends there's live zither music from 3 to 5). House specialties are fresh trout and local game (which fetches the higher prices on the menu). ⊠*Riess 6* ☎*08821/95440* 🖃*AE, MC, V* ☾*Closed Mon. and Dec. 1–15.*

$$–$$$ 🖾 **Hotel Waxenstein.** It's worth the 7 km (4½ mi) drive eastward from Garmisch-Partenkirchen to spend a night or a few at the delightful Waxenstein. The Toedts, who run the place, are obviously passionate about their work and their guests. The rooms are generous in size, with luxurious bathrooms. Furnishings combine Bavarian rustic with flights of fancy. The restaurant ($$–$$$) provides a breathtaking view of the Zugspitze, but the excellent food will keep you occupied, from the crispy bread and amuses bouches, to dishes such as gnocchi in ginger-pumpkin sauce, or veal fillet with foie gras. ⊠*Höhenrainweg 3, D-82491* ☎*08821/9840* 🖾*08821/8401* ⊕*www.waxenstein.de* ⇋*35 rooms, 6 suites* ♺*In-room: no a/c, dial-up. In-hotel: restaurant, bar, pool, sauna, beauty and wellness, some pets allowed* 🖃*V, MC, AE, DC* ⦿*BP.*

$$–$$$ ✕🖾 **Reindl's Partenkirchner Hof.** Owner Karl Reindl ranks among the
★ world's top hoteliers. His award-winning hotel is a real family concern, with daughter Marianne Holzinger in charge of the kitchen, which cooks up excellent Bavarian specialties and international gastronomical goodies, from roasted suckling pig to coq au vin. The light-filled bistro annex ($–$$) serves meals, coffee, and cake in an atmosphere that contrasts sharply with the heavier wood-and-velvet main building. Each guest room has pinewood furniture and a balcony or patio. Some of the double rooms are huge. An infra-red sauna and whirl-

2

EATING WELL IN THE BAVARIAN ALPS

Bavarian cooking originally fed a farming people, who spent their days out of doors doing heavy manual labor. *Knödel* (dumplings of old bread), pork dishes, sauerkraut, bread, and hearty soups were felt necessary to sustain a person facing the elements. The natural surroundings provided futher sustenance, in the form of fresh trout from brooks, *Renke* (pike-perch) from the lakes, venison, and mushrooms. This substantial fare was often washed down with beer, which was nourishment in itself, especially during the Lenten season, when the dark and powerful "Doppelbock" was on the market. Today this regimen will suit sporty types who have spent a day hiking in the mountains, skiing in the bracing air, or swimming or windsurfing in chilly lakes.

Bavaria is not immune to eclectic culinary trends, however: minimalist Asian daubs here, a touch of French sophistication and Italian elegance there, a little Tex-Mex to brighten a winter evening, even some sprinklings of curry. Menus often include large sections devoted to salads, and there are tasy vegetarian dishes even in the most conservative regions. Schnapps, which traditionally ended the meal, has gone from being a step above moonshine to a true delicacy extracted from local fruit by virtuoso distillers. Yes, Bavarian cooking—hearty, homey, and down-to-earth—is actually becoming lighter.

One area remains an exception: desserts. The selection of sinfully creamy cakes in the Konditorei, often enjoyed with whipped-cream-topped hot chocolate, continues to grow. These are irresistible, of course, especially when homemade. A heavenly experience might be a large portion of warm *Apfelstrudel* (apple- and nut-filled pastry) fresh from the oven in some remote mountain refuge.

---

pools soothe tired muscles. If you're planning to stay for several days, ask about specials. ⊠*Bahnhofstr. 15, D–82467* ☎*08821/943–870* 🖷*08821/9438–7250* ⊕*www.reindls.de* ⇆*35 rooms, 17 suites* ⌕*In-room: no a/c (some), in-room Wi-Fi (some). In-hotel: restaurant, bar, pool, gym, sauna, whirlpool, massages, bicycles, no-smoking rooms* ▭*AE, DC, MC, V* ❙⊙❙*BP.*

$ ✕▥**Gasthof Fraundorfer.** You can sled your way to dreamland in this beautiful old Bavarian Gasthof—some of the beds are carved like old-fashioned sleighs; others take the form of antique automobiles. The colorfully painted facade is covered with geraniums most of the year. The tavern-restaurant (¢–$), its walls covered with pictures and other ephemera, presents "Bavarian evenings" of folk entertainment every evening except Tuesdays. There's an Internet café across the street. ⊠*Ludwigstr. 24, D–82467* ☎*08821/9270* 🖷*08821/92799* ⊕*www. gasthof-fraundorfer.de* ⇆*20 rooms, 7 suites* ⌕*In-room: no a/c, dial-up. In-hotel: restaurant, some pets allowed (fee)* ▭*MC, V* ⊘*Closed late Nov.–early Dec.* ❙⊙❙*BP.*

$ ✕▥**Hotel-Gasthof Drei Mohren.** All the simple, homey comforts you'd expect can be found in this 150-year-old Bavarian inn tucked into the Partenkirchen village. All rooms have mountain views, and most are furnished with farmhouse-style painted beds and cupboards. A free bus to Garmisch and the cable-car stations will pick you up right outside the house. The restaurant ($–$$) serves solid fare, including a series of *Pfanderl,* large portions of meat and potatoes, or delicacies like venison in juniper sauce. ⊠*Ludwigstr. 65, D–82467* ☎*08821/9130* 🖷*08821/18974* ⊕*www.dreimohren.de* ➴*21 rooms, 2 apartments* 🖑*In-room: no a/c. In-hotel: restaurant, bar, public Internet, some pets allowed (fee)* ➯*AE, MC, V* ⦿|*BP.*

$–$$ 🏨**Edelweiss.** Like its namesake, the "nobly white" Alpine flower of *The Sound of Music* fame, this small downtown hotel has plenty of mountain charm. Inlaid with warm pinewood, it has Bavarian furnishings and individually decorated rooms. Breakfast buffet is included in the price. ⊠*Martinswinkelstr. 15–17, D–82467* ☎*08821/2454* 🖷*09621/4849* ⊕*www.hoteledelweiss.de* ➴*31 rooms* 🖑*In-room: no a/c. In-hotel: no-smoking rooms, some pets allowed (fee), no elevator* ➯*V* ⦿|*BP.*

SPORTS & THE OUTDOORS

HIKING &
WALKING
There are innumerable spectacular walks on 300 km (186 mi) of marked trails through the lower slopes' pinewoods and upland meadows. If you have the time and good walking shoes, try one of the two trails that lead to striking gorges. The **Höllentalklamm** route starts at the **Zugspitze Mountain railway terminal** (⊠*Olympiastr. 27*) in town and ends at the mountaintop (you'll want to turn back before reaching the summit unless you have mountaineering experience). The **Partnachklamm** route is quite challenging and takes you through a spectacular, tunneled water gorge (entrance fee), past a pretty little mountain lake, and far up the Zugspitze; to do all of it, you'll have to stay overnight in one of the huts along the way. Ride part of the way up in the **Eckbauer cable car** (€7.50 one way, €10 round-trip), which sets out from the Skistadion off Mittenwalderstrasse. The second cable car, the **Graseckbahn,** takes you right over the dramatic gorges (€3.50 one way, €5 round-trip). There's a handy inn at the top, where you can gather strength for the hour-long walk back down to the Graseckbahn station. Horse-drawn carriages also cover the first section of the route in summer; in winter you can skim along it in a sleigh. The carriages wait near the Skistadion. Or you can call the local coaching society, the **Lohnkutschevereinigung** (☎*08821/942–920*), for information.

Contact **Deutscher Alpenverein** (*German Alpine Association* ⊠*Von-Kahr-Str. 2–4, D–80997 Munich* ☎*089/140–030* ⊕*www.alpenverein. de*) for details on hiking and on staying in mountain huts.

SKIING &
SNOWBOARDING
Garmisch-Partenkirchen was the site of the 1936 Winter Olympics and remains Germany's premier winter-sports resort. The upper slopes of the Zugspitze and surrounding mountains challenge the best ski buffs and snowboarders, and there are also plenty of runs for intermediate skiers and families. The area is divided into two basic regions. The **Riffelriss** with the **Zugspitzplatt** is Germany's highest skiing area, with snow guaranteed from November to May. Access is via the **Zugspitzbahn** funicular. Cost for a day pass is €37, for a 2½-day pass €77 (valid from noon on the first day). The **CLASSIC-Gebiet,** or classical area, has 17 lifts in the

Alpspitz, Kreuzeck, and **Hausberg** region. Day passes cost €28, a two-day pass €48. The town has a number of ski schools and tour organizers. Skiers looking for instruction can try the **Skischule Alpin** (⊠ *Reintalstr. 8, Garmisch* ☏ *08821/945–676*). Cross-country skiers should check with the **Erste Skilanglaufschule Garmisch-Partenkirchen** (☏ *08821/1516*) at the eastern entrance of the Olympic stadium in Garmisch. For snowboarders, there's the **Snowboardschule Erwin Gruber** (⊠ *Mittenwalderstr. 47d, Garmisch* ☏ *08821/76490*). Telemark skiing is also popular in these rugged mountains. For information, contact the **Telemark Schule Leismüller** (⊠ *Waldeckstr. 7, Garmisch* ☏ *08821/752–696*).

The best place for information for all your snow-sports needs is the Alpine office at the tourist information office, **Alpine Auskunftstelle** (⊠ *Richard-Strauss-Pl. 2, Garmisch* ☏ *08821/180–744* ☉ *Mon.–Thurs. 4–6*).

NIGHTLIFE & THE ARTS

In season there's a busy **après-ski scene.** Many hotels have dance floors, and some have basement discos that pound away until the early hours. Bavarian folk dancing and zither music are regular features of nightlife. In summer there's entertainment every Saturday evening at the **Bayernhalle** (⊠ *Brauhausstr. 19*). Wednesday through Monday the cozy tavern-restaurant **Gasthof Fraundorfer** (⊠ *Ludwigstr. 24* ☏ *08821/9270*) hosts lots of yodeling and folk dancing. The younger, hipper crowd heads to the **Evergreen Lounge** to be heated up by DJs (⊠ *Klammstr. 47* ☏ *08821/72–626* ⊕ *www.disco-evergreen.de* ☉ *Wed.–Sat. 9–5*). Concerts are presented from Saturday to Thursday, mid-May through September, in the park bandstand in Garmisch, and on Friday in the Partenkirchen park. Tickets are available at **Garmisch-Partenkirchen-Ticket** (⊠ *Richard-Strauss-Pl. 2* ☏ *08821/752–545* ☏ *08821/752–547* ☉ *Weekdays 9–1 and 2–7, Sat. 9–1*).

The casino, **Spielbank Garmisch** (⊠ *Am Kurpark 10* ☏ *08821/95990*), is open daily 3 PM–2 AM and Saturday 3 PM–3 AM, with more than 100 slot machines and roulette, blackjack, and poker tables.

ETTAL

❷ *16 km (10 mi) north of Garmisch-Partenkirchen, 85 km (53 mi) south*
★ *of Munich.*

The village of Ettal is presided over by the massive bulk of **Kloster Ettal,** the great monastery founded in 1330 by Holy Roman Emperor Ludwig the Bavarian for a group of knights and a community of Benedictine monks. This is the largest Benedictine monastery in Germany; approximately 55 monks live here, including one from Compton, Los Angeles. The abbey was replaced with new buildings in the 18th century and now serves as a school. The original 10-sided church was brilliantly redecorated in 1744–53, becoming one of the foremost examples of Bavarian rococo. The church's chief treasure is its enormous dome fresco (83 feet wide), painted by Jacob Zeiller, circa 1751–52. The mass of swirling clouds and the pink-and-blue vision of heaven are typical of the rococo fondness for elaborate and glowing illusionistic ceiling painting.

Ettaler, a liqueur made from a centuries-old recipe, is still distilled at the monastery. It's made with more than 70 mountain herbs and has legendary health-giving properties. The ad tells it best: "Two monks know how it's made, 2 million Germans know how it tastes." You can visit the distillery right next to the church and buy bottles of the libation from the gift shop and bookstore. ☎08822/740 *for guided tour of church* 🎫*Free* ⊗*Daily 8–6.*

Besides its spirit and spirits, Ettal has made another local industry into an attraction: namely cheese, yogurt, and other milk derivatives. You can see cheese, butter, cream, and other dairy products in the making at the **Schaukäserei** or "public cheese manufacture." There is even a little buffet for a cheesy break. ⊠*Mandlweg 1* ☎08822/923–926 ⊕*www. milch-und-kas.de* 🎫*Free* ⊗*Tues.–Sat. 10–6, Sun. 12–5.*

WHERE TO STAY & EAT

¢–$ ✗**Edelweiss.** This friendly café and restaurant next to the monastery is an ideal spot for a light lunch or coffee and homemade cakes. ⊠*Kaiser-Ludwig-Pl. 3* ☎08822/92920 ⊟*No credit cards.*

$ ✗🔢 **Hotel Ludwig der Bayer.** Backed by mountains, this fine old hotel is run by the Benedictine order. There's nothing monastic about it, except for the exquisite religious carvings and motifs that adorn the walls. Most come from the monastery's carpentry shop, which also made much of the solid furniture in the comfortable bedrooms. The hotel has two excellent restaurants ($–$$) with rustic, Bavarian atmosphere and a vaulted tavern that serves sturdy fare and beer brewed at the monastery. The extensive wellness area includes a Finnish sauna, herbal steam bath, pool, solarium, a beauty section, and massage. ⊠*Kaiser-Ludwig-Pl. 10, D–82488* ☎08822/9150 🖶08822/9150 ⚓*70 rooms, 30 apartments* ⚭*In-room: no a/c. In-hotel: 2 restaurants, bars, tennis court, pool, gym, bicycles, some pets allowed (fee), no elevator* ⊟*MC, V* ⵏⵔ*BP.*

$ ✗🔢 **Posthotel.** Families are warmly welcomed at this traditional Gasthof in the center of town. There's a playground in the shady garden, and the Bavarian restaurant ($–$$), which is covered in warm wood paneling, has a children's menu. Breakfast buffet is included in the price. ⊠*Kaiser-Ludwig-Pl. 18, D–82488* ☎08822/3596 🖶08822/6971 ⊕*www.posthotel-ettal.de* ⚓*21 rooms, 4 apartments* ⚭*In-room: no a/c, no phone, in-hotel Wi-Fi. In-hotel: restaurant, gym, public Wi-Fi, no-smoking rooms, some pets allowed (fee)* ⊟*MC, V* ⊗*Closed Oct. 26–Dec. 18* ⵏⵔ*BP.*

SCHLOSS LINDERHOF

❸
★
10 km (6 mi) west of Ettal on B–23, 95 km (59 mi) south of Munich.

Built between 1870 and 1879 on the spectacular grounds of his father's hunting lodge, Schloss Linderhof was the only one of Ludwig II's royal residences to have been completed during the monarch's short life. It was the smallest of this ill-fated king's castles but his favorite country retreat among the various palaces at his disposal. Set in sylvan seclusion, between a reflecting pool and the green slopes of a gentle mountain, the charming, French-style, rococo confection is said to have been inspired by the Petit Trianon at Versailles. From an architectural standpoint it's a whimsical combination of conflicting styles, lavish on the outside, somewhat overly decorated on the inside. But the main inspiration came from the Sun King of France, Louis XIV, who is referred to in numerous bas reliefs, mosaics, paintings, and stucco pieces. Ludwig's bedroom is filled with brilliantly colored and gilded ornaments, the Hall of Mirrors is a shimmering dream world, and the dining room has a clever piece of 19th-century engineering—a table that rises from and descends to the kitchens below.

The formal gardens contain still more whimsical touches. There's a Moorish pavilion—bought wholesale from the 1867 Paris Universal Exposition—and a huge artificial grotto in which Ludwig had scenes from Wagner operas performed, with full lighting effects. It took the BASF chemical company much research to develop the proper glass for the blue lighting Ludwig desired. The gilded Neptune in front of the castle spouts a 100-foot water jet. According to hearsay, while staying at Linderhof the eccentric king would dress up as the legendary knight Lohengrin to be rowed in a swan boat on the grotto pond; in winter he took off on midnight sleigh rides behind six plumed horses and a platoon of outriders holding flaring torches. In winter be prepared for an approach road as snowbound as in Ludwig's day—careful driving is called for. ☎08822/92030 ⊕*www.schlosslinderhof.de* ✉*Summer €7, winter €6; palace grounds only in summer €3* ⊙*Apr.–Sept., daily 9–6; Oct.–Mar., daily 10–4; pavilion and grotto closed in winter.*

OBERAMMERGAU

❹ *20 km (12 mi) northwest of Garmisch-Partenkirchen, 4 km (2½ mi) northwest of Ettal, 90 km (56 mi) south of Munich.*

Its location alone, in an Alpine valley beneath a sentinel-like peak, makes this small town a major attraction (allow a half hour for the drive from Garmisch). Its main streets are lined with painted houses (such as the 1784 Pilatushaus on Ludwig-Thoma-Strasse), and in summer the village bursts with color as geraniums pour from every window box. Many of these lovely houses are occupied by families whose men are highly skilled in the art of wood carving, a craft that has flourished here since the early 12th century.

Oberammergau, however, is best known for its **Passion Play,** first presented in 1634 as an offering of thanks after the Black Death stopped just short of the village. In faithful accordance with a solemn vow, it will next be performed in the year 2010, as it has every 10 years since 1680. Its 16 acts, which take 5½ hours, depict the final days of Christ, from the Last Supper through the Crucifixion and Resurrection. It's presented daily on a partly open-air stage against a mountain backdrop from late May to late September. The entire village is swept up in the production, with some 1,500 residents directly involved in its preparation and presentation. Men grow beards in the hope of capturing a key role; young women have been known to put off their weddings—the role of Mary went only to unmarried girls until 1990, when, amid much local controversy, a 31-year-old mother of two was given the part.

The immense theater, the **Oberammergau Passionsspielhaus,** in which the Passion Play is performed every 10 years, can be toured. Visitors are given a glimpse of the costumes, the sceneries, the stage, and even the auditorium. ⊠*Passionstheater, Passionswiese* ☎*08822/945–8833* ☜*€4; combined ticket with museum €6.* ☉*Summer daily 10–5, winter irregular.*

You'll find many wood-carvers at work in town, and shop windows are crammed with their creations. From June through October a workshop is open free to the public at the **Pilatushaus** (⊠*Ludwig-Thoma-Str. 10* ☎*08822/92310 tourist office*); working potters and painters can also be seen. Pilatushaus was completed in 1775, and the frescoes—considered among the most beautiful in town—were done by Franz Seraph Zwinck, one of the greatest *Lüftlmalerei* painters. The house is named for the fresco over the front door depicting Christ before Pilate. A collection of reverse glass paintings depicting religious and secular scenes has been moved here from the Heimatmuseum. Contact the tourist office to sign up for a weeklong course in wood carving (classes are in German), which costs between €429 and €579, depending on whether you stay in a B&B or a hotel.

The **Oberammergau Museum** has historic examples of the wood craftsman's art and an outstanding collection of Christmas crèches, which date from the mid-18th century. Numerous exhibits also document the wax and wax-embossing art, which also flourishes in Oberammergau. ⊠*Dorfstr. 8* ☎*08822/94136* ☜*€4 (includes the Pilatushaus)* ☉*Apr.–Oct., Dec.–Feb., Tues.–Sun. 10–5.*

The 18th-century **St. Peter and St. Paul Church** is regarded as the finest work of rococo architect Josef Schmutzer, and has striking frescoes by Matthäus Günther and Franz Seraph Zwinck (in the organ loft). Schmutzer's son, Franz Xaver Schmutzer, did a lot of the stuccowork. ⊠*Pfarrpl. 1* ☎*No phone* ☉*Daily 9* AM*–dusk.*

WHERE TO STAY & EAT

$–$$$ ✕**Doppers.** It looks rustic and Bavarian from the outside, and the small barbecue terrace suggests weighty local foods. But, with the exception of various steaks, Doppers specializes in Thai dishes with red curry, for example, which will add to the warming effect of the old green Kachelofen in the ground-floor rooms. ⊠*Ludwig-Thoma-Str. 11* ☎*08822/935–615* ☉*No lunch.*

¢–$$ ✕**Ammergauer Stubn.** A homey restaurant with pink tablecloths and a lot of wood, the Stubn has a comprehensive menu that serves both Bavarian specialties and international dishes. You can expect nice roasts and some Swabian dishes, such as *Maultaschen,* a large, meat-filled ravioli. ⊠ *Wittelsbach Hotel, Dorfstr. 21* ☏*08822/92800* ⊟*AE, DC, MC* ⊙*Closed Tues. and Nov.–mid-Dec. No lunch.*

$-$$ ✕▦ **Hotel Landhaus Feldmeier.** This quiet family-run hotel, idyllically set just outside the village, has mostly spacious rooms with modern pinewood furniture. All have geranium-bedecked balconies, with views of the village and mountains. The rustic restaurant ($$-$$$) is one of the region's best. You can dine on the sunny, covered terrace in summer. Only hotel guests can use credit cards in the restaurant. ⊠*Ettalerstr. 29, D–82487* ☏*08822/3011* 🖷*08822/6631* ⊕*www.hotel-feldmeier. de* ⛶*22 rooms, 4 apartments* ⛐*In-room: no a/c. In-hotel: restaurant, gym, public Internet, no-smoking rooms, some pets allowed (fee), no elevator* ⊟*MC, V* ⊙*Closed mid-Nov.–mid-Dec.* ⵏⵔ*BP.*

$-$$ ✕▦ **Hotel Turmwirt.** Rich wood paneling reaches from floor to ceiling
★ in this transformed 18th-century inn, set in the shadow of Oberammergau's mountain, the Kofel. The hotel's own band presents regular folk evenings in the restaurant ($-$$). The *Ammergauer Pfanne*, a combination of meats and sauces, will take care of even industrial-size hunger. Rooms have corner lounge areas, and most come with balconies and sweeping mountain views. Prices are based on length of stay, so you'll pay less if you stay longer. ⊠*Ettalerstr. 2, D–82487* ☏*08822/92600* 🖷*08822/1437* ⊕*www.turmwirt.de* ⛶*44 rooms* ⛐*In-room: no a/c. In-hotel: restaurant, public Internet, no-smoking rooms, some pets allowed (fee), no elevator* ⊟*AE, DC, MC, V* ⊙*Closed Jan. 7–21* ⵏⵔ*BP.*

$ ✕▦ **Alte Post.** You can enjoy carefully prepared local cuisine (¢–$) on the original pine tables in this 350-year-old inn. There's a special children's menu, and in summer meals are also served in the beer garden. The front terrace of this delightful old building is a great place to watch traffic, both pedestrian and automotive. A part of the café has been reserved for Web surfing. The rooms are simply appointed, with tasteful rustic furniture. ⊠*Dorfstr. 19, D–82487* ☏*08822/9100* 🖷*08822/910–100* ⛶*37 rooms* ⛐*In-room: Wi-Fi, no a/c. In-hotel: restaurant, public Internet, no-smoking rooms, some pets allowed (fee), no elevator* ⊟*DC, V* ⊙*Closed Nov.–mid-Dec.* ⵏⵔ*BP.*

$ ✕▦ **Gasthaus zum Stern.** This is a traditional place (around 500 years old), with coffered ceilings, thick walls, an old Kachelofen that heats the dining room beyond endurance on cold winter days, and smiling waitresses in dirndls. The food ($-$$) is hearty, traditional Bavarian. For a quieter dinner or lunch, reserve a space in the Bäckerstube. ⊠*Dorfstr. 33, D–82487* ☏*08822/867* 🖷*08822/7027* ⛶*12 rooms* ⛐*In-room: no a/c, no phone. In-hotel: restaurant, some pets allowed, no elevator* ⊟*AE, DC, MC, V* ⊙*Restaurant closed Wed.* ⵏⵔ*BP.*

THE ARTS

Though the Passion Play theater was traditionally not used for anything other than the Passion Play (next performance, 2010), Oberammergauers decided that using it for opera or other theatrical events during the 10-year pause between the religious performances might be a good idea. The first stagings of Verdi's *Nabucco* and Mozart's *Magic Flute* in 2002 established a new tradition. Other passion plays are also performed here. Ticket prices are between €19 and €49. For reservations, call 08822/923–158.

MITTENWALD

⑤ *20 km (12 mi) southeast of Garmisch, 105 km (66 mi) south of Munich.*

Many regard Mittenwald as the most beautiful town in the Bavarian Alps. It has somehow avoided the architectural sins found in other Alpine villages by maintaining a balance between conservation and the needs of tourism. Its medieval prosperity is reflected on its main street, **Obermarkt,** which has splendid houses with ornately carved gables and brilliantly painted facades. Goethe called it "a picture book come alive," and it still is. The town has even re-created the stream that once flowed through the market square, and the main road was detoured around Mittenwald, markedly raising the quality of life in town.

In the Middle Ages Mittenwald was the staging point for goods shipped from the wealthy city-state of Venice by way of the Brenner Pass and Innsbruck. From Mittenwald, goods were transferred to rafts, which carried them down the Isar River to Munich. In the mid-17th century, however, the international trade route was moved to a different pass, and the fortunes of Mittenwald declined.

In 1684 Matthias Klotz, a farmer's son turned master violin maker, returned from a 20-year stay in Cremona, Italy. There, along with Antonio Stradivari, he had studied under Nicolo Amati, who gave the violin its present form. Klotz taught the art of violin making to his brothers and friends; before long, half the men in the village were crafting the instruments using woods from neighboring forests. Mittenwald became known as the Village of a Thousand Violins, and stringed instruments—violins, violas, and cellos—were shipped around the world. In the right weather—sunny, dry—you may even catch the odd sight of laundry lines hung with new violins out to receive their natural dark hue. The violin has made Mittenwald a small cultural oasis in the middle of the Alps. Not only is there an annual violin- (and viola-, cello-, and bow-) building contest each year in June, with concerts and lectures, but also an organ festival in the church of St. Peter and St. Paul held from the end of July to the end of September. The town also boasts a violin-making school.

The **Geigenbau und Heimatmuseum** *(Violin and Local Museum)* describes in fascinating detail the history of violin making in Mittenwald. Ask the museum curator to direct you to the nearest of several violin makers—they'll be happy to demonstrate the skills handed down to them. ✉*Ballenhausg. 3* ☎*08823/2511* 💶*€4* ⊙*Mid-May–Oct., Tues.–Sun. 10–5, Nov.—mid-May, 11–4.*

On the back of the altar in the 18th-century **St. Peter and St. Paul Church** (as in Oberammergau, built by Josef Schmutzer and decorated by Matthäus Günther), you'll find Matthias Klotz's name, carved there by the violin maker himself. ■**TIP→ Note that on some of the ceiling frescoes,** the angels are playing violins, violas da gamba, and lutes. In front of the church, Klotz is memorialized as an artist at work in a vivid bronze sculpted by Ferdinand von Miller (1813–79), creator of the mighty Bavaria monument in Munich. The church, with its elaborate and joyful stuccowork coiling and curling its way around the interior, is one of the most important rococo structures in Bavaria. Note its Gothic choir loft, added in the 18th century. The bold frescoes on its exterior are characteristic of *Lüftlmalerei*, a style that reached its height in Mittenwald. Images, usually religious motifs, were painted on the wet stucco exteriors of houses and churches. On nearby streets you can see other fine examples on the facades of three famous houses: the Goethehaus, the Pilgerhaus, and the Pichlerhaus. Among the artists working here was the great Franz Seraph Zwinck. ⊠*Ballenhausg., next to Geigenbau und Heimatmuseum.*

WHERE TO STAY & EAT

$–$$$
★
✕**Arnspitze.** Get a table at the large picture window and soak in the towering Karwendel mountain range as you ponder a menu that combines the best traditional ingredients with international touches. Chef and owner Herbert Wipfelder looks beyond the edge of his plate all the way to Asia, if need be, to find inspiration. The fish pot-au-feu has a Mediterranean flair; the jugged hare in red wine is truly Bavarian. The restaurant also offers accommodations in a separate house. ⊠*Innsbrucker Str. 68* ☎*08823/2425* ⊟*AE* ⊙*Closed Nov.–mid-Dec. and Tues. and Wed.*

$
✕**Osteria Viola.** Eggplant medallions, creative risottos, and a complete truffle menu (€38) provide a refreshing change from the local Bavarian fare. The setting is also a departure from the expected beams and wooden ceilings; the no-smoking room in the back has faux-leather upholstery and the pictures of great composers on the blue walls. ⊠*Obermarkt 31* ☎*08823/3849* ⊟*V, MC, AE, DC.*

$–$$
✕▥**Post.** Stagecoaches carrying travelers and mail across the Alps stopped here as far back as the 17th century. The hotel retains much of its historic charm. The elegant rooms come in various styles, from modern to art nouveau to Bavarian rustic. The indoor swimming pool has views of the Karwendel peaks, and a small rose garden is an inviting spot for coffee and cake. The lounge-bar, with its dark woods and green-velvet upholstered armchairs, lightens up when the open fire is crackling and live music gets you on the dance floor. You can have dinner here in the wine tavern or at the low-beam Postklause ($–$$). The food in each is excellent, with an emphasis on Bavarian fare such as roasts and great *Semmelknödel* (bread dumplings). ⊠*Obermarkt 9, D–82481* ☎*08823/938–2333* 🖶*08823/938–2999* ⊕*www.posthotel-mittenwald.de* ⇔*74 rooms, 7 suites* ⌂*In-room: no a/c, dial-up. In-hotel: 2 restaurants, bar, pool, no-smoking rooms, some pets allowed (fee)* ⊟*MC, V* ⊺◉*BP.*

$
✕▥**Alpenrose.** Once part of a monastery and later given one of the town's most beautiful painted baroque facades, the Alpenrose is one of the area's handsomest hotels. The typical Bavarian bedrooms and public rooms have lots of wood paneling, farmhouse cupboards, and finely woven fabrics. The restaurant ($–$$) devotes the entire month

of October to venison dishes, for which it has become renowned. A zither player strums away most evenings in the Josefi wine cellar. ⊠*Obermarkt 1, D–82481* ☎*08823/92700* 🖷*08823/3720* ⊕*www. hotel-alpenrose-mittenwald.de* ⮩*16 rooms, 2 apartments* ♿*In-room: no a/c. In-hotel: restaurant, bar, public Internet, some pets allowed (fee), no elevator* ⊟*AE, DC, MC, V* ⧖|*BP.*

$ ✕🖾**Gasthof Stern.** This white house with brilliant blue shutters is right in the middle of Mittenwald. The painted furniture is not antique but reminiscent of old peasant Bavaria, and the featherbeds are incredibly soft. Locals meet in the dining room (¢–$) for loud conversation, and the beer garden is a pleasant, familial place to while away the hours with a *Bauernschmaus,* a plate of sausage with sauerkraut and home-made liver dumplings. The restaurant is closed on Thursday. More than one night at the inn makes the price cheaper. ⊠*Fritz-Plössl-Pl. 2, D–82481* ☎*08823/8358* 🖷*08823/94322* ⊕*www.stern-mittenwald. de* ⮩*5 rooms* ♿*In-room: no a/c, no phone. In-hotel: restaurant, bar, some pets allowed, no elevator* ⊟*No credit cards* ⧖|*BP.*

$ 🖾**Bichlerhof.** Carved oak furniture gives the rooms of this Alpine-style hotel a solid German feel. A breakfast buffet is served until 11 AM and will keep the hardiest hiker going all day. Although the restaurant serves only breakfast, there's no shortage of taverns in the area. Most guest rooms have mountain views. ⊠*Adolf-Baader-Str. 5, D–82481* ☎*08823/9190* 🖷*08823/4584* ⊕*www.bichlerhof-mittenwald. de* ⮩*30 rooms* ♿*In-room: no a/c, dial-up. In-hotel: pool, gym, no-smoking rooms, some pets allowed (fee)* ⊟*AE, DC, MC, V* ⧖|*BP.*

SPORTS & THE OUTDOORS

Mittenwald lies literally in the shadow of the mighty **Karwendel** Alpine range, which rises to a height of nearly 8,000 feet. ■**TIP**➔ **There are a number of small lakes in the hills surrounding Mittenwald. You can either walk to the closer ones or rent bikes and adventure farther afield. The information center across the street from the train station has maps, and they can help you select a route.**

The **Dammkar** run is nearly 8 km (5 mi) long and offers some of the best free-riding skiing, telemarking, and snowboarding in the German Alps. A **cable car** (☎*08823/8480* 🖾*€12.50 one way, €20 round-trip, day pass €25* ⊙*Dec.–Oct., daily 8:30–5*) carries hikers and skiers to a height of 7,180 feet, the beginning of numerous trails down, or farther up into the Karwendel range. You can book a guide with **Bergerlebnis und Wanderschule Oberes Isartal** (☎*08651/5835*). Skiers, cross-country and downhill, and snowboarders can find all they need, including equipment and instruction, at the **Erste Schischule Mittenwald** (⊠*Bahnhofsparkpl., parking next to train station* ☎*08823/3582 or 08823/8548*).

SHOPPING

It's not the kind of gift every visitor wants to take home, but if you'd like a violin, a cello, or even a double bass, the Alpine resort of Mittenwald can oblige. There are more than 30 craftsmen whose work is coveted by musicians throughout the world. If you're buying or even just feeling curious, call on **Anton Maller** (⊠*Obermarkt 2* ☎*08823/5865*).

2

He's been making violins and other stringed instruments for more than 25 years. The **Geigenbau Leonhardt** (✉ *Mühlenweg 53a* ☎ *08823/8010*) is another good place to purchase one of the town's famous stringed instruments. For traditional Bavarian costumes—dirndls, embroidered shirts and blouses, and lederhosen—try **Trachten Werner** (✉ *Hochstr. 1* ☎ *08823/3785*). Find out where all the milk from the local cows goes with a visit to **Gabriele Schneider's SchokoLaden** (✉ *Dekan-Karl-Pl. 15* ☎ *08823/938–939* ⊕ *www.schokoladen-mittenwald.de*), a homemade chocolate shop.

EN ROUTE

One of the most beautiful stretches of the Deutsche Alpenstrasse follows the course of the fast-flowing Isar River and is lined with fir forests and rocky peaks. A toll road (€2) runs from Wallgau (7 km [4½ mi] north of Mittenwald at the junction of the road north to Benediktbeuren) 15 km (9 mi) to Vorderiss, but the booths are not always manned. Vorderiss is at the western end of the Sylvenstein dam-lake, whose mysterious waters cover a submerged village. Halfway along the lake the road divides, and you can drive either east to the Achen Pass, which cuts through Austria (there is no official border, but make sure you have your passport just in case) and on to Tegernsee, or north to the Alpine resort of Lenggries and to the beautiful spa town of Bad Tölz.

BAD TÖLZ

❻ *14 km (8 mi) north of Sylvenstein Lake, 48 km (30 mi) south of Munich.*

Bad Tölz's new town, dating from the mid-19th century, sprang up with the discovery of iodine-laden springs, which allowed the locals to call their town *Bad* (bath or spa) Tölz. You can take the waters, either by drinking a cupful from the local springs or going all the way with a full course of health treatments at a specially equipped hotel. ■**TIP→**If you can, visit on a Wednesday or a Friday morning—market days—when stalls stretch along the main street to the Isar River and on the Jungmayr-Fritzplatz.

This town clings to its ancient customs more tightly than any other Bavarian community. It is not uncommon to see people wearing traditional clothing as their daily dress. If you're in Bad Tölz on November 6, you'll witness one of the most colorful traditions of the Bavarian Alpine area: the Leonhardiritt equestrian procession, which marks the anniversary of the death in 559 of St. Leonhard, the patron saint of animals, specifically horses. The procession ends north of town at an 18th-century chapel on the Kalvarienberg, above the Isar River.

★ The **Alpamare,** Bad Tölz's very attractive spa complex, pumps spa water into its pools, one of which is disguised as a South Sea beach complete with surf. Its five waterslides include a 1,082-foot-long adventure run. Another—the Alpa-Canyon—has 90-degree drops, and only the hardiest swimmers are advised to try it. A nightmarish dark tunnel is aptly named the Thriller. They have a variety of prices for the various individual attractions, or combo tickets for more than one. ⊠*Ludwigstr. 13* ☎*08041/509–999* ⊕*www.alpamare.de* 🎫*4-hr ticket €25; €19 after 5* PM ⊙*Daily 9* AM*–10* PM.

The **Heimatmuseum,** in the Altes Rathaus (Old Town Hall), has many fine examples of Bauernmöbel (farmhouse furniture), as well as a fascinating exhibit on the history of the town and its environs. ⊠*Marktstr. 48* ☎*08041/504–688* 🎫*€2.50* ⊙*Mar.–Jan., Tues.–Sun. 10–4.*

WHERE TO STAY & EAT

$$–$$$$
★
✕🏨**Hotel Jodquellenhof-Alpamare.** The *Jodquellen* are the iodine springs that have made Bad Tölz wealthy. You can take advantage of these revitalizing waters at this luxurious spa, where the emphasis is on fitness. Vegetarian and low-calorie entrées are served in the restaurant ($$–$$$$). The imposing 19th-century building, with private access to the Alpamare Lido, contains stylish rooms, with granite and marble bathrooms. The room price includes full use of the spa facilities. There are discounts for children. ⊠*Ludwigstr. 13–15, D–83646* ☎*08041/5090* 🖨*08041/509–555* ⊕*www.jodquellenhof.com* ➷*71 rooms* ♿*In-room: no a/c, dial-up, in-hotel Wi-Fi. In-hotel: restaurant, pool, spa, public Wi-Fi, no elevator* ⊟*AE, DC, MC, V* ⦿*BP.*

$–$$
🏨**Hotel Kolbergarten.** Located right near the old town and surrounded by a quiet garden with old trees, this hotel offers comfortable rooms, each carefully done in a particular style such as baroque or Biedermeier. The grand restaurant ($$) in fin de siècle style offers a wide range of gourmet dishes created by the Viennese chef Johann Mikschy, from sashimi of yellow-fin tuna, to veal boiled with grape leaves. The wine list will take you around the world. ⊠*Fröhlichg. 5, D–83646* ☎*08041/78920* 🖨*08041/9069* ⊕*www.hotel-kolbergarten.de* ➷*12 rooms, 2 suites* ♿*In-room: no a/c, dial-up. In-hotel: public Internet, no-smoking rooms, some pets allowed* ⊟*AE, DC, MC, V* ⦿*BP.*

NIGHTLIFE & THE ARTS

Bad Tölz is world renowned for its outstanding **boys' choir** (☎*08041/78670 for program details from Städtische Kurverwaltung*). When it's not on tour, the choir gives regular concerts in the Kurhaus.

Tom's Bar (⊠*Demmeljochstr. 42*) has '60s furnishings with modern music (DJs, theme nights), reasonable prices, and plenty of space.

The **Kult/Advokatenhaus** (⊠*Wachterstr. 16. 42*) has a rather wide range of themes, and it features live music in the terrific setting of an old brewery, with barrel vaults and painted brick walls.

SPORTS & THE OUTDOORS

Bad Tölz's local mountain, the **Blomberg,** 3 km (2 mi) west of town, has moderately difficult ski runs and can also be tackled on a toboggan in winter and in summer. The winter run of 5 km (3 mi) is the longest in Bavaria, although the artificial concrete channel used in summer snakes only 3,938 feet down the mountain. A ski-lift ride to the start of the run and toboggan rental are included in the price. ☎*08041/3726* ⊕*www. blombergbahn.de* 🎫*€4 per toboggan ride* ⊙*Jan.–Oct., daily 9–4; Nov.–Dec., summer toboggan run hrs depend on weather conditions.*

SHOPPING

■ TIP→ Bad Tölz is famous for its painted furniture, particularly farmhouse cupboards and chests. Several local shops specialize in this type of *Bauernmöbel* (farmhouse furniture, usually hand carved from pine) and will usually handle export formalities. Ask at your hotel or tourist information for a recommendation on where to shop. One to try: **Antiquitäten Schwarzwälder** (⌧*Badstr. 2* ☎*08041/41222*).

TEGERNSEE

❼ *16 km (10 mi) east of Bad Tölz, 50 km (31 mi) south of Munich.*
★

The beautiful shores of the Tegernsee are among the most expensive property in all of Germany. The interest in the region shown by King Maximilian I of Bavaria at the beginning of the 19th century attracted VIPs and artists, which led to a boom that has never really faded. Most accommodations and restaurants, however, still have reasonable prices, and there are plenty of activities for everyone. Tegernsee's wooded shores, rising gently to scalable mountain peaks of no more than 6,300 feet, invite hikers, walkers, and picnicking families. The lake itself draws swimmers and yachters. In fall the russet-clad trees provide a colorful contrast to the snowcapped mountains. There are three main towns on the lake: Tegernsee, Rottach-Egern, and Bad Wiessee.

★ On the eastern shore of the lake, the laid-back town of Tegernsee is home to a large **Benedictine monastery** (⌧*Schlosspl., Tegernsee*). Founded in the 8th century, this was one of the most productive cultural centers in southern Germany; the Minnesänger (musician and poet) Walther von der Vogelweide (1170–1230) was a welcome guest. Not so welcome were Magyar invaders who laid waste to the monastery in the 10th century. During the Middle Ages the monastery made a lively business producing stained-glass windows thanks to a nearby quartz quarry, and in the 16th century it became a major center of printing. The late-Gothic **church** was refurbished in Italian baroque style in the 18th century. The frescoes are by Hans Georg Asam, whose work also graces the Benediktbeuren monastery. Secularization sealed the monastery's fate at the beginning of the 19th century: almost half the buildings were torn down. Maximilian I bought the surviving ones and had Leo von Klenze redo them for use as a summer retreat.

Today there is a high school on the property, and students write their exams beneath inspiring baroque frescoes in what was the monastery. The **Herzogliches Bräustüberl,** a brewery and beer hall, is also on-site. ■ TIP→ Try a stein of their legendary Tergernseer Helles beer.

The **Olaf Gulbransson Museum** is devoted to the Norwegian painter Olaf Gulbrannson, who went to Munich in 1902 and worked as a caricaturist for the satirical magazine *Simplicissimus*. His poignant caricatures and numerous works of satire depict noisy politicians and snooty social upper-crusters as well as other subjects. The museum is housed in a discreet modern building set back from the main lakeside road of

Tegernsee. ⊠ *Im Kurgarten, Tegernsee* ☎ *08022/3338* ⊕ *www.olaf-gulbransson-museum.de* ☜ *€4* ⊙ *Tues.–Sun. 10–5.*

Maximilian showed off this corner of his kingdom to Czar Alexander I of Russia and Emperor Franz I of Austria during their journey to the Congress of Verona in October 1821. You can follow their steps through the woods to one of the loveliest lookout points in Bavaria, the **Grosses Paraplui.** A plaque marks the spot where they admired the open expanse of the Tegernsee and the mountains beyond. The path starts opposite Schlossplatz in Tegernsee town and is well marked.

Rottach-Egern, the fashionable and upscale resort at the southern end of the lake, has classy shops, chic restaurants, and expensive boutiques. Rottach-Egern's church, **St. Laurentius,** is worth seeing for its baroque influences.

While at the Rottach-Egern tourist office (*Kuramt*), have a look at the collection of horse-drawn vehicles at the adjoining **Kutschen-, Wagen- und Schlittenmuseum.** It contains beautifully restored coaches, sleds, oxcarts, and all the implements of the wagon driver's trade. ⊠ *Nördliche Hauptstr. 9, Rottach-Egern* ☎ *08022/671–341* ☜ *€2* ⊙ *May–Oct., Tues.–Sun. 2–5.*

WHERE TO STAY & EAT

$–$$$$ ✕ **Freihaus Brenner.** Proprietor Josef Brenner has brought a taste of nouvelle cuisine to the Tegernsee. His attractive restaurant commands fine views from high above Bad Wiessee. Try any of his suggested dishes, ranging from roast pheasant in wine sauce to fresh lake fish. ⊠ *Freihaushöhe 4, Bad Wiessee* ☎ *08022/82004* ⊕ *www.freihaus-brenner.de* ▭ *MC, V* ⊙ *Closed Tues.*

$–$$ ✕ **Weinhaus Moschner.** You're pretty much expected to drink wine in this dark, old tavern on the edge of ritzy Rottach-Egern, though beer from the monastery brewery is also served. The menu has a wide range of options, from sturdy smoked pork to homemade ravioli filled with grilled salmon. But nobody comes here just to eat. You are welcome to join the locals at a rough wooden table in the log-wall tavern taproom, order a glass of ale or Franconian wine, and leave the fine dining until tomorrow. ⊠ *Kisslingerstr. 2, Rottach-Egern* ☎ *08022/5522* ▭ *AE, DC, MC, V* ⊙ *Closed Mon. and Tues.*

¢–$ ✕ **Herzogliches Bräustüberl.** Once part of Tegernsee's Benedictine monastery, then a royal retreat, the Bräustüberl is now an immensely popular beer hall and brewery. Only basic Bavarian snacks (sausages, pretzels, all the way up to steak tartare) are served in this crowded place, but hearty meals can be had in the adjoining **Schlossgaststätte** ($–$$). In summer, quaff your beer beneath the huge chestnuts and admire the delightful view of the lake and mountains. ⊠ *Schlosspl. 1, Tegernsee* ☎ *08022/4141* ⊸ *Reservations not accepted* ▭ *No credit cards* ⊙ *Closed Nov.*

$$$–$$$$
Fodor'sChoice
★ ✕▣ **Bischoff am See.** Owners Petra and Markus Bischoff have their heart in their hotel, and it shows in every detail. Each room is individually designed, understated, and luxurious, with either a private sauna or a whirlpool. The bar, breakfast room, restaurant, and terrace have a

splendid view of the lake. The restaurant ($$$–$$$$; closed Monday and Tuesday) serves unique specialties, often created in-house, and has 1,250 wines on its wine list. Every fourth Thursday in the month is sushi night. ⊠*Schwaighofstr. 53, Tegernsee, D–83684* ☎*08022/3966* 🖶*08022/1720* ⊕*www.bischoff-am-see.de* ↩*7 rooms, 5 suites* ♿*In-room: no a/c (some). In-hotel: restaurant, bar, no-smoking rooms, some pets allowed (fee)* ⊟*MC, V* ⌶⃝*BP.*

$$–$$$$ ✕⌂ **Hotel Bayern.** The elegant, turreted Bayern and its two spacious annexes sit high above the Tegernsee, backed by the wooded slopes of Neureuth Mountain. Rooms overlooking the lake are in demand despite their relatively high cost, so book early. All guests can enjoy panoramic views of the lake and mountains from the extensive terrace fronting the main building. You can dine in the hotel's stylish little restaurant ($$$–$$$$) or the cozy tavern. The extensive Bayern spa includes a heavenly musical tub and a colored light and aroma solarium. ⊠*Neureuthstr. 23, Tegernsee, D–83684* ☎*08022/1820* 🖶*08022/3775* ⊕*www.hotel-bayern.de* ↩*63 rooms, 10 suites* ♿*In-room: no a/c, dial-up. In-hotel: 2 restaurants, bar, pool, spa, no-smoking rooms, some pets allowed (fee)* ⊟*AE, MC, V* ⌶⃝*BP.*

$$–$$$ ✕⌂ **Landhaus Wilhelmy.** Inspiration is the word that comes to mind while enjoying tea and cake in the little garden of this old inn in Bad Wiessee. Although everything is modern, including the compact wellness center in the basement, the Wilhelmy takes its guests back to a less-frantic era. The Ziegelbauers, who have restored the buildings, know how to make you feel at home. Classical music accompanies unpretentious yet tasty meals in the restaurant ($$–$$$$); try the fish specialties or the light guinea fowl with herb rice. ⊠*Freihausstr. 15, Bad Wiessee, D–83707* ☎*08022/98680* 🖶*08022/9868–233* ⊕*www.romantik-hotel.de* ↩*20 rooms, 4 suites* ♿*In-room: no a/c. In-hotel: restaurant, public Wi-Fi, no-smoking rooms, sauna, steam room, beauty, massage, some pets allowed, no elevator* ⊟*AE, MC, V, DC* ⌶⃝*BP.*

$–$$ ✕⌂ **Seehotel Zur Post.** The lake views from most rooms are somewhat compromised by the main road outside, but a central location, a winter garden, a terrace, and a little beer garden are pluses. The restaurant (¢–$), with a panoramic view of the mountains and the lake, serves fresh fish and seasonal dishes; the "venison weeks" draw diners from far and wide. ⊠*Seestr. 3, Tegernsee, D–83684* ☎*08022/66550* 🖶*08022/1699* ⊕*www.seehotel-zur-post.de* ↩*43 rooms* ♿*In-room: no a/c. In-hotel: restaurant, no-smoking rooms, public Internet, some pets allowed (fee), no elevator* ⊟*DC, MC, V* ⌶⃝*BP.*

NIGHTLIFE & THE ARTS

Every resort has its **spa orchestra**—in the summer they play daily in the music-box-style bandstands that dot the lakeside promenades. A strong Tegernsee tradition is the summerlong program of **festivals,** some set deep in the forest. Tegernsee's lake festival in August, when sailing clubs deck their boats with garlands and lanterns, is an unforgettable experience.

Bad Wiessee has a brand-new **casino** near the entrance of town coming from Gmund (☎*08022/98350*) that's open Sunday–Thursday 3 PM–3 AM and Friday and Saturday 3 PM–4 AM. It is the biggest and liveliest venue in town for the after-dark scene.

The **Bischoff am See** (⊠*Schweighoferstr. 53* ☎08022/3966), on the lake shore in Tegernsee, has a sensational terrace bar with prices to match one of Bavaria's finest views.

SPORTS & THE OUTDOORS

For the best vista in the area, climb **Wallberg**, the 5,700-foot mountain at the south end of the Tegernsee. It's a hard four-hour hike or a short 15-minute cable car ride up (€8 one way, €13 round-trip). At the summit are a restaurant and sun terrace and several trailheads; in winter the skiing is excellent.

Contact the **tourist office** (☎08022/180–140 ⊕*www.tegernsee.de*) in the town of Tegernsee for hiking maps.

GOLF　Besides swimming, hiking, and skiing, the Tegernsee area has become a fine place for golfing. The **Tegernseer GOLFCLUB e. V** (⊠*Bad Wiessee D-83707* ☎08022/8769) has an 18-hole course overlooking the lake with a clubhouse and excellent restaurant. It also has fine apartments for rent.

SHOPPING

In Bad Tölz, **Schöttl** (⊠*61a Marktstr., Bad Tölz*) offers a wide assortment of traditional regional items, from trinkets to clothing. To get there, follow the lovely Marktstrasse up from the river and watch for the oversize top hat at the corner of Hindenburgstrasse. **Greif** (⊠*Nördliche Hauptstr. 24, Rottach-Egern* ☎08022/5540) has a fine selection of tastefully modern Bavarian fashions and a large stock of handwoven fabrics that you can either buy or have a costume fitted from. At her workshop just outside Gmund, **Marianne Winter-Andres** (⊠*Miesbacherstr. 88, Gmund* ☎08022/74643) creates a wide and attractive range of high-quality pottery at sensible prices.

SCHLIERSEE

❽ *20 km (12 mi) east of Tegernsee, 55 km (34 mi) southeast of Munich.*

Schliersee is smaller, quieter, and less fashionable than Tegernsee but hardly less beautiful. The different histories of the Tegernsee and the Schliersee are made clear in the names local people have long given them: the Tegernsee is *Herrensee* (Masters' Lake), while the Schliersee is *Bauernsee* (Peasants' Lake), although today Schliersee has come up in the world somewhat. There are walking and ski trails on the mountain slopes that ring its placid waters. The lake is shallow and often freezes over in winter, when the tiny island in its center is a favorite hiking destination. The one drawback in town is the heavy and fast traffic; Schliersee is on the road to the skiing areas of Sudelfeld and Spitzingsee.

Schliersee was the site of a monastery, built in the 8th century by a group of noblemen. It subsequently became a choral academy, which eventually moved to Munich. Today only the restored 17th-century **Schliersee church,** in the middle of town, recalls this piece of local history. The church has some frescoes and stuccowork by Johann Baptist Zimmermann.

WHERE TO STAY & EAT

¢–$ ✕**Zum Hofhaus am See.** What better place to enjoy a meal than in a small beer garden on the shore? The Hofhaus radiates friendly intimacy. Down-to-earth food, such as hocks or fresh forest mushrooms in cream with an herbed dumpling, is the order of the day. If the fishburger is on the menu, try it. In winter the Hofhaus offers fondue as a specialty. ⊠*Mesnerg. 2* ☎*08026/94499* ⊟*No credit cards.*

$ ▦**Gästehaus Franke am See.** Light, clean rooms with simple no-nonsense furniture can be very pleasant as a change from all the heavy dark beams and wood paneling you may have seen on your journey. The house's garden is a few steps from the lake. The Franke is small, giving it a nice family feel. ⊠*Seestr. 8, D–83727* ☎*08026/4097* 🖷*08026/4098* ⊕*www.gaestehaus-franke-schliersee.de* 🛏*7 rooms, 2 suites* 🔧*In-room: no a/c. In-hotel: some pets allowed, no elevator* ⊟*No credit cards* ℝℂℙ.

SPITZINGSEE

⊙ *10 km (6 mi) south of Schliersee, 65 km (40 mi) southeast of Munich.*

Arguably the most beautiful of this group of Bavarian lakes, the Spitzingsee is cradled 3,500 feet up between the Taubenstein, Rosskopf, and Stumpfling peaks, and the drive here is spectacular. The lake is usually frozen over in winter and almost buried in snow. In summer it's warm enough for a swim. Walking in this area is breathtaking in every season and in every sense. The skiing is very good, too. The only downside is the overrun town of Spitzingsee, whose modern architecture violates almost every rule of aesthetics.

WHERE TO STAY & EAT

¢–$ ✕**Alte Wurzhütte.** If you can't sit outside on the terrace and enjoy a dreamy view of the lake, then you'll have to make do with the cozy, Bavarian log-cabin atmosphere inside. Dishes here, such as Bavarian duck with red cabbage and a monster potato dumpling, are nice and heavy and come at excellent prices. Simple and functional rooms are available in the property's two adjacent buildings. ⊠*Rosskopfweg 1* ☎*08026/60680* ⊟*V, MC (for the lodgings only).*

$$–$$$$ ✕▦**Arabella Sheraton Alpenhotel.** For an out-of-the-way break in the mountains, head for this luxurious hotel on the shore of the Spitzingsee—even though its architecture is an eyesore. Rooms meet the high standards of comfort expected from the hotel chain that runs the establishment. If you can't stay overnight, come for a leisurely lunch ($$–$$$) at the **König Ludwig Stuben** or for a fondue night or theme buffet. Try the lake fish or the venison with elderberry sauce and cabbage. For lighter Italian fare, you can enjoy **Osteria L'Oliva**, with a menu of pasta, salads, and dishes from the grill. ⊠*Seeweg 7, D–83727* ☎*08026/7980* 🖷*08026/798–879* ⊕*www.arabellasheraton.de* 🛏*120 rooms, 13 suites* 🔧*In-room: no a/c, dial-up (some). In-hotel: 2 restau-*

rants, bar, tennis courts, pool, gym, public Wi-Fi, no-smoking rooms, some pets allowed (fee) ☐AE, DC, MC, V ❙❍❙BP.

BAYRISCHZELL

❿ *10 km (6 mi) east of Schliersee, 65 km (40 mi) southeast of Munich.*

Bayrischzell is in an attractive family-resort area and is much quieter than Spitzingsee. The wide-open slopes of the Sudelfeld Mountain are ideal for carefree skiing; in summer and fall you can explore countless upland walking trails. Access to the Sudelfeld area costs €2 per car.

The town sits at the end of a wide valley overlooked by the 6,000-foot **Wendelstein** mountain, which draws expert skiers. At its summit is a tiny stone-and-slate-roof chapel that's much in demand for wedding ceremonies. The cross above the entrance was carried up the mountain by Max Kleiber, who designed the 19th-century church. An instructive **geopark**, laid out beneath the summit, explains the 250-million-year geological history of the area on 36 graphic signboards. You can reach the summit from two directions: the cable car sets out from Osterhofen on the Bayrischzell-Munich road and costs €17.50 round-trip, €10.30 one way (its last descent is at 4 PM). The cable car closes for two weeks in mid-April. The historic cog railway leaves from Brannenburg, on the north side of the mountain, between Bayrischzell and the Inn Valley autobahn, and a one-way trip costs €15. The cog is closed in November and the first three weeks of December. ■ **TIP→ A round-trip, combination ticket, with trips on both the cable car and the cog, costs €23.50.**

A few miles east of Bayrischzell on the Sudelfeld Road is the **Tatzel-wurm** gorge and waterfall, named for a winged dragon that supposedly inhabits these parts. Dragon or not, this can be an eerie place to drive at dusk. A hiking trail is signposted. From the gorge, the road drops sharply to the valley of the Inn River, leading to the busy ski resort of Oberaudorf.

WHERE TO STAY & EAT

$$ ✕▥ **Hotel Feuriger Tatzelwurm.** This archetypal old Bavarian inn (with a modern wing) is named after the nearby Tatzelwurm Gorge and is ideally placed for hikes or ski trips. The inn sits in isolated splendor above a forest pond, some 980 feet from the main Oberaudorf-Bayrischzell road. Bavarian dishes (also vegetarian) are served in the warren of paneled dining rooms (¢–$$$$), one of which is dominated by a historic tile stove. The two-person *Jadgherrenplatte Brünnstein* will let you sample the game of the area (both people need to be ravenous to finish off this plate). The Tatzelwurm also serves its own beer. The spa area has everything anyone could desire. Price includes breakfast buffet and wellness area. ✉*Am Tatzelwurm, Oberaudorf/Bayrischzell, D–82080* ☎*08034/30080* ☐*08034/7170* ⊕*www.tatzelwurm.de* ⇆*45 rooms* ⌂*In-room: no a/c, dial-up. In-hotel: restaurant, spa, bicycles, no-smoking rooms, public Wi-Fi, some pets allowed (fee)* ☐DC, MC, V ❙❍❙BP.

2

$ ✕🍴 **Wendelstein.** This large restaurant ($) in the middle of Bayrischzell fills up quickly on winter evenings. On warm summer days there's always the beer garden, shaded by old chestnut trees. The generous portions come at reasonable prices. If you are not into slabs of meat, you can try some of the vegetarian dishes, such as a schnitzel of celery. Rooms here are simple but comfortable. ✉ *Ursprungstr. 1, D-83735 Bayrischzell* ☎ *08023/80890* 🖷 *08023/808–969* ⊕ *www.gasthof-wendelstein. de* 🛏 *18 rooms* 🚿 *In-room: no a/ c. In-hotel: restaurant, bar, public Internet, no-smoking rooms, some pets allowed (fee)* ⊟ *AE, MC, V* ⊗ *Restaurant closed Nov.–mid-Dec. and Mon.* 🍴 *BP.*

> ### HIKING
>
> Well-marked and well-groomed hiking trails lead from the glorious countryside, along rivers and lakes, through woods, and high into the Bavarian Alps. If you just want an afternoon stroll, head for the lower slopes. If you're a serious hiker, make for the mountain trails of the Zugspitze, in Garmisch-Partenkirchen; the heights above Oberammergau, Berchtesgaden, or Bad Reichenhall; or the lovely Walchensee. Well-marked trails near the Schliersee or Tegernsee (lakes) lead steadily uphill and to mountaintop inns. A special treat is a hike to the Tatzelwurm Gorge near Bayrischzell.

The Inn River valley, an ancient trade route, is the most important road link between Germany and Italy. The wide, green Inn gushes here, and in the parish church of St. Bartholomew, at **Rossholzen** (16 km [10 mi] north of Oberaudorf), you can see memorials and painted tributes to the local people who have lost their lives in its chilly waters. The church has a baroque altar incorporating vivid Gothic elements. A simple tavern adjacent to the church offers an ideal opportunity for a break on the Alpine Road.

ROSENHEIM

⑪ *34 km (21 mi) north of Bayrischzell, 55 km (34 mi) east of Munich.*

Bustling Rosenheim is a medieval market town that has kept much of its history while at the same time developing into a major center of commercial and industrial activity between Munich and Salzburg. The arcaded streets of low-eaved houses are characteristic of Inn Valley towns. Lake Chiemsee is nearby, and the area has a handful of rural lakes of its own (Simssee, Hofstättersee, and Rinssee). Leisure activities and culture at lower prices than in Munich have made the area very popular. Traffic is at times very heavy as a result. Avoid driving through town during the morning rush hour (around 8–9), around midday, and between 4:30 and 6:30.

⚠ **Rosenheim and its surroundings are ideal for day trips as far as Munich and Salzburg or the Alps.** Munich, for example, is just 30 minutes away by train. You might consider using Rosenheim as a base for explorations in the region.

The old restored locomotive shed, the **Lokschuppen** ($\boxtimes$*Rathausstr. 24* $\textcircled{=}$*08031/365–9032* $\odot$*Weekdays 9–6, weekends 10–6*), attracts crowds from as far away as Salzburg and Munich to its special exhibitions (mostly of art).

The Inn River was a major trade artery that bestowed a fair amount of wealth onto Rosenheim, especially in the Middle Ages. It not only served the purpose of transportation but also created jobs thanks to fishing, shipping, bridge-building, shipbuilding, and the like. The **Inn Museum** tells the story of the river, from geology to business. $\boxtimes$*Innstr. 74* $\textcircled{=}$*08031/31511* $\textcircled{=}$*€3* $\odot$*Apr.–Oct., Fri. 9–noon, weekends 10–4.*

Wood is another traditional big business around Rosenheim. **Das Holztechnische Museum** documents how it's grown and how it's used, for example in interior decoration, transportation, architecture, and art. $\boxtimes$*Max-Josephs-Pl. 4* $\textcircled{=}$*08031/16900* $\textcircled{=}$*€2* $\odot$*Tues.–Sat. 10–5.*

WHERE TO STAY & EAT

$ ✕⊞ **Fortuna.** This modern hotel at the entrance of Rosenheim (when arriving from the autobahn) has its focus on comfort and good value. Rooms are done in minimalist style, in contrast perhaps to the restaurant (¢–$). A large Italian menu with everything from simple pizza to grilled fish is a nice change in the Pork-Roast Belt of Germany. $\boxtimes$*Hochplattenstr. 42, D-83026* $\textcircled{=}$*08031/616–363* $\textcircled{=}$*08031/6163–6400* $\oplus$*www.hotel-fortuna.de* $\leftrightsquigarrow$*18 rooms* $\triangle$*In-room: dial-up. In-hotel: restaurant, some pets allowed (fee), no elevator* $\equiv$*MC, V* ⦿|*BP.*

$$ ⊞ **Hotel Lindner.** This ancient castle, with foundations going back to the 9th century, is located in the pretty spa town of Bad Aibling, about 8 km (5 mi) west of Rosenheim. It has been in the Lindner family for over 150 years. Adjectives that apply to the property include comfortable, ample, inviting, and elegant. The restaurant attracts everyone from the local card players to the traveling businessperson for delicious culinary creations, from weighty lamb dishes to halibut on white asparagus, or vegetarian delights. On warm days meals can be enjoyed on the lawn behind the hotel. Wines, schnapps, and the hotel's homemade jams can be purchased on location. $\boxtimes$*Marienplatz 5, D-83043 Bad Aibling* $\textcircled{=}$*08061/90630* $\textcircled{=}$*08061/30535* $\oplus$*www.romantikhotel-lindner. de* $\leftrightsquigarrow$*26 rooms* $\triangle$*In-room: no a/c, Wi-Fi (some). In-hotel: restaurant, bar, parking, no-smoking rooms, library, garden, bicycles, some pets allowed, no elevator* $\equiv$*V, MC, AE.*

CHIEMSEE

⑫ *20 km (12 mi) east of Rosenheim, 80 km (50 mi) east of Munich.*

Chiemsee is north of the Deutsche Alpenstrasse, but it demands a detour, if only to visit King Ludwig's huge palace on one of its idyllic islands. It's the largest Bavarian lake, and although it's surrounded by reedy flatlands, the nearby mountains provide a majestic backdrop. The town of **Prien** is the lake's principal resort. ■ **TIP→ The tourist offices of Prien and Aschau offer an €18 transportation package covering a boat**

2

trip, a round-trip rail ticket between the two resorts, and a round-trip ride by cable car to the top of Kampen Mountain, above Aschau.

Fodor's Choice ★ Despite its distance from Munich, the beautiful Chiemsee drew Bavarian royalty to its shores. Its dreamlike, melancholy air caught the imagination of King Ludwig II, and it was on one of the lake's three islands that he built his third and last castle, sumptuous **Schloss Herrenchiemsee.** The palace was modeled after Louis XIV's Versailles, but this was due to more than simple admiration: Ludwig, whose name was the German equivalent of Louis, was keen to establish that he, too, possessed the absolute authority of his namesake, the Sun King. As with most of Ludwig's projects, the building was never completed, and Ludwig spent only nine days in the castle. Moreover, Herrenchiemsee broke the state coffers and Ludwig's private ones as well. The gold leaf that seems to cover more than half of the rooms is especially thin. Nonetheless, what remains is impressive—and ostentatious. Regular ferries out to the island depart from Stock, Prien's harbor. If you want to make the journey in style, board the original 1887 steam train from Prien to Stock to pick up the ferry. A horse-drawn carriage takes you to the palace itself.

Most spectacular is the Hall of Mirrors, a dazzling gallery where candle-lighted concerts are held in summer. Also of interest are the ornate bedrooms Ludwig planned, the "self-rising" table that ascended from the kitchen quarters, the elaborately painted bathroom with a small pool for a tub, and the formal gardens. The south wing houses a **museum** containing Ludwig's christening robe and death mask, as well as other artifacts of his life. While the palace was being built, Ludwig stayed in a royal suite of apartments in a former monastery building on the island, the Altes Schloss. Germany's postwar constitution was drawn up here in 1948, and this episode of the country's history is the centerpiece of the museum housed in the ancient building, the **Museum im Alten Schloss** (€7). *08051/68870 palace ⊕www.herren-chiemsee.de ⌸Palace, including Museum im Alten Schloss €7 ⊙Mid-Mar.–late Oct., daily 9–6; late Oct.–mid-Mar., daily 10–4:15; English-language palace tours daily at 11:45 and 2:25.*

Boats going between Stock and Herrenchiemsee Island also call at the small retreat of **Fraueninsel** *(Ladies' Island)*. The **Benedictine convent** there, founded 1,200 years ago, now serves as a school. One of its earliest abbesses, Irmengard, daughter of King Ludwig der Deutsche, died here in the 9th century. Her grave in the convent chapel was discovered in 1961, the same year that early frescoes there were brought to light. The chapel is open daily from dawn to dusk. Otherwise, the island has just a few private houses, a couple of shops, and a hotel.

OFF THE BEATEN PATH

Amerang. There are two interesting museums in this town northwest of Chiemsee. In the **Museum für Deutsche Automobilgeschichte** *(Museum of German Automobile History)* the display of 220 automobiles begins with an 1886 Benz and culminates in contemporary models. Items on display range from the BMW 250 Isetta—the "rolling egg"—to a 600-hp 935 Porsche. The world's largest small-gauge model-railway panorama is also spread out here over nearly 6,000 square feet. ⊠ *Wasserburger Str. 38* ☎ *08075/8141* ⊕ *www.efa-automuseum.de* 🖾 *€6.50* ☉ *Late Mar.–Oct., Tues.–Sun. 10–6 (last entry at 5).* The **Bauernhausmuseum** *(Farmhouse Museum)* consists of four beautiful farmhouses with a bakery, beehives, sawmill, and blacksmith's workshop. It's worth seeing to find out more about everyday life in the Chiemgau over the last several hundred years. The oldest building in the cluster is from 1525. Every Sunday afternoon an 85-year-old roper shows off his craft, as does a lace maker. On alternate Sundays, spinning, felt making, and blacksmithing are demonstrated. You can take in the idyllic surroundings from the beer garden. ⊠ *Im Hopfgarten* ☎ *08075/915–090* ⊕ *www.bauernhausmuseum-amerang.de* 🖾 *€3* ☉ *Mid-Mar.–Nov. 5, Tues.–Sun. 9–6 (last entry at 5).*

WHERE TO STAY & EAT

$–$$ ✕ **Wirth von Amerang.** Theme restaurants are an up-and-coming busi-
★   ness in Bavaria, and the Wirth is the spearhead. The interior design comes very close to medieval, with brick stoves of handmade bricks, dripping candles, and a floor resembling packed clay. The food is definitely Bavarian, with *Knödel* (dumplings) and pork roast, hocks, and a top-notch potato soup. Reservations are recommended. You may want to purchase the pumpkin-seed oil or a homemade schnapps. ⊠ *Postweg 4, Amerang* ☎ *08075/185–918* ⊕ *www.wirth-von-amerang.de* ⊟ *No credit cards* ☉ *No lunch Nov.–Mar.*

$$ ✕🖾 **Inselhotel zur Linde.** Catch a boat to this enchanting inn on the car-free Fraueninsel: but remember, if you miss the last connection to the mainland (at 9 PM), you'll have to stay the night. The island is by and large a credit-card-free zone, so be sure to bring cash. Rooms are simply furnished and decorated with brightly colored fabrics. The Linde is one of Bavaria's oldest hotels, founded in 1396 as a refuge for pilgrims. Artists have favored the inn for years, and one of the tables in the small Fischerstüberl dining room ($–$$) is reserved for them. This is the best place to try fish from the lake. ⊠ *Fraueninsel im Chiemsee 1, D–83256* ☎ *08054/90366* 🖾 *08054/7299* ⊕ *www.inselhotel-zurlinde.de* 🛏 *14 rooms* ⌂ *In-room: no a/c. In-hotel: restaurant, bar, public Internet, no elevator* ⊟ *MC, V* ☉ *Closed mid-Jan.–mid-Mar.* ⦿ *BP.*

$–$$ ✕🖾 **Hotel Luitpold am See.** Boats to the Chiemsee islands tie up right outside your window at this handsome old Prien hotel, which organizes shipboard disco evenings as part of its entertainment program. Rooms have either traditional pinewood furniture, including carved cupboards and bedsteads, or are modern and sleek (in the new annex). Fish from the lake is served at the pleasant restaurant ($–$$). ⊠ *Seestr. 110, Prien am Chiemsee, D–83209* ☎ *08051/609–100* 🖾 *08051/609–175* ⊕ *www.luitpold-am-see.de* 🛏 *79 rooms* ⌂ *In-room: no a/c. In-hotel: 2 restaurants, public Internet, no-smoking rooms, some pets allowed (fee), no elevator* ⊟ *AE, DC, MC, V* ⦿ *BP.*

$–$$ ✕🖾 **Schlosshotel Herrenchiemsee.** This handsome mansion on the island of Herrenchiemsee predates King Ludwig's palace, which is a 15-minute walk through the woods. The rooms aren't palatial but are comfortable. A big plus is the pavilionlike restaurant ($–$$), which serves fresh fish. If you're here just to eat, make sure to catch the last boat to the mainland (9 PM)—otherwise you'll be sleeping on this traffic-free island. ⊠ *Herrenchiemsee, D–83209* ☎ *08051/1509* 🖷 *08051/1509* 🛏 *8 rooms, 6 with bath or shower, 1 suite* ⚒ *In-room: no a/c, no phone. In-hotel: restaurant, some pets allowed, no elevator* ▤ *AE, DC, MC, V* ⊘ *Hotel closed Oct.–Easter* ⦿*CP.*

SPORTS & THE OUTDOORS

There are boatyards all around the lake and several windsurfing schools. The **Mistral-Windsurfing-Center** (⊠ *Waldstr. 20* ☎ *08054/909–906*), at Gstadt am Chiemsee, has been in operation for decades. From

BOATING & SAILING

All the Bavarian Alpine lakes have sailing schools that rent sailboards as well as various other types of boats. At Tegernsee you can hire motorboats at the pier in front of the Schloss Cafe, in the Tegernsee town center. Chiemsee, with its wide stretch of water whipped by Alpine winds, is a favorite for both sailing enthusiasts and windsurfers. There are boatyards all around the lake and a very good windsurfing school at Bernau.

its boatyard the average windsurfer can make it with ease to the next island. The gentle hills of the region are ideal for golf. **Chiemsee Golf-Club Prien e.V** (☎ *08051/62215*), in Prien, has a year-round 9-hole course. **SportLukas** (⊠ *Hauptstr. 3, D–83259 Schleching* ☎ *08649/243*) provides equipment for any kind of sport imaginable, from skiing to kayaking, climbing to curling, and it organizes tours. For those wanting to learn windsurfing or to extend their skills, the **Surfschule Chiemsee** (⊠ *Ludwig-Thoma-Str. 15a, D–83233 Bernau* ☎ *08051/8877*) provides lessons and offers a package deal including board and bike rentals.

ASCHAU

⑬ *10 km (6 mi) south of Chiemsee, 75 km (46 mi) east of Munich.*

Aschau is an enchanting red-roof village nestled in a wide valley of the Chiemgauer Alps. Its **Schloss Hohenaschau** is one of the few medieval castles in southern Germany to have been restored in the 17th century in baroque style. For the regional exhibition on Bavaria's nobility in 2008 (April through November), several rooms will be open to the public for the first time. These rooms include the spectacular Laubensaal, which was lavishly painted by 17th-century Italian artists. Chamber-music concerts are presented regularly in the Rittersaal (Knights' Hall) during the summer. The **Prientalmuseum** (Museum of the Prien Valley), with historical documents on the region, is in the former deacon's house. Exhibitions by contemporary international artists are also on display. ☎ *08052/904–937* 🖷 *Castle €3* ⊘ *May–Sept., Tues.–Fri. tours at 9:30, 10:30, and 11:30; Apr. and Oct., Thurs. at 9:30, 10:30, and 11:30; museum during tour times and Sun. 1:30–5.*

WHERE TO STAY & EAT

$$$–$$$$
Fodor'sChoice
★

✕▥ **Residenz Heinz Winkler.** Star chef Heinz Winkler has turned a sturdy village inn into one of Germany's most extraordinary hotel-restaurant complexes. Rooms in the main house are noble in proportions and furnishings, and the maisonette-style suites in the annexes are cozy and romantic. All have views of the mountains. The restaurant ($$$$) has kept with ease the awards that Winkler won when in charge of Munich's Tantris. A grand piano and a harp add harmony to this deliciously sophisticated scene. ⊠*Kirchpl. 1, D–83229* ☎*08052/17990* 🖶*08052/179–966* ⊕*www.residenz-heinz-winkler.de* ☜*32 rooms, 13 suites* ⟨*In-room: no a/c, dial-up. In-hotel: restaurant, bar, pool, spa, some pets allowed (fee)* ⊟*AE, DC, MC, V* ⦿❘*BP.*

$ 🖫 **Hotel Bonnschlössl.** This turreted country palace is set in its own park studded with centuries-old trees. In good weather breakfast is served on the balustraded terrace. The hotel is 6 km (4 mi) north of Aschau and has a similarly enchanting sister property in the nearby village of Bernau, the Gasthof Alter Wirt. Both the Schloss and the Gasthof are protected by preservation orders. Emperor Maximilian I stayed overnight at the Gasthof in 1503 on his way to besiege the castle of Marquartstein. ⊠*Kirchpl. 9, D–83233 Bernau* ☎*08051/89011* 🖶*08051/89103* ⊕*www.bonnschloessl.de* ☜*22 rooms* ⟨*In-room: no a/c. In-hotel: restaurant, bar, spa, no-smoking rooms, some pets allowed* ⊟*MC, V* ⊗*Closed Mon.* ⦿❘*BP.*

BAD REICHENHALL

⑭   *50 km (30 mi) east of Aschau, 20 km (12 mi) west of Salzburg.*

Bad Reichenhall is remarkably well located, near the mountains for hiking and skiing, and near Salzburg in Austria for a lively cultural scene. The town shares a remote corner of Bavaria with another prominent resort, Berchtesgaden. Although the latter is more famous, Bad Reichenhall is older, with saline springs that made the town rich. Salt is so much a part of the town that you can practically taste it in the air. Europe's largest source of brine was first tapped here in pre-Christian times; salt mining during the Middle Ages supported the economies of cities as far away as Munich and Passau. The town prospered from a spa in the early 20th century. Lately, it has successfully recycled itself from a somewhat sleepy and stodgy "cure town" to a modern, attractive center of wellness.

The pride and joy of the Reichenhallers is the steep, craggy mountain appropriately named the **Predigtstuhl** *(Preaching Pulpit)*, which stands at 5,164 feet, southeast of town. A ride to the top offers a splendid view of the area. You can hike, ski in winter, or just enjoy a meal at the **Berghotel Predigtdstuhl** ($–$$). The cable-car ride costs €9 one way, €17 round-trip. Departures begin at 9:30 AM and continue (as needed) until the last person is off the mountain. ⊠*Südtiroler Pl. 1* ☎*08651/2127* ⊕*www.predigtstuhl-bahn.de.*

Hotels here base spa treatments on the health-giving properties of the saline springs and the black mud from the area's waterlogged moors. The waters can also be taken in the elegant, pillared **Wandelhalle** pavilion of the attractive spa gardens throughout the year. Breathing salt-laden air is a remedy for various lung conditions. All you need to do is walk along the 540-foot Gradierwerk, a massive wood-and-concrete construction that produces a fine salty mist by trickling brine down a 40-foot wall of dense black-thorn bundles. ✉*Salzburgerstr.* ⊙*Mon.–Sat. 8–12:30 and 3–5, Sun. 10–12:30.*

★ Part of Bad Reichenhall's revival included building a new spa facility, the brand new "spa and fitness resort" **Rupertus Therme.** Pools, saunas, and steam rooms are rounded off with a host of special applications using salt, essential oils, mud packs, and massages. ✉*Friedrich-Ebert-Allee 21* ☏*01805/606–706* ⊕*www.rupertustherme.de* ✆€ *22, includes sauna area for the day* ⊙*Daily 9–10.*

The ancient church **St. Zeno** is dedicated to the patron saint of those imperiled by floods and the dangers of the deep, an ironic note in a town that flourishes on the riches of its underground springs. This 12th-century basilica, the largest in Bavaria, was remodeled in the 16th and 17th centuries, but some of the original Romanesque cloisters remain, although these can be seen only during services and from 11 to noon on Sunday and holidays. ✉*Kirchpl. 1.*

> ## WHITE GOLD
>
> Salt, or white gold as it was known in medieval times, has played a key role in the history of both Bad Reichenhall and Berchtesgaden. Organized salt production in the region began around 450 BC and even included a 30-km (20-mi) wooden pipeline for salt built in the early 1600s. It wasn't until the early 19th century, however, that the town began utilizing its position and geological advantages to attract tourists. The production of salt continues to this day, as does the flow of travelers on the search for the healing saline pools.

In the early 19th century, King Ludwig I built an elaborate saltworks and spa house—the **Alte Saline und Quellenhaus**—in vaulted, pseudomedieval style. Their pump installations, which still run, are astonishing examples of 19th-century engineering. A "saline" **chapel** is part of the spa's facilities and was built in exotic Byzantine style. An interesting museum in the same complex looks at the history of the salt trade. The Alte Saline also houses a small **glass foundry** (☏*08651/69738* ⊕*www.riedl-glaskunst.de* ✆*Free* ⊙ *Weekdays 9–6, Sat. 9:30–1*), run by the famous company Riedl, makers of fine tableware. Glassblowers and engravers display their art in a small self-service restaurant, and children can try their mouths, so to speak, at glassblowing. The showroom has many articles for sale, notably glass globes used to ensure your potted plants are being slowly watered while you are away. There are tours through the whole saltworks, including visits to the museum. ✉*Salinen Str.* ☏*08651/7002–146* ⊕*www.salzwelt.de* ✆*€5.50, combined ticket with Berchtesgaden salt mine €15.50* ⊙*May–Oct., daily 10–11:30 and 2–4; Nov.–Apr., Tues., Fri., and first Sat. in the month 2–4.*

WHERE TO STAY & EAT

¢–$ ✗**Obermühle.** Tucked away off the main road leading from Bad Reichenhall to the autobahn, this 16th-century mill is a well-kept secret. Fish is the specialty here, though meats (the game in season is noteworthy) are also on the menu. The terrace is an inviting place for a few helpings of excellent homemade cakes. ⊠ *Tumpenstr. 11* ☎ *08651/2193* ▭ *No credit cards* ⊘ *Closed Mon. and Tues.*

$$–$$$ ✕⊞ **Parkhotel Luisenbad.** If you fancy spoiling yourself in a typical Ger-
Fodor'sChoice   man fin-de-siècle spa hotel, this is *the* place—a fine porticoed and pil-
★   lared building whose imposing pastel-pink facade promises luxury within. Rooms are large, furnished in deep-cushioned, dark-wood comfort, most with flower-filled balconies or loggias. The elegant restaurant ($–$$) serves international and traditional Bavarian cuisines with an emphasis on seafood (scallops or tuna steak, for example), and a pine-panel tavern, Die Holzstubn'n, pours excellent local brew. ⊠ *Ludwigstr. 33, D–83435* ☎ *08651/6040* 🖷 *08651/62928* ⊕ *www. parkhotel.de* ⤳ *70 rooms, 8 suites* ⌂ *In-room: no a/c, Wi-Fi. In-hotel: restaurant, bar, pool, gym, bicycles, public Internet, some pets allowed (fee)* ▭ *DC, MC, V* ❑BP.

$ ✕⊞ **Bürgerbräu.** Each dining area in this old brewery inn reflects the social class that once met here: politicos, peasants, burghers, and salt miners. Reichenhallers from all walks of life still meet here to enjoy good conversation, hearty beer, and excellent food. Rooms at the inn are simple but airy and modern, and best of all, you're in the middle of town. ⊠ *Am Rathauspl., D–83435* ☎ *08651/6089* 🖷 *08651/608–504* ⊕ *www.brauereigasthof-buergerbraeu.de* ⤳ *32 rooms* ⌂ *In-room: no a/c. In-hotel: restaurant, Wi-Fi, some pets allowed (fee), no elevator* ▭ *AE, DC, MC, V* ❑BP.

⊞ **Hotel-Pension Erika.** This four-story villa, painted a staid red, has been family-run since 1898, and it shows in the best sense. Everything radiates comfort, from the light-filled dining room to the generous garden. Owner Anton Oberarzbacher occasionally cooks dinner, using herbs from his own garden. The pedestrian zone in town is a minute away. ⊠ *Adolf-Schmid-Str. 3, D–83435* ☎ *08651/95360* 🖷 *08651/953–6200* ⊕ *www.hotel-pension-erika.de* ⤳ *32 rooms, 1 suite* ⌂ *In-room: no a/c, dial-up. In-hotel: some pets allowed* ▭ *AE, MC, V* ⊘ *Closed Nov.– Feb. Restaurant closed Sun.*

$ ⊡ **Pension Hubertus.** This delightfully traditional family-run lodging
★   stands on the shore of the tiny Thumsee, 5 km (3 mi) from the town center. The Hubertus's private grounds lead down to the lake, where guests can swim or boat (the water is bracingly cool). Rooms, some with balconies overlooking the lake, are furnished with hand-carved beds and cupboards. Excellent meals or coffee can be taken at the neighboring rustic **Madlbauer** ($–$$). There are special rates in the off-season (October–April). ⊠ *Am Thumsee 5, D–83435* ☎ *08651/2252* 🖷 *08651/63845* ⊕ *www.hubertus-thumsee.de* ⤳ *18 rooms* ⌂ *In-room: no a/c, no phone (some). In-hotel: gym, no-smoking rooms, some pets allowed (fee), no elevator* ▭ *AE, DC, MC, V* ❑CP.

NIGHTLIFE & THE ARTS

Bad Reichenhall is proud of its long musical tradition and of its orchestra, founded more than a century ago. It performs six days a week throughout the year in the chandelier-hung Kurgastzentrum Theater or, when weather permits, in the open-air pavilion, and at a special Mozart Week in March. Call the **Orchesterbüro** (☎ *08651/8661* 🖷 *08651/710– 551*) for program details.

As a spa town and winter resort, Bad Reichenhall is a natural for night haunts. The big draw is the elegant **casino** (⊠ *Wittelsbacherstr. 17* ☎ *08651/95800* ▨ *€2.50, free with a Kurkarte; ask for one at your hotel.* Jacket and tie), open daily 3 PM–1 or 2 AM depending on business. For some traditional ballroom dancing to live music in the evenings, head for the **Tanzcafe am Kurgarten.** Occasionally they also show soccer games. (⊠ *Salzburger Str. 7. 17* ☎ *08651/1691*).

SPORTS & THE OUTDOORS

Though Berchtesgaden definitely has the pull for skiers, Bad Reichenhall is proud of its Predigtstuhl, which towers over the town to the south. Besides fresh air and great views, it offers some skiing, lots of hiking, biking, and even rock climbing. The tourist-information office on Wittelsbacherstrasse, just a couple of hundred yards from the train station, has all of the necessary information regarding the numerous sporting activities possible in Bad Reichenhall and its surrounding area.

SHOPPING

Using flowers and herbs grown in the Bavarian Alps, the **Josef Mack Company** (⊠ *Ludwigstr. 36* ☎ *08651/78280*) has made medicinal herbal preparations since 1856. **Leuthenmayr** (⊠ *Ludwigstr. 27* ☎ *08651/2869*) is a youngster in the business, selling its "cure-all" dwarf-pine oil since 1908. Your sweet tooth will be fully satisfied at the confection emporium of **Paul Reber** (⊠ *Ludwigstr. 10–12* ☎ *08651/60030*), makers of the famous chocolate and marzipan *Mozartkugel,* and many other dietary bombs. Candle-making is a local specialty, and **Kerzenwelt Donabauer** (⊠ *Reichenhaller Str. 15, Piding* ☎ *08651/8143*), just outside Bad Reichenhall, has a selection of more than 1,000 decorative items in wax. It also has a free wax museum depicting fairy-tale characters.

BERCHTESGADEN

⑮ *18 km (11 mi) south of Bad Reichenhall, 20 km (12 mi) south of Salzburg.*

Berchtesgaden's reputation is unjustly rooted in its brief association with Adolf Hitler, who dreamed besottedly of his "1,000-year Reich" from the mountaintop where millions of tourists before and after him drank in only the superb beauty of the Alpine panorama. The historic old market town and mountain resort has great charm. In winter it's a fine place for skiing and snowboarding; in summer it becomes one of the region's most popular (and crowded) resorts. An ornate palace and working salt mine make up some of the diversions in this heavenly setting.

Salt was once the basis of Berchtesgaden's wealth. In the 12th century Emperor Barbarossa gave mining rights to a Benedictine abbey that had been founded here a century earlier. The abbey was secularized early in the 19th century, when it was taken over by the Wittelsbach rulers. Salt is still important today because of all the local wellness centers.

The entire area has been declared a "health resort region" (*Kurgebiet*) and was put on the UNESCO biosphere list.

At the sleek and classy **Watzmann Therme** you'll find fragrant steam rooms, saunas with infrared cabins for sore muscles, an elegant pool, whirlpools, and more. If you happen to be staying a few days, you might catch a tai chi course, enjoy a bio-release facial massage, or partake in an evening of relaxing underwater exercises. ⊠ *Bergwerkstr. 54* ☎ *08652/94640* ⊕ *www.watzmann-therme.de* ⊠ *2 hrs €8.30, 4 hrs €10.80, day pass including sauna €15.30* ☉ *Daily 10–10.*

The last royal resident of the Berchtesgaden abbey, Crown Prince Rupprecht (who died here in 1955), furnished it with rare family treasures that now form the basis of a permanent collection—the **Königliches Schloss Berchtesgaden Museum.** Fine Renaissance rooms exhibit the prince's sacred art, which is particularly rich in wood sculptures by such great late-Gothic artists as Tilman Riemenschneider and Veit Stoss. You can also visit the abbey's original, cavernous 13th-century dormitory and cool cloisters. ⊠ *Schlosspl. 2* ☎ *08652/947–980* ⊕ *www.hausbayern.com* ⊠ *€7 with tour* ☉ *Mid-May–mid-Oct., Sun.–Fri. 10–1 and 2–4; mid-Oct.–mid-May, weekdays 11–2.*

The **Heimatmuseum,** in the Schloss Adelsheim, displays examples of wood carving and other local crafts. Wood carving in Berchtesgaden dates to long before Oberammergau established itself as the premier wood-carving center of the Alps. ⊠ *Schroffenbergallee 6* ☎ *08652/4410* ⊕ *www.heimatmuseum-berchtesgaden.de* ⊠ *€2.50* ☉ *Dec.–Oct., Tues.–Sun. 10–4.*

★ The **Salzbergwerk** *(salt mine)* is one of the chief attractions of the region. In the days when the mine was owned by Berchtesgaden's princely rulers, only select guests were allowed to see how the source of the city's wealth was extracted from the earth. Today, during a 90-minute tour, you can sit astride a miniature train that transports you nearly 1 km (½ mi) into the mountain to an enormous chamber where the salt is mined. Included in the tour are rides down the wooden chutes used by miners to get from one level to another and a boat ride on an underground saline lake the size of a football field. You may wish to partake in the special four-hour **brine dinners** down in the mines (€75). These are very popular, so be sure to book early ⊠ *2 km (1 mi) from center of Berchtesgaden on B–305 Salzburg Rd.* ☎ *08652/600–220* ⊕ *www.salzbergwerk-berchtesgaden.de* ⊠ *€9, combined ticket with Bad Reichenhall's saline museum €15.50* ☉ *May–mid-Oct., daily 9–5; mid-Oct.–Apr., Mon.–Sat. 11:30–3.*

⑯ The **Obersalzberg,** site of Hitler's luxurious mountain retreat, is part of the north slope of the Hoher Goll, high above Berchtesgaden. It was a remote mountain community of farmers and foresters before Hitler's deputy, Martin Bormann, selected the site for a complex of Alpine homes for top Nazi leaders. Hitler's chalet, the Berghof, and all the others were destroyed in 1945, with the exception of a hotel that had been taken over by the Nazis, the Hotel zum Türken. Beneath the hotel is a section of the labyrinth of tunnels built as a last retreat for Hitler and his cronies; the macabre, murky **bunkers** (⊡€3 ◎ *May–Oct., Tues.–Sun. 9–5; Nov.–Apr., daily 10–3*) can be visited. Nearby, the **Dokumentation Obersalzberg** (⊠*Salzbergstr. 41* ☎*08652/947–960* ⊕*www.obersalzberg.de* ⊡€3 ◎ *Apr.–Oct., Tues.–Sun. 9–5; Nov.–Mar., Tues.–Sun. 10–3*) documents the Third Reich's history by specific themes with rare archival material. Beyond Obersalzberg, the hairpin bends of Germany's highest road come to the base of the 6,000-foot peak on which sits the **Kehlsteinhaus** (☎*08652/2969* ⊕*www.kehlsteinhaus.de*), also known as the Adlerhorst (Eagle's Nest), Hitler's personal retreat and his official guesthouse. It was Martin Bormann's gift to the Führer on Hitler's 50th birthday. The road leading to it, built in 1937–39, climbs more than 2,000 dizzying feet in less than 6 km (4 mi). A tunnel in the mountain will bring you to an elevator that whisks you up to what appears to be the top of the world (you can walk up in about a half hour). There are refreshment rooms and a restaurant. The round-trip from Berchtesgaden's post office by bus and elevator costs €16.20 per person. The bus runs mid-May through September, daily from 9 to 4:50. By car you can travel only as far as the Obersalzberg bus station. From there the round-trip fare is €14.50. The full round-trip takes one hour.

WHERE TO STAY & EAT

$ ✕⊡ **Alpenhotel Denninglehen.** Nonsmokers appreciate the special dining room set aside just for them in this mountain hotel's restaurant. The house was built in 1981 in Alpine style, with lots of wood paneling, heavy beams, and wide balconies with cascades of geraniums in summer. Skiers enjoy the fact that the slopes are about 200 yards away. The restaurant has a large fireplace to warm up winter evenings. The menu ($–$$$) is regional (the usual schnitzels and roasts) with a few items from the French repertoire (a fine steak in pepper sauce, for example). Price includes breakfast buffet and use of the wellness facilities. ⊠*Am Priesterstein 7, Berchtesgaden-Oberau, D-83471* ☎*08652/97890* ⊟*08652/64710* ⊕*www.denninglehen.de* ♿*In-room: no a/c. In-hotel: restaurant, pool, no-smoking rooms, some pets allowed (fee)* ⊟*MC* ◎*Closed last 2 wks in Jan.* ❿*BP.*

$ ✕⊡ **Hotel Grünberger.** Only a few strides from the train station in the town center, the Grünberger overlooks the River Ache—it even has a private terrace beside the river you can relax on. The cozy rooms have farmhouse-style furnishings and some antiques. The wellness area has in-house acupuncture and traditional Chinese medicine treatments. The hotel restaurant focuses on German fare with some international dishes to lighten the load. Those who need to check e-mail head to the Internet café nearby. ⊠*Hansererweg 1, D-83471* ☎*08652/976– 590* ⊟*08652/62254* ⊕*www.hotel-gruenberger.de* ⇆*65 rooms* ♿*In-room: no a/c, no phone, no TV (some). In-hotel: restaurant, bar, pool, no-smoking rooms* ⊟*MC, V* ◎*Closed Nov.–mid-Dec.* ❿*BP.*

$$ ⊡ **Hotel zum Türken.** The view alone is worth the 10-minute journey from Berchtesgaden to this hotel. Confiscated during World War II by the Nazis, the hotel is at the foot of the road to Hitler's mountaintop retreat. Beneath it are remains of Nazi wartime bunkers. The decor, though fittingly rustic, is a bit dated. There's no restaurant, although

evening meals can be ordered in advance. ✉*Hintereck 2, Obersalz-berg-Berchtesgaden, D–83471* ☎*08652/2428* 🖷*08652/4710* ⊕*www. hotel-zum-tuerken.de* ⤴*17 rooms, 12 with bath or shower* ♿*In-room: no a/c, no phone (some). In-hotel: no-smoking rooms, some pets allowed, no elevator* ▤*AE, DC, MC, V* ⊘*Closed Nov.–Dec. 20* ❖*BP.*

$–$$ 🏨 **Stoll's Hotel Alpina.** Set above the Königsee in the delightful little vil-lage of Schönau, the Alpina offers rural solitude and easy access to Ber-chtesgaden. Families are catered to with apartments, a resident doctor, and a playroom. The hotel also has an annex about a half a mile away, the Sporthotel, where rooms are somewhat cheaper. ✉*Ulmenweg 14, Schönau, D–83471* ☎*08652/65090* 🖷*08652/61608* ⊕*www.stolls-hotel-alpina.de* ⤴*52 rooms, 8 apartments* ♿*In-room: no a/c, dial-up (some). In-hotel: restaurant, pool, some pets allowed (fee), no elevator* ▤*AE, DC, MC, V* ⊘*Closed early Nov.–mid-Dec.* ❖*BP.*

$ 🏨 **Hotel Wittelsbach.** This is one of the oldest (built in 1892) and most traditional lodgings in the area, so it is wise to reserve well ahead of time. The small rooms have dark pinewood furnishings and deep red and green drapes and carpets. Ask for one with a balcony. The breakfast room has a mountain view. If you have to send thoughts back home, there's an Internet terminal available. ✉*Maximilianstr. 16, D–83471* ☎*08652/96380* 🖷*08652/66304* ⊕*www.hotel-wittelsbach. com* ⤴*26 rooms, 3 apartments* ♿*In-room: no a/c. In-hotel: public Internet, some pets allowed* ▤*AE, DC, MC, V* ❖*BP.*

▌OFF THE
BEATEN
PATH
Schellenberg Eishöhlen. Germany's largest ice caves lie 10 km (6 mi) north of Berchtesgaden. By car take B–305, or take the bus (€4) from the Berchtesgaden post office to the village of Marktschellenberg. From there you can reach the caves on foot by walking 2½ hours along the clearly marked route. A guided tour of the caves takes one hour. On the way to Marktschellenberg watch for the **Almbachklamm,** a narrow valley good for hikes. At its entrance is an old (1683) mill for mak-ing and polishing marbles. ☎*08652/944–5300* ⊕*www.eishoehle.net* 🎫*€5* ⊘*Tours June–Oct. 10–4.*

SPORTS & THE OUTDOORS

Buried as it is in the Alps, Berchtesgaden is a place for the active. The Rossfeld ski area is one of the favorites, thanks to almost guaranteed natural snow. The piste down to Oberau is nearly 6 km (4 mi) long (with bus service at the end to take you back to Berchtesgaden). There is a separate snowboarding piste as well. Berchtesgaden also has many cross-country trails and telemark opportunities. The other popular area is on the slopes of the Götschenkopf, which is used for world cup races. Snow is usually artificial, but the floodlit slopes at night and a lively après-ski scene make up for the lesser quality.

In summer, hikers, power-walkers, and paragliders take over the region. The Obersalzberg even has a summer sledding track. Avid hikers should ask for a map featuring the refuges (Berghütten) in the mountains, where one can spend the night either in a separate room or a bunk. Simple, solid meals are offered. In some of the smaller refuges you will have to bring your own food. For more information, check out ⊕*www.berchtesgaden.de*. And though the Königsee is beautiful to look at, only cold-water swimmers will appreciate its frigid waters.

Germany's highest course, the **Berchtesgaden Golf Club** (⊠*Salzbergstr. 33* ☎*08652/2100*), is on a 3,300-foot plateau of the Obersalzberg. Only fit players should attempt the demanding 9-hole course. Seven Berchtesgaden hotels offer their guests a 30% reduction on the €25 greens fee—contact the tourist office or the club for details.

Whatever your mountain-related needs, whether it's climbing and hiking in summer or cross-country tours in winter, you'll find it at the **Erste Bergschule Berchtesgadenerland** (⊠*Silbergstr. 25, Strub* ☎*08652/2420 May–Oct., 08652/5371 Nov.–Apr.* 🖷*08652/2420*).

SHOPPING

The **Berchtesgadener Handwerkskunst** (⊠*Schlosspl. 1½* ☎*08652/979–790*) offers handicrafts—such as wooden boxes, woven tablecloths, wood carvings, and Christmas-tree decorations—from Berchtesgaden, the surrounding region, and other parts of Bavaria.

BERCHTESGADEN NATIONAL PARK

⑰ *5 km (3 mi) south of Berchtesgaden.*

The deep, mysterious, and fabled Königsee is the most photographed panorama in Germany. Together with its much smaller sister, the Obersee, it's nestled within the Berchtesgaden National Park, 210 square km (82 square mi) of wild mountain country where flora and fauna have been left to develop as nature intended. No roads penetrate the area, and even the mountain paths are difficult to follow. The park administration organizes guided tours of the area from June through September. *Nationalparkhaus* ⊠*Franziskanerpl. 7, D–83471 Berchtesgaden* ☎*08652/64343* ⊕*www.nationalpark-berchtesgaden.de*.

★ One less strenuous way into the Berchtesgaden National Park is by boat. A fleet of 21 excursion boats, electrically driven so that no noise disturbs the peace, operates on the **Königsee** *(King Lake)*. Only the skipper of the boat is allowed to shatter the silence—his trumpet fanfare demonstrates a remarkable echo as notes reverberate between the almost vertical cliffs that plunge into the dark green water. A cross on a rocky promontory marks the spot where a boatload of pilgrims hit the cliffs and sank more than 100 years ago. The voyagers were on their way to the tiny, twin-tower baroque chapel of St. Bartholomä, built in the 17th century on a peninsula where an early-Gothic church once stood. The princely rulers of Berchtesgaden built a hunting lodge at the side of the chapel; a tavern and restaurant now occupy its rooms.

Smaller than the Königsee but equally beautiful, the **Obersee** can be reached by a 15-minute walk from the second stop (Salet) on the boat tour. The lake's backdrop of jagged mountains and precipitous cliffs is broken by a waterfall, the Rothbachfall, that plunges more than 1,000 feet to the valley floor.

Boat service (☎ *08652/96360* ⊕ *www.bayerische-seenschifffahrt.de*) on the Königsee runs year-round, except when the lake freezes. A round-trip to St. Bartholomä and Salet, the landing stage for the Obersee, lasts almost two hours, without stops, and costs €14. A round-trip to St. Bartholomä lasts a little over an hour and costs €11.50. In summer the Berchtesgaden tourist office organizes evening cruises on the Königsee, which includes a concert in St. Bartholomä Church and a four-course dinner in the neighboring hunting lodge.

BAVARIAN ALPS ESSENTIALS

TRANSPORTATION

BY AIR

Munich, 95 km (59 mi) northwest of Garmisch-Partenkirchen, is the gateway to the Bavarian Alps. If you're staying in Berchtesgaden, consider the closer airport in Salzburg, Austria, although it has fewer international flights.

Information Salzburg Airport (SZ6) (☎ *0662/8580* ⊕ *www.salzburg-airport.com*).

BY BOAT

Passenger boats operate on all the major Bavarian lakes. They're mostly excursion boats, and many run only in summer. However, there's year-round service on the Chiemsee. Eight boats operate year-round on the Tegernsee, connecting the towns of Tegernsee, Rottach-Egern, Bad Wiessee, and Gmund.

BY BUS

The Alpine region is not well served by long-distance buses. On the other hand, there's a fairly good network of local buses, but they tend to run at commuter times. Inquire at any local train station, travel agent, or at your hotel, or log onto the German Railways' itinerary-planning site, ⊕ *www.bahn.de*. Larger resorts operate buses to outlying areas. The Wendelstein region, for example, is serviced by the Wendelstein Ringlinie, offering fares from a simple €8.50 per day to more complex ones involving skiing tickets. It connects the skiing areas of Sudelfeld with Bayrischzell, the Tatzelwurm Gorge, Bad Aibling near Rosenheim, and other towns and areas. Your hotel reception should be able to help. Remember, too, to pick up a "Kurkarte" in some places: this allows you discounts on a variety of services, including local transportation. Garmisch-Partenkirchen runs night buses to and from Murnau, Oberammergau, Mittenwald, and Krün. Night buses also run between Murnau and Oberammergau. The cost is €2.50.

BY CAR

A car is obviously the best way—though not the only way—to get around in the Bavarian Alps. The region lends itself to amazing scenic drives and myriad stops in quaint little towns. For orientation, three autobahns reach into the Bavarian Alps: A–7 comes in from the northwest (Frankfurt, Stuttgart, Ulm) and ends near Füssen in the western Bavarian Alps; A–95 runs from Munich to Garmisch-Partenkirchen; take A–8 from Munich for Tegernsee, Schliersee, and Chiemsee and for Berchtesgaden. All provide speedy access to a network of well-paved country roads that penetrate high into the mountains. (Germany's highest road runs above Berchtesgaden at more than 5,000 feet.)

Note that on weekends and at the start and end of national holidays, traffic jams up the end of A–95 near Garmisch-Partenkirchen. A–8 carries a tremendous amount of traffic into Austria and points east. It can become a long parking lot on weekends and holidays. The two major climbs around the Irschenberg and Bernau are particularly affected. The driving style is fast, and tailgating is common, though it is inexcusable and strictly illegal. ⚠ **Do not engage in any one-upmanship. If an accident ensues, you will be held responsible.** Remember, too, the "guideline speed" (Richtgeschwindigkeit) on the A–8 is 110 kmh (68 mph). If an accident occurs at higher speeds, your insurance will not necessarily cover it.

BY TRAIN

Most Alpine resorts are connected with Munich by regular express and slower services. With some careful planning, you can perhaps save yourself the expense of renting a car and the hassle of driving on dangerous autobahns. If you have an itinerary, check out the possibilities at www.bahn.de.

Trains to Garmisch-Partenkirchen depart hourly from Munich's Hauptbahnhof. Garmisch-Partenkirchen and Mittenwald are on the InterCity Express network, which has regular direct service to all regions of the country. (Klais, just outside Garmisch, is Germany's highest-altitude InterCity train station.) A train from Munich also connects to Gmund on Tegernsee. Bad Reichenhall, Berchtesgaden, Prien, and Rosenheim are linked directly to north German cities by long-distance express service. You can also travel between the mountain towns by train: this can at times go faster than driving, owing to traffic and weather conditions. It also gives you a chance to meet people.

■ TIP→ **If you're making a day trip to the Zugspitze from Munich, Augsburg, or any other southern Bavarian center, take advantage of the Bayern Ticket, a very attractive deal offered by Deutsche Bahn.** The ticket includes discounted rail fare to Garmisch-Partenkirchen and discounts on Zugspitze transportation of up to 10%. The ticket costs €27 and is valid from 9 AM on the day of validation until 3 AM that night. A group of five can travel with one ticket. There is a "single" version for €19. Only "regional" trains can be used, however, so make sure you plan ahead a little. Ask at the train station for details, as the offers are always changing.

CONTACTS & RESOURCES

TOUR OPTIONS

BERCHTESGADEN In Berchtesgaden, the Schwaiger bus company runs tours of the area and across the Austrian border as far as Salzburg. An American couple runs Berchtesgaden Mini-bus Tours out of the local tourist office, opposite the railroad station.

Information Berchtesgaden Mini-bus Tours (☎ *08652/64971*). **Schwaiger** (☎ *08652/2525*).

GARMISCH- Bus tours to King Ludwig II's castles at Neuschwanstein and Linder-
PARTENKIRCHEN hof and to the Ettal Monastery, near Oberammergau, are offered by DER travel agencies. Local agencies in Garmisch also run tours to Neuschwanstein, Linderhof, and Ettal and into the neighboring Austrian Tyrol.

The Garmisch mountain railway company, the Bayerische Zugspitzbahn, offers special excursions to the top of the Zugspitze, Germany's highest mountain, by cog rail and/or cable car.

Information Bayerische Zugspitzbahn (☎ *08821/7970*). **DER** (✉ *Garmisch-Partenkirchen* ☎ *08821/55125*). **Dominikus Kümmerle** (☎ *08821/4955*). **Hans Biersack** (☎ *08821/4920*). **Hilmar Röser** (☎ *08821/2926*). **Weiss-Blau-Reisen** (☎ *08821/3766*).

VISITOR INFORMATION

The Bavarian regional tourist office in Munich, Tourismusverband München Oberbayern, provides general information about Upper Bavaria and the Bavarian Alps.

Contacts Aschau (✉ *Verkehrsamt, Kampenwandstr. 38, D–83229* ☎ *08052/904–937* ⊕ *www.aschau.de*). **Bad Reichenhall** (✉ *Kur-und-Verkehrsverein, im Kurgastzentrum, Wittelsbacherstr. 15, D–83424* ☎ *08651/606–303* ⊕ *www.bad-reichenhall.de*). **Bad Tölz** (✉ *Tourist Information, Max-Höfler-Pl. 1, D–83646* ☎ *08041/78670* ⊕ *www.bad-toelz.de*). **Bad Wiessee** (✉ *Tourist-Information, Adrian-Stoop-Str. 20, D–837004* ☎ *08022/86030* ⊕ *www.bad-wiessee.de*). **Bayrischzell** (✉ *Kirchpl. 2, 🖰 Postfach 2, Kurverwaltung, D–83735* ☎ *08023/648* ⊕ *www.bayrischzell.de*). **Berchtesgaden** (✉ *Kurdirektion, D–83471* ☎ *08652/9670* ⊕ *www.berchtesgadener-land.com*). **Chiemsee** (✉ *Kur- und Tourismusbüro Chiemsee, Alte Rathausstr. 11, D–83209 Prien* ☎ *08051/69050* ⊕ *www.chiemsee.de*). **Ettal** (✉ *Verkehrsamt, Kaiser-Ludwig-Pl., D–82488* ☎ *08822/3534*). **Garmisch-Partenkirchen** (✉ *Verkehrsamt der Kurverwaltung, Richard-Strauss-Pl. 2, D–82467* ☎ *08821/180–420* ⊕ *www.garmisch-partenkirchen.de*). **Mittenwald** (✉ *Kurverwaltung, Dammkarstr. 3, D–82481* ☎ *08823/33981* ⊕ *www.mittenwald.de*). **Oberammergau** (✉ *Verkehrsamt, Eugen-Papst-Str. 9a, D–82487* ☎ *08822/92310* 🖰 *08822/923–190* ⊕ *www.oberammergau.de*). **Rottach-Egern/Tegernsee** (✉ *Kuramt, Hauptstr. 2, D–83684* ☎ *08022/180–149* ⊕ *www.tegernsee.de*). **Tourismusverband München Oberbayern** (✉ *Bodenseestr. 113, D–81243 Munich* ☎ *089/829–2180* ⊕ *www.oberbayern-tourismus.de/*).

The Romantic Road

WORD OF MOUTH

". . . the highlight [of Würzburg] must certainly be the Residenz, a baroque castle built by Balthasar Neumann, which I found to be more beautiful than even Versailles. . . . If you want a high energy, lots of activity kind of holiday, I don't think Würzburg is for you. It's quite laid back, the kind of place for leisurely strolls around the old town."

—Mariannah

"Rothenburg . . . has more cameras per square foot than Disneyland USA. Many other towns and cities—Würzburg [and] Weikersheim among them—retain a more authentic atmosphere and a mostly German identity."

—Russ

Updated by
Uli Ehrhardt

OF ALL THE TOURIST ROUTES that crisscross Germany, none rivals the aptly named Romantische Strasse, or Romantic Road. The scenery is more pastoral than spectacular, but the route is memorable for the medieval towns, villages, castles, and churches that anchor its 355-km (220-mi) length. Many of these are tucked away beyond low hills, their spires and towers just visible through the greenery.

The road runs south from Würzburg, in northern Bavaria, to Füssen, on the border of Austria. You can, of course, follow it in the opposite direction, as a number of bus tours do. Either way, among the major sights you'll see are one of Europe's most scintillating baroque palaces, in Würzburg, and perhaps the best-preserved medieval town on the continent, Rothenburg-ob-der-Tauber. Then there's the handsome Renaissance city of Augsburg. Finally, the fantastical highlight will be Ludwig II's castle, Neuschwanstein.

The Romantic Road concept developed as West Germany rebuilt its tourist industry after World War II. A public-relations wizard coined the catchy title for a historic passage through Bavaria and Baden-Württemberg that could be advertised as a unit. In 1950 the Romantic Road was born. The name itself isn't meant to attract lovebirds but, rather, uses the word *romance* as meaning wonderful, fabulous, and imaginative. And, of course, the Romantic Road started as a road on which the Romans traveled.

Along the way, the road crosses centuries-old battlefields. The most cataclysmic conflict, the Thirty Years' War, destroyed the region's economic base in the 17th century. The depletion of resources prevented improvements that would have modernized the area—thereby assuring the survival of the historic towns' now charmingly quaint infrastructures.

EXPLORING THE ROMANTIC ROAD

The Romantic Road runs from the vineyard-hung slopes of the Main River valley at Würzburg to the snow-covered mountains overlooking Füssen in the Allgäuer Alps. For much of its route it follows two enchanting rivers, the Tauber and the Lech, and at one point crosses the great Danube, still a surprisingly narrow river this far from the end of its journey in the Black Sea. The city of Augsburg marks the natural halfway point of the Romantic Road. South of Augsburg, the road climbs gradually into the Alpine foothills, and the landscape changes from the lush green of Franconian river valleys to mountain-backed meadows and forests.

ABOUT THE RESTAURANTS

During peak season, restaurants along the Romantic Road tend to be crowded, especially in the larger towns. ■TIP➔ **You may want to plan your mealtimes around visits to smaller villages, where there are fewer people and the restaurants are pleasant.** The food will be more basic Franconian or Swabian, but it will also be generally less expensive than in the well-known towns. You may find that some of the small,

TOP REASONS TO GO

Würzburg's Baroque Masterpiece: When the prince-bishops decided after 450 years to descend from their lofty hilltop fortress into the city proper, they employed the best artists of their time, including Neumann and Tiepolo, to create the lavishly ostentatious Residenz palace.

An Overnight in a Medieval Town: Dodge the daytrippers by spending the night in Rothenburg-ob-der-Tauber. Patrol the city walls with the night watchman, explore the streets in the morning light (perfect for photos), then get out of town before the tour buses begin to arrive.

768 Steps: That's what it takes to reach the top platform of the highest church steeple in the world, but the incredible view from Ulm's Münster is worth the effort. On a clear day you can see the Austrian, German, and Swiss Alps in the distance, seventy miles away.

A Rococo Jewel: The opposite of Ulm's soaring Gothic cathedral is the Wieskirche, a name which means "church in the meadow." You get the most stunning views in the late afternoon, when the westering sun shines through the high windows, flooding the church with light and highlighting the details.

Neuschwanstein: Walt Disney may have spread the word about this castle, but the sight of the original, rising up against its theatrical backdrop of green mountainside, speaks for itself.

family-run restaurants close around 2 PM, or whenever the last lunch guests have left, and open again at 5 or 5:30 PM. Some serve cold cuts or coffee and cake during that time, but no hot food.

ABOUT THE HOTELS
With a few exceptions, the Romantic Road hotels are quiet and rustic, and you'll find high standards of comfort and cleanliness. If you plan to stay in one of the bigger hotels in the off-season, do ask for weekend rates. Make reservations as far in advance as possible if you plan to visit in summer. Hotels in Würzburg, Rothenburg, and Füssen are often full year-round. Augsburg hotels are in great demand during trade fairs in nearby Munich. Tourist information offices can usually help with accommodations, especially if you arrive early in the day.

WHAT IT COSTS IN EUROS					
	¢	$	$$	$$$	$$$$
RESTAURANTS	under €9	€9–€15	€16–€20	€21–€25	over €25
HOTELS	under €50	€50–€100	€101–€175	€176–€225	over €225

Restaurant prices are per person for a main course at dinner. Hotel prices are for two people in a standard double room, including tax and service.

TIMING
Late summer and early autumn are the best times to travel the Romantic Road, when the grapes ripen on the vines around Würzburg and the geraniums run riot on the medieval walls of towns such as Rothenburg

and Dinkelsbühl. You'll also miss the high-season summer crush of tourists. Otherwise, consider visiting the region in the depths of December, when Christmas markets pack the ancient squares of the Romantic Road towns and snow gives turreted Schloss Neuschwanstein a final magic touch.

NORTHERN ROMANTIC ROAD

The northern section of the Romantic Road skirts the wild, open countryside of the Spessart uplands before heading south through the plains of Swabia and along the lovely Tauber and Lech rivers.

WÜRZBURG

115 km (71 mi) east of Frankfurt.

The baroque city of Würzburg, the pearl of the Romantic Road, is a heady example of what happens when great genius teams up with great wealth. Beginning in the 10th century, Würzburg was ruled by powerful (and rich) prince-bishops, who created the city with all the remarkable attributes you see today.

The city is at the junction of two age-old trade routes in a calm valley backed by vineyard-covered hills. Festung Marienberg, a fortified castle on the steep hill across the Main River, overlooks the town. Constructed between 1200 and 1600, the fortress was the residence of the prince-bishops for 450 years.

Present-day Würzburg is by no means completely original. On March 16, 1945, seven weeks before Germany capitulated, Würzburg was all but obliterated by Allied saturation bombing. The 20-minute raid destroyed 87% of the city and killed at least 4,000 people. Reconstruction has returned most of the city's famous sights to their former splendor. Except for some buildings with modern shops, it remains a largely authentic restoration.

TIMING   You need two days to do full justice to Würzburg. The Residenz alone demands several hours of attention. If time is short, head for the Residenz as the doors open in the morning, before the first crowds assemble, and aim to complete your tour by lunchtime. Then continue to the nearby Juliusspital Weinstuben or one of the many traditional taverns in the area for lunch. In the afternoon explore central Würzburg. Next morning cross the Main River to visit the Festung Marienberg along with the Mainfränkisches Museum and the Fürstenbaumuseum.

MAIN ATTRACTIONS

12 **Alte Mainbrücke** *(Old Main Bridge).* Construction on this ancient structure, which crosses the Main River, began in 1473. Twin rows of infinitely graceful statues of saints line the bridge. They were placed here in 1730, at the height of Würzburg's baroque period. Note the *Patronna Franconiae* (commonly known as the Weeping Madonna). There's a beautiful view of the Marienberg Fortress from the bridge.

GREAT ITINERARIES

Würzburg and Augsburg are each worth two or three days of exploration, and such attractions as the minster of Ulm are time-consuming but rewarding diversions from the recognized Romantic Road.

Numbers in the text correspond to numbers in the margin and on the maps in this chapter.

IF YOU HAVE 3 DAYS: NORTH

Spend the first day in **Würzburg ❶–⓮**, strolling through the streets and enjoying the splendor of the city. The next morning, stop in **Bad Mergentheim ⓯**, once the home of the Teutonic Knights. Next, visit the castle of the counts of Hohenlohe in **Weikersheim ⓰**. Continue east to **Creglingen ⓱**, where you can admire the Tilman Riemenschneider altar in the **Herrgottskirche ⓲**. Continue toward **Rothenburg-ob-der-Tauber ⓳–㉖** for an overnight. Spend your final day in **Nördlingen ㉘** and **Augsburg ㉛–㊸**.

IF YOU HAVE 3 DAYS: SOUTH

Start your explorations with an overnight in **Rothenburg-ob-der-Tauber ⓳–㉖**. In the morning, make your way to **Nördlingen ㉘** and

Augsburg ㉛–㊸. Next morning continue south to the Wieskirche. Spend the night in 🚇 **Füssen ㊹**, and use your last day for a day trip to **Neuschwanstein and Hohenschwangau ㊸**.

IF YOU HAVE 5 DAYS

Tackle the entire length of the Romantic Road by just hitting the highlights: spend a night and day in 🚇 **Würzburg ❶–⓮**, with all its baroque splendor. The next afternoon, head south toward **Bad Mergentheim ⓯**, making a short stop before continuing on to 🚇 **Rothenburg-ob-der-Tauber ⓳–㉖**. Try to arrive in the evening, when the tour buses have left. Spend the evening roaming the streets, and the next morning look at the highlights. Spend the rest of the day exploring the towns of **Dinkelsbühl ㉗**, **Nördlingen ㉘**, and 🚇 **Augsburg ㉛–㊸**. The next morning, continue south toward 🚇 **Füssen ㊹**, first taking a detour at the small town of Steingaden, which has signs leading to the rococo Wieskirche. Spend your last nights in Füssen while you explore **Neuschwanstein and Hohenschwangau ㊸** during the day.

❾ **Dom St. Kilian** *(St. Kilian Basilica)*. Würzburg's Romanesque cathedral, the fourth largest of its kind in Germany, was begun in 1045. Step inside and you'll find yourself in a shimmering rococo treasure house. Prince-Bishop von Schönborn is buried here. His tomb is the work of his architect and builder Balthasar Neumann. Tilman Riemenschneider carved the tombstones of two other bishops buried at the cathedral. ✉ *Paradepl., south end of Schönbornstr.* ☎ *0931/321–1830* 🚇 *Tour* €2.50 ☉ *Easter–Oct., daily 8–6; Nov.–Easter, daily 8–noon and 2–6; guided tours May–Oct., Mon.–Sat. at 12:20, Sun. at 12:30.*

⓮ **Festung Marienberg** *(Marienberg Fortress)*. This complex was the original home of the prince-bishops, beginning in the 13th century. The oldest buildings—note especially the **Marienkirche** (Church of the Virgin Mary)—date from around 700, although excavations have disclosed

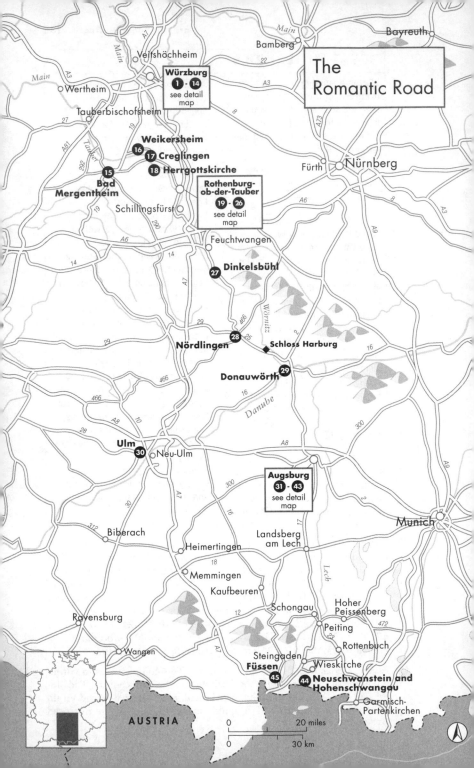

The
Romantic Road

Main · Bamberg · Bayreuth

Veitshöchheim

Würzburg
1 · **14**
see detail
map

Wertheim

Tauberbischofsheim

Weikersheim

16 **17** Creglingen

18 Herrgottskirche

Bad
Mergentheim **15**

Schillingsfürst

Rothenburg-
ob-der-Tauber
19 · **26**
see detail
map

Fürth · Nürnberg

Feuchtwangen

27 Dinkelsbühl

Wörnitz

28
Nördlingen **25** ◆ Schloss Harburg

Donauwörth **29**

Danube

Ulm **30**
Neu-Ulm

Augsburg
31 · **43**
see detail
map

Munich

Biberach

Heimertingen

Landsberg
am Lech

Lech

Memmingen

Kaufbeuren

Ravensburg

Schongau

Hoher
Peissenberg

Peiting

Rottenbuch

Wangen

Steingaden
Füssen
45

Wieskirche

44 **Neuschwanstein and**
Hohenschwangau

Garmisch-
Partenkirchen

AUSTRIA

0   20 miles

0   30 km

evidence that there was a settlement here in the Iron Age, 3,000 years ago. In addition to the rough-hewn medieval fortifications, there are a number of Renaissance and baroque apartments. ■TIP→ **To reach the hilltop Marienberg, you can make the fairly stiff climb on foot through vineyards or take bus number 9, starting at the Residenz, with several stops in the city.** It runs about every 40 minutes from April to October.

★ The highlight is the remarkable collection of art treasures in the **Mainfränkisches Museum** (*Main-Franconian Museum* ☎0931/205–940 ⊕*www.mainfraenkisches-museum. de* ☖€4 ☉*Apr.–Oct., Tues.–Sun. 10–5; Nov.–Mar., Tues.–Sun. 10–4*), which traces the city's rich and varied history. Be sure to visit the gallery devoted to Würzburg-born sculptor Tilman Riemenschneider, who lived from the late 15th to the early 16th century. Also on view are paintings by Tiepolo and Cranach the Elder, as well as exhibits of porcelain, firearms, antique toys, and ancient Greek and Roman art. Other exhibits include enormous old winepresses and exhibits about the history of Franconian wine making. From April through October, tours around the fortress are offered for €2 per person, starting from the Scherenberg Tor. The Marienberg collections are so vast that they spill over into another outstanding museum that is part of the fortress, the **Fürstenbaumuseum** (*Princes' Quarters Museum*), which traces 1,200 years of Würzburg's history. The holdings include breathtaking exhibits of local goldsmiths' art. ☖*Combined ticket for Mainfränkisches and Fürstenbau museums €5* ☉*Apr.–Oct., Tues.–Sun. 10–5.*

➍ **Juliusspital.** Founded in 1576 by Prince-Bishop Julius Echter as a home for the poor, the elderly, and the sick, this enormous edifice now houses an impressive restaurant serving wine from the institution's own vineyards. It also sells wineglasses. All profits from the restaurant are used to run the adjacent home for the elderly. ■TIP→ **A glass of wine is included in a weekly tour of the wine cellars.** ☒*Juliuspromenade 19* ☎*0931/393–1400* ☖*Tour €5* ☉*Daily 10 AM–midnight.*

➐ **Residenz** (*Residence*). The line of Würzburg's prince-bishops lived in this glorious baroque palace after moving down from the hilltop Festung Marienberg. Construction started in 1719 under the brilliant direction of Balthasar Neumann. Most of the interior decoration was entrusted to the Italian stuccoist Antonio Bossi and the Venetian painter Giovanni Battista Tiepolo. It's the spirit of the pleasure-loving prince-bishop

FodorsChoice
★

TOURING TIPS

Information: The city tourist office is in the Haus zum Falken on Marktplatz. They have a handy English-language tour map marked with a route through the Old Town.

Scenic Spots: From the Alte Mainbrücke (Old Main Bridge), you can look back at parts of the Old Town behind you or take in the spectacular view of the Marienberg Fortress up on the hill before you.

Scenic Spots: Take the wide view of the river and Würzburg from a vantage point high in Marienberg Fortress.

3

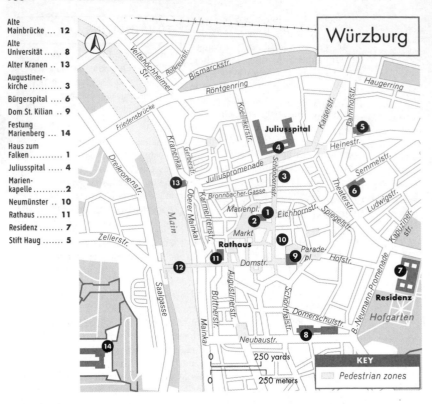

Johann Philipp Franz von Schönborn, however, that infuses the Residenz. Now considered one of Europe's most sumptuous palaces, this dazzling structure is a 10-minute walk from the railway station, along pedestrians-only Kaiserstrasse and then Theaterstrasse.

As you enter the building, the largest baroque staircase in the country, the **Treppenhaus,** greets you. Halfway up, the stairway splits and peels away 180 degrees to the left and to the right. Soaring above on the vaulting is Tiepolo's giant fresco *The Four Continents,* a gorgeous exercise in blue and pink, with allegorical figures at the corners representing the four continents known at the time (take a careful look at the elephant's trunk). Tiepolo immortalized himself and Balthasar Neumann as two of the figures—they're not too difficult to spot.
■ **TIP→** The fresco, which survived a devastating wartime bombing raid, is being restored bit by bit, so don't be surprised to find a small section covered by scaffolding.

Next, make your way to the **Weissersaal** (White Room) and then beyond to the grandest of the state rooms, the **Kaisersaal** (Throne Room). Tiepolo's frescoes show the 12th-century visit of Emperor Frederick Barbarossa, when he came to Würzburg to claim his bride. If you take part in the guided tour, you'll also see private chambers of

CLOSE UP

Germany's Master Sculptor

Tilman Riemenschneider, Germany's master of late-Gothic sculpture (1460–1531), lived an extraordinary life. His skill with wood and stone was recognized at an early age, and he soon presided over a major Würzburg workshop. Riemenschneider worked alone, however, on the life-size figures that dominate his sculptures. Details such as the folds of a robe or wrinkles upon a face highlight his grace and harmony of line.

At the height of his career Riemenschneider was appointed city counselor; later he became mayor of Würzburg. In 1523, however, he made the fateful error of siding with the small farmers and guild members in the Peasants' War. He was arrested and held for eight weeks in the dungeons of the Marienberg Fortress, above Würzburg, where he was frequently tortured. Most of his wealth was confiscated, and he returned home a broken man. He died in 1531.

For nearly three centuries he and his sculptures were all but forgotten. Only in 1822, when ditchdiggers uncovered the site of his grave, was Riemenschneider once again included among Germany's greatest artists. Today Riemenschneider is recognized as the giant of German sculpture. The richest collection of his works is in Würzburg, although other masterpieces are on view in churches and museums along the Romantic Road and in other parts of Germany. The renowned *Windsheim Altar of the Twelve Apostles* is in the Palatine Museum in Heidelberg.

the various former residents (guided tours in English are given daily at 11 and 3).

The **Hofkirche** demonstrates the prince-bishops' love of ostentation. Among the lavish marble, rich gilding, and delicate stuccowork, note the Tiepolo altarpieces, ethereal visions of *The Fall of the Angels* and *The Assumption of the Virgin*. Finally, tour the **Hofgarten**; the entrance is next to the chapel. The 18th-century formal garden has stately gushing fountains and trim ankle-high shrubs outlining geometric flower beds and gravel walks. ⊠ *Residenzpl.* ☏ *0931/355–170* ⊕ *www.residenz-wuerzburg.de* ⊠ *€5, including guided tour* ⊙ *Apr.–Oct., daily 9–5:30; Nov.–Mar., daily 10–4.*

ALSO WORTH SEEING

❽ Alte Universität *(Old University)*. Founded by Prince-Bishop Julius Echter and built in 1582, this rambling institution is one of Würzburg's most interesting Renaissance structures. ⊠ *Neubaustr. 1–9.*

⓭ Alter Kranen *(Old Crane)*. Near the Main River and north of the Old Main Bridge, the crane was erected in 1772–73 by Balthasar Neumann's son, Franz Ignaz Michael. It was used to unload boats; beside it is the old customs building.

❸ Augustinerkirche *(Church of St. Augustine)*. This baroque church, a work by Balthasar Neumann, was a 13th-century Dominican chapel. Neumann retained the soaring, graceful choir and commissioned Antonio Bossi to add colorful stuccowork to the rest of the church. ⊠ *Dominikanerpl. 2* ☏ *0931/30970* ⊙ *Daily 7–6.*

6 Bürgerspital (*Almshouse*). Wealthy burghers founded this refuge for the city's poor and needy in 1319; it now sells wine. The arcade courtyard is baroque in style. ■TIP→ From mid-March through October there's a weekly tour (Saturday at 2), which includes a glass of wine. ⊠*Theaterstr. 19* ☎*0931/35030* ⊕*www.buergerspital.de* ⊠*Tour €6.*

1 Haus zum Falken. The city's most splendid baroque mansion, formerly a humble inn, now houses the city tourist office. Its colorful rococo facade was added in 1751. ⊠*Am Marktpl. 9* ☎*0931/372—335* ⊙*Jan.–Mar., weekdays 10–4, Sat. 10–1; Apr.–Dec., weekdays 10–6, Sat.10–2; May–Oct., Sun. and holidays 10–2.*

2 Marienkapelle (*St. Mary's Chapel*). This tranquil Gothic church (1377–1480) tucked modestly away at one end of Würzburg's market square is almost lost amid the historic old facades. Balthasar Neumann lies buried here. ⊠*Marktpl.* ☎*0931/321–1830* ⊙*Daily 8–6.*

10 Neumünster (*New Minster*). Next to the Dom St. Kilian, this 11th-century Romanesque basilica was completed in 1716. The original church was built above the grave of the early Irish martyr St. Kilian, who brought Christianity to Würzburg and, with two companions, was put to death here in 689. Their missionary zeal bore fruit, however—17 years after their death a church was consecrated in their memory. By 742 Würzburg had become a diocese, and over the following centuries 39 flourishing churches were established throughout the city. ⊠*Schönbornstr.* ☎*0931/321–1830* ⊙*Daily 8–5.*

11 Rathaus. The Gothic town hall, once headquarters of the bishop's administrator, has been the center of municipal government since 1316. A permanent exhibition in the tower documents Würzburg's destruction by Allied bombs, some examples of which are on display. ⊠*Marktpl.* ☎*0931/370* ⊠*Free* ⊙*Weekdays 9–5, information only; tours May–Oct., Sat. at 11.*

5 Stift Haug. Franconia's first baroque church, designed by the Italian architect Antonio Petrini, was built between 1670 and 1691. Its elegant twin spires and central cupola make an impressive exterior. The altarpiece is a 1583 Crucifixion scene by Tintoretto. ⊠*Bahnhofstr. at Heinestr.* ☎*0931/54102* ⊙*Daily 8–6:30.*

WHERE TO STAY & EAT

$–$$$ ✕**Ratskeller.** The vaulted cellars of Würzburg's Rathaus shelter one of the city's most popular restaurants. Beer is served, but Franconian wine is what the regulars drink. The food is staunch Franconian fare. ⊠*Beim Grafeneckart, Langg. 1* ☎*0931/13021* ⊟*AE, DC, MC, V.*

¢–$$$ ✕**Wein- und Speisehaus zum Stachel.** On a warm spring or summer day
★ take a bench in the ancient courtyard of the Stachel, which is shaded by a canopy of vine leaves and enclosed by tall, ivy-covered walls. The entrées are satisfyingly Franconian, from lightly baked onion cake in season to hearty roast pork, and the atmosphere is satisfyingly unstuffy. ⊠*Gresseng. 1* ☎*0931/52770* ⊟*No credit cards.*

¢–$$ ✕**Backöfele.** More than 400 years of tradition are sustained by this old
Fodor'sChoice tavern. Hidden away behind huge wooden doors in a backstreet, the
★ Backöfele's cavelike interior is a popular meeting and eating place for

regulars and newcomers alike. The surprisingly varied menu includes local favorites such as suckling pig and marinated pot roast as well as some good fish. ⊠ *Ursulinerg. 2, D–97070* ☏*0931/59059* ⊟*MC, V.*

¢–$$ ✕ **Juliusspital Weinstuben.** This tavern serves wine from its own vineyard and good portions of basic Franconian fare. ■**TIP→ In summer you can enjoy your food and drinks on a quiet terrace in the courtyard.** ⊠ *Julius-promenade 19* ☏*0931/54080* ⊟*MC, V.*

$$–$$$ ✕⊡ **Hotel Greifensteiner Hof.** The modern Greifensteiner offers comfort-
★ able, individually furnished rooms in a quiet corner of the city, just off the market square. ■**TIP→ The cheaper doubles are small but lack no comforts or facilities.** The Fränkische Stuben (¢–$) has excellent cui-sine—mostly Franconian specialties. ⊠ *Dettelbacherg. 2, D–97070* ☏*0931/35170* 🖷*0931/57057* ⊕*www.greifensteiner-hof.de* ⤳*49 rooms* ⌂*In-room: no a/c (some), safe (some), Wi-Fi. In-hotel: 2 res-taurants, bar, public Wi-Fi, parking (fee), some pets allowed (fee), no-smoking rooms* ⊟*AE, DC, MC, V.*

$$ ✕⊡ **Hotel Walfisch.** Guest rooms are furnished in solid Franconian style with farmhouse cupboards, bright fabrics, and heavy drapes. You'll breakfast in a dining room on the bank of the Main with views of the vineyard-covered Marienberg. For lunch and dinner try the hotel's cozy Walfisch-Stube restaurant ($–$$). They don't serve their namesake (*Walfisch* means "whale"), but they do have other excellent fish as well as a good selection of white wines. ⊠ *Am Pleidenturm 5, D–97070* ☏*0931/35200* 🖷*0931/352–0500* ⊕*www.hotel-walfisch.com* ⤳*40 rooms* ⌂*In-room: safe (some), no a/c (some), Wi-Fi. In-hotel: restau-rant, public Wi-Fi, parking (fee), no-smoking rooms* ⊟*AE, DC, MC, V* ⊺⊚*CP.*

$$ ✕⊡ **Hotel Zur Stadt Mainz.** This traditional Franconian inn dates from the early 15th century. The cuisine (¢–$$$) is based on its own his-toric recipe book. Eel from the Main River and locally caught carp and pike are specialties. Homemade apple strudel is served with after-noon coffee; the breakfast buffet is enormous. Rooms are comfortably furnished, with old-fashioned touches such as gilt mirrors and heavy drapes. ⊠ *Semmelstr. 39, D–97070* ☏*0931/53155* 🖷*0931/58510* ⊕*www.hotel-stadtmainz.de* ⤳*15 rooms* ⌂*In-room: no a/c. In-hotel: restaurant, no elevator* ⊟*AE, MC, V* ⊙*Closed first 2 wks in Jan. No dinner Sun.* ⊺⊚*CP.*

$–$$ ✕⊡ **Ringhotel Wittelsbacher Höh.** Most of the cozy rooms in this historic redbrick mansion offer views of Würzburg and the vineyards. The res-taurant's wine list embraces most of the leading local vintages, and Fran-conian and Italian dishes ($–$$) pack the menu. In summer take a table on the terrace and soak up the view. ⊠ *Hexenbruchweg 10, D–97082* ☏*0931/453–040* 🖷*0931/415–458* ⊕*www.wuerzburg-hotel.de* ⤳*73 rooms, 1 suite* ⌂*In-room: no a/c, Wi-Fi. In-hotel: restaurant, public Wi-Fi, parking, some pets allowed (fee), no smoking rooms* ⊟*AE, DC, MC, V* ⊺⊚*CP.*

$–$$ ⊡ **Strauss.** Close to the river and the pedestrians-only center, the pink-stucco Strauss has been in the same family for more than 100 years. Rooms are simply furnished in light woods. The beamed restaurant Würtzburg serves Franconian cuisine. ✉*Juliuspromenade 5, D–97070* ☎*0931/30570* 🖷*0931/305–7555* ⊕*www.hotel-strauss.de* ➽*75 rooms, 3 suites* ⚿*In-room: no a/c, safe (some), Wi-Fi. In-hotel: restaurant, public Wi-Fi, parking (fee), some pets allowed (fee), no smoking rooms* ▤*AE, DC, MC, V* ⊘*Restaurant closed Tue., late Dec.–end Jan.*

$ 🛏**Spehnkuch.** What was once a large apartment with high-ceiling rooms is today a small, spotlessly clean, very price-worthy pension. It's just opposite the main railway station. ■**TIP➔ The only possible drawback is that the shower and toilet are located down the hall.** ✉*Röntgenstr. 7, D–97070* ☎*0931/54752* 🖷*0931/54760* ➽*7 rooms* ⚿*In-room: no a/c, no phone, no TV. In-hotel: no elevator* ▤*No credit cards* ⊘*Closed first week in Jan.* ꭥ❘*CP.*

FESTIVALS

Würzburg's cultural year starts with the International Film Weekend in January and ends with a Johann Sebastian Bach Festival in November. The annual jazz festival is also in November. Its annual Mozart Festival, **Mozartfest** (✉*Oeggstr. 2* ☎*0931/372–336* ⊕*www.mozart-fest-wuerzburg.de*), between May and June, attracts visitors from all over the world. Most concerts are held in the magnificent setting of the Residenz. The town hosts a series of wine festivals, such as the **Hofkeller Würzburg** (✉*Residenzpl. 3* ☎*0931/305–0931* ⊕*www.hofkeller.de*), the last week in June. For a list of festivities and more information, contact **Tourismus Würzburg** (✉*Am Congress Zentrum* ☎*0931/372–335* ⊕*www.wuerzburg.de*). **Mainfranken Theater Würzburg** (✉*Theaterstr. 21* ☎*0931/390–8124* ⊕*www.theaterwuerzburg.de*) also has information.

SPORTS & THE OUTDOORS

Wine lovers and hikers should visit the **Stein-Wein-Pfad**, a (signposted) trail through the vineyards that rises up from the northwest edge of Würzburg. A two-hour round-trip affords stunning views of the city as well as the chance to try the excellent local wines directly at the source. The starting point for the walk is the vineyard of **Weingut am Stein, Ludwig Knoll** (✉*Mittlerer Steinbergweg 5* ☎*0931/25808* ⊕*www.weingut-am-stein.de*), 10 minutes on foot from the main railway station.

SHOPPING

Würzburg is the true wine center of the Romantic Road. Visit any of the vineyards that rise from the Main River and choose a *Bocksbeutel*, the distinctive green, flagon-shape wine bottle of Franconia. It's claimed that the shape came about because wine-guzzling monks found it the easiest to hide under their robes. The **Haus des Frankenweins** (*House of Franconian Wine* ✉*Kranenkai 1* ☎*0931/390–110*) has wine tastings for individual visitors. Some 100 Franconian wines and a wide range of wine accessories are sold.

Die Murmel (✉*Augustinerstr. 7* ☎*0931/59349*) is the place to go if you're looking for a special toy. **Ebinger** (✉*Karmelitenstr. 23* ☎*0931/59449*) sells fine antique jewelry, clocks, watches, and silver. At the **Eckhaus** (✉*Langg. 8, off the Marktpl.* ☎*0931/12001*) you'll find high-quality

EATING WELL ON THE ROMANTIC ROAD

To sample the authentic food of this area, venture off the beaten track of the official Romantic Road into any small town with a nice-looking Gasthof. Order *Rinderbraten* (roast beef) with spaetzle (small boiled ribbons of rolled dough), or try *Maultaschen* (oversized Swabian ravioli), another typical regional dish.

Franconia (including Würzburg) is the sixth-largest wine-producing area of Germany. Franconian wines—half of which are Müller-Thurgau, a blending of Riesling and Sylvaner—are served in distinctive green, flagon-shape wine bottles. Riesling and red wines account for only about 5% of the total production of the Franconia wines.

Travel south on the Romantic Road from Würzburg, and you enter beer country. There is a wide range of Franconian and Bavarian brews available from *Räucherbier* (literally, "smoked beer") to the lighter ales of Augsburg. If this is your first time in Germany, beware of the potency of German beer. Even the regular ones are much stronger than the normal American brew. If you want a light beer, in most parts of Germany you ask for "Export"; a small one will be 0.3 liters, a big one 0.5 liters. In most beer tents you will be only served a Stein with one liter.

gifts. In summer the selection consists mostly of garden and terrace decorations; from October through December the store is filled with delightful Christmas ornaments and candles.

EN ROUTE

From Würzburg, follow the Romantic Road through Bavarian Franconia and Swabia and into the mountains of Upper Bavaria. For the first stretch, to Bad Mergentheim, B–19 takes you through the open countryside of the Hohenloher Plain.

BAD MERGENTHEIM

⑮ *38 km (23 mi) south of Würzburg.*

Between 1525 and 1809 Bad Mergentheim was the home of the Teutonic Knights, one of the most successful medieval orders of chivalry. In 1809 Napoléon expelled them as he marched toward his ultimately disastrous Russian campaign. The expulsion seemed to sound the death knell of the little town, but in 1826 a shepherd discovered mineral springs on the north bank of the river. They proved to be the strongest sodium sulfate and bitter saltwaters in Europe, with health-giving properties that ensured the town's future prosperity.

The **Deutschordensschloss,** the Teutonic Knights' former castle, at the eastern end of the town, has a museum that follows the history of the order. ⊠*Schloss 16* ☎*07931/52212* ⊕*www.deutschordensmuseum. de* 🖾*€4, guided tour €2* ۞*Apr.–Oct., Tues.–Sun. 11–5, tours Thurs. and Sun. at 3; Nov.–Mar., Tues.–Sun. 2–5.*

☪ The **Wildpark Bad Mergentheim,** a few miles outside Bad Mergentheim, is a wildlife park with Europe's largest selection of European species, including wolves and bears. ✉*B–290* ☎*07931/41344* ⊕*www.wild-tierpark.de* ⌚*€8* ⊙*Mid-Mar.–Oct., daily 9–6; Nov.–mid-Mar., week-ends 10:30–4.*

WHERE TO STAY & EAT

¢–$ ✕**Klotzbücher.** You can order 10 different kinds of beer—four from the tap—at the long wooden bar in this renovated Franconian brewery tavern. In the other room, paneled with dark wood, you can have the obligatory bratwurst at heavy wooden tables. In summer, head for the beer garden. ✉*Boxbergerstr. 6* ☎*07931/562–928* ▭*No credit cards* ⊙*Closed Wed.*

$$ ✕▥**Hotel Victoria.** An elegant lounge, complete with library and open fireplace, greets you as you enter this hotel. The restaurant Zirbelstube ($$–$$$$, dinner only) is known as one of the best in the region. In the Vinothek ($–$$), open all day, you can eat at the bar and watch the chefs prepare your next dish behind a huge glass partition. The hotel very conveniently has its own wineshop. ✉*Poststr. 2–4, D–97980* ☎*07931/5930* 🖶*07931/593–500* ⊕*www.victoria-hotel.de* ⇆*44 rooms, 4 suites* ⌂*In-room: no a/c, Wi-Fi (some). In-hotel: 2 restaurants, bar, public Wi-Fi, parking (fee), no-smoking rooms* ▭*AE, DC, MC, V* ⊙*Restaurant Zirbelstube closed Jan.–Feb.15, July 15–Aug., and Sun.* ⍾*CP.*

WEIKERSHEIM

⑯ *10 km (6 mi) east of Bad Mergentheim, 40 km (25 mi) south of Würzburg.*

The Tauber River town of Weikersheim is dominated by the **castle** of the counts of Hohenlohe. Its great hall is the scene each summer of an international youth music festival. The **Rittersaal** (Knights' Hall) contains life-size stucco wall sculptures of animals, reflecting the counts' love of hunting. In the cellars you can drink a glass of wine drawn from the huge casks that seem to prop up the building. Outside, stroll through the gardens and enjoy the view of the Tauber River. ⌚*€5, gardens only €2.50* ⊙*Apr.–Oct., daily 9–6; Nov.–Mar., daily 10–noon and 1–5.*

WHERE TO STAY & EAT

$–$$ ✕▥**Flair Hotel Laurentius.** This hotel is set in the row of houses on
★   the market square, dominated by the church on the one end and the entrance to the castle on the other. The vaulted ground floor of the Hotel Laurentius has a wine tavern as well as a very good restaurant ($–$$$; dinner only). The bistro (¢–$$), serving more regional food, is open all day every day. The rooms are comfortable. On the top floor are two exquisite junior suites with whirlpool tubs and big flat-screen TVs; one has a balcony and a view into the castle gardens. ■**TIP→ From the bistro terrace a door leads into a small regional farmers' market with excellent wines.** ✉*Marktpl. 5, D–97990* ☎*07934/91080* 🖶*07934/910–818* ⊕*www.hotel-laurentius.de* ⇆*13 rooms* ⌂*In-room: no a/c, Ethernet (some). In-hotel: 2 restaurants, bar, public Wi-Fi* ▭*AE, MC, V* ⊙*Restaurant closed Mon. and Tues.* ⍾*CP.*

CREGLINGEN

⑰ *20 km (12 mi) east of Weikersheim, 40 km (25 mi) south of Würzburg.*

The village of Creglingen has been an important pilgrimage site since the 14th century, when a farmer plowing his field had a vision of a heavenly host.

⑱
★ The **Herrgottskirche** *(Chapel of Our Lord)* is in the Herrgottstal (Valley of the Lord), 3 km (2 mi) south of Creglingen; the way there is well signposted. The chapel was built by the counts of Hohenlohe on the exact spot where the farmer had his vision, and in the early 16th century Riemenschneider carved an altarpiece for it. This enormous work, 33 feet high, depicts in minute detail the life and ascension of the Virgin Mary. Riemenschneider entrusted much of the background detail to the craftsmen of his Würzburg workshop, but he allowed no one but himself to attempt its life-size figures. Its intricate detail and attenuated figures are a high point of late-Gothic sculpture. ☎07933/508 ✆€2 ⊙*Apr.–Oct., daily 9:15–5:30; Nov.–Dec. and Feb.–Mar., Tues.–Sun. noon–4.*

The **Fingerhutmuseum** is opposite the Herrgottskirche. *Fingerhut* is German for "thimble," and this delightful, privately run museum has thousands of them, some dating from Roman times. ☎07933/370 ⊕*www. fingerhutmuseum.de* ✆€1.50 ⊙*Apr.–Oct., daily 10–noon and 2–5; Nov. and Mar., Tues.–Sun. 1–4.*

WHERE TO STAY

¢
⊛ ☒**Heuhotel Ferienbauernhof.** For a truly off-the-beaten-track experience, book a space in the hayloft of the Stahl family's farm in a suburb of Creglingen. Guests bed down in freshly turned hay in the farmhouse granary. Bed linen and blankets are provided. The overnight rate of €18 includes a cold supper and breakfast. For €44 you can swap the granary for one of three double rooms or even an apartment. ■**TIP→Children are particularly well catered to, with tours of the farmyard and their own playground.** ☒*Frauental-Weidenhof 1, D–97993* ☎07933/378 ☎07933/7515 ⊕*www.ferienpension-heuhotel.de* ⚙*In-room: no a/c, no TV. In-hotel: bicycles, no elevator, no-smoking rooms* ⊟*No credit cards* ☒CP.

ROTHENBURG-OB-DER-TAUBER

Fodor's Choice
★ *20 km (12 mi) southeast of Creglingen, 75 km (47 mi) west of Nürnberg.*

Rothenburg-ob-der-Tauber (literally, "red castle on the Tauber") is the kind of medieval town that even Walt Disney might have thought too picturesque to be true, with half-timber architecture galore and a wealth of fountains and flowers against a backdrop of towers and turrets. As late as the 17th century it was a small but thriving market town that had grown up around the ruins of two 12th-century churches destroyed by an earthquake. Then it was laid low economically by the

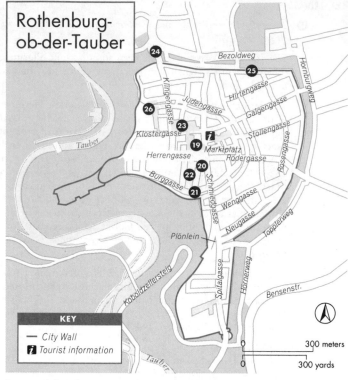

Rothenburg-
ob-der-Tauber

KEY
— *City Wall*
i *Tourist information*

300 meters
300 yards

havoc of the Thirty Years' War, and with its economic base devastated, the town slumbered until modern tourism rediscovered it. It's undoubtedly something of a tourist trap but genuine enough for all the hype.

There really is no place quite like it. Whether Rothenburg is at its most appealing in summer, when the balconies of its ancient houses are festooned with flowers, or in winter, when snow lies on its steep gables, is a matter of taste. Few people are likely to find this extraordinary little survivor from another age anything short of remarkable.

TIMING   Sights are dotted around town, and the streets don't lend themselves to a particular route. Be aware that crowds will affect the pace at which you can tour the town. Early morning is the only time to appreciate the place in relative calm. The best times to see the mechanical figures on the Rathaus wall are in the evening, at 8, 9, or 10.

WHAT TO SEE

20 **Herterichbrunnen** (*Herterich Fountain*). A *Schäfertanz* (Shepherds' Dance) was performed around the ornate Renaissance fountain on the central Marktplatz whenever Rothenburg celebrated a major event. The dance is still done, though it's now for the benefit of tourists. It takes place in front of the Rathaus several times a year, chiefly at Easter, on Whitsunday, and in September. ⊠*Marktpl..*

㉑ Mittelalterliches Kriminalmuseum *(Medieval Criminal Museum)*. The gruesome medieval implements of torture on display here are not for the fainthearted. The museum, the largest of its kind in Europe, also soberly documents the history of German legal processes in the Middle Ages. ✉ *Burgg. 3* ☎ *09861/5359* ⊕ *www.kriminalmuseum.rothenburg.de* 💲 *€4* ⊙ *Apr.–Oct., daily 9:30–6; Nov., Jan., and Feb., daily 2–4; Dec. and Mar., daily 10–4.*

㉒ Puppen und Spielzeugmuseum *(Doll and Toy Museum)*. This complex ⟳ of medieval and baroque buildings houses more than 1,000 dolls, the oldest dating from 1780, the newest from 1940, as well as a collection of dollhouses, model shops, and theaters guaranteed to charm every youngster. ✉ *Hofbronneng. 13* ☎ *09861/7330* 💲 *€4* ⊙ *Jan. and Feb., daily 11–5; Mar.–Dec., daily 9:30–6.*

㉙ Rathaus. Half of the town hall is Gothic, begun in 1240; the other half is neoclassical, started in 1572. Below the building are the **Historiengewölbe** (*Historic Vaults* 💲 *€2* ⊙ *Apr.–Oct., daily 9:30–5:30; Christmas market season, daily 1–4*), housing a museum that concentrates on the Thirty Years' War.

Tales of the *Meistertrunk* (Master Drink) and a mighty civil servant are still told in Rothenburg. The story originates from 1631, when the Protestant town was captured by Catholic forces during the Thirty Years' War. During the victory celebrations, the conquering general was embarrassed to find himself unable to drink a great tankard of wine in one go, as his manhood demanded. He volunteered to spare the town further destruction if any of the city councillors could drain the mighty 6-pint draft. The mayor took up the challenge and succeeded, and Rothenburg was preserved. The tankard itself is on display at the Reichsstadtmuseum. On the north side of the main square is a fine clock, placed there 50 years after the mayor's feat. A mechanical figure acts out the epic Master Drink daily on the hour from 11 to 3 and in the evening at 8, 9, and 10. The feat is also celebrated at two annual pageants, when townsfolk parade through the streets in 17th-century garb. The Rathaus tower offers a good view of the town. ✉ *Rathauspl.*

㉖ Reichsstadtmuseum *(Imperial City Museum)*. This city museum is two attractions in one. Its artifacts illustrate Rothenburg and its history. Among them is the great tankard, or *Pokal*, of the Meistertrunk. The setting of the museum is the other attraction; it's in a former Dominican convent, the oldest parts of which date from the 13th century. Tour the building to see the

TOURING TIPS

Information: The tourist office on the central Marktplatz has maps and information in many languages.

Scenic Spots: Plönlein, a small square south of Marktplatz, is an excellent spot for taking pictures of the small half-timber house in the foreground with a city gate on each side.

Scenic Spots: Climb the 220 steps of the Rathaustum (tower of the city hall) for a spectacular view of Rothenburg.

cloisters, the kitchens, and the dormitory; then see the collections. ✉ *Klosterhof 5* ☎ *09861/939–043* 🎫 *€3* 🕐 *Apr.–Oct., daily 10–5; Nov.–Mar., daily 1–5.*

㉔ St. Wolfgang. A historic parish church of Gothic origins with a baroque interior, St. Wolfgang's is most notable for the way it blends into the forbidding city wall. ✉ *Klingeng* ☎ *09861/40492* 🎫 *€1.50* 🕐 *Apr.– Oct., daily 10–1 and 2–5.*

㉕ Stadtmauer *(City Wall).* Rothenburg's city walls are more than 2 km (1 mi) long and provide an excellent way of circumnavigating the town from above. The walls' wooden walkway is covered by eaves. Stairs every 200 or 300 yards provide ready access. There are superb views of the tangle of pointed and tiled red roofs and of the rolling country beyond.

㉓ Stadtpfarrkirche St. Jakob *(Parish Church of St. James).* The church has some notable Riemenschneider sculptures, including the famous *Heiliges Blut* (Holy Blood) altar. Above the altar a crystal capsule is said to contain drops of Christ's blood. There are three 14th- and 15th-century stained-glass windows in the choir, and the Herlin-Altar is famous for its 15th-century painted panels. ✉ *Klosterg. 15* ☎ *09861/700–620* 🎫 *€2* 🕐 *Jan.–Mar. and Nov., daily 10–noon and 2–4; Apr.–Oct., daily 9–5; Dec., daily 10–4. English tour Sat. at 3.*

WHERE TO STAY & EAT

$$–$$$
★ ✕🏨 **Hotel Eisenhut.** It's fitting that the prettiest small town in Germany should have one of the prettiest small hotels. Every one of the 79 rooms is different—each with its own charming color scheme, most with antique furniture. ■ TIP→ **Try for one on the top floor toward the back overlooking the old town and the Tauber River valley.** The restaurant ($$–$$$), one of the region's best, offers impeccable service along with delicious food and a lovely view of the garden. In summer you'll want to eat on the terrace, surrounded by flowers. ✉ *Herrng. 3–5, D–91541* ☎ *09861/7050* 📠 *09861/70545* ⊕ *www.eisenhut.com* 🛏 *77 rooms, 2 suites* & *In-room: no a/c, Wi-Fi. In-hotel: restaurant, room service, bar, laundry service, public Wi-Fi, parking (fee), no-smoking rooms* ⊟ *AE, DC, MC, V* 🕐 *Closed early Jan.–early Mar.*

$$
★ ✕🏨 **Romantik-Hotel Markusturm.** The Markusturm began as a 13th-century custom house, an integral part of the city defense wall, and has since developed over the centuries into an inn and staging post and finally into a luxurious small hotel. Some rooms are beamed, others have Laura Ashley decor or gaily painted bedsteads, and some have valuable antiques from the Middle Ages. Try to book a reservation for dinner when you arrive, as the beamed, elegant restaurant ($–$$) may fill up. The fish is excellent—you may want to try it as part of their Romantic Gourmet dinner. Besides well selected wines you can order three kinds of home-brewed beer. In summer head for the patio. ✉ *Röderg. 1, D–91541* ☎ *09861/94280* 📠 *09861/113* ⊕ *www.markusturm. de* 🛏 *23 rooms, 2 suites* & *In-room: no a/c, Wi-Fi. In-hotel: restaurant, public Wi-Fi, parking (fee), no-smoking rooms* ⊟ *AE, DC, MC, V* ⎟◎⎟ *CP.*

$–$$ ✕⚏ **Hotel-Restaurant Burg Colmberg.** East of Rothenburg in Colmberg,
★ this castle turned hotel maintains a high standard of comfort within
its original medieval walls. As you enter the hotel, logs are burning in
the fireplace of the entrance hall, illuminating an original Tin Lizzy
from 1917. The restaurant Zur Remise ($–$$$) serves venison from
the castle's own hunting grounds. ⊠ *Burg 1–3, 18 km (11 mi) east
of Rothenburg, D–91598 Colmberg* ☎ *09803/91920* 🖷 *09803/262*
⊕ *www.burg-colmberg.de* 🖵 *24 rooms, 2 suites* ☖ *In-room: no a/c. In-
hotel: restaurant, bar, golf course, bicycles, no-smoking rooms* ☰ *AE,
MC, V* ⊘ *Closed Feb.* ⑩| *CP.*

$–$$ ⚏ **Burg-Hotel.** This exquisite little hotel abuts the town wall and was
FodorsChoice once part of a Rothenburg monastery. Most rooms have a view of the
★ Tauber Valley. All have plush furnishings, with antiques or fine repro-
ductions. The Steinway Cellar holds a grand piano. Breakfast is served
in good weather on the terrace on top of the town wall with an even
more stunning wide-angle view into the Tauber Valley and the hills
beyond. The owner and staff are gracious hosts. ⊠ *Klosterg. 1–3, D–
91541* ☎ *09861/94890* 🖷 *09861/948–940* ⊕ *www.burghotel.rothen-
burg.de* 🖵 *17 rooms* ☖ *In-room: no a/c, Wi-Fi. In-hotel: spa, laundry
service, public Wi-Fi, no-smoking rooms* ☰ *AE, DC, MC, V* ⑩| *CP.*

$–$$ ⚏ **Hotel Reichs-Küchenmeister.** Master chefs in the service of the Holy
Roman Emperor were the inspiration for the name of this historic
hotel-restaurant, one of the oldest trader's houses in Rothenburg. For
five generations it's been run by the same energetic family. Rooms are
furnished in a stylish mixture of old and new; light veneer pieces share
space with heavy oak bedsteads and painted cupboards. ⊠ *Kirchpl.
8–10, D–91541* ☎ *09861/9700* 🖷 *09861/970–409* ⊕ *www.reichskue-
chenmeister.com* 🖵 *45 rooms, 2 suites, 3 apartments* ☖ *In-room: no
a/c, Wi-Fi. In-hotel: restaurant, bar, public Wi-Fi, no-smoking rooms*
☰ *AE, MC, V* ⑩| *CP.*

$ ⚏ **Gasthof Klingentor.** This sturdy old staging post is outside the city
walls but still within a 10-minute walk of Rothenburg's historic center. Rooms are spacious and furnished in the local rustic style. Most
have en-suite facilities. Its inexpensive restaurant serves substantial
Franconian fare. A well-marked path for hiking or biking starts outside the front door. ⊠ *Mergentheimerstr. 14, D–91541* ☎ *09861/3468*
🖷 *09861/3492* ⊕ *www.hotel-klingentor.de* 🖵 *20 rooms, 16 with bath*
☖ *In-room: no a/c, no TV (some). In-hotel: restaurant, bar, no elevator,
no-smoking rooms* ☰ *MC, V* ⑩| *CP.*

$ ⚏ **Hotel-Gasthof Post.** This small family-run hotel, two minutes on
foot from the eastern city gate, must be one of the friendliest in town.
The rooms are simple but clean, and all have shower or bath. ⊠ *Ans-
bacherstr. 27, D–91541* ☎ *09861/938–880* 🖷 *09861/7896* ⊕ *www.
post-rothenburg.com* 🖵 *18 rooms* ☖ *In-room: no a/c. In-hotel: restau-
rant, no elevator* ☰ *DC, MC, V* ⑩| *CP.*

FESTIVALS

Highlights of Rothenburg's annual calendar are the **Meistertrunk Festival,** over the Whitsun weekend, celebrating the famous wager said
to have saved the town from destruction in the Thirty Years' War,
and the **Reichstadt-Festtage,** on the first weekend of September, com-

memorating Rothenburg's attainment of Free Imperial City status in 1274. Both are spectacular festivals, when thousands of townspeople and local horsemen reenact the events in period costume.

SHOPPING

On the old and atmospheric premises of the **Anneliese Friese** (⊠ *Grüner Markt 7–8, near the Rathaus* ☎ *09861/7166*) you'll find everything from cuckoo clocks and beer tankards to porcelain and glassware. If you are looking specifically for Hummel articles, try **Haus der Tausend Geschenke** (⊠ *Obere Schmiedeg. 13* ☎ *09861/4801*).

Käthe Wohlfahrt (⊠ *Herrng. 1* ☎ *09861/4090*) carries children's toys and seasonal decorations. The Christmas Village part of the store is a wonderland of mostly German-made toys and decorations. **Teddyland** (⊠ *Herrng. 10* ☎ *09861/8904*) has Germany's largest teddy bear population. More than 5,000 of them pack this extraordinary store. ■ **TIP→** Children adore the place, but be prepared: these are pedigree teddies, and they don't come cheap.

EN ROUTE

Schloss Schillingsfürst (⊠ *Schlosspl. 1* ☎ *09868/201* ⊕ *www.schloss-schillingsfuerst.de*), a baroque castle of the Princes of Hohenlohe-Schillingsfürst, is 20 km (12 mi) south of Rothenburg-ob-der-Tauber. Standing on an outcrop, it can be seen from miles away. ■ **TIP→ If you visit the castle, try to arrive in time for one of the demonstrations of Bavarian falconry, held in the courtyard.** You can watch eagles and falcons, on a single command, shoot down from the sky to catch their prey. The castle can be visited only with a guided tour at 10, noon, 2, or 4. The falconry show is at 11 and 3 (€7 for both tour and show) from March to October.

DINKELSBÜHL

㉗
★
26 km (16 mi) south of Schillingsfürst.

Within the walls of Dinkelsbühl, a beautifully preserved medieval town, the rush of traffic seems a lifetime away. There's less to see here than in Rothenburg, and the mood is much less tourist oriented. Like Rothenburg, Dinkelsbühl was caught up in the Thirty Years' War, and it also preserves a fanciful episode from those bloody times. An annual open-air-theater festival takes place from mid-June until mid-August.

The **Münster St. Georg** *(Minster St. George)* is the standout sight in town. At 235 feet in length it's large enough to be a cathedral, and it's among the best examples in Bavaria of the late-Gothic style. Note the complex fan vaulting that spreads sinuously across the ceiling. If you can face the climb, head up the 200-foot tower for amazing views over the jumble of rooftops. ⊠ *Marktpl.* ☎ *09851/2245* 🖃 *Tower €1.50* 🕙 *Church daily 9–noon and 2–5; tower May–Sept., Sat. 10–6, Sun. 1–6.*

WHERE TO STAY & EAT

$$ ✕🖃 **Hotel Deutsches Haus.** This medieval inn, with a facade of half-timber gables and flower boxes, has many rooms fitted with antique furniture. One of them has a romantic four-poster bed. Dine beneath heavy oak beams in the restaurant (¢–$$), where you can try the local specialty, a type of grain called Dinkel. It's very nutritious and often served roasted with potatoes and salmon. ⊠ *Weinmarkt 3, D–91550* ☎ *09851/6058* 🖶 *09851/7911* ⊕ *www.deutsches-haus-dkb.de* 🛏 *16 rooms, 2 suites* 🔥 *In-room: no a/c, dial-up (some). In-hotel: restaurant, bar, parking (fee), no-smoking rooms* ▤ *AE, DC, MC, V* 🕙 *Closed Jan. and Feb.* ❍❘ *CP.*

$–$$ ✕🖃 **Goldene Rose.** Since 1450 the inhabitants of Dinkelsbühl and their guests—among them Queen Victoria in 1891—have enjoyed good food and refreshing drinks in this half-timber house. Dark paneling in the restaurant ($–$$) creates the cozy atmosphere in which you can enjoy good regional cuisine, especially fish and game. Many of the comfortably furnished rooms have half-timber walls. ⊠ *Marktpl. 4, D–91550* ☎ *09851/57750* 🖶 *09851/577–575* ⊕ *www.hotel-goldene-rose.com* 🛏 *31 rooms* 🔥 *In-room: no a/c, Wi-Fi. In-hotel: restaurant, bar, public Wi-Fi, parking (fee), some pets allowed* ▤ *DC, MC, V* ❍❘ *CP.*

SHOPPING

Deleika (⊠ *Waldeck 33* ☎ *09857/97990*) makes barrel organs to order, although it won't deliver the monkey! The firm also has a museum of barrel organs and other mechanical instruments. It's just outside Dinkelsbühl. Call ahead. At **Dinkelsbüler Kunst-Stuben** (⊠ *Segringerstr. 52* ☎ *09851/6750*), the owner, Mr. Appelberg, sells his own drawings, paintings, and etchings of the town. **Jürgen Pleikies** (⊠ *Segringerstr. 53–55* ☎ *09851/7596*) is doing his part to restore his town's former reputation for fine earthenware; he also offers courses at the potter's wheel.

NÖRDLINGEN

❷❽ *32 km (20 mi) southeast of Dinkelsbühl, 70 km (43 mi) northwest of Augsburg.*

In Nördlingen the cry *"So G'sell so"*—"All's well"—still rings out every night across the ancient walls and turrets.

Sentries sound out the traditional message from the 300-foot tower of the central parish church of **St. Georg** at half-hour intervals between 10 PM and midnight. The tradition goes back to an incident during the Thirty Years' War, when an enemy attempted to slip into the town and was detected by a resident. You can climb the 365 steps up the tower—known locally as the Daniel—for an unsurpassed view of the town and countryside, including, on clear days, 99 villages. The ground plan of the town is two concentric circles. The inner circle of streets,

BICYCLING

One of the most interesting ways to get to know the Romantic Road is by bicycle, especially because the route, which mostly follows rivers, is relatively flat. Even if you pedal all the way from Würzburg to Füssen, you won't have to climb any mountains. In the Alpine foothills you'll have a few longer inclines, but even those can be managed by an average cyclist. Of course, if you'd rather avoid inclines altogether, start in Füssen and then roll back down in the opposite direction, following the River Lech.

There are three ways to explore the Romantic Road by bicycle. One is to venture out with as little baggage as possible, finding places to stay along the way. Another possibility is to have a tour operator book rooms for you and your group and transport your luggage. Or, you can do day trips. Most tourist offices and good hotels along the Romantic Road will supply bicycles, maps, and information for local and regional bike trips.

The Romantic Road office in Dinkelsbühl has a booklet with detailed maps for cycling, and signs mark the Romantic Road bicycle path (all 420 km [260 mi] of it) from beginning to end. In any town on the Romantic Road you can board the Deutsche Touring bus (with a trailer for bicycles), which travels the length of the Romantic Road daily.

whose central point is St. Georg, marks the earliest medieval boundary. A few hundred yards beyond it is the outer boundary, a wall built to accommodate expansion. Fortified with 11 towers and punctuated by five massive gates, it's one of the best-preserved town walls in Germany. ⊠ *Marktpl.* ☜ *Tower €1.50* ☉ *Daily 9–dusk.*

Nördlingen lies in the center of a huge, basinlike depression, the **Ries,** that until the beginning of this century was believed to be the remains of an extinct volcano. In 1960 it was proven by two Americans that the 24-km-wide (15-mi-wide) crater was caused by a meteorite at least 1 km (½ mi) in diameter. ■ **TIP→ The compressed rock, or** *Suevit,* **formed by the explosive impact of the meteorite was used to construct many of the town's buildings, including St. Georg's tower.**

WHERE TO STAY

$ ✕🖼 **Braunes Ross.** This Gasthaus in the central square, directly opposite the city tower, was first mentioned in city archives in 1481 as "a place to eat and drink." The Haubner family bought the house 517 years later, in 1998, and renovated it from top to bottom. It now features modern rooms with cable TV, phones, and private baths, and a cozy, Bavarian-style restaurant. ⊠ *Marktpl. 12, D–86720* ☏ *09081/290–120* 🖨 *09081/290–1228* 🛏 *14 rooms* ⟁ *In-room: no a/c. In-hotel: restaurant, some pets allowed* ☰ *MC, V* ❢⊙❢ *CP.*

$–$$ 🖼 **Kaiserhof-Hotel-Sonne.** The great German poet Goethe stayed here, only one in a long line of distinguished guests starting with Emperor Friedrich III in 1487. The vaulted-cellar wine tavern is a reminder of those days. The three honeymoon suites are furnished in 18th-century style, with hand-painted four-poster beds. The property is right in the center of the city, in the shadow of the big church tower. ⊠*Marktpl. 3, D–86720* ☎*09081/5067* 🖷*09081/29290* ⇥*40 rooms* ♿*In-room: no a/c, Wi-Fi (some). In-hotel: restaurant, bar, parking (no fee), public Wi-Fi, some pets allowed, no-smoking rooms* ☰*AE, MC, V* ⊘*Closed Nov. Restaurant closed Jan. and Feb., Sun. dinner, and Wed.* ❙❘❙*CP.*

$ 🔲**Hotel Goldene Rose.** This small, modern hotel is just inside the town wall and is ideal for those who wish to explore Nördlingen on foot. The in-house restaurant serves wholesome, inexpensive dishes. ⊠*Baldingerstr. 42, D–86720* ☎*09081/86019* 🖷*09081/24591* ⊕*www.goldene-rose-noerdlingen.de* ⇥*17 rooms, 1 apartment* ♿*In-room: no a/c. In-hotel: restaurant, parking (no fee), no-smoking rooms* ☰*MC, V* ❙❘❙*CP.*

SPORTS & THE OUTDOORS

Ever cycled around a huge meteor crater? You can do just that in the **Nördlingen Ries,** the basinlike depression left by a meteor that hit the area in prehistoric times. The **Nördlingen tourist office** (☎*09081/84116*) has a list of 10 recommended bike routes, including one 47-km (29-mi) trail around the northern part of the meteor crater.

DONAUWÖRTH

㉙ *11 km (7 mi) south of Harburg, 41 km (25 mi) north of Augsburg.*

At the old walled town of Donauwörth, the Wörnitz River meets the Danube. If you're driving, pull off into the clearly marked lot on B–25, just north of town. Below you sprawls a striking natural relief map of Donauwörth and its two rivers. The oldest part of town is on an island. A wood bridge connects it to the north bank and the single surviving town gate, the Riederstor. North of the gate is one of the finest avenues of the Romantic Road: Reichsstrasse (Empire Street), so named because it was once a vital link in the Road of the Holy Roman Empire between Nürnberg and Augsburg. The Fuggers, a famous family of traders and bankers from Augsburg, acquired a palatial home here in the 16th century; its fine Renaissance-style facade, under a steeply gabled roof, stands proudly at the upper end of Reichsstrasse.

Donauwörth is the home of the famous Käthe Kruse dolls, beloved for their sweet looks and frilly, floral outfits. You can buy them at several outlets in town, and they have their own museum, where more than 130 examples dating from 1912 are displayed in a specially reno-vated monastery building, the **Käthe-Kruse-Puppen-Museum.** ⊠*Pflegstr. 21a* ☎*0906/789–170* 🎫*€3* ⊘*May–Sept., Tues.–Sun. 11–5; Apr. and Oct., Tues.–Sun. 2–5; Nov.–Mar., Wed. and weekends 2–5.*

WHERE TO STAY

$–$$ 🔲**Parkhotel.** Members of the Landidyll chain of hotels have one fea-ture in common: an idyllic location. This one qualifies with its position high above Donauwörth. Most rooms have floor-to-ceiling win-dows with panoramic views. All are decorated in bright pastel tones and have wicker chairs and sofas. ⊠*Sternschanzenstr. 1, D–86609* ☎*0906/706–510* 🖷*0906/706–5180* ⊕*www.parkhotel-donauwoerth.*

de ⇌*45 rooms* ♿*In-room: no a/c, Wi-Fi. In-hotel: restaurant, bar,*
public Wi-Fi, parking (no fee), some pets allowed, no-smoking rooms
☰*AE, DC, MC, V* ⦿|*CP.*

ULM

㉚ *60 km (40 mi) west of Augsburg.*

Ulm isn't considered part of the Romantic Road, but it's definitely
worth visiting, if only for one reason: its mighty Münster, which has the
world's tallest church tower (536 feet). Ulm grew as a medieval trading
city thanks to its location on the Danube River. Today the proximity of
the Old Town to the river adds to Ulm's charm. In the Fisherman and
Tanner quarters the cobblestone alleys and stone-and-wood bridges
over the Blau (a small Danube tributary) are especially picturesque. To
get to Ulm from Donauwörth, take Highway B–16 west, connecting
with B–28. Or, from Augsburg, take a 40-minute ride on one of the
superfast ICE (Intercity Express) trains that run to Ulm every hour.

★ Ulm's **Münster,** the largest church in southern Germany, was unscathed
by wartime bombing. It stands over the huddled medieval gables of
Old Ulm, visible long before you hit the ugly suburbs encroaching on
the Swabian countryside. Its single, filigree tower challenges the physically fit to plod 536 feet up the 768 steps of a giddily twisting spiral
stone staircase to a spectacular observation point below the spire. On
clear days the highest steeple in the world will reward you with views
of the Swiss and Bavarian Alps, 160 km (100 mi) to the south. The
Münster was begun in the late-Gothic age (1377) and took five centuries to build, with completion in the neo-Gothic years of the late
19th century. It contains some notable treasures, including late-Gothic
choir stalls and a Renaissance altar. ■**TIP➔The mighty organ can be
heard in special recitals every Sunday at 11:15 from Easter until November.**
⊠*Münsterpl.* ☎*Tower €3, organ recitals €1.50* ⊘*Daily 9–5; organ
recitals May–Oct., daily at 11:30.*

The central **Marktplatz** is bordered by medieval houses with stepped
gables. Every Wednesday and Saturday, farmers from the surrounding area arrive by 6 AM to erect their stands and unload their produce.
Potatoes, vegetables, apples, pears, berries, honey, fresh eggs, poultry,
homemade bread, and all kinds of other edible things are carefully displayed. ■**TIP➔ If you plan to come, be sure to get here early; the market
packs up around noon.**

A reproduction of local tailor Ludwig Berblinger's flying machine hangs
inside the elaborately painted **Rathaus.** In 1811 Berblinger, a tailor and
local eccentric, cobbled together a pair of wings and made a big splash
by trying to fly across the river. He didn't make it, but he grabbed a
place in German history books for his efforts. ⊠*Marktpl. 1.*

German bread is world renowned, so it's not surprising that a national
museum is devoted to bread making. The **Museum der Brotkultur** *(German Bread Museum)* is housed in a former salt warehouse, just north of
the Münster. It's by no means as crusty or dry as some might fear, with

some often-amusing tableaux illustrating how bread has been baked over the centuries. ⊠*Salzstadelg. 10* ☎*0731/69955* ⊕*www.museum-brotkultur.de* 🎫*€4* ⊙*Daily 10–5.*

Complete your visit to Ulm with a walk down to the banks of the Danube, where you'll find long sections of the **old city wall** and fortifications intact.

WHERE TO STAY & EAT

$–$$

Fodor'sChoice

★

✕**Zur Forelle.** For more than 350 years the aptly named Forelle, which means "trout," has stood over the small clear River Blau, which flows through a large trout basin right under the restaurant. If you're not a trout fan, there are five other fish dishes available, as well as excellent venison, in season. ■**TIP→ On a nice summer evening try to get a table on the small terrace. You'll literally sit over the small river, with a weeping willow on one side, half-timber houses all around you, and the towering cathedral in the background.** ⊠*Fischerg. 25, D–89073* ☎*0731/63924* ▤*DC, MC, V.*

¢–$$

✕**Zunfthaus der Schiffleute.** The sturdy half-timber Zunfthaus (Guildhall) has stood here for more than 500 years, first as a fishermen's pub and now as a charming tavern-restaurant. Ulm's fishermen had their guild headquarters here, and when the nearby Danube flooded the fish swam right up to the door. Today they land on the menu. One of the "foreign" intruders on the menu is Bavarian white sausage, *Weisswurst.* The local beer is an excellent accompaniment. The minimum amount for credit cards is €25. ⊠*Fischerg. 31* ☎*0731/64411* ⊕*www.zunfthaus-ulm.de* ▤*AE, MC, V.*

$$–$$$

✕▥**Maritim.** Whether you come here to eat or stay, be prepared for incredible views. The elegant rooms and restaurants all offer breathtaking panoramas. In the main restaurant ($–$$) on the 16th floor, the international dishes are good and the view is amazing. Huge floor-to-ceiling windows reveal the Old Town of Ulm with the cathedral, the Danube, and the Swabian Alps all at your fingertips. The large, luxurious bar with cozy corners and live piano music every night has become a favorite with hotel and restaurant guests. Ask for weekend rates. ⊠*Basteistr. 40, D–89073* ☎*0731/9230* 📠*0731/923–1000* ⊕*www.maritim.de* 🛏*287 rooms* ⚿*In-room: no a/c, dial-up, Wi-Fi (some). In-hotel: 2 restaurants, bar, pool, gym, public Wi-Fi, parking (fee), no-smoking rooms* ▤*AE, DC, MC, V.*

$

▥**Hotel am Rathaus/Reblaus.** The owner's love for antique paintings, furniture, and dolls is evident throughout this hotel. Some of the rooms have antique furniture. In the annex, the half-timber Reblaus, most rooms have hand-painted cupboards. If you take a room toward the front, look up from your window and you'll see the cathedral with its huge spire a few hundred feet away. The hotel is behind the old historic Rathaus, on the fringe of the Old City, where you'll find more than a dozen restaurants and taverns. ⊠*Kroneng. 10, D–89073* ☎*0731/968–490* 📠*0731/968–4949* ⊕*www.rathausulm.de* 🛏*34 rooms* ⚿*In-room: no a/c, Wi-Fi. In-hotel: no elevator, public Wi-Fi, parking (no fee), no-smoking rooms* ▤*AE, DC* ⊙*Closed late Dec.–mid-Jan.* ▯◎▯*CP.*

AUGSBURG

41 km (25 mi) south of Donauwörth, 60 km (37 mi) west of Munich.

Augsburg is Bavaria's third-largest city, after Munich and Nürnberg. It dates to 15 years before the birth of Christ, when a son of the Roman emperor Augustus set up a military camp here on the banks of the Lech River. The settlement that grew up around it was known as Augusta, a name Italian visitors to the city still call it. It was granted city rights in 1156, and 200 years later was first mentioned in municipal records of the Fugger family, who were to Augsburg what the Medici family was to Florence.

TIMING   A walking tour of Augsburg is easy because signs on almost every street corner point the way to the chief sights. The signs are integrated into three-color, charted tours devised by the tourist board. You'll need a complete day to see Augsburg if you linger in any of the museums.

MAIN ATTRACTIONS

42 Dom St. Maria *(Cathedral of St. Mary)*. Augsburg's cathedral stands out within the city's panorama because of its square Gothic towers, which were built in the 9th century. A 10th-century Romanesque crypt, built in the time of Bishop Ulrich, also remains from the cathedral's early years. The 11th-century windows on the south side of the nave, depicting the prophets Jonah, Daniel, Hosea, Moses, and David, form the oldest cycle of stained glass in central Europe. Five important paintings by Hans Holbein the Elder adorn the altar.

The cathedral's treasures are on display at the **Diözesan Museum St. Afra** (⊠*Kornhausg. 3–5* ⊡*€ 4* ⊙*Tues.–Sat. 10–5, Sun. noon–6*). A short walk from the cathedral will take you to the quiet courtyards and small raised garden of the former episcopal residence, a series of 18th-century buildings in baroque and rococo styles that now serve as the Swabian regional government offices ⊠*Dompl.* ⊙*Daily 9–dusk.*

34 Fuggerei. This neat little settlement is the world's oldest social housing project, established by the Fugger family in 1516 to accommodate the city's deserving poor. The 104 homes still serve the same purpose; the annual rent of "one Rhenish guilder" (€1) hasn't changed, either. Residents must be Augsburg citizens, Catholic, and destitute through no fault of their own—and they must pray daily for their original benefactors, the Fugger family. ⊠*Jacoberstr..*

40 Maximilian-Museum. Augsburg's main museum houses a permanent exhibition of Augsburg arts and crafts in a 16th-century merchant's mansion. ⊠*Philippine-Welser-Str. 24* ⊡*€7* ⊙*Tues.–Sun. 10–5.*

32 Perlachturm *(Perlach Tower)*. This 258-foot-high plastered brick bell tower has foundations dating to the 11th century. Although it's a long climb to the top of the tower, the view over Augsburg and the countryside is worth the effort. ⊠*Rathauspl.* ⊞*No phone* ⊡*€2* ⊙*May–mid-Oct., daily 10–6; Dec., weekends noon–7.*

31 Rathaus. Augsburg's city hall was Germany's largest when it was built in the early 17th century; it's now regarded as the finest Renaissance secu-

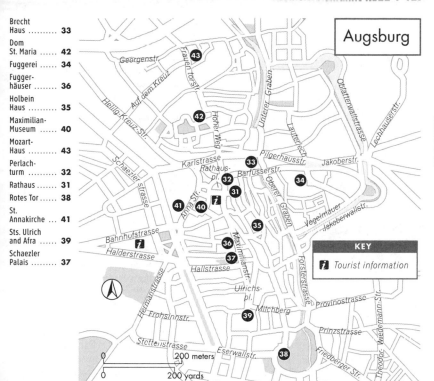

lar structure north of the Alps. Its **Goldenener Saal** (Golden Hall) was given its name because of its rich decoration—a gold-based harmony of wall frescoes, carved pillars, and coffered ceiling. ⊠*Rathauspl.* 🔊*€2* ⊗*10–6 on days when no official functions take place.*

39 Sts. Ulrich and Afra. Standing at the highest point of the city, this basilica was built on the site of a Roman cemetery where St. Afra was martyred in AD 304. The original structure was begun in the late-Gothic style in 1467; a baroque preaching hall was added in 1710 as the Protestant church of St. Ulrich. St. Afra is buried in the crypt, near the tomb of St. Ulrich, a 10th-century bishop who helped stop a Hungarian army at the gates of Augsburg in the Battle of the Lech River. The remains of a third patron of the church, St. Simpert, are preserved in one of the church's most elaborate side chapels. From the steps of the magnificent altar, look back along the high nave to the finely carved baroque wrought-iron and wood railing that borders the entrance. As you leave, look into the separate but adjacent church of St. Ulrich, the former chapter house that was reconstructed by the Lutherans after the Reformation. ⊠*Ulrichspl.* ⊗*Daily 9–dusk.*

37 Schaezler Palais. This elegant 18th-century city palace was built by the von Liebenhofens, a family of wealthy bankers. Schaezler was the name of a baron who married into the family. Today the palace rooms contain the **Deutsche Barockgalerie** (German Baroque Gallery), a major art collection that features works of the 17th and 18th centuries. The palace adjoins the former church of a Dominican monastery. A steel door behind the banquet hall leads into another world of high-vaulted ceilings, where the **Staatsgalerie Altdeutsche Meister,** a Bavarian state collection, highlights old-master paintings, among them a Dürer portrait of one of the Fuggers. ⊠ *Maximilianstr. 46* ☜€7 ⊙ *Tues.–Sun. 10–5.*

ALSO WORTH SEEING

63 Brecht Haus. This modest artisan's house was the birthplace of the renowned playwright Bertolt Brecht (1898–1956), author of *Mother Courage* and *The Threepenny Opera.* ⊠ *Auf dem Rain 7* ☜€2 ⊙ *Tues.–Sun. 10–5.*

66 Fuggerhäuser. The 16th-century former home and business quarters of the Fugger family now houses a restaurant in its cellar and offices on the upper floors. In the ground-floor entrance are busts of two of Augsburg's most industrious Fuggers, Raymund and Anton. Beyond a modern glass door is a quiet courtyard with colonnades, the Damenhof (Ladies' Courtyard), originally reserved for the Fugger women. ⊠ *Maximilianstr. 36–38.*

65 Holbein Haus. The rebuilt 16th-century home of painter Hans Holbein the Elder, one of Augsburg's most famous residents, is now a city art gallery, with changing exhibitions. ⊠ *Vorderer Lech 20* ☜ *Varies* ⊙ *May–Oct., Tues., Wed., and Fri.–Sun. 10–5, Thurs. 10–8; Nov.–Apr., Tues., Wed., and Fri.–Sun. 10–4, Thurs. 10–8.*

Maximilianstrasse. This main shopping street was once a medieval wine market. Most of the city's sights are on this thoroughfare or a short walk away. Two monumental and elaborate fountains punctuate the long street. At the north end is the **Merkur,** designed in 1599 by the Dutch master Adrian de Vries (after a Florentine sculpture by Giovanni da Bologna), which shows winged Mercury in his classic pose. Farther up Maximilianstrasse is another de Vries fountain: a bronze **Hercules** struggling to subdue the many-headed Hydra.

43 Mozart-Haus *(Mozart House).* Leopold Mozart, the father of Wolfgang Amadeus Mozart, was born in this bourgeois 17th-century residence; he was an accomplished composer and musician in his own right. The house now serves as a Mozart memorial and museum, with some fascinating contemporary documents on the Mozart family. ⊠ *Frauentorstr. 30* ☏ *0821/324–3894* ☜€ *3.50* ⊙ *Tues.–Sun. 10–5.*

TOURING TIPS

Information: Pick up maps in the tourist office on Maximilianstrasse 57.

Scenic Spots: There's an excellent view over the center of the city from the spot where Maximilianstrasse joins Rathausplatz (square of the city hall).

Scenic Spots: Climb the 258 steps of the Perlachturm (beside the city hall) for a spectacular vantage point over the city.

Snacks: Recuperate from the climb at the cafés and restaurants on Rathausplatz and Maximilianstrasse.

③ **Rotes Tor** *(Red Gate)*. The city's most important medieval gate once straddled the main trading road to Italy. It provides the backdrop to an open-air opera and operetta festival in June and July. ✉ *Eserwallstr.*

④ **St. Annakirche** *(St. Anna's Church)*. This site was formerly part of a Carmelite monastery, where Martin Luther stayed in 1518 during his meetings with Cardinal Cajetanus, the papal legate sent from Rome to persuade the reformer to renounce his heretical views. Luther refused, and the place where he publicly declared his rejection of papal pressure is marked with a plaque on Maximilianstrasse. ■**TIP→You can wander through the quiet cloisters, dating from the 14th century, and view the chapel used by the Fugger family until the Reformation.** ✉ *Anna-Str., west of Rathauspl.* ☉ *Tues.–Sat. 10–12:30 and 3–6, Sun. noon–6.*

WHERE TO STAY & EAT

$$–$$$
Fodor'sChoice
★

✕**Die Ecke.** Situated on an *Ecke* (corner) of the small square right behind Augsburg's city hall, the Ecke is valued for the imaginative variety of its cuisine and the scope of its wine list. In season, the venison dishes are among Bavaria's best. The fish, in particular the *Zander* (green pike) or the trout sautéed in butter and lightly dressed with herbs and lemon, is magnificent and complemented nicely by the Riesling Gimmeldinger Meersspinne, the house wine for 40 years. In summer ask for a table on the patio. ✉ *Elias-Holl-Pl. 2, D–86150* ☎ *0821/510–600* ⌕ *For dinner, reservations essential* ▭ *AE, DC, MC, V.*

$$–$$$
✕▦**Steigenberger Drei Mohren Hotel.** Kings and princes, Napoléon and the Duke of Wellington, have all slept here. Except for the modern fourth- and fifth-floor rooms, all the rooms maintain a luxurious, traditional style. Ask for weekend rates. Dining options include the elegant, Mediterranean-style restaurant Maximilian's ($$–$$$) and Bistro 3M ($–$$). The Sunday Jazz Brunch at Maximilian's has been a town favorite since the late '90s. Bistro 3M is thoroughly French, and the food is excellent. ✉ *Maximilianstr. 40, D–86150* ☎ *0821/50360* 🖷 *0821/157–864* ⊕ *www.augsburg.steigenberger.de* ⌕ *106 rooms, 5 suites* ⌂ *In-room: no a/c (some), Wi-Fi. In-hotel: 2 restaurants, bar, laundry service, public Wi-Fi, some pets allowed (fee), no-smoking rooms* ▭ *AE, DC, MC, V.*

$$
✕▦**Privat Hotel Riegele.** The hotel is just opposite the main railway station. The tavern-restaurant ($–$$), the Bräustüble, is a local favorite. The food is good German cooking and the service is efficient and friendly. Public rooms and some bedrooms have plush armchairs, deep-pile rugs, and heavy drapes. Ask for weekend rates. ✉ *Viktoriastr. 4, D–86150* ☎ *0821/509–000* 🖷 *0821/517–746* ⊕ *www.hotel-riegele.de* ⌕ *27 rooms, 1 apartment* ⌂ *In-room: no a/c, Wi-Fi. In-hotel: restaurant, laundry service, public Wi-Fi, some pets allowed (free), no smoking rooms* ▭ *AE, DC, MC, V* ☉ *No dinner Sun.* ⦿*CP.*

$–$$
★

✕▦**Romantikhotel Augsburger Hof.** A preservation order protects the beautiful Renaissance facade of this charming old Augsburg mansion. Rather than remake an old-world atmosphere inside, the owners opted for a cheerful but classic look with natural wood finishes and flowered curtains. The restaurant ($–$$$) serves excellent Swabian specialties and international dishes. In season, try the duck. The cathedral is around the corner; the town center is a five-minute stroll. ⊠*Auf dem Kreuz 2, D–86152* ☎*0821/343–050* 🖷*0821/343–0555* ⊕*www. augsburger-hof.de* ☞*36 rooms* ⌂*In-room: no a/c, Wi-Fi. In-hotel: restaurant, bar, laundry service, public Wi-Fi, parking (fee), some pets allowed (fee), no-smoking rooms* ☰*AE, DC, MC, V* ¶⊖*CP.*

$–$$ 🏨 **Dom Hotel.** Just around the corner from Augsburg's cathedral, this
★   snug establishment has personality. ■**TIP➔ Ask for one of the attic rooms, where you'll sleep under beam ceilings and wake to a rooftop view of the city.** Or try for one of the rooms on the top floor that have a small terrace facing the cathedral. A garden terrace borders the old city walls, and in summer you'll have your breakfast in the garden under old chestnut trees. ⊠*Frauentorstr. 8, D–86152* ☎*0821/343– 930* 🖷*0821/3439–3200* ⊕*www.domhotel-augsburg.de* ☞*44 rooms, 8 suites* ⌂*In-room: no a/c, Wi-Fi. In-hotel: room service, pool, gym, parking (no fee), no-smoking rooms* ☰*AE, DC, MC, V* ⊗*Closed late Dec.–mid-Jan.* ¶⊖*CP.*

$ 🏨 **Hotel-Garni Schlössle.** From the main railroad station, a 10-minute ride on tram Number 3 to the end of the line at Stadtbergen brings you to this friendly, family-run hotel. Rooms under the steep eaves are particularly cozy. The location offers fresh country air, walks, and sporting facilities (a golf course is within a good tee-shot's range). ⊠*Bauernstr. 37, Stadtbergen D–86391* ☎*0821/243–930* 🖷*0821/437–451* ☞*14 rooms* ⌂*In-room: no a/c. In-hotel: no-smoking rooms* ☰*MC, V* ¶⊖*CP.*

THE ARTS

Augsburg has chamber and symphony orchestras, as well as ballet and opera companies. The city stages a Mozart Festival of international stature in September. The **Kongresshalle** (⊠*Göggingerstr. 10* ☎*0821/324–2348*) presents music and dance performances from September through July.

Augsburg's annual open-air **opera and operetta** (☎*0821/502–070 city tourist office*) season takes place in June and July. Productions move to the romantic inner courtyard of the **Fugger Palace** for part of July and August. Phone the city tourist office for details.

🄲 Children love the city's excellent **Augsburger Puppenkiste** (*Puppet theater* ⊠*Spitalg. 15, next to Rotes Tor* ☎*0821/4503–450*).

EN ROUTE Leaving Augsburg southward on B–17—the southern stretch of the Romantic Road—you'll drive across the Lech battlefield, where Hungarian invaders were stopped in 955. Rich Bavarian pastures extend as far as the Lech River, which the Romantic Road meets at the historic town of Landsberg.

TOWARD THE ALPS

South of Augsburg, the Romantic Road climbs gradually into the foothills of the Bavarian Alps, which burst into view between Landsberg and Schongau. The route ends dramatically at the northern wall of the Alps at Füssen, on the Austrian border. Landsberg was founded by the

Bavarian ruler Heinrich der Löwe (Henry the Lion) in the 12th century and grew wealthy from the salt trade. Solid old houses are packed within its turreted walls; the early-18th-century Rathaus is one of the finest in the region.

Schongau has virtually intact wall fortifications, complete with towers and gates. In medieval and Renaissance times the town was an important trading post on the route from Italy to Augsburg. The steeply gabled 16th-century Ballenhaus was a warehouse before it was elevated to the rank of Rathaus. A popular Märchenwald ("fairy-tale forest") lies 1½ km (1 mi) outside Schongau, suitably set in a clearing in the woods. It comes complete with mechanical models of fairy-tale scenes, deer enclosures, and an old-time miniature railway.

NEUSCHWANSTEIN & HOHENSCHWANGAU

44 *93 km (60 mi) south of Augsburg, 105 km (65 mi) southwest of Munich.*

These two famous castles belonging to the Wittelbachs, one historic and the other nearly "make-believe," are 1 km (½ mi) across a valley from each other, near the town of Schwangau. Bavaria's King Ludwig II (1845–86) spent much of his youth at Schloss Hohenschwangau (Hohenschwangau Castle). It's said that its neo-Gothic atmosphere provided the primary influences that shaped his wildly romantic Schloss Neuschwanstein (Neuschwanstein Castle), the fairy-tale castle he built after he became king and which has since become one of Germany's most recognized sights.

PLANNING YOUR VISIT

Timing: The best time to see either castle without waiting a long time is a weekday between January and April. The prettiest time, however, is in fall. ■**TIP**➔ Bear in mind that more than 1 million people pass through one or both castles every year. If you visit in summer, get there early.

Tickets: Tickets are for timed entry, and the average wait to enter Neuschwanstein is one hour. With a deposit or credit-card number you can book your tickets in advance for either castle through the **ticket center** (✉*Alpseestr. 12, D–87645 Hohenschwangau* ☎*08362/930–830* 🖷*08362/930–8320* ⊕*www.hohenschwangau.de*). You can change entrance times or cancel up to two hours before the confirmed entrance time.

Directions: From Schwangau (5 km [3 mi] north of Füssen, 91 km [59 mi] south of Augsburg, 103 km [64 mi] southwest of Munich), follow the road signs marked KONIGSCHLÖSSER (King's Castles). After 3 km (2 mi) you come to Hohenschwangau, a small village consisting of a few houses, some good hotels, and five spacious parking lots (parking €4.50). You have to park in one of them and then walk to the ticket center serving both castles. If you are staying in Füssen, take the bus to Hohenschwangau. The clearly-marked bus leaves from the train station in Füssen every hour from morning to night and the cost is €1.60 per person one way.

Provisions: The main street of the small village Hohenschwangau is lined with restaurants and quick eateries of all categories.

NEUSCHWANSTEIN

Fodor'sChoice
★

Neuschwanstein was conceived by a set designer instead of an architect, thanks to King Ludwig II's deep love of the theater. The castle soars from its mountainside like a stage creation—it should hardly come as a surprise that Walt Disney took it as the model for his castle in the movie *Sleeping Beauty* and later for the Disneyland castle itself.

The life of this spectacular castle's king reads like one of the great Gothic mysteries of the 19th century, and the castle symbolizes that life. Yet during the 17 years from the start of Schloss Neuschwanstein's construction until King Ludwig's death, the king spent less than six months in the country residence, and the interior was never finished. The Byzantine-style throne room is without a throne; Ludwig died before one could be installed. However, the walls of the rooms leading to Ludwig's bedroom are painted with murals depicting characters from Wagner's operas—Siegfried and the Nibelungen, Lohengrin, Tristan, and others. Ludwig's bed and its canopy are made of intricately carved oak. A small corridor behind the bedroom was made as a ghostly grotto, reminiscent of Wagner's *Tannhäuser*. **Chamber concerts** (☎08362/81980) are held in September in the gaily decorated minstrels' hall—one room, at least, that was completed as Ludwig conceived it. On the walls outside the castle's gift shop are plans and photos of the castle's construction. There are some spectacular walks around the castle. The delicate **Marienbrücke** (Mary's Bridge) is spun like a medieval maiden's hair across a deep, narrow gorge. From this vantage point there are giddy views of the castle and the great Upper Bavarian Plain beyond.

To reach Neuschwanstein from the ticket center below, take one of the clearly marked paths (about a 40-minute uphill walk) or one of the horse-drawn carriages that leave from Hotel Müller (uphill €5, downhill €2.50). A shuttle bus leaves from the Hotel Lisl (uphill €1.80, downhill €1) and takes you halfway up the hill to an outlook called Aussichtspunkt Jugend. From there it's a 10-minute downhill walk to the castle or a 5-minute uphill walk to Marienbrücke. ⊠ *Neuschwansteinstr. 20* ☎*08362/930–830* ⊕*www.neuschwanstein.de* ✆*€9, including guided tour; ticket for both castles €17* ☉ *Apr.–Sept., daily 8–5; Oct.–Mar., daily 9–3.*

HOHENSCHWANGAU

★ Hohenschwangau was built by the knights of Schwangau in the 12th century. It was remodeled later by King Ludwig II's father, the Bavarian crown prince (and later king) Maximilian, between 1832 and 1836. Unlike Ludwig's more famous castle across the valley, Neuschwanstein, the somewhat garishly yellow Schloss Hohenschwangau has the feeling of a noble home, where comforts would be valued as much as outward splendor. It was here that the young Ludwig met the composer Richard Wagner. Their friendship shaped and deepened the future king's interest in theater, music, and German mythology—the mythology Wagner drew upon for his *Ring* cycle of operas.

3

After obtaining your ticket at the ticket center in the village, you can take a 25-minute walk up either of two clearly marked paths to the castle, or board one of the horse-drawn carriages that leave from Hotel Müller (uphill €3.50, downhill €1.50). *€9, including guided tour; ticket for both castles €17* ☎*08362/930–830* ⊕*www.hohenschwangau.de* ⊙*Apr.–Sept., daily 8–5; Oct.–Mar., daily 9–3.*

■ OFF THE BEATEN PATH

Wieskirche. This church—a glorious example of German rococo architecture—stands in an Alpine meadow just off the Romantic Road. In the village of Steingaden (22 km [14 mi] north of Füssen on the B–17 or, if you come from the north, 74 km [46 mi] south of Augsburg), turn east and follow the signs to Wieskirche. Its yellow-and-white walls and steep red roof are set off by the dark backdrop of the Trauchgauer Mountains. The architect Dominicus Zimmermann, former mayor of Landsberg and creator of much of that town's rococo architecture, built the church in 1745 on the spot where six years earlier a local woman claimed to have seen tears running down the face of a picture of Christ. Although the church was dedicated as the Pilgrimage Church of the Scourged Christ, it's now known simply as the Wieskirche (Church of the Meadow). **■ TIP➔ Visit it on a bright day if you can, when light streaming through its high windows displays the full glory of the glittering interior.** A complex oval plan is animated by brilliantly colored stuccowork, statues, and gilt. A luminous ceiling fresco completes the decoration. Concerts are presented in the church from the end of June through the beginning of August. Contact the **Pfarramt Wieskirche** (☎*08862/932–930 Pastor's office* ⊕*www.wieskirche.de*) for details. *Free* ⊙*Daily 8–dusk.*

WHERE TO STAY & EAT

$$ ✕⊞**Hotel Müller.** Between the two Schwangau castles, the Müller fits beautifully into the stunning landscape, its creamy Bavarian baroque facade complemented by the green mountain forest. Inside, the baroque influence is everywhere, from the finely furnished bedrooms to the chandelier-hung public rooms and restaurant (¢–$$). The mahogany-paneled, glazed veranda (with open fireplace) provides a magnificent view of Hohenschwangau Castle. Round your day off with a local specialty such as the *Allgäuer Lendentopf* (sirloin) served with spaetzle. ✉*Alpseestr. 16, D–87643 Hohenschwangau* ☎*08362/81990* 📠*08362/819–913* ⊕*www.hotel-mueller.de* ⇨*39 rooms, 4 suites* ⚒*In-room: no a/c. In-hotel: 2 restaurants, bar, public Wi-Fi, parking* *(no fee), some pets allowed (no fee), no-smoking rooms* ▤AE, DC, MC, V ⊘ *Closed mid–Feb. to late Mar.* ⅢCP.

$$ ╳▥ **Schlosshotel Lisl und Jägerhaus.** These jointly run 19th-century properties are across the street from one another, and share views of the nearby castles. The intimate Jägerhaus has five suites and six double rooms, all decorated with floral wallpaper and drapery. The bathrooms have swan-motif golden fixtures. The Lisl's rooms have bright blue carpeting and fabrics. The restaurant, Salon Wittelsbacher (¢–$$$), provides a view of Neuschwanstein as well as a tasty dish of *Tafelspitz* (boiled beef with horseradish). ⊠*Neuschwansteinstr. 1–3, D–87643* ☎*08362/8870* 🖷*08362/81107* ⊕*www.lisl.de* ⟿*42 rooms, 5 suites* ⟁*In-room: no a/c. In-hotel: 2 restaurants, bar, laundry service, some pets allowed (fee), parking (no fee)* ▤AE, MC, V ⊘*Closed Jan.–mid-Feb.*

FÜSSEN

㊺ *5 km (3 mi) southwest of Schwangau, 110 km (68 mi) south of Munich.*

Füssen is beautifully located at the foot of the mountains that separate Bavaria from the Austrian Tyrol. The Lech River, which accompanies much of the final section of the Romantic Road, embraces the town as it rushes northward.

The town's **Hohes Schloss** *(High Castle)* is one of the best-preserved late-Gothic castles in Germany. It was built on the site of the Roman fortress that once guarded this Alpine section of the Via Claudia, the trade route from Rome to the Danube. Evidence of Roman occupation of the area has been uncovered at the foot of the nearby Tegelberg Mountain, and the **excavations** next to the Tegelberg cable-car station are open for visits daily. The Hohes Schloss was the seat of Bavarian rulers before Emperor Heinrich VII mortgaged it and the rest of the town to the bishop of Augsburg for 400 pieces of silver. The mortgage was never redeemed, and Füssen remained the property of the Augsburg episcopate until secularization in the early 19th century. The bishops of Augsburg used the castle as their summer Alpine residence. It has a spectacular 16th-century **Rittersaal** (Knights' Hall) with a carved ceiling, and a princes' chamber with a Gothic tile stove. ⊠*Magnuspl. 10* ☎*08362/940–162* 🖾*€2.50* ⊘*Apr.–Oct., Tues.–Sun. 11–4; Nov.–Mar., Tues.–Sun. 2–4.*

The summer presence of the bishops of Augsburg ensured that Füssen received an impressive number of baroque and rococo churches. Füssen's **Rathaus** was once a Benedictine abbey, built in the 9th century at the site of the grave of St. Magnus, who spent most of his life ministering in the area. A Romanesque crypt beneath the baroque abbey church has a partially preserved 10th-century fresco, the oldest in Bavaria. In summer, chamber concerts are held in the high-ceiling baroque splendor of the former abbey's **Fürstensaal** (Princes' Hall). Program details are available from the tourist office. ⊠*Lechalde 3.*

The Fairy-Tale King

King Ludwig II (1845–86), the enigmatic presence indelibly associated with Bavaria, was one of the last rulers of the Wittelsbach dynasty, which ruled Bavaria from 1180 to 1918. Though his family had created grandiose architecture in Munich, Ludwig II disliked the city and preferred isolation in the countryside, where he constructed monumental edifices born of fanciful imagination and spent most of the royal purse on his endeavors. Although he was also a great lover of literature, theater, and opera (he was Richard Wagner's great patron), it is his fairy-tale-like castles that are his legacy.

Ludwig II reigned from 1864 to 1886, all the while avoiding political duties whenever possible. By 1878 he had completed his Schloss Linderhof retreat and immediately began Schloss Herrenchiemsee, a tribute to Versailles and Louis XIV (⇨ *see Chapter 2*). The grandest of his extravagant projects is Neuschwanstein, one of Germany's top attractions and concrete proof of the king's eccentricity. In 1886, before Neuschwanstein was finished, members of the government became convinced that Ludwig had taken leave of his senses. A medical commission declared the king insane and forced him to abdicate. Within two days of incarceration in the Berg Castle, on Starnbergersee (⇨ *see Side Trips from Munich in Chapter 1*), Ludwig and his doctor were found drowned in the lake's shallow waters. Their deaths are still a mystery.

Füssen's main shopping street, called **Reichenstrasse,** was, like Augsburg's Maximilianstrasse, once part of the Roman Via Claudia. This cobblestone walkway is lined with high-gabled medieval houses and backed by the bulwarks of the castle and the easternmost buttresses of the Allgäu Alps.

WHERE TO STAY & EAT

¢ ✕ **Markthalle.** This is a farmers' market where you can grab a quick bite and drink at very reasonable prices. Try the fish soup. There are even a few tables. The building started in 1483 as the *Kornhaus* (grain storage) and then became the *Feuerhaus* (fire station). ⊠*Schrannenpl. 1* ▭*No credit cards* ⊘*Closed Sun. No dinner Sat.*

$–$$ ✕▦ **Hotel Hirsch.** A mother-and-daughter team provides friendly service at this traditional Füssen hotel. Outside the majestic building is its trademark stag (*Hirsch* in German); inside, the decor is Bavarian. You can stay in the King Ludwig room with his pictures on the walls and books about him to read, or stay with King Maximilian or with Spitzweg, a famous German artist who painted in Füssen. Both restaurants (¢–$$) serve an interesting variety of seasonal and local specialties. In season try venison or wild duck with blue cabbage and dumpling. If it's on the menu the trout is excellent, as it comes fresh from the local rivers. ⊠*Kaiser-Maximilian-Pl. 7, D–87629* ☎*08362/93980* 🖷*08362/939–877* ⊕*www.hotelhirsch.de* ⬈*58 rooms* ⌂*In-room: no a/c. In-hotel: 2 restaurants, bar, parking (no fee), some pets allowed (no fee), no-smoking rooms* ▭*AE, DC, MC, V* ⊘*Closed Jan.* †⊙*CP.*

$ ✗🖼Altstadthotel Zum Hechten. Geraniums flower most of the year on this comfortable inn's balconies. It's one of the town's oldest lodgings and is directly below the castle. Some rooms have en-suite facilities. In one of the two restaurants (¢–$), which have sturdy, round tables and colorfully frescoed walls, vegetarian meals are served. ⊠*Ritterstr. 6, D–87629* ☎*08362/91600* 🖷*08362/916–099* ⊕*www.hotel-hechten. com* ⇝*36 rooms, 30 with bath or shower* ⚇*In-room: no a/c, Wi-Fi (some). In-hotel: 2 restaurants, public Wi-Fi, parking (no fee), some pets allowed, no smoking rooms* ⊟*AE, MC, V* ⦿|*CP.*

SPORTS & THE OUTDOORS
Pleasure boats cruise Forggensee lake mid-June–early October. Alpine winds ensure good sailing and windsurfing. The **Forgensee-Yachtschule** (⊠*Seestr. 10, Dietringen* ☎*08367/471* ⊕*www.segeln-info.de*) offers sailing courses of up to two weeks' duration, with hotel or apartment accommodations. There are also boatyards and jetties with craft for rent at Waltenhofen.

There's good downhill skiing in the mountains above Füssen. Cross-country enthusiasts are catered to with more than 20 km (12 mi) of trails. Füssen's highest peak, the Tegelberg, has a ski school, **Skischule Tegelberg A. Geiger** (⊕*www.skischule-tegelberg.de* ☎*08362/8455*).

THE ROMANTIC ROAD ESSENTIALS

TRANSPORTATION

BY AIR
The major international airports serving the Romantic Road are Frankfurt and Munich. Regional airports include Nürnberg and Augsburg.

Contacts Airport Nürnberg (⊠*Flughafenstr. 100, D–90411* ☎*0911/93700* ⊕ *www.airport-nuernberg.de*). **Augsburg Airport** (⊠*Flughafenstr. 1, D–86169* ☎*0821/270–8111* ⊕ *www.augsburg-airport.de*).

BY BUS
From April through October daily bus service covers the northern stretch of the Romantic Road, between Frankfurt and Munich. A second bus covers the section of the route between Dinkelsbühl and Füssen. All buses stop at the major sights along the road. Deutsche Touring also operates six more extensive tours along the Romantic Road and along the region's other major holiday route, the Burgenstrasse. Reservations are essential; contact Deutsche Touring. Local buses cover much of the route but are infrequent and slow.

Information Deutsche Touring (⊠*Am Römerhof 17, D–60486 Frankfurt am Main* ☎*069/790–3501* ⊕ *www.touring-germany.com*).

BY CAR
Würzburg is the northernmost city of the Romantic Road and the natural starting point for a tour. It's on the Frankfurt–Nürnberg autobahn,

A–3, and is 115 km (71 mi) from Frankfurt. If you're using Munich as a gateway, Augsburg is 60 km (37 mi) from Munich via A–8.

The Romantic Road is most easily traveled by car, starting from Würzburg as outlined above and following country highway B–27 south to meet Roads B–290, B–19, B–292, and B–25 along the Wörnitz River.

The roads are busy and have only two lanes, so figure on covering no more than 70 km (40 mi) each hour, particularly in summer. The 40-km (24-mi) section of the route that's the least "romantic," the A–2 between Augsburg and Donauwörth, is also heavily used by trucks and other large vehicles traveling to northern Bavaria, so expect delays. For route maps, with roads and sights highlighted, contact the Touristik-Arbeitsgemeinschaft Romantische Strasse (Central Tourist Information Romantic Road) (⇨ *see Visitor Information*).

BY TRAIN

Infrequent trains link most major towns of the Romantic Road, but both Würzburg and Augsburg are on the InterCity and high-speed InterCity Express routes and have fast, frequent service to and from Berlin, Frankfurt, Munich, Stuttgart, and Hamburg. Deutsche Bahn offers special weekend excursion rates covering travel from most German railroad stations to Würzburg and hotel accommodations for up to four nights. Details are available at any train station.

CONTACTS & RESOURCES

TOUR OPTIONS

Many of the cities and towns on the Romantic Road offer guided tours, either on foot or by bus. Details are available from local tourist information offices. Following are a few of the most interesting guided tours.

Augsburg has self-guided walking tours, with routes posted on color-coded signs throughout the downtown area. From mid-May to mid-October a bus tour (€9.50) starts from the Rathaus at 10, from Thursday through Sunday, and walking tours (€7) set out from the Rathaus daily at 2. From November until April this walking tour takes place only on Saturday. All tours are conducted in German and English.

Contacts **Augsburg** (✉ *Tourist-Information, Maximilianstr. 57, D–86150* ☎ *0821/502–070* ⊕ *www.regio-augsburg.de*).

DINKELSBÜHL In Dinkelsbühl you can join guided tours from Easter through October at 2:30 PM or at 8:30 PM for €3, or you can patrol the illuminated old town with the night watchman at 9 PM free of charge. Weather permitting, you can drive around the old town in horse-drawn carriages (April–October) for €5. Tours in English are by reservation only and cost €45. All tours start from the Münster St. Georg.

Contacts **Dinkelsbühl** (✉ *Tourist-Information, Marktpl., D–91550* ☎ *09851/90240* ⊕ *www.dinkelsbuehl.de*).

ROTHENBURG-
OB-DER-
TAUBER

The costumed night watchman conducts a nightly tour of the town, leading the way with a lantern. From Easter to December a one-hour tour in English begins at 8 PM and costs €6 (a 90-minute daytime tour begins at 2 PM). All tours start at the Marktplatz (Market Square); at least two people are required for the tour. Private group tours with the night watchman can be arranged through www.nightwatchman. de. Art, patrician houses, and church theme tours for groups (€70 in English, €60 in German) can be arranged by the tourist office.

Contacts Rothenburg-ob-der-Tauber (⊠ *Tourist-Information, Rathaus, Marktpl. 2, D–91541* ☎ *09861/40492* ⊕ *www.rothenburg.com*).

ULM

The tourist office's 90-minute tour includes a visit to the Münster, the Old Town Hall, the Fischerviertel (Fishermen's Quarter), and the Danube riverbank. From April through October there are tours at 10 and 2:30 Monday–Saturday, 11:30 and 2:30 Sunday; from November through March tours are at 10 and 2:30 on Saturday and 11:30 and 2:30 on Sunday. The departure point is the tourist office (Stadthaus) on Münsterplatz; the cost is €6. From May to mid-October you can view Ulm from on-board the motor cruiser *Ulmer Spatz*. There are 50-minute cruises at 2 and 3 daily (€8). The boats tie up at the Metzgerturm, a two-minute walk from the city hall.

Contacts Ulm (⊠ *Tourist-Information, Münsterpl. 50 (Stadthaus), D–89073* ☎ *0731/161–2830* ⊕ *www.tourismus.ulm.de*).

WÜRZBURG

One-hour guided strolls through the old town in English start at the Haus zum Falken tourist office and take place from mid-June to mid-September, daily at 6:30 PM. Tickets (€5) can be purchased from the guide. German-speaking guided walking tours start at the Haus zum Falken tourist office from April through October, daily at 10:30 AM. The 90-minute tours cost €6. If you'd rather guide yourself, pick up a map from the same tourist office and follow the extremely helpful directions marked throughout the city by distinctive signposts. Two-hour bus tours of the city start at the main railway station from April through October, Monday–Saturday at 2 and Sunday and holidays at 10:30. The fare is €9. Look for the sign STADTRUNDFAHRTEN (guided city tours).

The Würzburger Personenschiffahrt Kurth & Schiebe operates excursions. A wine tasting (€8) is offered as you glide past the vineyards. Veitshöchheimer Personenschiffahrt offers daily service from Würzburg to Veitshöchheim, once the summer residence of the bishops of Würzburg.

Information Veitshöchheimer Personenschiffahrt (⊠ *Obere Maing. 8, D–97209 Veitshöchheim* ☎ *0931/55633*). **Würzburger Personenschiffahrt Kurth & Schiebe** (⊠ *St.-Norbert-Str. 9, D–97299Zell* ☎ *0931/58573*).

BICYCLE
TOURS

From April through September, Velotours offers a five-day trip from Würzburg to Rothenburg for €350 per person and a five-day trip from Rothenburg to Donauwörth for €350 per person. These two trips can be combined for a nine-day tour for €700. The tour operator Alpenland-Touristik offers several guided six- to eight-day bike tours starting from Landsberg am Lech into the Alpine foothills.

Information Alpenland–Touristik (⌂ Box 10-13-13, D–86899 Landsberg ☎ 08191/308–620 ☎ 08191/4913 ⊕ www.alpenlandtouristik.de). **Velotours** (✉ Ernst-Sachsstr. 1, D–78467Konstanz ☎ 07531/98280 ☎ 07531/982–898 ⊕ www.velotours.de).

VISITOR INFORMATION

A central tourist office based in Dinkelsbühl covers the entire Romantic Road: Touristik-Arbeitsgemeinschaft Romantische Strasse. Its brochure describes all the attractions along the Romantic Road.

Information Touristik-Arbeitsgemeinschaft Romantische Strasse (Central Tourist Information Romantic Road) (✉ Segringerstr. 19 D–91550 Dinkelsbühl ☎ 09851/551–387 ☎ 09851/551–388 ⊕ www.romantischestrasse.de). **Augsburg** (✉ Tourist-Information, Maximilianstr. 57, D–86150 ☎ 0821/502–070 ⊕ www.regio-augsburg.de). **Bad Mergentheim** (✉ Städtisches Kultur-und Verkehrsamt, Marktpl. 3, D–96980 ☎ 07931/57135 ⊕ www.bad-mergentheim.de). **Dinkelsbühl** (✉ Tourist-Information, Marktpl., D–91550 ☎ 09851/90240 ⊕ www.dinkelsbuehl.de). **Donauwörth** (✉ Städtisches Verkehrs-und Kulturamt, Rathausg. 1, D–86609 ☎ 0906/789–151 ⊕ www.donauwoerth.de). **Füssen** (✉ Kurverwaltung, Kaiser-Maximilian-Pl. 1, D–87629 ☎ 08362/93850 ⊕ www.fuessen.de). **Harburg** (✉ Fremdenverkehrsverein, Schlossstr. 1, D–86655 ☎ 09080/96990). **Nördlingen** (✉ Städtisches Verkehrsamt, Marktpl. 2, D–86720 ☎ 09081/84116 ⊕ www.noerdlingen.de). **Rothenburg-ob-der-Tauber** (✉ Tourist-Information, Rathaus, Marktpl. 2, D–91541 ☎ 09861/40492 ⊕ www.rothenburg.de). **Ulm** (✉ Tourist-Information, Münsterpl. 50 [Stadthaus], D–89073 ☎ 0731/161–2830 ⊕ www.tourismus.ulm.de). **Weikersheim** (✉ Städtisches Kultur-und Verkehrsamt, Marktpl. 12, D–97990 ☎ 07934/10255 ☎ 07934/10558 ⊕ www.weikersheim.de). **Würzburg** (✉ Fremdenverkehrsamt, Am Congress-Centrum, D–97070 ☎ 0931/372–335 ⊕ www.wuerzburg.de).

Franconia & the German Danube

WORD OF MOUTH

"[Franconia] is a delightful area to explore . . . there are endless little treasures of landscape and architecture . . . not to mention the gorgeous wines and regional delicacies in what is, by the way, the least expensive part of the country for the visitor."

—harzer

"Bamberg is an absolute gem, with a well-preserved Altstadt. It's actually a real, living city—not just maintained for tourists."

—RufusTFirefly

"Regensburg is vastly overlooked, and if you make it that far, drive another hour and visit Passau on the Austrian border at the confluence of three rivers. It was postcard pretty."

—cstepane

Updated by
Uli Ehrhardt

ALL THAT IS LEFT OF the huge, ancient kingdom of the Franks is the region known today as Franken (Franconia), stretching from the Bohemian Forest on the Czech border to the outskirts of Frankfurt. The Franks were not only tough warriors but also hard workers, sharp tradespeople, and burghers with a good political nose. The name *frank* means bold, wild, and courageous in the old Frankish tongue. It was only in the early 19th century, following Napoléon's conquest of what is now southern Germany, that the area was incorporated into northern Bavaria.

Although many proud Franconians would dispute it, this historic homeland of the Franks, one of the oldest Germanic peoples, is now unmistakably part of Bavaria. Franconian towns such as Bayreuth, Coburg, and Bamberg are practically places of cultural pilgrimage. Rebuilt Nürnberg (Nuremberg in English) is the epitome of German medieval beauty, though its name recalls both the Third Reich's huge rallies at the Zeppelinfeld and its henchmen's trials held in the city between 1945 and 1950.

Franconia is hardly an overrun tourist destination, yet its long and rich history, its landscapes and leisure activities (including skiing, golfing, hiking, and cycling), and its gastronomic specialties place it high on the enjoyment scale.

EXPLORING FRANCONIA & THE GERMAN DANUBE

Franconia's northern border is marked by the Main River, which is seen as the dividing line between northern and southern Germany. Its southern border ends at the Danube, where Lower Bavaria (Niederbayern) begins. Despite its extensive geographic spread, however, Franconia is a homogeneous region of rolling agricultural landscapes and thick forests climbing the mountains of the Fichtelgebirge. Nürnberg is a major destination in the area, and the towns of Bayreuth, Coburg, and Bamberg are an easy day trip from one another.

The Danube River passes through the Bavarian Forest on its way from Germany to Austria. West of Regensburg, river cruises and cyclists follow its path.

ABOUT THE RESTAURANTS & HOTELS

Many restaurants in the rural parts of this region serve hot meals only between 11:30 AM and 2 PM, and 6 PM and 9 PM. ■TIP→*Durchgehend warme Küche* **means that hot meals are also served between lunch and dinner.**

Make reservations well in advance for hotels in all the larger towns and cities if you plan to visit anytime between June and September. During the Nürnberg Toy Fair at the beginning of February rooms are rare and at a premium. If you're visiting Bayreuth during the annual Wagner Festival, in July and August, consider making reservations up to a year in advance. Remember, too, that during the festival, prices can be double the normal rates.

TOP REASONS TO GO

A Living Altstadt: This one isn't just for the tourists. Bamberg may be a UNESCO World Heritage site, but it's also a vibrant town living very much in the present.

The Fortress at Nürnberg: Holy Roman Emperors once resided in the vast complex of the Kaiserburg, which has fabulous views over the entire city.

The Bridge in Regensburg: The Golden Gate Bridge may be better known today, but the 12th century Steinerne Brücke (Stone Bridge) was its match in terms of engineering ingenuity and importance in its day.

"God's Ballroom": Vierzehnheiligen, a church on the Main north of Bamberg, is spectacular both inside and out. Fourteen columns, commemorating a vision of Christ and 14 saints, preside over the scene of swirling rococo decoration and light that earned the nickname "God's Ballroom."

An Organ Concert in Passau: Dom St. Stephan has the largest church organ in the world: 17,774 pipes all told. You can listen to the mighty sound they create at weekday concerts.

WHAT IT COSTS IN EUROS					
	¢	$	$$	$$$	$$$$
RESTAURANTS	under €9	€9–€15	€16–€20	€21–€25	over €25
HOTELS	under €50	€50–€100	€101–€175	€176–€225	over €225

Restaurant prices are per person for a main course at dinner. Hotel prices are for two people in a standard double room, including tax and service.

TIMING
Summer is the best time to explore Franconia, though spring and fall are also fine when the weather cooperates. Avoid the cold and wet months from November to March; many hotels and restaurants close, and no matter how pretty, many towns do seem quite dreary. If you're in Nürnberg in December, you're in time for one of Germany's largest and loveliest Christmas markets.

NORTHERN FRANCONIA

Three major German cultural centers lie within easy reach of one another: Coburg, a town with blood links to royal dynasties throughout Europe; Bamberg, with its own claim to German royal history and an Old Town area designated a UNESCO World Heritage site; and Bayreuth, where composer Richard Wagner finally settled, making it a place of musical pilgrimage for Wagner fans from all over the world.

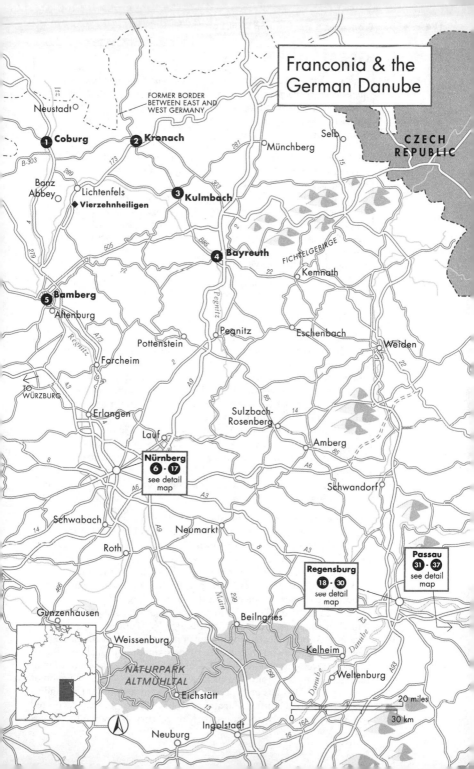

Franconia & the German Danube

FORMER BORDER
BETWEEN EAST AND
WEST GERMANY

Neustadt

1 **Coburg**

2 **Kronach**

Münchberg

Selb

**CZECH
REPUBLIC**

Banz
Abbey

Lichtenfels

Vierzehnheiligen

3 **Kulmbach**

4 **Bayreuth**

FICHTELGEBIRGE

Kemnath

5 **Bamberg**

Altenburg

Pegnitz

Eschenbach

Weiden

Pottenstein

Pegnitz

Forcheim

TO
WÜRZBURG

Erlangen

Lauf

Sulzbach-
Rosenberg

Amberg

Nürnberg

6 - **17**
see detail
map

Schwandorf

Schwabach

Neumarkt

Roth

Passau

31 - **37**
see detail
map

Regensburg

18 - **30**
see detail
map

Gunzenhausen

Beilngries

Kelheim

Weissenburg

**NATURPARK
ALTMÜHLTAL**

Danube

Weltenburg

Eichstätt

0   20 miles

0   30 km

Neuburg

Ingolstadt

GREAT ITINERARIES

Numbers in the text correspond to numbers in the margin and on the *Franconia & the German Danube, Nürnberg, Regensburg, and Passau* maps.

IF YOU HAVE 3 DAYS
Make ▣Nürnberg ❻–❼ your base and take day trips on each of the three days to **Bayreuth** ❹ (an imperative visit whether or not it's Wagner Festival season); **Bamberg** ❺, once the seat of one of the most powerful ruling families in the country; and **Coburg** ❶, home

of the Saxe-Coburg duchy. Each town is only a 50- to 70-minute drive away.

IF YOU HAVE 5 DAYS
Follow the 3 day itinerary and on the fourth day travel to ▣**Regensburg** ⓲–㉚, another city that has retained its original splendor. From here you can take a day trip to **Passau** ㉛–㉟. Make sure that you leave enough time to take a boat trip to view these cities from the waters of the Danube.

COBURG

❶ *105 km (65 mi) north of Nürnberg.*

Coburg is a surprisingly little-known treasure that was founded in the 11th century and remained in the possession of the dukes of Saxe-Coburg-Gotha until 1918; the present duke still lives here. The remarkable Saxe-Coburg dynasty established itself as something of a royal stud farm, providing a seemingly inexhaustible supply of blue-blood marriage partners to ruling houses the length and breadth of Europe. The most famous of these royal mates was Prince Albert (1819–1861), who married the English Queen Victoria, after which she gained special renown in Coburg. Their numerous children, married off to other kings, queens, and emperors, helped to spread the tried-and-tested Saxe-Coburg stock even farther afield. Despite all the history that sweats from each sandstone ashlar, Coburg is a modern and bustling town.

★ The **Veste Coburg** fortress, one of the largest and most impressive in the country, is Coburg's main attraction. The brooding bulk of the castle guards the town from a 1,484-foot hill. Construction began around 1055, but with progressive rebuilding and remodeling, today's predominantly late-Gothic–early-Renaissance edifice bears little resemblance to the original crude fortress. One part of the castle harbors the **Kunstsammlungen,** a grand set of collections including art, with works by Dürer, Cranach, and Hans Holbein, among others; sculpture from the school of the great Tilman Riemenschneider (1460–1531); furniture and textiles; magnificent weapons, armor, and tournament garb spanning four centuries (in the so-called **Herzoginbau,** or Duchess's Building); carriages and ornate sleighs; and more. The room where Martin Luther lived for six months in 1530 while he observed the goings-on of the Augsburg Diet has an especially dignified atmosphere. The **Jagdintarsien-Zimmer** (Hunting Marquetry Room), an elaborately decorated room that dates back to the early 17th century, has some of the finest woodwork in southern Germany. Finally, there's the **Carl-Eduard-Bau** (Carl-Eduard Building), which contains a valuable antique glass collection, mostly from the baroque age. Inquire at the ticket office for tours and reduced family tickets. ☎*09561/8790* ⊕*www.kunst-sammlungen-coburg.de* 📧*€3.30* ☉*Museums Apr.–Oct., daily 10–5; Nov.–Mar., Tues.–Sun. 1–4.*

NEED A BREAK? Relax and soak up centuries of history while sampling a Coburg beer at the **Burgschänke** (⊠*Veste Coburg* ☎*09561/80980*), Veste Coburg's own tavern. The basic menu has traditional dishes. The tavern is closed Monday and January–mid-February.

Coburg's **Marktplatz** *(Market Square)* has a statue of Prince Albert, the high-minded consort, standing proudly surrounded by gracious Renaissance and baroque buildings. The **Stadhaus,** former seat of the local dukes, begun in 1500, is the most imposing structure here. A forest of ornate gables and spires projects from its well-proportioned facade. Opposite is the **Rathaus** (Town Hall). ■**TIP→ Look on the building's tympanum for the statue of the Bratwurstmännla (it's actually St. Mauritius in armor); the staff he carries is said to be the official length against which the town's famous bratwursts are measured.** These tasty sausages, roasted on pinecone fires, are available on the market square.

Prince Albert spent much of his childhood in **Schloss Ehrenburg,** the ducal palace. Built in the mid-16th century, it has been greatly altered over the years, principally following a fire in the early 19th century. Duke Ernst I invited Karl Friedrich Schinkel from Berlin to redo the palace in the then-popular Gothic style. Some of the original Renaissance features were kept. The rooms of the castle are quite special, especially those upstairs, where the ceilings are heavily decorated with stucco and the floors have wonderful patterns of various woods. The Hall of Giants is named for the larger-than-life caryatids that support the ceiling; the favorite sight downstairs is Queen Victoria's flush toilet, which was the first one installed in Germany. Here, too, the ceiling is worth noting for its playful, gentle stuccowork. The baroque chapel attached to Ehrenburg is often used for weddings. ⊠*Schlosspl.* ☎*09561/80880* ⊕*www.sgvcoburg.de* 📧*€3, combined ticket with Schloss Rosenau €4.50* ☉*Tour Tues.–Sun. 10–3 on the hr.*

Perched on a hill 5 km (3 mi) to the west of Coburg is **Schloss Callenberg,** until 1231 the main castle of the Knights of Callenberg. In the 16th century it was taken over by the Coburgs. From 1842 on it served as the summer residence of the hereditary Coburg prince and later Duke Ernst II. It holds a number of important collections, including that of the Windsor gallery; arts and crafts from Holland, Germany, and Italy from the Renaissance to the 19th century; precious baroque, Empire, and Biedermeier furniture; table and standing clocks from three centuries; a selection of weapons; and various handicrafts. The best way to reach the castle is by car via Baiersdorf or by Bus 5 from the Marktplatz. ⊠*Callenberg* ☎*09561/55150* ⊕*www.schloss-callenberg.de* 📧*€4* ☉*Daily 11–5.*

WHERE TO STAY & EAT

¢–$ ✗**Ratskeller.** The local specialties taste better here beneath the old vaults and within earshot of the Coburg marketplace. Try the sauerbraten, along with a glass of crisp Franconian white wine. The prices become a little higher in the evening, and the menu adds a few more dishes. ⊠*Markt 1* ☏*09561/92400* ⊟*No credit cards.*

$–$$ ✗▥**Hotel Festungshof.** Duke Carl Eduard had this guest mansion built right outside the Veste in Coburg. This turn-of-the-20th-century building has comfortably (if not very imaginatively) furnished rooms. The café (¢–$$$) has a generous terrace, and the beer garden seats 300. A bus will take you to the town center, or you can take a 20-minute walk through the castle garden and the wooded landscape to reach the market square. ⊠*Rosenauerstr. 30, D–96450* ☏*09561/80290* 🖷*09561/802–933* ⊕*www.hotel-festungshof.de* ➴*14 rooms* ⌂*In-room: no a/c. In-hotel: restaurant, bar, parking, some pets allowed, no-smoking rooms* ⊟*MC, V* ☉*No dinner Sun., no lunch Mon.* ⦿❘*BP.*

¢–$ ✗▥**Goldene Rose.** One of the region's oldest, this agreeable inn is located about 5 km (3 mi) southeast of Coburg. The interior has simple wooden paneling and floors. On a warm summer evening, however, the beer garden (¢–$$) is the best place to enjoy traditional Franconian dishes, or a plate of homemade sausages, and meet some of the locals. Rooms are well appointed and comfortable—the wooden theme is continued, but the style is definitely modern. ⊠*Coburgerstr. 31, Grub am Forst, D–96271* ☏*09560/92250* 🖷*09560/1423* ⊕*www.goldene-rose. de* ➴*14 rooms* ⌂*In-room: no a/c, Wi-Fi. In-hotel: restaurant, bar, public Wi-Fi, parking (fee), no-smoking rooms* ⊟*MC, V* ☉*Restaurant closed Mon.* ⦿❘*BP.*

$$ ▥**Romantic Hotel Goldene Traube.** The first guests were welcomed to this hotel in 1756. Rooms are individually decorated, and for dining you can choose between the elegant restaurant Meer und Mehr (The Sea and More) or the cozy Weinstüble.After a day of sightseeing, relax in the sauna complex with solarium or with one of the vintages from the small wine boutique just opposite the reception. ⊠*Am Viktoriabrunnen 2, D–96450* ☏*09561/8760* 🖷*09561/876–222* ⊕*www. goldenetraube.com* ➴*72 rooms, 1 suite* ⌂*In-room: no a/c. In-hotel: restaurant, bar, gym, bicycles, public Wi-Fi, parking (fee), some pets allowed, no-smoking rooms* ⊟*AE, DC, MC, V* ⦿❘*BP.*

$–$$ ▥**Hotel Mercure Coburg.** You can expect modern, clean, well-designed rooms that are airy and functional at the Mercure. This link in the Mercure/Accor chain is about 15 minutes, on foot, east of Coburg's center. ⊠*Ketschendorfer Str. 86, D–96450* ☏*09561/8210* 🖷*09561/821–444* ⊕*www.mercure.com* ➴*123 rooms* ⌂*In-room: no a/c, Wi-Fi (some). In-hotel: laundry service, public Wi-Fi, parking (fee), some pets allowed, no-smoking rooms* ⊟*AE, DC, MC, V* ⦿❘*BP.*

FESTIVALS

Coburg's **Brazilian Samba Festival** is a three-day bacchanal held in mid-July. Check the Coburg tourist office's Web site for this and other events.

SHOPPING

■TIP➔Coburg is full of culinary delights; its *Schmätzen* (gingerbread) and *Elizenkuchen* (almond cake) are famous. You'll find home-baked versions in any of the many excellent **patisseries** or at a Grossman store (there are three in Coburg). Rödental, northeast of Coburg, is the home of the world-famous M. I. Hummel figurines, made by the Göbel porcelain manufacturer. There's a **Hummel Museum** (✉ *Coburgerstr. 7, Rödental* ☎ *09563/92303* ⊕ *www.goebel.de*) devoted to them, and 18th- and 19th-century porcelain from other manufacturers. The museum is open weekdays 9–5 and Saturday 9–noon. Besides the museum's store, there are several retail outlets in the village.

EN ROUTE Near the village of Rödental, 9 km (5½ mi) northeast of Coburg, the 550-year-old **Schloss Rosenau** sits in all its neo-Gothic glory in the midst of an English-style park. Prince Albert was born here in 1819, and one room is devoted entirely to Albert and his queen, Victoria. Much of the castle furniture was made especially for the Saxe-Coburg family by noted Viennese craftsmen. In the garden's Orangerie is the **Museum für Modernes Glas** (Museum of Modern Glass), which displays nearly 40 years' worth of glass sculptures (dating from 1950 to 1990) that contrast sharply with the venerable architecture of the castle itself. ☎ *09563/1606* ⊕ *www.kunstsammlungen-coburg.de* 🎟 *Castle €4, museum €1* ⊗ *Tours Apr.–Oct., daily at 10, 11, noon, 2, 3, and 4.*

KRONACH

❷ *23 km (15 mi) east of Coburg, 120 km (74 mi) north of Nürnberg.*

Kronach is a charming little gateway to the natural splendor of the Frankenwald region.

In its old medieval section, the **Obere Stadt** *(Upper Town)* , harmonious sandstone houses are surrounded by old walls and surmounted by a majestic fortress. Kronach is best known as the birthplace of Renaissance painter Lucas Cranach the Elder (1472–1553), but there's a running argument as to which house he was born in—Am Marktplatz 1 or in the house called Am Scharfen Eck, at Lucas-Cranach-Strasse 38. The latter was for more than a hundred years a meeting place for locals, where they had their beer and where today you can enjoy a very good, inexpensive Franconian meal. ■TIP➔On the last weekend in June, Kronach celebrates its past with a medieval festival featuring authentic garb, food, and troubadours.

FodorśChoice ★ **Festung Rosenberg** *(Rosenberg Fortress)* is a few minutes' walk from the town center. As you stand below its mighty walls, it's easy to see why it was never taken by enemy forces. During World War I it served as a POW camp with no less a figure than Charles de Gaulle as a "guest." Today Rosenberg houses a youth hostel and, more importantly, the **Fränkische Galerie** (the Franconian Gallery), an extension of the Bavarian National Museum in Munich, featuring paintings and sculpted works from the Middle Ages and the Renaissance. Lucas Cranach the Elder and Tilman Riemenschneider are represented, as well as artists from the Dürer School and the Bamberg School. In July and August the central courtyard is an atmospheric backdrop for performances of Goethe's *Faust*. The grounds of the fortress are also used by wood sculptors in the summer. ☎09261/60410 ⊕*www.kronach. de* ☞€3.50 ⊙*Fortress Apr.–Oct., Tues.–Sun. 9:30–5:30; Nov.–Mar., Tues.–Sun. 10–2.*

KULMBACH

❸ *19 km (12 mi) southeast of Kronach.*

A quarter of Kulmbachers earn their living directly or indirectly from beer. A special local brew available only in winter and during the Lenten season is *Eisbock,* a dark beer that is frozen as part of the brewing process to make it stronger. Kulmbach celebrates its beer every year in a nine-day festival that starts on the last Saturday in July. The main festival site, a mammoth tent, is called the *Festspulhaus*—literally, "festival swill house"—a none-too-subtle dig at nearby Bayreuth and its tony *Festspielhaus,* where Wagner's operas are performed.

The **Kulmbacher Brewery** (⊠*Lichtenfelserstr.* ☎09221/7050), a merger of four Kulmbach breweries, produces among others the strongest beer in the world—the *Doppelbock* Kulminator 28—which takes nine months to brew and has an alcohol content of more than 11%. The brewery runs the **Bayerisches Brauereimuseum Kulmbach** *(Kulmbach Brewery Museum)* jointly with the nearby Mönchshof-Bräu brewery and inn. ⊠*Hoferstr. 20* ☎09221/4264 ☞*Tour €5* ⊙*Tues.–Sun. 10–5.*

☼ The **Plassenburg,** the town's castle and symbol, is the most important Renaissance castle in the country. It stands on a rise overlooking Kulmbach, a 20-minute hike from the Old Town. The first building here, begun in the mid-12th century, was torched by marauding Bavarians who were eager to put a stop to the ambitions of Duke Albrecht Alcibiades—a man who spent several years murdering, plundering, and pillaging his way through Franconia. His successors built today's castle, starting in about 1560. Externally there's little to suggest the graceful Renaissance interior, but as you enter the main courtyard, the scene changes abruptly. The tiered space of the courtyard is covered with precisely carved figures, medallions, and other intricate ornaments, the whole comprising one of the most remarkable and delicate architectural ensembles in Europe. Inside, the **Deutsches Zinnfigurenmuseum** (Tin Figures Museum), with more than 300,000 miniature statuettes and tin soldiers, holds the largest collection of its kind in the world. The figures are arranged in scenes from all periods of history. During the day you cannot drive up to the castle. There is a shuttle bus that leaves from the main square every half hour from 9 to 6; cost is €2. ☎09221/947–505 ☞€4 ⊙*Apr.–Oct., daily 9–6, Nov.–Mar. 10–4.*

OFF THE BEATEN PATH

☼ **Neuenmarkt.** In this "railway village" near Kulmbach, more than 25 beautifully preserved gleaming locomotives huff and puff in a living railroad museum. Every now and then a nostalgic train will take you to the Brewery Museum in Kulmbach. Or you can enjoy a round trip to Marktschorgast that takes you up the very steep "schiefe Ebene" stretch (literally, slanting level). The museum also has model trains set up in incredibly detailed replicas of landscapes. ☒*Birkenstr. 5* ☏*09227/5700* ⊕*www.dampflok-museum.de* ☎€ *5* ⊙*Tues.–Sun. 10–5.*

WHERE TO STAY

$–$$ ☷**Hotel Kronprinz.** This old hotel tucked away in the middle of Kulmbach's Old Town, right in the shadow of Plassenburg Castle, covers all basic needs, though the furnishings are somewhat bland except in the higher-priced rooms. The café serves snacks and cakes. ☒*Fischerg. 4–6, D–95326* ☏*09221/92180* ☎*09221/921–836* ⊕*www.kronprinz-kulmbach.de* ⮐*22 rooms* ⌂*In-room: no a/c. In-hotel: restaurant, bar, no-smoking rooms* ⊙*Closed Dec. 24–29* ⊟*AE, DC, MC, V* ♚|*BP.*

> ### KULMBACH BREWS
>
> In a country where brewing and beer drinking break all records, Kulmbach produces more beer per capita than anywhere else: 9,000 pints for each man, woman, and child. The locals claim it's the sparkling-clear springwater from the nearby Fichtelgebirge hills that makes their beer so special.

4

BAYREUTH

❹ *24 km (15 mi) south of Kulmbach, 80 km (50 mi) northeast of Nürnberg.*

The small town of Bayreuth, pronounced "bye-*roit,*" owes its fame to the music giant Richard Wagner (1813–83). The 19th-century composer and musical revolutionary finally settled here after a lifetime of rootless shifting through Europe. Here he built his great theater, the Festspielhaus, as a suitable setting for his grand operas on mythological Germanic themes. The annual Wagner Festival dates to 1876, and brings droves of Wagner fans who push prices sky-high, fill hotels to bursting, and earn themselves much-sought-after social kudos in the process. The festival is held from late July until late August, so unless you plan to visit the town specifically for it, this is the time to stay away.

★ The **Neues Schloss** *(New Palace)* is a glamorous 18th-century palace built by the Margravine Wilhelmine, sister of Frederick the Great of Prussia and a woman of enormous energy and decided tastes. Though Wagner is the man most closely associated with Bayreuth, his choice of this setting is largely due to the work of this woman, who lived 100 years before him. Wilhelmine devoured books, wrote plays and operas (which she directed and, of course, acted in), and had buildings constructed, transforming much of the town and bringing it near bankruptcy. Her distinctive touch is evident at the palace, built when a mysterious fire conveniently destroyed parts of the original palace. Anyone with a taste for the wilder flights of rococo decoration will love it. Some rooms have been given over to one of Europe's finest collections of faience. ☒*Ludwigstr. 21* ☏*0921/759–6921* ☎€*4* ⊙*Apr.–Sept., daily 9–6; Oct.–Mar., Tues.–Sun. 10–4.*

Another great architectural legacy of Wilhelmine is the **Markgräfliches Opernhaus** *(Margravial Opera House).* Built between 1745 and 1748, it is a rococo jewel, sumptuously decorated in red, gold, and blue. Apollo and the nine Muses cavort across the frescoed ceiling. It was this delicate 500-seat theater that originally drew Wagner to Bayreuth; he felt that it might prove a suitable setting for his own operas. It's a wonderful setting for the concerts and operas of Bayreuth's "other" musical festivals, which in fact go on virtually throughout the year. Visitors are treated to a sound-and-light show. ⊠ *Opernstr.* ☎ *0921/759–6922* 🖼 *€5* ⊘ *Apr.–Sept., daily 9–5; Oct.–Mar., daily 10–3. Sound-and-light shows daily in opera house every 45 min starting at 9:15 in summer and 10:15 in winter. Closed during performances and on rehearsal days.*

Near the center of town, in the 1887 Maisel Brewery building, the **Brauerei und Büttnerei-Museum** *(Brewery and Coopers Museum)* reveals the tradition of the brewing trade over the past two centuries with a focus on the Maisel's trade, of course. The brewery operated until 1981, when its much bigger home was completed next door. ∎ **TIP→ After the 60-minute tour, you can quaff a cool, freshly tapped beer in the museum's pub, which has traditional Bavarian Weissbier (wheat beer).** ⊠ *Kulmbacherstr. 40* ☎ *0921/401–234* ⊕ *www.maisel.com* 🖼 *€4* ⊘ *Tour daily at 2* PM; *individual tours by prior arrangement.*

The **Altes Schloss Eremitage,** 5 km (3 mi) north of Bayreuth on B–85, makes an appealing departure from the sonorous and austere Wagnerian mood of much of the town. It's an early-18th-century palace, built as a summer palace and remodeled in 1740 by the Margravine Wilhelmine. Although her taste is not much in evidence in the drab exterior, the interior, alive with light and color, displays her guiding hand in every elegant line. The extraordinary **Japanischer Saal** (Japanese Room), filled with Asian treasures and chinoiserie furniture, is the finest room. The park and gardens, partly formal, partly natural, are enjoyable for idle strolling. Fountain displays take place at the two fake grottoes at the top of the hour, 10–5 daily. ☎ *0921/759–6937* 🖼 *Schloss €3, park free* ⊘ *Schloss Apr.–Sept., daily 9–6.*

WAGNER IN BAYREUTH

The **Festspielhaus** *(Festival Theater)* is by no means beautiful. In fact, this high temple of the Wagner cult is surprisingly plain. The spartan look is explained partly by Wagner's desire to achieve perfect acoustics. The wood seats have no upholstering, for example, and the walls are bare. The stage is enormous, capable of holding the huge casts required for Wagner's largest operas. Performances take place only during the annual Wagner Festival, still masterminded by descendants of the composer. ⊠ *Festspielhügel 1* ☎ *0921/78780* 🖼 *€5* ⊘ *Tour Dec.–Oct., Tues.–Sun. at 10, 11, 2, and 3. Closed during rehearsals and afternoons during festival.*

"Wahnfried," built by Wagner in 1874 and the only house he ever owned, is now the **Richard-Wagner-Museum.** It's a simple, austere neoclassical building whose name, "peace from madness," was well

4

earned. Wagner lived here with his wife, Cosima, daughter of pianist Franz Liszt, and they were both laid to rest here. King Ludwig II of Bavaria, the young and impressionable "Fairy-Tale King" who gave Wagner so much financial support, is remembered in a bust before the entrance. The exhibits, arranged along a well-marked tour through the house, require a great deal of German-language reading, but it's a must for Wagner fans. The original scores of such masterpieces as *Parsifal, Tristan und Isolde, Lohengrin, Der Fliegende Holländer,* and *Götterdämmerung* are on display. You can also see designs for productions of his operas, as well as his piano and huge library. A multimedia display lets you watch and listen to various productions of his operas. The little house where Franz Liszt lived and died is right next door and can be visited with your Richard-Wagner-Museum ticket, but be sure to express your interest in advance. It, too, is heavy on the paper, but the last rooms—with pictures, photos, and silhouettes of the master, his students, acolytes, and friends—are well worth the detour. ⊠ *Richard-Wagner-Str. 48* ☎ *0921/757–2816* ⊕ *www.wagnermuseum.de* 🖃 *€4, during festival €4.50* ☉ *Apr.–Oct., daily 9–5; Nov.–Mar., daily 10–5.*

WHERE TO STAY & EAT

¢–$ ✕ **Oskar.** A huge glass ceiling gives the large dining room a light atmo-
★ sphere even in winter. In summer, try for a table in the beer garden to enjoy fine Franconian specialties and continental dishes. The kitchen uses the freshest produce. The room fills up at night and during Sunday brunch, especially if a jazz band is playing in one of the alcoves. ⊠ *Maximilianstr. 33* ☎ *0921/516–0553* 🖃 *No credit cards.*

¢–$ ✕ **Wolffenzacher.** This self-described "nostalgic inn" harks back to the days when the local *Wirtshaus* (inn-pub) was the meeting place for everyone from the mayor's scribes to the local carpenters. Beer and hearty food are shared at wooden tables either in the rustic interior or out in the shady beer garden (in the middle of town), weather permitting. The hearty Franconian specialties are counterbalanced by a few lighter French and Italian dishes. ⊠ *Sternenpl. 5* ☎ *0921/64552* 🖃 *MC, V.*

$$–$$$ ✕🏠 **Schlosshotel Thiergarten.** Staying at this 250-year-old former hunting lodge is like being at your favorite aunt's, if she were an elderly millionaire. Rooms are individually furnished and have a plush, lived-in feel. The intimate Kaminhalle, with an ornate fireplace, and the Venezianischer Salon, dominated by a glittering 300-year-old Venetian chandelier, offer regional and international cuisine ($$–$$$$). The fabulous setting may outshine the food, but dining here, you will feel a bit like royalty yourself. The hotel is 8 km (5 mi) from Bayreuth in the Thiergarten suburb. ⊠ *Oberthiergärtenstr. 36, D–95448* ☎ *09209/9840* 🖨 *09209/98429* ⊕ *www.schlosshotel-thiergarten.de* ⇆ *8 rooms, 1 suite* ⚷ *In-room: no a/c, Wi-Fi. In-hotel: restaurant, bar, pool, public Internet, parking, some pets allowed, no-smoking rooms* 🖃 *AE, DC, MC, V* ⚹ *BP.*

$–$$ ✕🏠 **Goldener Anker.** No question about it, this is *the* place to stay in
★ Bayreuth. The hotel is right next to the Markgräfliches Opernhaus and has been entertaining composers, singers, conductors, and players for hundreds of years. The establishment has been run by the same family

EATING WELL IN FRANCONIA

Franconia is known for its good and filling food and for its simple and atmospheric *Gasthäuser*. Pork is a staple, served either as *Schweinsbraten* (a plain roast) or sauerbraten (marinated) with *Knödel* (dumplings made from either bread or potatoes). The specialties in Nürnberg, Coburg, and Regensburg are the Bratwürste—short, spiced sausages. The Nürnberg variety is known all over Germany; they are even on the menu in the ICE trains. You can have them grilled or heated in a stock of onions and wine (*saurer Zipfel*).

On the sweet side, try the *Dampfnudel*, a kind of sweet yeast-dough dumpling that is tasty and filling. Loved all over Germany, especially at Christmas time, are the Nürnberger Lebkuchen, a sort of gingerbread.

Not to be missed are Franconia's liquid refreshments from both the grape and the grain. Franconian wines, usually white and sold in distinctive flagons called *Bocksbeutel*, are renowned for their special bouquet (Silvaner is the traditional grape). The region has the largest concentration of local breweries in the world (Bamberg alone has 10, Bayreuth 7), producing a wide range of brews, the most distinctive of which is the dark, smoky *Rauchbier* and the even darker and stronger *Schwärzla*. Then of course there is Kulmbach, with the strongest beer in the world—the *Doppelbock* Kulminator 28—which takes nine months to brew and has an alcohol content of more than 11%.

since 1753. Some rooms are small; others have a royal splendor. One huge suite has a spiral staircase leading up to the bedroom. All are individually decorated, and many have antique pieces. The restaurant ($$– $$$$) is justly popular. Book your room far in advance. ⊠*Opernstr. 6, D–95444* ☎*0921/65051* 🖷*0921/65500* ⊕*www.anker-bayreuth. de* ⬦*38 rooms, 2 suites* ♿*In-room: no a/c, Ethernet (some). In-hotel: restaurant, public Wi-Fi, parking (fee), some pets allowed, no-smoking rooms* ▤*AE, DC, MC, V* ☻*Restaurant closed Mon., Tues., and Dec. 20–Jan. 15* ¶⊙|*BP.*

$–$$ ✕🏨**Hotel Lohmühle.** The old part of this hotel is in Bayreuth's only half-timber house, a former sawmill by a stream. It's just a two-minute walk to the town center. The rooms are rustic with visible beams; the newer, neighboring building has correspondingly modern rooms. Between the two is a gallery with a bar where you can enjoy a small aperitif before trying some of the restaurant's traditional, hearty cooking ($$–$$$), such as Schäufele or carp. ⊠*Badstr. 37, D–95445* ☎*0921/53060* 🖷*0921/530–6469* ⊕*www.hotel-lohmuehle.de* ⬦*42 rooms* ♿*In-room: no a/c, Wi-Fi (some). In-hotel: restaurant, bar, public Wi-Fi, some pets allowed, no-smoking rooms* ▤*AE, DC, MC, V* ☻*No dinner Sun.* ¶⊙|*BP.*

NIGHTLIFE & THE ARTS

Opera lovers swear that there are few more intense operatic experiences than the annual **Wagner Festival** in Bayreuth, held July and August. For tickets write to the **Bayreuther Festspiele Kartenbüro** (✉*Postfach 100262, D–95402 Bayreuth* ☎*0921/78780*), but be warned: the waiting list is years long. You'll do best if you plan your visit a couple of years in advance. Rooms can be nearly impossible to find during the festival, too. If you don't get Wagner tickets, console yourself with visits to the exquisite 18th-century **Markgräfliches Opernhaus** (✉ *Opernstr.* ☎ *0921/759–6922*). In May the *Fränkische Festwochen* (Franconian Festival Weeks) take the stage with works of Wagner, of course, but also Paganini and Mozart.

SHOPPING

The **Hofgarten Passage,** off Richard-Wagner-Strasse, is one of the fanciest shopping arcades in the region; it's full of smart boutiques selling anything from German high fashion to simple local craftwork.

EN ROUTE The B–22 highway cuts through the **Fränkische Schweiz**—or Franconian Switzerland—which got its name from its fir-clad upland landscape. Just north of Hollfeld, 23 km (14 mi) west of Bayreuth, the Jurassic rock of the region breaks through the surface in a bizarre, craggy formation known as the Felsgarten (Rock Garden).

4

BAMBERG

5 Fodor'sChoice ★

65 km (40 mi) west of Bayreuth, 80 km (50 mi) north of Nürnberg.

Few towns in Germany survived the war with as little damage as Bamberg, which is on the Regnitz River. ■ **TIP→ This former residence of one of Germany's most powerful imperial dynasties is on UNESCO's World Heritage Site list.** Bamberg, originally nothing more than a fortress in the hands of the Babenberg dynasty (later contracted to Bamberg), rose to prominence in the 11th century thanks to the political and economic drive of its most famous offspring, Holy Roman Emperor Heinrich II. He transformed the imperial residence into a flourishing episcopal city. His cathedral, consecrated in 1237, still dominates the historic area. For a short period Heinrich II proclaimed Bamberg the capital of the Holy Roman Empire of the German Nation. Moreover, Bamberg earned fame as the second city to introduce book printing, in 1460.

Bamberg's historic core, the **Altes Rathaus** *(Old Town Hall)*, is tucked snugly on a small island in the Regnitz. To the west of the river is the so-called Bishops' Town; to the east, Burghers' Town. This rickety, extravagantly decorated building was built in this unusual place so that the burghers of Bamberg could avoid paying real-estate taxes to their bishops and archbishops. The excellent collection of porcelain here is a vast sampling of 18th-century styles, from almost sober Meissens with bucolic Watteau scenes to simple but rare Haguenau pieces from Alsace and faience from Strasbourg. ✉ *Obere Brücke 1* ☎ *0951/871–871* 💶 *€4* ⏱ *Tues.–Sun. 9:30–4:30.*

NEED A BREAK? Before heading up the hill to the main sights in the Bishops' Town, take a break with coffee, cake, small meals, or cocktails in the half-timber **Rathaus-Schänke** (✉ *Obere Brücke 3* ☎ *0951/208–0890*). It overlooks the river on the Burghers' Town side of the Town Hall.

The **Neue Residenz** *(New Residence)* is a glittering baroque palace that was once the home of the prince-electors. Their plans to extend the immense palace even further is evident at the corner on Obere Karolinenstrasse, where the ashlar bonding was left open to accept another wing. The most memorable room in the palace is the **Kaisersaal** (Throne Room), complete with impressive ceiling frescoes and elaborate stuccowork. The rose garden behind the Neue Residenz provides an aromatic and romantic spot for a stroll with a view of Bamberg's roof landscape.

The palace is also home to the **Staatsbibliothek** (State Library) (⊕*www. Staatsbibliothek-bamberg.de* ◷ *Weekdays 9–5, Sat. 9–noon* ⊠*Free).* Among the thousands of books and illuminated manuscripts here are the original prayer books belonging to Heinrich II and his wife, a 5th-century codex of the Roman historian Livy, and manuscripts by the 16th-century painters Dürer and Cranach. You have to take a tour to see the Residenz itself, but you can visit the library free of charge at any time during its open hours. ⊠*Neue Residenz, Dompl. 8* ☎*0951/955– 030* ⊠*€4* ◷*Neue Residenz by tour only, Apr.–Sept., daily 9–6; Oct.– Mar., daily 10–4.*

★ Bamberg's great **Dom** *(Cathedral)* is one of the country's most important, a building that tells not only the town's story but that of Germany as well. The first building here was begun by Heinrich II in 1003, and it was in this partially completed cathedral that he was crowned Holy Roman Emperor in 1012. In 1237 it was destroyed by fire, and the present late-Romanesque—early-Gothic building was begun. The dominant features are the massive towers at each corner. Heading into the dark interior, you'll find a striking collection of monuments and art treasures. The most famous piece is the **Bamberger Reiter** (Bamberg Rider), an equestrian statue carved—no one knows by whom—around 1230 and thought to be an allegory of chivalrous virtue or a representation of King Stephen of Hungary. Compare it with the mass of carved figures huddled in the tympana above the church portals. In the center of the nave you'll find another masterpiece, the massive tomb of Heinrich and his wife, Kunigunde. It's the work of Tilman Riemenschneider. Pope Clement II is also buried in the cathedral, in an imposing tomb beneath the high altar; he's the only pope to be buried north of the Alps. ⊠*Dompl.* ☎*0951/502–330* ◷*Nov.–Mar., daily 10–5; Apr.–Oct., daily 10–6. No visits during services.*

The **Diözesanmuseum** *(Cathedral Museum)*, directly next to the cathedral, contains one of many nails and splinters of wood reputed to be from the cross of Jesus. The "star-spangled" cloak stitched with gold that was given to Emperor Heinrich II by an Italian prince is among the finest items displayed. More macabre exhibits in this rich ecclesiastical collection are the elaborately mounted skulls of Heinrich and Kunigunde. The building itself was designed by Balthasar Neumann (1687–1753), the architect of Vierzehnheiligen, and constructed between 1730 and 1733. ⊠*Dompl. 5* ☎*0951/502–325* ⊠*€3* ◷*Tues.–Sun. 10–5; tour in English by prior arrangement.*

Bamberg's wealthy burghers built no fewer than 50 churches. Among the very special ones is the Church of Our Lady, known simply as **Obere Pfarre** *(Upper Parish)*, whose history goes back to around 1325. It's unusual because it's still entirely Gothic from the outside. Also, the grand choir, which was added at a later period, is lacking windows. And then there's the odd, squarish box perched atop the tower. This watchman's abode served to cut the tower short before it grew taller than the neighboring cathedral, thereby avoiding a great scandal. The interior is heavily baroque. Note the slanted floor, which allowed crowds of pilgrims to see the object of their veneration, a 14th-century Madonna. Don't miss the *Ascension of Mary* by Tintoretto at the rear of the church. Around Christmas, the Obere Pfarre is the site of the city's greatest Nativity scene. Avoid the church during services, unless you're worshipping. ⊠ *Untere Seelg.* ☉ *Daily 7–7.*

St. Michael, a former Benedictine monastery, has been gazing over Bamberg since about 1015. After being overwhelmed by so much baroque elsewhere, entering this haven of simplicity is quite an experience. The entire choir is intricately carved, but the ceiling is gently decorated with very exact depictions of 578 flowers and healing herbs. The tomb of St. Otto is in a little chapel off the transept, and the stained-glass windows hold symbols of death and transfiguration. The monastery is now used as a home for the aged. One tract, however, was taken over by the **Franconian Brewery Museum**, which exhibits everything that has to do with beer, from the making of malt to recipes. ⊠ *Michelsberg 10f* 🕾 *0951/53016* 🎫 *Museum €3* ☉ *Apr.–Oct., Wed.–Sun. 1–5.*

NEAR BAMBERG

Fodor'sChoice ★ **Vierzehnheiligen.** On the east side of the Main north of Bamberg is a tall, elegant yellow-sandstone edifice whose interior represents one of the great examples of rococo decoration. The church was built by Balthasar Neumann (architect of the Residenz at Würzburg) between 1743 and 1772 to commemorate a vision of Christ and 14 saints— *vierzehn Heiligen*—that appeared to a shepherd in 1445. The interior, known as "God's ballroom," is supported by 14 columns. In the middle of the church is the Gnadenaltar (Mercy Altar) featuring the 14 saints. Thanks to clever play with light, light colors, and fanciful gold-and-blue trimmings, the interior seems to be in perpetual motion. Guided tours of the church are given on request; a donation is expected. On Saturday afternoon and all day Sunday the road leading to the church is closed and you have to walk the last half mile. ⊠ *36 km (22 mi) north of Bamberg via B–173* 🕾 *09571/95080* ⊕ *www.vierzehnheiligen.de* ☉ *Mar.–Oct., daily 7–6; Nov.–Feb., daily 8–5.*

Kloster Banz *(Banz Abbey).* This abbey, which some call the "holy mountain of Bavaria," proudly crowns the west bank of the Main north of Bamberg. There had been a monastery here since 1069, but the present buildings—now a political-seminar center and think tank—date from the end of the 17th century. The highlight of the complex is the **Klosterkirche** (Abbey Church), the work of architect Leonard Dientzenhofer and his brother, the stuccoist Johann Dientzenhofer (1663–1726). Balthasar Neumann later contributed a good deal of work.

Concerts are occasionally held in the church, including some by members of the renowned "Bamberger Symphoniker." To get to Banz from Vierzehnheiligen, drive south to Unnersdorf, where you can cross the river. ☎09573/7311 ⊙ *May–Oct., daily 9–5; Nov.–Apr., daily 9–noon; call to request a tour.*

WHERE TO STAY & EAT

¢–$ ✕ **Bischofsmühle.** It doesn't always have to be beer in Bamberg. The old mill, its grinding wheel providing a sonorous backdrop for patrons, specializes in wines from Franconia and elsewhere. The menu offers Franconian specialties such as the French-derived *Böfflamott,* or beef stew. ⊠ *Geyerswörthstr. 4* ☎0951/27570 ☐ *No credit cards* ⊙ *Closed Wed.*

¢–$ ✕ **Klosterbräu.** This massive old stone-and-half-timber house has been standing since 1533. Regulars nurse their dark, smoky beer called Schwärzla near the big stove. If you like the brew, you can buy a 5-liter bottle as well as other bottled beers and the corresponding beer steins at the counter. The cuisine is basic, robust, filling, and tasty, with such items as a bowl of beans with a slab of smoked pork, or marinated pork kidneys with boiled potatoes. ⊠ *Obere Mühlbrücke* ☎0951/52265 ☐ *No credit cards.*

$$ ✕🏨 **Hotel-Restaurant St. Nepomuk.** This half-timber house seems to float
Fodor's Choice over the Regnitz. The dining room, with its podium fireplace, discreet
★ lights, and serene atmosphere, has a direct view of the river. The Grüner family makes a special effort to bring not only high-quality food to the restaurant ($$$) but a world of excellent wines as well. The individually decorated rooms are comfortable, and many have quite a view of the water and the old town hall on its island. ⊠ *Obere Mühlbrücke 9, D–96049* ☎0951/98420 🖷0951/984–2100 ⊕ *www.hotel-nepomuk. de* ➾47 rooms ⚬ *In-room: no a/c, Wi-Fi. In-hotel: restaurant, public Wi-Fi, parking (fee), some pets allowed, no-smoking rooms* ☐*MC, V* ⫿◎⫿*BP.*

$$ ✕🏨 **Romantik Hotel Weinhaus Messerschmitt.** Willy Messerschmitt of avia-
★ tion fame grew up in this beautiful late-baroque house with a steep-eaved, green-shutter stucco exterior. The very comfortable hotel has spacious and luxurious rooms, some with exposed beams and many of them lighted by chandeliers. You'll dine under beams and a coffered ceiling in the excellent Messerschmitt restaurant ($$–$$$), one of Bamberg's most popular culinary havens for Franconian specialties. ⊠ *Langestr. 41, D–96047* ☎0951/297–800 🖷0951/297–8029 ⊕ *www.hotel-messerschmitt.de* ➾67 rooms ⚬ *In-room: no a/c. In-hotel: restaurant, bar, some pets allowed, no-smoking rooms* ☐*AE, DC, MC, V* ⫿◎⫿*BP.*

THE ARTS

The **Sinfonie an der Regnitz** (⊠*Muss-Str. 20* ☎0951/964–7200), a fine riverside concert hall, is home to Bamberg's world-class resident symphony orchestra. The **Hoffmann Theater** (⊠*Schillerpl. 5* ☎0951/873030) has opera and operetta from September through July. The city's first-class choir, **Capella Antiqua Bambergensis,** concentrates on ancient music. Throughout the summer organ concerts are given Saturdays at noon in the **Dom.** For program details and tickets to all cultural events, call ☏0951/297–6200.

SHOPPING

■**TIP➜ If you happen to be traveling around Christmastime, make sure you keep an eye out for crèches, a Bamberg specialty.** Of the many shops in Bamberg, the **AGIL** (✉*Schranne 14* ☏*0951/519–0389*) may be the one you'll want to visit for an unusual souvenir.

EN ROUTE

From Bamberg you can take either the fast autobahn (A–73) south to Nürnberg or the parallel country road (B–4) that follows the Main-Donau Canal (running parallel to the Regnitz River at this point) and joins A–73 just under 25 km (15 mi) later at Forchheim-Nord.

Eighteen kilometers (11 mi) south of Bamberg in the village of Buttenheim is a little blue-and-white half-timber house where Löb Strauss was born—in egregious poverty—in 1826. Take the tape-recorded tour of the **Levi-Strauss Museum** (✉*Marktstr. 33* ☏*09545/442–602* ⊕*www. levi-strauss-museum.de* 🎫*€2.60* ⊙*Tues. and Thurs. 2–6, weekends 11–5 and by appointment*) and learn how Löb emigrated to the United States, changed his name to Levi, and became the first name in denim. The stone-washed color of the house's beams, by the way, is the original 17th-century color.

NÜRNBERG (NUREMBERG)

Nürnberg (Nuremberg in English) is the principal city of Franconia and the second-largest city in Bavaria. With a recorded history stretching back to 1050, it's among the most historic of Germany's cities; the core of the Old Town, through which the Pegnitz River flows, is still surrounded by its original medieval walls. Nürnberg has always taken a leading role in German affairs. It was here, for example, that the Holy Roman Emperors traditionally held the first Diet, or convention of the estates, of their incumbency. And it was here, too, that Hitler staged the most grandiose Nazi rallies; later, this was the site of the Allies' war trials, where top-ranking Nazis were charged with—and almost without exception convicted of—crimes against humanity. The rebuilding of Nürnberg after the war was virtually a miracle, considering the 90% destruction of the Old Town. Nürnberg, in 2001, became the world's first city to receive the UNESCO prize for Human Rights Education.

As a major intersection on the medieval trade routes, Nürnberg became a wealthy town where the arts and sciences flowered. Albrecht Dürer (1471–1528), the first indisputable genius of the Renaissance in Germany, was born here in 1471. He married in 1509 and bought a house in the city where he lived and worked for the rest of his life. Other leading Nürnberg artists of the Renaissance include painter Michael Wolgemut (a teacher of Dürer), stonecutter Adam Kraft, and the brass founder Peter Vischer. The tradition of the Meistersinger also flourished here in the 16th century, thanks to the high standard set by the local cobbler Hans Sachs (1494–1576). The Meistersinger were poets and musicians who turned songwriting into a special craft with a wealth

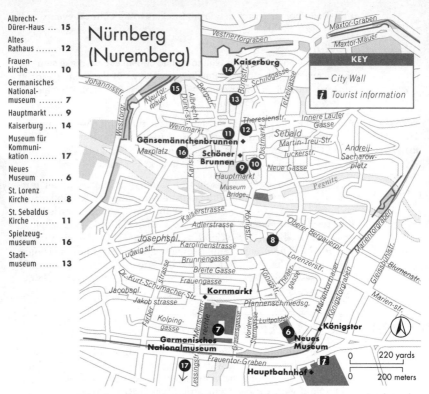

of rules and regulations. They were celebrated three centuries later by Wagner in his *Meistersinger von Nürnberg*.

The Thirty Years' War and the shift to sea routes for transportation led to the city's long decline, which ended only in the early 19th century when the first railroad opened in Nürnberg. Among a great host of inventions associated with the city, the most significant are the pocket watch, gun casting, the clarinet, and the geographic globe (the first of which was made before Columbus discovered the Americas). Among Nürnberg's famous products are *Lebkuchen* (gingerbread of sorts) and Faber-Castell pencils.

EXPLORING NÜRNBERG'S OLD TOWN

Walls, finished in 1452, surround Nürnberg's Old Town. Year-round floodlighting adds to the brooding romance of their moats, sturdy gateways, and watchtowers.

You'll need a full day to walk around Nürnberg's Old Town, two if you wish to take more time at its fascinating museums and churches. Most of the major sights are within a few minutes' walk of each other. The Kaiserburg is a must-visit on any trip to Nürnberg.

MAIN ATTRACTIONS

15 **Albrecht-Dürer-Haus** *(Albrecht Dürer*
★ *House).* The great painter Albrecht
Dürer lived here from 1509 until his
death in 1528. This beautifully preserved late-medieval house is typical of the prosperous merchants'
homes that once filled Nürnberg.
Dürer, who enriched German art
with Italianate elements, was more
than a painter. He raised the wood-
cut, a notoriously difficult medium,
to new heights of technical sophistication, combining great skill with a
haunting, immensely detailed drawing style and complex, allegorical
subject matter while earning a good
living at the same time. A number
of original prints adorn the walls,
and printing techniques using the
old press are demonstrated in the
studio. An excellent opportunity to
find out about life in the house of
Dürer is the Saturday 2 PM tour with a guide role-playing Agnes Dürer,
Dürer's wife. ✉*Albrecht-Dürer-Str. 39* ☏*0911/231–2568* 💶*€5, with
tour €7.50* ⏱*Tues., Wed., and Fri.–Sun. 10–5, Thurs. 10–8; guided tour
in English Sat. at 2.*

TOURING TIPS

Information: The tourist office at
the Hauptbahnhof, the main train
station, has maps and brochures.

Scenic Spots: The ramparts of
the Kaiserburg offer a spectacular
view over this medieval gem of
a town.

Scenic Spots: Where the König-
strasse crosses the Pegnitz River
is one of the most photogenic
points of the city. At Museums-
brücke, the former hospital Heilig-Geist-Spital, now a restaurant,
broods over the waters.

Snacks: Look to the restaurants
and bars around the Hauptmarkt
for refreshment.

7 **Germanisches Nationalmuseum** *(German National Museum).* You could
Fodor'sChoice spend days visiting this vast museum, which showcases the country's
★ cultural and scientific achievements, ethnic background, and history.
It's the largest of its kind in Germany and perhaps the best arranged.
The museum is in what was once a Carthusian monastery, complete
with cloisters and monastic outbuildings. The extensions, however, are
modern. The exhibition begins outside, with the tall, sleek pillars of
the Strasse der Menschenrechte (Street of Human Rights), designed
by Israeli artist Dani Karavan. Thirty columns are inscribed with the
articles from the Declaration of Human Rights. There are few aspects
of German culture, from the Stone Age to the 19th century, that are not
covered by the museum, and quantity and quality are evenly matched.
One highlight is the superb collection of Renaissance German paintings (with Dürer, Cranach, and Altdorfer well represented). Others
may prefer the exquisite medieval ecclesiastical exhibits—manuscripts,
altarpieces, statuary, stained glass, jewel-encrusted reliquaries—the
collections of arms and armor, the scientific instruments, or the toys.
✉*Kartäuserg. 1* ☏*0911/13310* 🌐*www.gnm.de* 💶*€6* ⏱*Tues. and
Thurs.–Sun. 10–6, Wed. 10–9.*

**NEED A
BREAK?**
Opposite the Germanisches Nationalmuseum is **Vivere** (✉*Kartäuserg.
12* ☏*0911/244–9774* ⏱*Closed Mon.*). Al dente pasta or meat and fish
dishes with excellent wines will revive you after the long hours spent
in the museum.

⑭ Kaiserburg *(Imperial Castle)*. The city's main attraction is a grand yet
Fodor'sChoice playful collection of buildings standing just inside the city walls; it was
★ once the residence of the Holy Roman Emperors. The complex comprises three separate groups. The oldest, dating from around 1050, is
the **Burggrafenburg** (Castellan's Castle), with a craggy old pentagonal
tower and the bailiff's house. It stands in the center of the complex.
To the east is the **Kaiserstallung** (Imperial Stables), built in the 15th
century as a granary and now serving as a youth hostel. The real interest of this vast complex of ancient buildings, however, centers on the
westernmost part of the fortress, which begins at the **Sinwell Turm**
(Sinwell Tower). The **Kaiserburg Museum** is here, a subsidiary of the
Germanisches Nationalmuseum that displays ancient armors and has
exhibits relating to horsemanship in the imperial era and to the history
of the fortress. This section of the castle also has a wonderful Romanesque **Doppelkappelle** (Double Chapel). The upper part—richer, larger,
and more ornate than the lower chapel—was where the emperor and
his family worshiped. Also visit the **Rittersaal** (Knights' Hall) and
the **Kaisersaal** (Throne Room). Their heavy oak beams, painted ceilings, and sparse interiors have changed little since they were built in
the 15th century. ⊠ *Burgstr.* ☎ *0911/24465–9115* 🖃 *€6* ☉ *Apr.–Sept.,
daily 9–6; Oct.–Mar., daily 10–4.*

⑥ Neues Museum *(New Museum)*. Anything but medieval, this museum
★ is devoted to international design since 1945. The collection, supplemented by changing exhibitions, is in a slick, modern edifice that
achieves the perfect synthesis between old and new. It's mostly built
of traditional pink-sandstone ashlars, while the facade is a flowing,
transparent composition of glass. The interior is a work of art in
itself—cool stone, with a ramp that slowly spirals up to the gallery.
Extraordinary things await, including a Joseph Beuys installation (*Ausfegen,* or *Sweep-out*) and *Avalanche* by François Morellet, a striking
collection of violet, argon-gas-filled fluorescent tubes. The café-restaurant adjoining the museum contains modern art, silver-wrapped candies, and video projections. ⊠ *Luitpoldstr. 5* ☎ *0911/240–200* 🖃 *€4*
☉ *Tues.–Fri. 10–8, weekends 10–6.*

ALSO WORTH SEEING

⑫ Altes Rathaus *(Old Town Hall)*. This ancient building on Rathausplatz
abuts the rear of St. Sebaldus Kirche; it was erected in 1332, destroyed
in World War II, and subsequently restored. Its intact medieval dungeons, consisting of 12 small rooms and one large torture chamber
called the **Lochgefängnis** (or the Chapel, owing to the vaulted ceilings), provide insight into the gruesome applications of medieval
law. **Gänsemännchenbrunnen** (Gooseman's Fountain) faces the Altes
Rathaus. This lovely Renaissance bronze fountain, cast in 1550, is a
work of rare elegance and great technical sophistication. ⊠ *Rathauspl.
2* ☎ *0911/231–2690* 🖃 *€3, minimum of 5 people for tours* ☉ *Tues.–
Sun. 10–4.*

⑩ Frauenkirche *(Church of Our Lady)*. The fine late-Gothic Frauenkirche
was built in 1350, with the approval of Holy Roman Emperor Charles
IV, on the site of a synagogue that was burned down during a 1349

pogrom. The modern tabernacle beneath the main altar was designed to look like a Torah scroll as a kind of memorial to that despicable act. The church's real attraction is the **Männleinlaufen,** a clock dating from 1509, which is set in its facade. It's one of those colorful mechanical marvels at which Germans have long excelled. ■ TIP→ Every day at noon the seven electors of the Holy Roman Empire glide out of the clock to bow to Emperor Charles IV before sliding back under cover. It's worth scheduling your morning to catch the display. ⊠ *Hauptmarkt* ⊙ *Mon.–Sat. 9–6, Sun. 12:30–6.*

⑨ Hauptmarkt *(Main Market).* Nürnberg's central market square was at one time the city's Jewish Quarter. When the people of Nürnberg petitioned their emperor, Charles IV, for a big central market, the emperor was in desperate need of money and, above all, political support. The Jewish Quarter was the preferred site, but as the official protector of the Jewish people, the emperor could not just openly take away their property. Instead, he instigated a pogrom that left the Jewish Quarter in flames and more than 500 dead. He then razed the ruins and resettled the remaining Jews.

Towering over the northwestern corner of the Hauptmarkt, **Schöner Brunnen** (Beautiful Fountain) looks as though it should be on the summit of some lofty cathedral. Carved around the year 1400, the elegant 60-foot-high Gothic fountain is adorned with 40 figures arranged in tiers—prophets, saints, local noblemen, sundry electors of the Holy Roman Empire, and one or two strays such as Julius Caesar and Alexander the Great. ■ TIP→ A gold ring is set into the railing surrounding the fountain, reportedly placed there by an apprentice carver. Touching it is said to bring good luck. A market still operates in the Hauptmarkt. Its colorful stands are piled high with produce, fruit, bread, homemade cheeses and sausages, sweets, and anything else you might need for a snack or picnic. It's here that the Christkindlesmarkt is held.

Jüdisches Museum Franken. The everyday life of the Jewish community in Franconia and Fürth is examined in this Jewish museum: books, seder plates, coat hangers, old statutes concerning Jews, and children's toys are among the exhibits. Among the most famous members of the Fürth community was Henry Kissinger, born here in 1923. Changing exhibitions relate to contemporary Jewish life in Germany, and in the basement is the mikwe, the ritual bath, which was used by the family who lived here centuries ago. A subsidiary to the museum, which houses special exhibitions, is in the former synagogue in nearby Schnaittach. To get to the museum from Nürnberg, you can take the U1 U-bahn to the Rathaus stop. ⊠ *Königstr. 89, 10 km (6 mi) west of Nürnberg, Fürth* ☎ *0911/770–577* ⊕ *www.juedisches-museum.org* ✆ *€5* ⊙ *Wed.–Sun. 10–5, Tues. 10–8.*

⑰ Museum für Kommunikation *(Communication Museum).* Two museums have been amalgamated under a single roof here, the German Railway Museum and the Museum of Communication—in short, museums about how people get in touch. The first train to run in Germany did so on December 7, 1835, from Nürnberg to nearby Fürth. A model of the epochal train is here, along with a series of original 19th- and early-20th-century trains and stagecoaches. Philatelists will want to check out some of the 40,000-odd stamps in the extensive exhibits on the German postal system. You can also find out about the history of sending messages—from old coaches to optical fiber networks. ⊠*Lessingstr. 6* ☎*0911/219–2428* ☞*€4* ⊙*Tues.–Sun. 9–5.*

❽ St. Lorenz Kirche *(St. Laurence Church).* In a city with several striking churches, St. Lorenz is considered by many to be the most beautiful. It was begun around 1250 and completed in about 1477; it later became a Lutheran church. Two towers flank the main entrance of the sizable church, which is covered with a forest of carvings. In the lofty interior, note the works by sculptors Adam Kraft and Veit Stoss: Kraft's great stone tabernacle, to the left of the altar, and Stoss's *Annunciation,* at the east end of the nave, are their finest works. There are many other carvings throughout the building, testimony to the artistic wealth of late-medieval Nürnberg. ⊠*Lorenzer Pl.* ⊙*Mon.–Sat. 9–5, Sun. noon–4.*

⓫ St. Sebaldus Kirche *(St. Sebaldus Church).* Although St. Sebaldus lacks the quantity of art treasures found in its rival St. Lorenz, its nave and choir are among the purest examples of Gothic ecclesiastical architecture in Germany: elegant, tall, and airy. Veit Stoss carved the crucifixion group at the east end of the nave, while the elaborate bronze shrine, containing the remains of St. Sebaldus himself, was cast by Peter Vischer and his five sons around 1520. Not to be missed is the **Sebaldus Chörlein,** an ornate Gothic oriel that was added to the Sebaldus parish house in 1361 (the original is in the Germanisches Nationalmuseum). ⊠*Albrecht-Dürer-Pl. 1* ☎*0911/214–2500* ⊙*Daily 10–5.*

⓰ Spielzeugmuseum *(Toy Museum).* Young and old are captivated by this
☺ playful museum, which has a few exhibits dating from the Renaissance; most, however, are from the 19th century. Simple dolls vie with mechanical toys of extraordinary complexity, such as a wooden Ferris wheel from the Erz Mountains adorned with little colored lights. The top floor displays Barbies and intricate Lego constructions. ⊠*Karlstr. 13–15* ☎*0911/231–3164* ☞*€5* ⊙*Tues.–Sun. 10–5.*

⓭ Stadtmuseum *(City Museum).* This city history museum is in the Fembohaus, a dignified patrician dwelling completed in 1598. It's one of the finest Renaissance mansions in Nürnberg. Each room explores another aspect of Nürnberg history, from crafts to gastronomy. The 50-minute multivision show provides a comprehensive look at the city's long history. ⊠*Burgstr. 15* ☎*0911/231–2595* ☞*€7* ⊙*Tues.–Sun. 10–5.*

■ OFF THE BEATEN PATH
☺ **Tiergarten Nürnberg.** The well-stocked Nürnberg Zoo has a dolphinarium where dolphins perform to the delight of children; it's worth the extra admission fee. The zoo is on the northwest edge of town; reach it by taking the No. 5 streetcar from the city center. ⊠*Am Tiergarten 30* ☎*0911/54546* ⊕*www.tiergarten.nuernberg.de* ☞*€7.50, dolphinarium €4.50* ⊙*Zoo and dolphinarium Apr.–Sept., daily 8–7:30; Oct.–Mar., daily 9–5; dolphin show daily at 11, 2, and 4.*

EXPLORING NÜRNBERG'S NAZI SIGHTS

To reach the Documentation Center by public transit, take streetcar Number 9 from the Hauptbahnhof; the Center is the final stop on the line. If you are driving, follow Regensburger Strasse in the direction of Regensburg until you reach Bayernstrasse. Plan for at least an hour to tour the exhibition.

Documentation Centre Nazi Party Rally Grounds. On the eastern outskirts of the city, the **Ausstellung Faszination und Gewalt** (Fascination and Terror Exhibition) documents the political, social, and architectural history of the Nazi Party. The 19-room exhibition is within a horse-shoe-shape Congressional Hall that was intended to harbor a crowd of 50,000; the Nazis never completed it. The Nazis did make famous use of the nearby Zeppelin Field, the enormous parade grounds where Hitler addressed his largest Nazi rallies. Today it sometimes shakes to the amplified beat of pop concerts. ☎*0911/231–5666* ⊕*www.museen. nuernberg.de* ☑*€5* ⊙*Museum daily 9–6, weekends 10–6.*

The Nürnberg Trials. Nazi leaders and German organizations were put on trial here in 1945 and 1946 during the first international war-crimes trials, conducted by the Allied victors of World War II. The trials were held in the Landgericht (Regional Court) in courtroom No. 600 and resulted in 11 death sentences, among other convictions. The guided tours are in German, but English-language material is available. Take the U1 subway line to Bärenschanze. The building can be visited only on weekends, when the court is not in session. ☑*Bärenschanzstr. 72* ☎*0911/231–8411* ⊕*www.museen.nuernberg.de* ☑*€5* ⊙*Weekends 1–4, guided tours every hr on the hr.*

WHERE TO STAY & EAT

$$–$$$$
Fodor's Choice
★
✕**Essigbrätlein.** The oldest restaurant in Nürnberg is also the top restaurant in the city and among the best in Germany. Built in 1550, it was originally used as a meeting place for wine merchants. Today its tiny but elegant period interior caters to the distinguishing gourmet with a taste for special spice mixes (owner Andrée Köthe's hobby). The menu changes daily. ☑*Weinmarkt 3, D-90403* ☎*0911/225–131* ⚠*Reservations essential* ▤*AE, DC, MC, V* ⊙*Closed Sun., Mon., and late Aug.*

$–$$$
★
✕**Heilig-Geist-Spital.** Heavy wood furnishings and a choice of more than 100 wines make this huge, 650-year-old wine tavern—built as the refectory of the city hospital—a popular spot. Try for a table in one of the alcoves, where you can see the river below you as you eat your fish. The menu also includes grilled pork chops, panfried potatoes, and other Franconian dishes. ☑*Spitalg. 16* ☎*0911/221–761* ▤*AE, DC, MC, V.*

¢–$
★
✕**Historische Bratwurst-Küche Zum Gulden Stern.** The city council meets here occasionally to decide upon the official size and weight of the Nürnberg bratwurst. It's a fitting venue for such a decision, given that this house, built in 1375, holds the oldest bratwurst restaurant in the world. The famous Nürnberg bratwursts are always freshly roasted

on a beechwood fire; the boiled variation is prepared in a tasty stock of Franconian wine and onions. ⊠*Zirkelschmiedg. 26* ☎*0911/205–9288* ⊟*DC, MC, V.*

$$$–$$$$ ⚹⌗ **Le Meridien Grand Hotel.** Across the square from the central railway
★ station is this stately building with the calling card Grand Hotel arching over its entranceway. The spacious and imposing lobby with marble pillars feels grand and welcoming. Since 1896 kings, politicians, and celebrities have soaked up the luxury of large rooms and tubs in marble bathrooms. On Friday and Saturday evenings and on Sundays at noon, locals arrive for the candlelight dinner or exquisite brunch ($$–$$$) with live piano music in the restaurant of glittering glass and marble. The trout is a standout in an impressive list of fish dishes, and the lamb is a good pick from the meat entrées. Be sure to ask for weekend rates. ⊠*Bahnhofstr. 1, D-90402* ☎*0911/23220* ⧗*0911/232–2444* ⊕*www. nuremberg.lemeridien.com* ☙*186 rooms, 5 suites* ♨*In-room: ethernet. In-hotel: restaurant, bar, laundry service, concierge, public Internet, public Wi-Fi, parking (fee), some pets allowed, no-smoking rooms* ⊟*AE, DC, MC, V.*

$ ⚹⌗ **Hotel-Weinhaus Steichele.** An 18th-century bakery has skillfully converted into this hotel, which has been managed by the same family for four generations. It's handily close to the main train station, on a quiet street of the old walled town. The cozy rooms are decorated in rustic Bavarian style. Two wood-paneled, traditionally furnished taverns ($–$$$) serve Franconian fare with an excellent fish menu. ⊠*Knorrstr. 2–8, D-90402* ☎*0911/202–280* ⧗*0911/221–914* ⊕*www.steichele. de* ☙*56 rooms* ♨*In-room: no a/c. In-hotel: restaurant, bar, laundry service, some pets allowed* ⊟*AE, DC, MC, V* ⍩*BP.*

$–$$ ⌗ **Agneshof.** This comfortable hotel is north of the Old Town between the fortress and St. Sebaldus Church. Interiors are very modern and tastefully done. The hotel also has a small wellness section and even some lounges for sunning in the small garden. ⊠*Agnesg. 10, D-90403* ☎*0911/214–440* ⧗*0911/2144–4144* ⊕*www.agneshof-nuernberg.de* ☙*72 rooms* ♨*In-room: no a/c, safe, Wi-Fi. In-hotel: bar, laundry service, public Wi-Fi, parking (fee), some pets allowed, no-smoking rooms* ⊟*AE, DC, MC, V* ⍩*BP.*

$–$$ ⌗ **Burghotel Stammhaus.** The service is familial and friendly at this little family-run hotel, where accommodations are small but cozy. If you need more space, ask about the wedding suite. The breakfast room with its balcony overlooking the houses of the Old Town has a charm all its own. ⊠*Schildg. 14, D–90403* ☎*0911/203–040* ⧗*0911/226–503* ⊕*www.burghotel-stamm.de* ☙*22 rooms* ♨*In-room: no a/c, Wi-Fi. In-hotel: pool, public Wi-Fi, parking (fee), some pets allowed, no-smoking rooms* ⊟*AE, DC, MC, V* ⍩*BP.*

$–$$ ⌗ **Hotel Drei Raben.** Legends and tales of Nürnberg form the leitmotif
★ running through the designer rooms at this hotel. One room celebrates the local soccer team with a table-soccer game; in another room sandstone friezes recall sights in the city. There are also standard rooms in the lower price category. The reception room, with its pods, is modeled after *2001: A Space Odyssey,* yet doesn't seem overbearingly modern. It's three minutes from the train station, just within the Old Town

walls. ⊠*Königstr. 63, D–90402* ☏*0911/274–380* 🖶*0911/232–611* ⊕*www.hotel-drei-raben.de* ➲*25 rooms* ♿*In-room: no a/c, Wi-Fi. In-hotel: bar, public Wi-Fi, some pets allowed, no-smoking rooms* ▤*AE, DC, MC, V* ⦿*BP.*

FESTIVALS

Nürnberg is rich in special events and celebrations. By far the most famous is the **Christkindlesmarkt** (Christ-Child Market), an enormous pre-Christmas fair that runs from the Friday before Advent to Christmas Eve. One of the highlights is the candle procession, held every second Thursday of the market season, during which thousands of children parade through the city streets.

Nürnberg has an annual summer festival, **Sommer in Nürnberg,** from May through September, with more than 200 events. Its international organ festival in June and July is regarded as Europe's finest. From May through August classical music concerts are given in the Rittersaal of the **Kaiserburg.** In June and July open-air concerts are given in the Kaiserburg's Serenadenhof. For details, call ☏0911/244–6590.

SHOPPING

Step into the **Handwerkerhof,** in the tower at the Old Town gate (Am Königstor) opposite the main railway station, and you'll think you're back in the Middle Ages. Craftspeople are busy at work in a "medieval mall," turning out the kind of handiwork that has been produced in Nürnberg for centuries: pewter, glassware, basketwork, wood carvings, and, of course, toys. The Lebkuchen specialist **Lebkuchen-Schmidt** has a shop here as well. The mall is open mid-March–December 24, weekdays 10–6:30, Saturday 10–4. December 1–24 the mall is also open Sunday 10–6:30.

THE GERMAN DANUBE

For many people, the sound of the Danube River (Donau in German) is the melody of *The Blue Danube,* the waltz written by Austrian Johann Strauss. The famous 2,988-km-long (1,800-mi-long) river originates in Germany's Black Forest and flows through ten countries. In Germany it's mostly a rather unremarkable stream as it passes through cities such as Ulm on its southeastern route. However, that changes at Kelheim, just west of Regensburg, where the Main-Donau Canal (completed in 1992) brings big river barges all the way from the North Sea. The river becomes sizable in Regensburg, where the ancient Steinerne Brücke (Stone Bridge) needs 15 spans of 30 to 48 feet each to bridge the water. Here everything from small pleasure boats to cruise liners joins the commercial traffic. In the university town of Passau, two more rivers join the waters of the Danube before Europe's longest river continues into Austria.

REGENSBURG

85 km (52 mi) southeast of Nürnberg, 120 km (74 mi) northwest of Munich.

Few visitors to Bavaria venture this far off the well-trod tourist trails, and even Germans are surprised when they discover medieval Regensburg. ■**TIP→ The town escaped World War II with no major damage, and it is one of the best-preserved medieval cities in Germany.**

Regensburg's story begins with the Celts around 500 BC. In AD 179, as an original marble inscription in the Historisches Museum proclaims, it became a Roman military post called Castra Regina. The Porta Praetoria, or gateway, built by the Romans, remains in the Old Town, and whenever you see huge ashlars incorporated into buildings, you are looking at bits of the old Roman settlement. When Bavarian tribes migrated to the area in the 6th century, they occupied what remained of the Roman town and, apparently on the basis of its Latin name, called it Regensburg. Anglo-Saxon missionaries led by St. Boniface in 739 made the town a bishopric before heading down the Danube to convert the heathen in even more far-flung lands. Charlemagne, first of the Holy Roman Emperors, arrived at the end of the 8th century and incorporated Regensburg into his burgeoning domain. Regensburg benefited from the fact that the Danube wasn't navigable to the west of it, and thus it was able to control trade as goods traveled between Germany and Central Europe.

By the Middle Ages Regensburg had become a political, economic, and intellectual center. For many centuries it was the most important city in southeast Germany, serving as the seat of the Perpetual Imperial Diet from 1663 until 1806, when Napoléon ordered the dismantlement of the Holy Roman Empire.

Today the ancient and hallowed walls of Regensburg continue to buzz with life. Students from the university fill the restaurants and pubs, and locals do their daily shopping and errand-running in the inner city, where small shops and stores have managed to keep international consumer chains out.

EXPLORING REGENSBURG

Regensburg is compact; its Old Town center is about 1 square mi. All of its attractions lie on the south side of the Danube, so you won't have to cross it more than once—and then only to admire the city from the north bank.

Any serious tour of Regensburg includes an unusually large number of places of worship. If your spirits wilt at the thought of inspecting them all, you should at least see the Dom (cathedral), famous for its Domspatzen (boys' choir—the literal translation is "cathedral sparrows"). You'll need about another two hours or more to explore Schloss Emmeram and St. Emmeram Church.

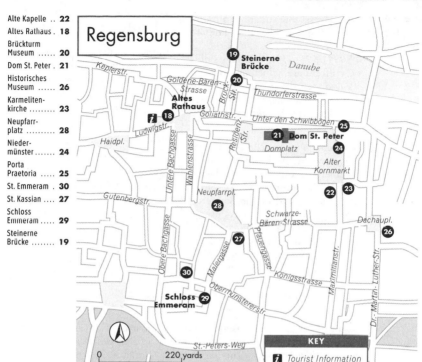

MAIN ATTRACTIONS

18 **Altes Rathaus** *(Old Town Hall).* The picture-book complex of medieval, half-timber buildings, with windows large and small, and flowers in tubs, is one of the best-preserved town halls in the country, as well as one of the most historically important. It was here, in the imposing Gothic **Reichssaal** (Imperial Hall), that the Perpetual Imperial Diet met from 1663 to 1806. This parliament of sorts consisted of the emperor, the electors (seven or eight), the princes (about 50), and the burghers, who assembled to discuss and determine the affairs of the far-reaching German lands. The hall is sumptuously appointed with tapestries, flags, and heraldic designs. Note the wood ceiling, built in 1408, and the different elevations for the various estates. The Reichssaal is occasionally used for concerts. The neighboring **Ratsaal** (Council Room) is where the electors met for their consultations. The cellar holds the actual torture chamber of the city; the **Fragstatt** (Questioning Room); and the execution room, called the **Armesünderstübchen** (Poor Sinners' Room). Any prisoner who withstood three degrees of questioning without confessing was considered innocent and released—which tells you something about medieval notions of justice. ✉*Rathauspl.* ☎*0941/507–4411* 💷*€6* ☉*Guided tours in English May–Sept., Mon.–Sat. at 3.*

NEED A
BREAK?

Just across the square from the Altes Rathaus is the **Prinzess Confiserie Café** (⊠*Rathauspl. 2* ☎*0941/595–310*), Germany's oldest coffeehouse, which first opened its doors to the general public in 1686. The homemade chocolates are highly recommended, as are the rich cakes.

② Brückturm Museum *(Bridge Tower Museum)*. With its tiny windows, weathered tiles, and pink plaster, this 17th-century tower stands at the south end of the Steinerne Brücke. The tower displays a host of items relating to the construction and history of the old bridge. It also offers a gorgeous view of the Regensburg roof landscape. The brooding building with a massive roof to the left of the Brückturm is an old salt warehouse. ⊠*Steinerne Brücke* ☎*0941/507–5888* 💶€2 ⊗*Apr.–Oct., daily 10–5; call ahead to ask about English tours.*

TOURING TIPS

Information: The tourist office adjacent to the Altes Rathaus at the very center of town, on medieval Rathausplatz, has maps and brochures.

Scenic Spots: The Steinerne Brücke (Stone Bridge) has an unforgettable view of Regensburg's Old Town center.

Snacks: Don't miss the ancient Historische Wurstküche, a tavern nestling between the river and the bridge. It's crowded at lunchtime, but it has the best sausages.

② Dom St. Peter *(St. Peter's Cathedral)*. Regensburg's transcendent cathedral, modeled on the airy, vertical lines of French Gothic architecture, is something of a rarity this far south in Germany. Begun in the 13th century, it stands on the site of a much earlier Carolingian church. Remarkably, the cathedral can hold 6,000 people, three times the population of Regensburg when building began. Construction dragged on for almost 600 years until Ludwig I of Bavaria, then ruler of Regensburg, finally had the towers built. These had to be replaced in the mid-1950s. Behind the Dom is a little workshop where a team of 15 stonecutters is busy full-time during the summer recutting and restoring parts of the cathedral.

Before heading into the Dom, take time to admire the intricate and frothy carvings of its facade. Inside, the glowing 14th-century stained glass in the choir and the exquisitely detailed statues of the archangel Gabriel and the Virgin in the crossing (the intersection of the nave and the transepts) are among the church's outstanding features. ⊠*Dompl.* ☎*0941/586–5500* 💶*Tour, only in German (for tours in English call ahead), €3* ⊗*Cathedral tour daily at 2.*

Be sure to visit the **Kreuzgang** *(Cloisters)*, reached via the garden. There you'll find a small octagonal chapel, the Allerheiligenkapelle (All Saints' Chapel), a Romanesque building that is all sturdy grace and massive walls, a work by Italian masons from the mid-12th century. You can barely make out the faded remains of stylized 11th-century frescoes on its ancient walls. The equally ancient shell of St. Stephan's Church, the cloisters, the chapel, and the Alter Dom (Old Cathedral), are included in the Cathedral tour. The **Domschatzmuseum** *(Cathedral*

Museum) contains valuable treasures going back to the 11th century. Some of the vestments and the monstrances, which are fine examples of eight centuries' worth of the goldsmith's trade, are still used during special services. The entrance is in the nave. ⊠*Dompl.* ☎*0941/57645* 🎫€*2* ⊙*Apr.–Oct., Tues.–Sat. 10–5, Sun. noon–5; Dec.–Mar., Fri. and Sat. 10–4, Sun. noon–4.*

NEED A BREAK?

The restaurant **Haus Heuport** (⊠*Dompl. 7* ☎*0941/599–9297*), opposite the entrance of the Dom, is in one of the old and grand private ballrooms of the city. The service is excellent, and the tables at the windows have a wonderful view of the Dom. In summer head for the bistro area in the courtyard for snack fare, such as sandwiches and salads.

㉖ **Historisches Museum** *(Historical Museum).* The municipal museum vividly relates the cultural history of Regensburg. It's one of the highlights ★ of the city, both for its unusual and beautiful setting—a former Gothic monastery—and for its wide-ranging collections, from Roman artifacts to Renaissance tapestries and remains from Regensburg's 16th-century Jewish ghetto. The most significant exhibits are the paintings by Albrecht Altdorfer (1480–1538), a native of Regensburg and, along with Cranach, Grünewald, and Dürer, one of the leading painters of the German Renaissance. Altdorfer's work has the same sense of heightened reality found in that of his contemporaries, in which the lessons of Italian painting are used to produce an emotional rather than a rational effect. His paintings would not have seemed out of place among those of 19th-century Romantics. Far from seeing the world around him as essentially hostile, or at least alien, he saw it as something intrinsically beautiful, whether wild or domesticated. Altdorfer made two drawings of the old synagogue of Regensburg, priceless documents that are on exhibit here. ⊠*Dachaupl. 2–4* ☎*0941/507–2448* 🎫€*2.20* ⊙*Tues.– Sun. 12–4.*

㉙ **Schloss Emmeram** *(Emmeram Palace).* Formerly a Benedictine monastery, this is the ancestral home of the princely Thurn und Taxis family, who made their fame and fortune after being granted the right to carry official and private mail throughout the empire and Spain by Emperor Maximilian I (1493–1519) and by Philip I, king of Spain, who ruled during the same period. Their business extended over the centuries into the Low Countries (Holland, Belgium, and Luxembourg), Hungary, and Italy. The little horn that still symbolizes the post office in several European countries comes from the Thurn und Taxis coat of arms. For a while Schloss Emmeram was heavily featured in the gossip columns thanks to the wild parties and somewhat extravagant lifestyle of the young dowager Princess Gloria von Thurn und Taxis. After the death of her husband, Prince Johannes, in 1990, she had to auction off belongings in order to pay inheritance taxes. Ultimately a deal was cut, allowing her to keep many of the palace's treasures as long they were put on display.

The **Thurn und Taxis Palace,** with its splendid ballroom and throne room, allows you to witness the setting of courtly life in the 19th century. A visit usually includes the fine **Kreuzgang** (cloister) of the former

Benedictine abbey of St. Emmeram. The items in the **Thurn und Taxis Museum,** which is part of the Bavarian National Museum in Munich, have been carefully selected for their fine craftsmanship—be it dueling pistols, a plain marshal's staff, a boudoir, or a snuffbox. The palace's **Marstallmuseum** (former royal stables) holds the family's coaches and carriages as well as related items. ☎*0941/504–8133* ⊙*Museum Apr.– Oct., 1–5. Tours of palace and cloisters Apr.–Oct., weekdays at 11, 2, 3, and 4, weekends at 10* 🖾*Museum €4.50, palace and cloisters €11.50.*

⑲ **Steinerne Brücke** *(Stone Bridge).* This impressive old bridge resting on
Fodor'sChoice massive pontoons is Regensburg's most celebrated sight. It was com-
★ pleted in 1146 and was rightfully considered a miraculous piece of engineering at the time. As the only crossing point over the Danube for miles, it effectively cemented Regensburg's control over trade. The significance of the little statue on the bridge is a mystery, but the figure seems to be a witness to the legendary rivalry between the master builders of the bridge and those of the Dom.

ALSO WORTH SEEING

㉒ **Alte Kapelle** *(Old Chapel).* The Carolingian structure was erected in the 9th century. Its dowdy exterior gives little hint of the joyous rococo treasures within—extravagant concoctions of sinuous gilt stucco, rich marble, and giddy frescoes, the whole illuminated by light pouring in from the upper windows. ⊠*Alter Kornmarkt 8* ☎*No phone* ⊙*Daily 9–dusk.*

㉓ **Karmelitenkirche** *(Church of the Carmelites).* This lovely church, in the baroque style from crypt to cupola, stands next to the Alte Kapelle. It has a finely decorated facade designed by the 17th-century Italian master Carlo Lurago. ⊠*Alter Kornmarkt.*

㉘ **Neupfarrplatz.** This oversize open square was once a Jewish ghetto. Hard economic times and superstition led to their eviction by decree in 1519. While the synagogue was being torn down, one worker survived a very bad fall. A church was promptly built to celebrate the miracle, and before long a pilgrimage began. The **Neupfarrkirche** (New Parish Church) was built as well to accommodate the flow of pilgrims. During the Reformation, the Parish Church was given to the Protestants, hence its bare-bones interior. In the late 1990s, excavation work (for the power company) on the square uncovered well-kept cellars and, to the west of the church, the old synagogue, including the foundations of its Romanesque predecessor. Archaeologists salvaged the few items they could from the old stones (including a stash of 684 gold coins) and, not knowing what to do with the sea of foundations, ultimately carefully reburied them. Recovered items were carefully restored and are on exhibit in the Historisches Museum. Only one small underground area to the south of the church, the **Document,** accommodates viewing of the foundations. In a former cellar, surrounded by the original walls, visitors can watch a short video reconstructing life in the old Jewish ghetto. Over the old synagogue, the Israeli artist Dani Karavan designed a stylized plaza where people can sit and meet. Call the educational institution VHS for a tour of the Document (reservations are requested). For spontaneous visits, tickets are available at Tabak Götz on the western side of the square, at Neupfarrplatz 3. ☒*Neupfarrpl.* ☏*0941/507–2433 for tours led by VHS* ⊕*www.vhs-regensburg.de* ☒*Document € 5* ⊙*Church daily 9–dusk, Document tour Thurs.–Sat. at 2:30.*

NEED A BREAK?

A Dampfnudel is a kind of sweet yeast-dough dumpling that is tasty and filling. The best in Bavaria can be had at **Dampfnudel Uli** (☒ *Watmarkt 4* ☏*0941/53297* ⊙*Tues.–Fri. 10–6, Sat. 10–3*), a little establishment in a former chapel. The decoration is incredibly eclectic, from Bavarian crafts to a portrait of Ronald Reagan inscribed "To Uli Deutzer, with best wishes, Ronald Reagan."

4

㉔ **Niedermünster.** This 12th-century building with a baroque interior was originally the church of a community of nuns, all of them from noble families. ☒*Alter Kornmarkt 5* ☏*0941/586–5500.*

㉕ **Porta Praetoria.** The rough-hewn former gate to the old Roman camp, built in AD 179, is one of the most interesting relics of Roman times in Regensburg. Look through the grille on its east side to see a section of the original Roman street, about 10 feet below today's street level. ☒*North side of Alter Kornmarkt.*

㉚ **St. Emmeram.** The family church of the princely Thurn und Taxis family stands across from their ancestral palace, the Schloss Emmeram. The foundations of the church date to the 7th and 8th centuries. A richly decorated baroque interior was added in 1730 by the Asam brothers. St. Emmeram contains the graves of the 7th-century martyred Regensburg bishop Emmeram and the 10th-century saint Wolfgang. ☒*Emmeramspl. 3* ☏*0941/51030* ⊙*Mon.–Thurs. and Sat. 10–4:30, Fri. 1–4:30, Sun. noon–4:30.*

㉗ **St. Kassian.** Regensburg's oldest church was founded in the 8th century. Don't be fooled by its dour exterior; inside, it's filled with delicate rococo decoration. ☒*St. Kassianpl. 1* ☏*No phone* ⊙*Daily 9–5:30.*

WHERE TO STAY & EAT

¢–$ ✕**Café Felix.** A modern bi-level café and bar, Felix offers everything from sandwiches to steaks, and buzzes with activity from breakfast until the early hours. Light from an arty chandelier and torch-like fixtures bounces off the many large framed mirrors. The crowd tends to be young. ☒*Fröhliche-Türkenstr. 6* ☏*0941/59059* ▭*No credit cards.*

¢–$ ✕**Leerer Beutel.** Excellent international cuisine—from antipasti to solid pork roast—is served in a pleasant vaulted room supported by massive rough-hewn beams. The restaurant is in a huge warehouse that's also a venue for concerts, exhibitions, and film screenings, making it a good place to start or end an evening. ☒*Bertoldstr. 9* ☏*0941/58997* ▭*AE, DC, MC, V.*

¢ ✕**Historische Wurstküche.** Succulent Regensburger sausages—the best in town—are prepared right before your eyes on an open beechwood charcoal grill in this tiny kitchen. If you want to eat them inside in the tiny dining room, you'll have to squeeze past the cook to get there. On the walls—outside and in—are plaques recording the levels the river reached in the various floods that have doused the restaurant's kitchen in the past 100 years. ⊠*Thundorferstr. 3, just by the stone bridge* ☎*0941/466–210* ⊟*No credit cards.*

$$ ✕⊞ **Hotel-Restaurant Bischofshof am Dom.** This is one of Germany's most historic hostelries, a former bishop's palace where you can sleep in an apartment that includes part of a Roman gateway. Other chambers are only slightly less historic, and some have seen emperors and princes as guests. The hotel's restaurant (¢–$) serves fine regional cuisine (including the famous Regensburger sausages) at reasonable prices. The beer comes from a brewery founded in 1649. ⊠*Krauterermarkt 3, D–93047* ☎*0941/58460* 🖷*0941/584–6146* ⊕*www.hotel-bischofshof.de* ⇆*55 rooms, 3 suites* ⚅*In-room: no a/c. In-hotel: restaurant, bar, parking (fee), some pets allowed, no-smoking rooms* ⊟*AE, DC, MC, V.*

$–$$ ✕⊞ **Hôtel Orphée.** It's difficult to choose from among the very spacious
Fodor's Choice rooms at this establishment. You may decide to take an attic room with
★ large wooden beams or an elegant room with stucco ceilings on the first floor. There's also a huge bedroom-salon (€20 extra) with a bathroom where the tub resides in the center. The French bistro–style restaurant ($$–$$$) prepares a selection of crepes, salads, and tasty meat dishes. There is also a Petit Hotel Orphée on the next street; you get your key at the Grand Hôtel Orphée. A Country Manor Orphée is on the other side of the river about 2 km (1 mi) away. ⊠*Untere Bachg. 8, D–93047* ☎*0941/596–020* 🖷*0941/5960–2199* ⊕*www.hotel-orphee.de* ⇆*15 rooms* ⚅*In-room: no a/c, Wi-Fi. In-hotel: restaurant, bar, public Wi-Fi, parking (fee), some pets allowed, no-smoking rooms* ⊟*MC, V.*

$–$$ ⊞ **Kaiserhof am Dom.** Renaissance windows punctuate the green facade of this historic city mansion. The rooms are 20th-century modern. Try for one with a view of the cathedral, which stands directly across the street. Breakfast is served beneath the high-vaulted ceiling of the former 14th-century chapel. ⊠*Kramg. 10–12, D–93047* ☎*0941/585–350* 🖷*0941/585–3595* ⊕*www.kaiserhof-am-dom.de* ⇆*30 rooms* ⚅*In-room: no a/c, Wi-Fi. In-hotel: public Wi-Fi, some pets allowed* ⊟*AE, DC, MC, V* ⊘*Closed Dec. 21–Jan. 8.*

$ ⊞ **Am Peterstor.** The clean and basic rooms of this popular hotel in the heart of the Old Town are an unbeatable value. The many local eateries, including the excellent Café Felix a few doors away, more than compensate for the lack of an in-house restaurant. ⊠*Fröhliche-Türken-Str. 12, D–93047* ☎*0941/54545* 🖷*0941/54542* ⊕*www.hotel-am-peterstor.de* ⇆*36 rooms* ⚅*In-room: no a/c, no phone* ⊟*MC, V.*

$ ⊞ **Hotel Münchner Hof.** The original arches of the ancient building are visible in some of the rooms at this little hotel. It is in a block near the Neupfarrkirche. The restaurant is quiet and comfortable, serving Bavarian specialties and good Munich beer. The bottom line: you get top service at a good price, and Regensburg is at your feet. ⊠*Tändlerg. 9, D–93047* ☎*0941/58440* 🖷*0941/561–709* ⊕*www.muenchner-hof. de* ⇆*53 rooms* ⚅*In-room: no a/c, Wi-Fi. In-hotel: restaurant, public Wi-Fi, some pets allowed, no-smoking rooms* ⊟*AE, DC, MC, V.*

SHOPPING

The winding alleyways of the Altstadt are packed with boutiques, ateliers, jewelers, and other small shops offering a vast array of arts and crafts. You may also want to visit the daily market (Monday through Saturday 9–4) at the Neupfarrplatz, where you can buy regional specialties such as *Radi* (juicy radish roots), which local people love to wash down with a glass of wheat beer.

NIGHTLIFE & THE ARTS

Regensburg offers a range of musical experiences, though none so moving as a choral performance at the cathedral. ■TIP→ **Listening to the Regensburger Domspatzen, the boys' choir at the cathedral, can be a remarkable experience, and it's worth scheduling your visit to the city to hear them. The best-sung mass is held on Sunday at 9 AM.** If you're around in summer, look out for the Citizens Festival (Bürgerfest) and the Bavarian Jazz Festival (Bayreisches Jazzfest; www.bayernjazz.de) in July, both in the Old Town.

The kind of friendly, mixed nightlife that has become hard to find in some cities is alive and well in this small university city in the many *Kneipen,* bar-cum-pub-cum-bistros or -restaurants, such as the Leerer Beutel. Ask around to discover the latest in spot.

NEAR REGENSBURG

★ **Walhalla.** Walhalla (11 km [7 mi] east of Regensburg) is an excursion from Regensburg you won't want to miss, especially if you have an interest in the wilder expressions of 19th-century German nationalism. Walhalla—a name resonant with Nordic mythology—was where the god Odin received the souls of dead heroes. Ludwig I erected this monumental temple in 1840 to honor important German personages from ages past. In keeping with the neoclassic style then prevailing, the Greek-style Doric temple is actually a copy of the Parthenon in Athens. The expanses of costly marble are evidence of both the financial resources and the craftsmanship at Ludwig's command. Walhalla may be kitschy, but the fantastic view it affords over the Danube and the wide countryside is definitely worth a look.

A boat ride from the Steinerne Brücke in Regensburg is the best way to go. On the return trip, you can steer the huge boat about half a mile, and, for €5 extra, you can earn an "Honorary Danube Boat Captain" certificate. Kids and grown-ups love it (*see details on river cruises in the Essentials section at the end of this chapter*). To get to the temple from the river, you'll have to climb 358 marble steps.

To drive to it, take the Danube Valley country road (unnumbered) east from Regensburg 8 km (5 mi) to Donaustauf. The Walhalla temple is 1 km (½ mi) outside the village and well signposted.

Stiftskirche Sts. Georg und Martin (*Abbey Church of Sts. George and Martin*). In Weltenburg (25 km [15 mi] southwest of Regensburg) you'll find the great Stiftskirche Sts. Georg und Martin, on the bank of the Danube River. The most dramatic approach to the abbey is by boat from Kelheim, 10 km (6 mi) downstream. On the stunning ride the boat winds between towering limestone cliffs that rise straight up from the tree-lined riverbanks. The abbey, constructed between 1716 and 1718, is commonly regarded as the masterpiece of the brothers Cosmas Damian and Egid Quirin Asam, two leading baroque architects and decorators of Bavaria. Their extraordinary composition of painted figures whirling on the ceiling, lavish and brilliantly polished marble, highly wrought statuary, and stucco figures dancing in rhythmic arabesques across the curving walls is the epitome of Bavarian baroque. Note especially the bronze equestrian statue of St. George above the high altar, reaching down imperiously with his flamelike, twisted gilt sword to dispatch the winged dragon at his feet. In Kehlheim there are two boat companies that offer trips to Kloster Weltenburg every 30 minutes in summer. You cannot miss the landing stages and the huge parking lot. ⊙ *Daily 9–dusk.*

EN ROUTE   It's about a two-hour drive on the autobahn between Regensburg and Passau. Be forewarned, however, that if your trip coincides with a German holiday, it can be stop-and-go traffic for hours along this stretch. Halfway between Regensburg and Passau, the village of Metten is a worthwhile diversion or break. After you visit the monastery, stop to refuel at Cafe am Kloster (Marktpaltz 1, ☎ 0991/9989380). Once you are seated in the beer garden, the quality and the prices may well tempt you to linger longer than you had anticipated.

Metten's **Benedictine monastery,** founded in the 9th century by Charlemagne, is an outstanding example of baroque art. The 18th-century library has a collection of 160,000 books whose gilt leather spines are complemented by the heroic splendor of their surroundings—Herculean figures support the frescoed, vaulted ceiling, and allegorical paintings and fine stuccowork identify different categories of books. In the church is Cosmas Damian Asam's altarpiece *Lucifer Destroyed by St. Michael*; created around 1720, it has vivid coloring and a swirling composition that are typical of the time. ⊠ *7 km (4½ mi) west of Deggendorf* ☎0991/91080 ⊠€3 ⊙ *Guided tours Tues.–Sun. at 10 and 3.*

PASSAU

137 km (86 mi) southeast of Regensburg, 179 km (111 mi) northeast of Munich.

Flanking the borders of Austria and the Czech Republic, Passau dates back more than 2,500 years. Originally settled by the Celts, then by the Romans, Passau later passed into the possession of prince-bishops whose domains stretched into present-day Hungary. At its height, the Passau episcopate was the largest in the entire Holy Roman Empire.

Passau's location is truly unique. Nowhere else in the world do three rivers—the Ilz from the north, the Danube from the west, and the Inn from the south—meet. Wedged between the Inn and the Danube, the Old Town is a maze of narrow cobblestone streets lined with beautifully preserved burgher and patrician houses and riddled with churches.

Many streets have been closed to traffic, enhancing the appeal of an Old Town stroll.

Passau can be toured leisurely in the course of one day. Try to visit the Dom at noon to hear a recital on its great organ, the world's largest. Early morning is the best time to catch the light falling from the east on the Old Town walls and the confluence of the three rivers.

WHAT TO SEE

35 **Dom St. Stephan** *(St. Stephan's Cathedral)* rises majestically on the high-

Fodor's Choice est point of the earliest-settled part of the city. A baptismal church ★ stood here in the 6th century. Two hundred years later, when Passau became a bishop's seat, the first basilica was built. It was dedicated to St. Stephan and became the original mother church of St. Stephan's Cathedral in Vienna. A fire reduced the medieval basilica to smoking ruins in 1662; it was then rebuilt by Italian master architect Carlo Lurago. What you see today is the largest baroque basilica north of the Alps, complete with an octagonal dome and flanking towers. Little in its marble- and stucco-encrusted interior reminds you of Germany, and much proclaims the exuberance of Rome. Beneath the dome is the largest church organ assembly in the world. Built between 1924 and 1928 and enlarged in 1979–80, it claims no fewer than 17,774 pipes and 233 stops. The church also houses the most powerful bell chimes in southern Germany. ⊠ *Dompl.* ☎ *0851/3930* ⌨ *Concerts midday €4, evening €8* ⊗ *Daily 8–11 and 12:30–6; Tours May–Oct., weekdays at 12:30; Nov.–Apr., at noon.*

34 **Domplatz** *(Cathedral Square).* This large square in front of the Dom is bordered by sturdy 17th- and 18th-century buildings, including the **Alte Residenz,** the former bishop's palace and now a courthouse. The fine statue depicts Bavarian king Maximilian Joseph I.

33 **Domschatz- und Diözesanmuseum** *(Cathedral Treasury and Diocesan Museum).* The cathedral museum houses one of Bavaria's largest collections of religious treasures, the legacy of Passau's rich episcopal history. The museum is part of the **Neue Residenz,** which has a stately baroque entrance opening onto a magnificent staircase—a scintillating study in marble, fresco, and stucco. ⊠ *Residenzpl.* ⌨ *€1.50* ⊗ *Apr.–Oct., Mon.–Sat. 10–4.*

32 **Glasmuseum** *(Glass Museum).* The world's most comprehensive collection of Bohemian glass is housed in the lovely Hotel Wilder Mann. The history of Central Europe's glassmaking is captured in 30,000 items, from baroque to art deco, spread over 35 rooms. ⊠ *Am Rathauspl.* ☎ *0851/35071* ⌨ *€5* ⊗ *Daily 1–5.*

31 **Rathaus.** Passau's 14th-century city hall sits like a Venetian merchant's house on a small square fronting the Danube. It was the home of a wealthy German merchant before being declared the seat of city government after a 1298 uprising. Two assembly rooms have wall paintings depicting scenes from local history and lore, including the (fictional) arrival in the city of Siegfried's fair Kriemhild, from the Nibelungen fable. ■TIP→ **The Rathaus tower has Bavaria's largest glockenspiel, which**

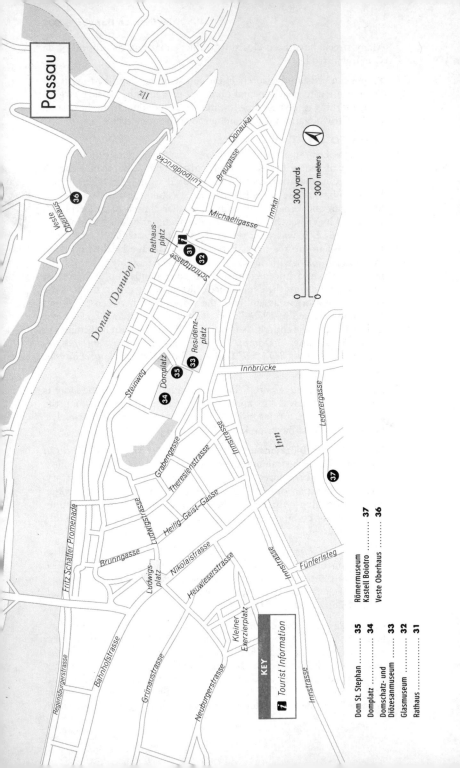

Passau

Donau (Danube)

Illz

Veste Oberhaus

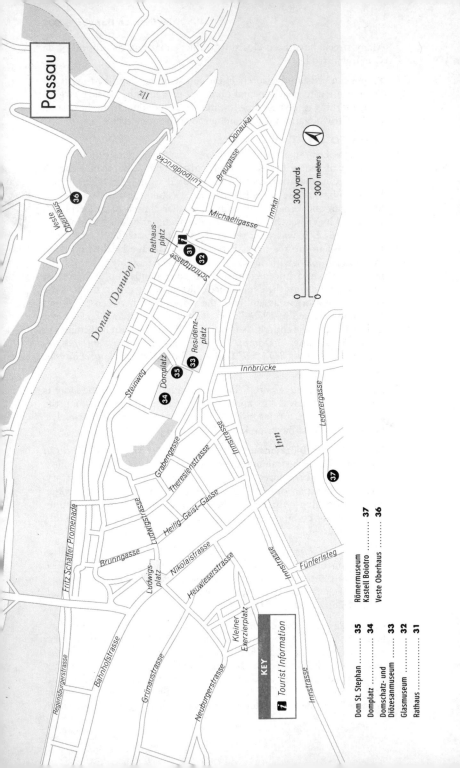36

Rathaus-platz

Schrottgasse

Luitpoldbrücke

Donaukai

Braugasse

Michaeligasse

Innkai

Steinweg

Domplatz

Residenz-platz

Grabengasse

Theresienstrasse

Innstrasse

Innbrücke

Inn

Ledergasse

Fünferlsteg

Fritz Schäffer Promenade

Ludwigstrasse

Heilig-Geist-Gasse

Brunngasse

Ludwigs-platz

Nikolaistrasse

Heuwieserstrasse

Kleiner Exerzierplatz

Bahnhofstrasse

Regensburgerstrasse

Grünaustrasse

Neuburgerstrasse

Innstrasse

34
35
33

31
32
1

37

300 yards

300 meters

KEY

🛈 Tourist Information

Dom St. Stephan **35**

Domplatz **34**

Domschatz- und
Diözesanmuseum **33**

Glasmuseum **32**

Rathaus **31**

Römermuseum
Kastell Boiotro **37**

Veste Oberhaus **36**

plays daily at 10:30, 2, and 7:25, with an additional performance at 3:30 on Saturday. ⊠*Rathauspl.* ☎*0851/3960* 💳*€1.50* ⊙*Apr.–Oct. and late Dec.–early Jan., daily 10–4.*

㊲ Römermuseum Kastell Boiotro *(Roman Museum).* A stout fortress with five defense towers and walls more than 12 feet thick came to light as archaeologists excavated the site of a 17th-century pilgrimage church on a hill known as Mariahilfberg, on the south bank of the Inn. The Roman citadel Boiotro was discovered along with a Roman well, its water still plentiful and fresh. Pottery, lead figures, and other artifacts from the area are housed in this museum at the edge of the site.

⊠*Ledererg. 43* ☎*0851/34769* 💳*€3* ⊙*Mar.–Nov., Tues.–Sun. 10–4.*

㊱ Veste Oberhaus *(Upper House Stronghold).* The powerful fortress and summer castle commissioned by Bishop Ulrich II in 1219 looks over Passau from an impregnable site on the other side of the river, opposite the Rathaus. Today the Veste Oberhaus is Passau's most important museum, containing exhibits that illustrate the city's 2,000-year history. ■**TIP➔ From the terrace of its café-restaurant (open Easter–October), there's a magnificent view of Passau and the convergence of the three rivers.** ⊠*Oberhausleitenstiege* ☎*0851/493–3512* 💳*Museum €6* ⊙*Mar.–Oct., weekdays 9–5, weekends 10–6* 🚌*Bus from Rathauspl. to museum Apr.–Nov. every ½ hr 10:30–5.*

WHERE TO STAY & EAT

$–$$ ✕**Gasthaus zur blauen Donau.** Passau's esteemed chef Richard Kerscher turned this old house with thick walls and recessed windows into a simple but stylish restaurant. The first-floor dining room has a commanding view of the Danube. His delicacies are all based on traditional German recipes. ⊠*Höllg. 14* ☎*0851/490–8660* 🚫*No credit cards.*

¢–$$ ✕**Blauer Bock.** This is one of Passau's oldest houses (first mentioned in city records in 1257) and has been welcoming travelers since 1875. The Danube flows by the tavern windows, and in summer you can watch the river traffic from a beer garden. The food is traditional; you'll find pork and potatoes in every variety. The tavern also offers accommodation in tastefully fitted rooms. ⊠*Höllg. 20* ☎*0851/34637* 💳*MC, V.*

¢–$$ ✕**Peschl Terrasse.** The beer you sip on the high, sunny terrace overlooking the Danube is brought fresh from the Old Town brewery below, which, along with this traditional Bavarian restaurant, has been in the same family since 1855. ⊠*Rosstränke 4* ☎*0851/2489* 💳*DC, MC, V.*

$$ **Hotel König.** Though built in 1984, the König blends successfully with the graceful Italian-style buildings alongside the elegant Danube waterfront. Rooms are large and airy; most have a fine view of the river. ⊠ *Untere Donaulände 1, D–94032* ☎*0851/3850* 🖷*0851/385–460* ⊕*www.hotel-koenig.de* ⇆*61 rooms* ⚬*In-room: no a/c, Wi-Fi (some). In-hotel: bar, public Wi-Fi, parking (fee), some pets allowed, no-smoking rooms* ⊟*AE, DC, MC, V.*

$–$$ **Hotel Wilder Mann.** Passau's most historic hotel dates from the 11th century and shares prominence with the ancient city hall on the waterfront market square. Empress Elizabeth of Austria and American astronaut Neil Armstrong have been among its guests. On beds of carved oak you'll sleep beneath chandeliers and richly stuccoed ceilings. For sheer indulgence, ask for either the King Ludwig or Sissi (Empress Elisabeth) suite. The esteemed Glasmuseum is within the hotel. ⊠*Am Rathauspl. 1, D–94032* ☎*0851/35071* 🖷*0851/31712* ⊕*www.rotel-tours.de* ⇆*48 rooms, 5 suites* ⚬*In-room: no a/c, Wi-Fi (some). In-hotel: public Wi-Fi, parking (fee), no-smoking rooms* ⊟*AE, DC, MC, V.*

$–$$ **Schloss Ort.** This 13th-century castle's large rooms have views of the Inn River, which flows beneath the hotel's stout walls. The rooms are decorated in a variety of styles with old-fashioned four-poster beds or modern wrought-iron details. The restaurant is closed in winter and on Mondays, but the kitchen will always oblige hungry hotel guests. In summer the garden terrace is a delightful place to eat and watch the river. ⊠*Ort 11, D–94032* ☎*0851/34072* 🖷*0851/31817* ⊕*www. schlosshotel-passau.de* ⇆*18 rooms* ⚬*In-room: no a/c. In-hotel: restaurant, parking (fee), some pets allowed, no-smoking rooms* ⊟*DC, MC, V.*

¢ **Rotel Inn.** "Rotels" are usually hotels on wheels, an idea developed by a local entrepreneur to accommodate tour groups in North Africa and Asia. The first permanent Rotel Inn is on the banks of the Danube in central Passau and resembles an ocean liner. Its rooms are truly ship-shape—hardly any wider than the bed inside—but they're clean, decorated in a pop-art style, and amazingly cheap. The building's unique design—a red, white, and blue facade with flowing roof lines—has actually been patented. It's definitely for young travelers but also fun for families. ⊠*Am Hauptbahnhof/Donauufer, D–94032* ☎*0851/95160* 🖷*0851/951–610* ⊕*www.rotel-tours.de* ⇆*100 rooms* ⚬*In-room: no a/c* ⊟*No credit cards* ⊙*Closed Oct.–late Apr.*

CYCLING

Cyclists can choose between eight long-distance paths along the rivers Danube (as far as Vienna) and Inn (tracing the river to its source in the Swiss Engadine). Bikes are permitted on most Danube boats and local trains for a small fee (usually €2) so you can cover part of the journey by river or rail. **Fahrrad-Laden Passau** (⊠*Rosstränke 12* ☎*0851/722–26*) is the best address in Passau for renting and repairing bicycles.

FESTIVALS

Passau is the cultural center of Lower Bavaria. Its **Europäische Wochen** *(European Weeks)* festival—featuring everything from opera to pantomime—is a major event on the European music calendar. Now into its 53rd year, the festival runs from June to July. For program details and reservations, write the **Kartenzentrale der Europäischen Wochen Passau** (✉ *Dr.-Hans-Kapfinger-Str. 22, D–94032 Passau* ☎ *0851/560–960* ⊕ *www.europaeische-wochen-passau.de*).

FRANCONIA & THE GERMAN DANUBE ESSENTIALS

4

TRANSPORTATION

BY AIR

The major international airport serving Franconia and the German Danube is Munich. A regional airport is Nürnberg.

Contact Airport Nürnberg (✉ *Flughafenstr. 100, D–90411* ☎ *0911/93700* ⊕ *www.airport-nuernberg.de*).

BY CAR

Franconia is served by five main autobahns: A–7 from Hamburg, A–3 from Köln and Frankfurt, A–81 from Stuttgart, A–6 from Heilbronn, and A–9 from Munich. Nürnberg is 167 km (104 mi) north of Munich and 222 km (138 mi) southeast of Frankfurt. Regensburg and Passau are reached on the A–3 from Nürnberg.

BY TRAIN

Nürnberg is a stop on the high-speed InterCity Express north–south routes, and there are hourly trains from Munich direct to Nürnberg. Regular InterCity services connect Nürnberg and Regensburg with Frankfurt and other major German cities. Trains run hourly from Frankfurt to Munich, with a stop at Nürnberg. The trip takes about three hours to Munich, two hours to Nürnberg. There are hourly trains from Munich to Regensburg.

Some InterCity trains stop in Bamberg, which is most speedily reached from Munich. Local trains from Nürnberg connect with Bayreuth and areas of southern Franconia. Regensburg and Passau are on the EC line from Nürnberg to Vienna.

CONTACTS & RESOURCES

TOUR OPTIONS

BOAT TOURS There are about 15 different lines that operate cruises on the Main River and the Main-Donau Canal in summer. In Bamberg, Personenschiffahrt Kropf boats leave daily from March through October beginning at 11 AM for short cruises on the Regnitz River and the Main-Donau Canal; the cost is €7.

In Regensburg all boats depart from the Steinerne Brücke. The most popular excursions are boat trips to Ludwig I's imposing Greek-style Doric temple of Walhalla. There are daily sailings to Walhalla from Easter through October. The round-trip costs €8 and takes three hours. Don't bother with the trip upriver from Regensburg to Kehlheim.

In Passau cruises on the three rivers begin and end at the Danube jetties on Fritz-Schäffer Promenade. A two-hour Danube cruise aboard the *Sissi* costs €11; cruises run daily at 11:15 and 2:45 from early May to the end of September. DDSG offers two-day cruises from Passau to Vienna, as well as Danube cruise connections via Budapest all the way to the Black Sea.

Information DDSG (✉ *Im Ort 14a, D–94032 Passau* ☎ *0431/58880* ⊕ *www. ddsg-blue-danube.at*).

Ludwig Wurm (✉ *Donaustr. 71, D–94342 Irlbach* ☎ *09424/1341* ⊕ *www.donaus-chiffahrt-wurm.de*). **Personenschiffahrt Klinger** (✉ *Thundorfstr. 1, D–93047 Regensburg* ☎ *0941/55359* ⊕ *www.schifffahrtklinger.de*). **Personenschiffahrt Kropf** (✉ *Kapuzinerstr. 5, Bamberg* ☎ *0951/26679*).

VISITOR INFORMATION

Information **Franconia Tourist Board** (✉ *Tourismusverband Franken e.V., Wilhelminenstr. 6, D–90461 Nürnberg* ☎ *0911/941–510*). **Bamberg** (✉ *Fremden-verkehrsamt, Geyerswörthstr. 3, D–96047* ☎ *0951/297–6200* ⊕ *www.bamberg. info*). **Bayreuth** (✉ *Fremdenverkehrsverein, Luitpoldpl. 9, D–95444* ☎ *0921/88588* ⊕ *www.bayreuth.de*). **Coburg** (✉ *Fremdenverkehrs- und Kongressbetrieb, Herrng. 4, D–96450* ☎ *09561/74180* ⊕ *www.coburg-tourist.de*). **Kronach** (✉ *Marktpl., D–96317* ☎ *09261/97236* ⊕ *www.kronach.de*). **Kulmbach** (✉ *Fremdenverkehrsbüro, Stadthalle, Sutte 2, D–95326* ☎ *09221/95880* ⊕ *www.kulmbach.de*). **Nürnberg** (✉ *Congress- und Tourismus-Zentrale Frauentorgraben 3, D–90443* ☎ *0911/23360* ⊕ *www.nuernberg.de*). **Passau** (✉ *Tourist-Information Passau, Rathauspl. 3, D–94032* ☎ *0851/955–980* ⊕ *www.passau.de*). **Regensburg** (✉ *Altes Rathaus, D–93047* ☎ *0941/507–4410* ⊕ *www.regensburg.de*).

Salzburg

WORD OF MOUTH

"And be SURE to have the peach soufflé at the Stiftskeller St. Peter (next to St. Peter's Church). It is the oldest restaurant in Austria (it dates to before ad803)."

—cherrybob

"Last time we were in Salzburg we took the cheesy but fun 'Sound of Music Tour.' We really enjoyed the day since they showed us places where they had filmed scenes around Salzburg, then took us out into the countryside to small towns that had different things to do with the movie."

—tomc

Updated by
Horst Erwin
Reischenböck

ART LOVERS CALL SALZBURG the Golden City of High Baroque; historians refer to it as the Florence of the North or the German Rome; and, of course, music lovers know it as the birthplace of one of the world's most beloved composers, Wolfgang Amadeus Mozart (1756–91). Salzburg did Mozart no particular honor in his lifetime, it is making up for it now. Since 1920 the world-famous Salzburger Festspiele (Salzburg Festival) have honored "Wolferl" with performances of his works by the world's greatest musicians. To see and hear them, crowds pack the city from the last week in July until the end of August.

But many who come to this golden city of High Baroque first hear the instantly recognizable strains that beloved Hollywood extravaganza *The Sound of Music,* filmed here in 1964. One can hardly imagine taking in the Mirabell Gardens, the Pferdeschwemme fountain, Nonnberg Convent, the Residenzplatz, and all the other filmed locations without imagining Maria and the von Trapp children trilling their hearts out. Oddly enough, just like Mozart, the Trapp family—who escaped the Third Reich by fleeing their beloved country—were little appreciated at home; Austria was the only place on the planet where the film failed, closing after a single week's showing in Vienna and Salzburg.

Salzburg lies on both banks of the Salzach River, at the point where it squeezes between two mountains, the Kapuzinerberg on one side, the Mönchsberg on the other. In broader view are many beautiful Alpine peaks. Added to these many gifts of Mother Nature, man's contribution is a trove of buildings worthy of such surroundings. Salzburg's rulers pursued construction on a grand scale ever since Wolf-Dietrich von Raitenau—the "Medici prince-archbishop who preached in stone"—began his regime in the latter part of the 16th century. At the age of only 28, Wolf-Dietrich envisioned "his" Salzburg to be the Rome of the Alps, with a town cathedral grander than St. Peter's, a Residenz as splendid as a Roman palace, and his private Mirabell Gardens flaunting the most fashionable styles of Italianate horticulture. After he was deposed by the rulers of Bavaria, other cultured prince-archbishops took over. Johann Ernst von Thun and Franz Anton von Harrach commanded the masters of Viennese Baroque, Fischer von Erlach and Lukas von Hildebrandt, to complete Wolf-Dietrich's vision. The result is that Salzburg's many fine buildings blend into a harmonious whole. Perhaps nowhere else in the world is there so cohesive a flowering of baroque architecture.

But Salzburg isn't stuck in the past. The city is home to the Museum der Moderne, an avant-garde showcase that stands on the very spot where Julie Andrews "do-re-mi"-d with the von Trapp brood; where once the fusty Café Winkler stood atop the Mönchsberg mount, a modern, cubical museum of cutting-edge art now commands one of the grandest views of the city.

TOP REASONS TO GO

The view from Fortress Hohensalzburg: Go up to the fortress on the peak and realize what the already romantic visitors in the 19th century enjoyed so much—the soul-stirring combination of gorgeous architecture in a stunning natural location.

A pilgrimage to the Rome of the North: See the magnificent baroque churches built not only to honor God but also to document the importance of the ruling prince-archbishops during the 17th century.

Concerts, operas, and more: Feel the spirit of 1,300 years of musical history as you listen to the music of Wolfgang Amadeus Mozart, the greatest composer who ever lived, in the Marble Hall of Mirabell Palace.

Or perhaps you would prefer an opera performed by marionettes or a mass sung in the cathedral. You will run out of time, not options, in Salzburg.

Medieval city: After exploring the Altstadt's grand churches and squares, cross the river Salzach to take in the completely different atmosphere of the narrow, 16th-century Steingasse, where working people once lived and shops, galleries, and clubs now beckon.

Rulers' delights: Drive, bike, walk, or take the boat out to Schloss Hellbrunn, a Renaissance-inspired pleasure palace with trick fountains and the gazebo that witnessed so much wooing in *The Sound of Music*.

EXPLORING SALZBURG

Most of Salzburg's sights are within a comparatively small area. The Altstadt (Old City) is squeezed between the jutting outcrop of the Mönchsberg and the Salzach River. The cathedral and interconnecting squares surrounding it form what used to be the religious center, around which the major churches and the old archbishops' residence are arranged. (Note that entrance into all Salzburg churches is free.) The rest of the Old City belonged to the wealthy burghers: the Getreidegasse, the Alter Markt (old market), the town hall, and the tall, plain burghers' houses (like Mozart's Birthplace). The Mönchsberg cliffs emerge unexpectedly behind the Old City, crowned to the east by the Hohensalzburg Fortress. Across the river, in the small area between the cliffs of the Kapuzinerberg and the riverbank, is Steingasse, a narrow medieval street where working people lived. Northwest of the Kapuzinerberg lie Mirabell Palace and its gardens.

It's best to begin by exploring the architectural and cultural riches of the Old City, then go on to the fortress and after that cross the river to inspect the other bank. Ideally, you need two days to do it all. ■TIP➜ If you are doing this spectacular city in just one day, there is a flip-book approach to Salzburg 101: take a walking tour run by city guides every day at 12:15, setting out from the tourist information office, Information Mozartplatz, at Mozart Square (closed on some Sundays during off-season).

THE ALTSTADT: IN MOZART'S FOOTSTEPS

Intent on becoming a patron of the arts, the prince-archbishop Wolf-Dietrich lavished much of his wealth on rebuilding Salzburg into a beautiful and baroque city in the late 16th and early 17th centuries. In turn, his grand townscape came to inspire the young Joannes Chrysostomus Wolfgangus Amadeus (Theophilus) Mozart. Born in Salzburg on January 27, 1756, Mozart crammed a prodigious number of compositions into the 35 years of his life, many of which he spent in Salzburg (he moved to Vienna in 1781). The Altstadt (or Old Town) has a bevy of important Mozart sights, ranging from his birthplace on the Getreidegasse to the abbey of St. Peter's, where his "Great Mass in C Minor" was first performed.

TIMING   Other than exploring by horse-drawn cabs (*Fiakers*), available for rental at Residenzplatz, most of your exploring will be done on foot, since this historic section of town bans cars. The center city is compact, so you can easily cover it in one day. Note that many churches close at 6 PM, so unless you're catching a concert at one of them, be sure to visit during the daylight hours.

WHAT TO SEE

⑩ Alter Markt *(Old Market)*. Right in the heart of the Old City is the Alter Markt, the old marketplace and center of secular life in past centuries. The square is lined with 17th-century middle-class houses, colorfully hued in shades of pink, pale blue, and yellow ocher. Look in at the old royal pharmacy, the **Hofapotheke,** whose ornate black-and-gold rococo interior was built in 1760. Inside, you'll sense a curious apothecarial smell, traced to the shelves lined with old pots and jars (labeled in Latin). These are not just for show: this pharmacy is still operating today. You can even have your blood pressure taken—but preferably not after drinking a *Doppelter Einspänner* (black coffee with whipped cream, served in a glass) in the famous Café Tomaselli just opposite. In warm weather the café's terrace provides a wonderful spot for watching the world go by. Next to the coffeehouse you'll find the **smallest house in Salzburg,** now a crystal shop.

⑤ Dom *(Cathedral)*. When you walk through the arches leading from Res-★   idenzplatz into **Domplatz,** you're entering one of Salzburg's most beautiful urban set pieces. In the center rises the Virgin's Column, and at one side is the cathedral, considered to be the first early-Italian baroque building north of the Alps, and one of the finest. Its facade is marble, its towers reach 250 feet into the air, and it holds 10,000 people (standing …). There has been a cathedral on this spot since the 8th century, but the present structure dates from the 17th century. Archbishop Wolf-Dietrich took advantage of the old Romanesque-Gothic cathedral's destruction by fire in 1598 to demolish the remains and make plans for a huge new structure facing onto the Residenzplatz. His successor, Markus Sittikus, and the new court architect, Santino Solari, started the present cathedral in 1614; it was consecrated with great ceremony in 1628 during the Thirty Years' War.

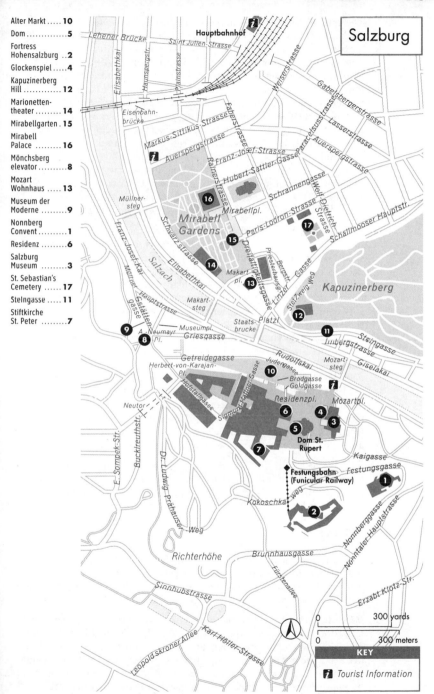

5

The church's simple sepia-and-white interior, a peaceful counterpoint to the usual baroque splendor, dates from a later renovation. To see remains of the old cathedral, go down the steps from the left-side aisle into the crypt where the archbishops from 1600 on are buried. Mozart was christened, the day after he was born, at the 14th-century font here, and he later served as organist from 1779 to 1781. Some of his compositions, such as the *Coronation Mass,* were written for the cathedral. ■TIP➔ On Sunday and all catholic holidays, mass is sung at 10 AM—the most glorious time to experience the cathedral's full splendor. This is the only house of worship in the world with no fewer than five independent fixed organs, which are sometimes played together during special church-music concerts. Many of the church's treasures are in a special museum on the premises. ⊠ *Domplatz* ☎ *0662/844189* 🖷 *0662/840442* ⊕ *www.kirchen.net/dommuseum* ⊠ *Museum: €4.50* ⊙ *Early May–late Oct., Mon.–Sat. 10–5, Sun. and holidays 1–6.*

★ **Getreidegasse.** For centuries this has been the main shopping street in the Old City center. According to historians, the name means "trade street"—not "grain street," as many people believe. Today it is the address of elegant fashion houses, international shoe chains, and a McDonald's (note its wrought-iron sign with classy bronze lettering: like all the other shops, it has conformed with Salzburg's strict Old City conservation laws). Other than coming to shop, crowds flock to this street because house No. 9 is Mozart's birthplace, the **Mozarts Geburtshaus.** In summer the street is as densely packed with people as a corncob with kernels. You can always escape for a while through one of the many arcades—mostly flower-bedecked and opening into delightful little courtyards—that link the Getreidegasse to the river and the Universitätsplatz. At No. 37 you'll find one of the most glamorous hotels in the world, the Goldener Hirsch—just look for its filigree-iron sign showing a leaping stag with gilded antlers. The southern end of Getreidegasse becomes Judengasse, part of the former Jewish ghetto area, which is also festooned with more of Salzburg's famous wrought-iron signs.

❹ Glockenspiel *(Carillon).* The famous carillon tower is perched on top of the **Neue Residenz** (New Residence), Prince-Archbishop Wolf-Dietrich's government palace. The carillon is a later addition, brought from today's Belgium in 1695 and finally put in working order in 1704. The 35 bells play classical tunes (usually by Mozart or Michael Haydn) at 7 AM, 11 AM, and 6 PM—with charm and ingenuity often making up for the occasional musical inaccuracy. From Easter to October, the bells are immediately followed by a resounding retort from perhaps the oldest mechanical musical instrument in the world, the 200-pipe "Bull" organ housed in the Hohensalzburg Fortress across town. ⊠ *Mozartplatz 1.*

❽ Mönchsberg Elevator. Just around the corner from the Pferdeschwemme horse-fountain, at Neumayr Platz, you'll find the Mönchsberg elevator, which carries you up through solid rock not only to the new **Museum der Moderne** but also to wooded paths that are great for walking and gasping—there are spectacular vistas of Salzburg. In summer this can be a marvelous—and quick—way to escape the tiny crowded streets of

the Old City. ✉ *Gstättengasse 13* 🎫 *Round-trip €2.90, one-way €1.80*
🕐 *Open Oct.–May, daily 9–9; June–Sept., daily 9 AM–11 PM.*

⑨ Museum der Moderne. Enjoying one of Salzburg's most famous scenic
spots, the dramatic museum of modern and contemporary art reposes
atop the sheer cliff face of the Mönchsberg. The setting was immortalized in *The Sound of Music*—this is where Julie and the kids start war-
bling "Doe, a deer, a female deer ..." Clad in minimalist white marble,
the museum (2004) was designed by Friedrich Hoff Zwink of Munich.
It has three exhibition levels, which bracket a restaurant with a large
terrace—now, as always, the place to enjoy the most spectacular view
over the city while sipping a coffee. ■ TIP➔ **Visit in the evening to see
the city illuminated.** The museum has an impressive calendar of tempo-
rary exhibitions of cutting-edge contemporary art. ✉ *Mönchsberg 32*
☎ *0662/842220* ⊕ *www.museumdermoderne.at* 🎫 *€8* 🕐 *Tues.–Sun.
10–6, Wed. 10–9.*

⑥ Residenz. At the very heart of baroque Salzburg, the Residenz over-
★ looks the spacious Residenzplatz and its famous fountain. The palace
in its present condition was built between 1600 and 1619 as the home
of Wolf-Dietrich, the most powerful of Salzburg's prince-archbishops.
The Kaisersaal (Imperial Hall) and the Rittersaal (Knight's Hall), one
of the city's most regal concert halls, can be seen along with the rest of
the magnificent **State Rooms** on a self-guided tour with headphones.
Upstairs on the third floor is the **Residenzgalerie**, a princely art collection specializing in 17th-century Dutch and Flemish art and 19th-
century paintings of Salzburg. On the state room floor, Mozart's opera
La Finta Semplice was premiered in 1769 in the Guard Room. Mozart
often did duty here, as, at age 14, he became the first violinist of the
court orchestra. Today the reception rooms of the Residenz are often
used for official functions, banquets, and concerts, and therefore might
not always be open for visitors. ✉ *Residenzplatz 1* ☎ *0662/8042–
2690, 0662/840451 art collection* ⊕ *www.residenzgalerie.at/* 🎫 *€7.30
for both museums; art collection only: €5* 🕐 *Daily 10–5, closed 2 wks
before Easter. Tours by arrangement. Art collection: daily 10–5, closed
early Feb.–mid-Mar. and Wed., Oct.–Mar.*

③ Salzburg Museum *(Neugebäude).* Salzburg's mammoth 17th-century
Fodor's Choice Neue Residenz (New Residence) was Prince-Archbishop Wolf-Dietri-
★ ch's "overflow" palace (he couldn't fit his entire archiepiscopal court
into the main Residenz across the plaza). It features 10 state reception
rooms that were among the first attempts at a *stil Renaissance* in the
North, and it's now the splendid home of the collections of the former Carolino-Augusteum Museum. These include Hallstatt Age relics,
remains of the town's ancient Roman ruins, and the famous Celtic
bronze flagon found earlier this century on the Dürrnberg near Hallein
(15 km [10 mi] south of Salzburg). The collection of Old Master paintings ranges from Gothic altarpieces to wonderful "view" paintings of
18th- and 19th-century Salzburg. Pride of place is given to the spectacular **Sattler Panorama**, one of the few remaining 360-degree paintings
in the world, which shows the city of Salzburg in the early 19th century.

⊠*Mozartplatz 1* ☎*0662/620808–200* 🖷*0662/620808–220* ⊕*www. smca.at* 🖻*€8* ⊙*Mon.–Wed. and Fri.–Sun. 9–5, Thurs. 9–8.*

❼ Stiftkirche St. Peter *(Collegiate Church of St. Peter)*. The most sumptuous
★ church in Salzburg, St. Peter's is where Mozart's famed *Great Mass in C Minor* premiered in 1783, with his wife, Constanze, singing the lead soprano role. Wolfgang often directed the orchestra and choir here, and also played the organ. During every season of the city's summer music festival in August, the *Great Mass in C Minor* is performed here during a special church music concert. The front portal of what was originally a Romanesque basilica dates from 1245. Inside, the low-ceiling aisles are charmingly painted in rococo candy-box style. The porch has beautiful Romanesque vaulted arches from the original structure built in the 12th century; the interior was decorated in the characteristically voluptuous late-baroque style when additions were made in the 1770s. Note the side chapel by the entrance, with the unusual crèche portraying the Flight into Egypt and the Massacre of the Innocents. Behind the Rupert Altar is the "Felsengrab," a rockface tomb where—according to a legend—St. Rupert himself was originally buried. To go from the sacred to the profane, head for the abbey's legendary Weinkeller restaurant, adjacent to the church. ⊠*St. Peter Bezirk* ☎*0662/844578–0* 🖻*Free* ⊙*Apr.–Sept., daily 6:30* AM–7 PM; *Oct.–Mar., daily 6:30* AM–6 PM.

ACROSS THE RIVER SALZACH: FROM THE FORTRESS TO THE NEW TOWN

According to a popular saying in Salzburg, "If you can see the fortress, it's just about to rain; if you can't see it, it's already raining." Fortunately there are plenty of days when spectacular views can be had of Salzburg and the surrounding countryside from the top of this castle. Looking across the River Salzach to the Neustadt (New Town) area of historic Salzburg, you can pick out the Mirabell Palace and Gardens, the Landestheater, the Mozart Residence and the Mozarteum, the Church of the Holy Trinity, and the Kapuzinerkloster perched atop the Kapuzinerberg. Ranging from the "acropolis" of the city—the medieval Fortress Hohensalzburg—to the celebrated Salzburg Marionette Theater, this part of Salzburg encapsulates the city's charm.

TIMING   Allow half a day for the fortress, to explore it fully both inside and out. If you don't plan an intermission at one of the restaurants on the Mönchsberg, you can stock up on provisions at Fasties (Pfeifergasse 3, near Kajetanerplatz). Call the Mozarteum to see if there will be evening recitals in their two concert halls; hearing the *Haffner* or another of Mozart's symphonies could be a wonderfully fitting conclusion to your day.

WHAT TO SEE
❷ Fortress Hohensalzburg. Founded in 1077, the Hohensalzburg is Salz-
Ⓒ burg's acropolis and the largest preserved medieval fortress in Central
★ Europe. Brooding over the city from atop the Festungsberg, it was originally founded by Salzburg's Archbishop Gebhard, who had supported the pope in the investiture controversy against the Holy Roman

Emperor. Over the centuries the archbishops gradually enlarged the castle, using it originally only sometimes as a residence, then as a siege-proof haven against invaders and their own rebellious subjects. The exterior may look grim, but inside there are lavish state rooms, such as the glittering **Golden Room,** the **Burgmuseum**—a collection of medieval art—and the **Rainer's Museum,** with its brutish arms and armor. Politics and Church are in full force here: there's a torture chamber not far from the exquisite late-Gothic **St. George's Chapel** (although, in fact, the implements on view came from another castle and were not used here). The 200-pipe organ from the beginning of the 16th century, played during the warmer months daily after the carillon in the Neugebäude, is best heard from a respectful distance, as it's called "the Bull" for good reason. ■**TIP→** Climb up the 100 tiny steps to the Reckturm, a grand lookout post with a sweeping view of Salzburg and the mountains. Children will love coming here, especially as some rooms of the castle are now given over to a special exhibition, the **Welt der Marionetten,** which offers a fascinating view into the world of marionettes—a great preview of the treats in store at the nearby Marionettentheater.

To reach the fortress, walk up the zigzag path that begins just beyond the Stieglkeller on Festungsgasse. Note that you don't need a ticket to walk the footpath. The more-than-110-year-old **Festungsbahn** (*funicular railway* ⊠*Festungsgasse 4* ☎*0662/842682* ⊕*www.festungsbahn.at* ⊙*Every 10 min Oct.–Mar., daily 9–5; May–Sept., daily 9–9*) is the easy way up (advisable with young children). It is behind St. Peter's Cemetery. A round-trip pass including the entrance fee to all the museums in the fortress is €9.50, and a one-way ticket down is €2.10.■**TIP→** Visitor lines to the fortress can be long, so try to come early. ⊠*Fortress Hohensalzburg, Mönchsberg 34* ☎*0662/842430–11* ⊕*www.salzburg-burgen.at* ☞*Fortress including all museums €6.90* ⊙*Mid-Mar.–mid-June, daily 9–6; mid-June–mid-Sept., daily 8:30–8; mid-Sept.–mid-Mar., daily 9–5.*

⑫ **Kapuzinerberg Hill.** Directly opposite the Mönchsberg on the other side of the river, Kapuzinerberg Hill is crowned by several interesting sights. By ascending a stone staircase near Steingasse 9 you can start your climb up the peak. At the top of the first flight of steps is a tiny chapel, **St. Johann am Imberg,** built in 1681. Farther on are a signpost and gate to the **Hettwer Bastion,** part of the old city walls. ■**TIP→** Hettwer Bastion is one of the most spectacular viewpoints in Salzburg. At the summit is the gold-beige **Kapuzinerkloster** (Capuchin Monastery), originally a fortification built to protect the one bridge crossing the river, which dates from the time of Prince-Archbishop Wolf-Dietrich. It is still an active monastery and thus cannot be visited (except for the church). The road downward—note the Stations of the Cross along the path—is called Stefan Zweig Weg, after the great Austrian writer who rented the **Paschingerschlössl** house (on the Kapuzinerberg to the left of the monastery) until 1934, when he left Austria after the Nazis murdered chancellor Dollfuss.

⑭ **Marionettentheater** (*Marionette Theater*). The Salzburger Marionettentheater is both the world's greatest marionette theater and—surprise!—a sublime theatrical experience. Many critics have noted that viewers quickly forget the strings controlling the puppets, which assume lifelike dimensions and provide a very real dramatic experience. The Marionettentheater is identified above all with Mozart's operas, which seem particularly suited to the skilled puppetry; a delightful production of *Così fan tutte* captures the humor of the work better than most stage versions. The theater itself is a rococo concoction. The company is famous for its world tours, but is usually in Salzburg around Christmas, during the late-January Mozart Week, at Easter, and from May to September (schedule subject to change). ⊠*Schwarzstrasse 24* ☎*0662/872406–0* ᕎ*0662/882141* ⊕*www.marionetten.at* ᕎ*€18–€35* ⊙*Box office Mon.–Sat. 9–1 and 2 hrs before performance; Salzburg season May–Sept., Christmas, Mozart Week (Jan.), Easter.*

⑮ **Mirabellgarten** *(Mirabell Gardens).* While there are at least four
ᐖ entrances to the Mirabell Gardens—from the Makartplatz (framed
Fodor's Choice by the statues of Roman gods), the Schwarzstrasse, and the Rainer-
★ strasse—you'll want to enter from the Rainerstrasse and head for the Rosenhügel (Rosebush Hill): you'll arrive at the top of the steps where Julie Andrews and her seven charges showed off their singing ability in *The Sound of Music.* This is also an ideal vantage point from which to admire the formal gardens and one of the best views of Salzburg. The center of the gardens—one of Europe's most beautiful parks—is dominated by four large groups of statues representing the elements water, fire, air, and earth, and designed by Ottavio Mosto, who came to live in Salzburg from Padua. The most famous part of the Mirabell Gardens is the **Zwerglgarten** (Dwarfs' Garden), where you'll find 12 statues of "Danubian" dwarves sculpted in marble—the real-life models for which were presented to the bishop by the landgrave of Göttweig. Prince-Archbishop Franz Anton von Harrach had the stone figures made for a kind of stone theater below. The **Heckentheater** (Hedge Theater) is an enchanting natural stage setting that dates from 1700. The Mirabell Gardens are open daily 7 AM–8 PM.

Art lovers will make a beeline for the **Barockmuseum** (⊠*Orangeriegarten* ☎*0662/877432*), beside the Orangery of the Mirabell Gardens. It houses a collection of late-17th- and 18th-century paintings, sketches, and models illustrating the extravagant vision of life of the baroque era—the signature style of Salzburg. Works by Giordano, Bernini, and Rottmayr are the collection's highlights. The museum is open Tuesday to Saturday, 9 to noon and 2 to 5, and Sunday and holidays 10 to 1; admission is €3.

⑯ **Mirabell Palace.** The "Taj Mahal of Salzburg," Schloss Mirabell was built in 1606 by the immensely wealthy and powerful Prince-Archbishop Wolf-Dietrich for his mistress, Salomé Alt, and their 15 children. Such was the palace's beauty that it was taken over by succeeding prince-archbishops; Franz Anton von Harrach gave the place a baroque facelift in 1727. A disastrous fire hit in 1818, but happily, three of the most spectacular set-pieces of the palace—the Chapel, the Marble Hall, and the Angel Staircase—survived. The Marble Hall is now used for civil wedding ceremonies, and is regarded as the most beautiful registry office in the world. The young Mozart and his sister gave concerts here, and he also composed *Tafelmusik* (Table Music) to accompany the prince's meals. ■TIP➔ **Candlelight chamber music concerts in the Marble Hall provide an ideal combination of performance and atmosphere.** Beside the chapel in the northeast corner, the only other part of the palace to survive the fire was the magnificent marble Angel Staircase. Outdoor concerts are held at the palace and gardens May though August, Sunday mornings at 10:30 and Wednesday evenings at 8:30. ☒ *Off Makartplatz* ☎ *0662/889–87–330* 🖃 *Free* ☉ *Weekdays 8–6.*

⑬ Mozart Wohnhaus *(Mozart Residence).* The Mozart family moved from their cramped quarters in Getreidegasse to this house on the Hannibal Platz, as it was then known, in 1773. Wolfgang Amadeus Mozart lived here until 1780, his sister Nannerl stayed here until she married in 1784, and their father Leopold lived here until his death in 1787. During the first Allied bomb attack on Salzburg in October 1944, the house was partially destroyed, but was reconstructed in 1996. Mozart composed the "Salzburg Symphonies" here, as well as all five violin concertos, church music and some sonatas, and parts of his early operatic masterpieces, including *Idomeneo*. Besides an interesting collection of musical instruments, among the exhibits are books from Leopold Mozart's library. Autograph manuscripts and letters can be viewed, by prior arrangement only, in the cellar vaults. ☒ *Makartplatz 8* ☎ *0662/874227–40* 🖨 *0662/872924* ⊕ *www.mozarteum.at* 🖃 *Mozart residence €6.50, combined ticket for Mozart residence and birthplace €10* ☉ *Sept.–June, daily 9–5:30; July and Aug., daily 9–6:30.*

❶ Nonnberg Convent. Just below the south side of the Fortress Hohensalzburg—and best visited in tandem with it—the Stift Nonnberg was founded right after 700 by St. Rupert, and his niece St. Erentrudis was the first abbess. ■TIP➔ **Spend the extra €.50 to illuminate the frescos just below the steeple. They are some of the oldest in Austria, painted in the Byzantine style during the 10th century.** The church is more famous these days as "Maria's convent"—both the one in *The Sound of Music* and that of the real Maria. She returned to marry her Captain von Trapp here in the Gothic church. (No filming was done here—"Nonnberg" was re-created in the film studios of Salzburg-Parsch.) Each evening in May at 7 the nuns sing a 15-minute service called Maiandacht in the old Gregorian chant. Parts of the private quarters for the nuns, which include some lovely, intricate woodcarving, can be seen by prior arrangement. ☒ *Nonnberggasse 2* ☎ *0662/841607–0* ☉ *Fall–spring, daily 7–5; summer, daily 7–7.*

⑰ St. Sebastian's Cemetery. Memorably recreated for the escape scene in *The Sound of Music* on a Hollywood soundstage, final resting place for many members of the Mozart family, and situated in the shadows of St. Sebastian's Church, the Friedhof St. Sebastian is one of the most peaceful spots in Salzburg. Prince-Archbishop Wolf-Dietrich commissioned the cemetery in 1600 to replace the old cathedral graveyard, which he planned to demolish. It was built in the style of an Italian *campo santo,* (sacred field) with arcades on four sides, and in the center of the square he had the Gabriel Chapel, an unusual, brightly tiled Mannerist mausoleum, built for himself, in which he was interred in 1617 (now closed for visitors). Around the chapel is the grave of Mozart's widow, Constanze. According to the latest research, Mozart's father Leopold came to rest in the unmarked community grave here, too. If the gate is closed, enter through the back entrance around the corner in the courtyard. ⊠ *Linzergasse* ☉ *Daily 9–6.*

⑪ **Steingasse.** This narrow medieval street, walled in on one side by the bare cliffs of the Kapuzinerberg, was originally the ancient Roman entrance into the city from the south. The houses stood along the riverfront before the Salzach was regulated. Nowadays it's a fascinating mixture of artists' workshops, antiques shops, and trendy nightclubs, but with its tall houses the street still manages to convey an idea of how life used to be in the Middle Ages. The **Steintor** marks the entrance to the oldest section of the street; here on summer afternoons the light can be particularly striking. House No. 23 on the right still has deep, slanted peep-windows for guarding the gate. House No. 31 is the birthplace of Josef Mohr, the poet of "Silent Night, Holy Night" fame (not No. 9, as is incorrectly noted on the wall).

WHERE TO EAT

Salzburg has some of the best—and most expensive—restaurants in Austria, but the city is also plentifully supplied with pleasant, more modest eateries. You can get not only good, solid Austrian food, but also exceptional Italian dishes and newer-than-now *neue Küche* (nouvelle cuisine) delights. There are certain dining experiences that are quintessentially Salzburgian, including restaurants perched on the town's peaks that offer "food with a view"—in some cases, it's too bad the food isn't up to the view—or rustic inns that offer "Alpine evenings" with entertainment. Some of the most distinctive places in town are the fabled hotel restaurants, such as those of the Goldener Hirsch or the "Ratsherrenkeller" of the Hotel Elefant (⇨ *Where to Stay).*

For fast food, Salzburgers love their broiled-sausage street-stands. Some say the most delicious are to be found at the Balkan Grill at Getreidegasse 33 (its recipe for spicy Bosna sausage has always been a secret). ■TIP➔ For a quick lunch on weekdays, visit the market in front of the Kollegienkirche—a lot of stands offer a large variety of boiled sausages for any taste, ranging from mild to spiced.

Many restaurants are open all day; otherwise, lunch is served from approximately 11 to 2 and dinner from 6 to 10. In more expensive restaurants it's always best to make a reservation. At festival time most restaurants are open seven days a week, and have generally more flexible late dining hours.

WHAT IT COSTS IN EUROS				
	¢	$	$$	$$$	$$$$
AT DINNER	under €7	€7–€12	€13–€17	€18–€22	over €22

Prices are per person for a main course at dinner.

$$$$ ✕**Gasthof Hohlwegwirt.** It's worth a detour on the way to Hallein along
★ the B159 Salzachtal-Bundesstrasse about 10 km (6 mi) south of Salzburg to dine at this inviting inn, run by the same family for more than 130 years. Chef Ernst Kronreif uses recipes from his legendary mother, Ida: spring for the delicious *Butternockerlsuppe* (soup-broth with buttered dumplings), the *Kalbsbries* (calf's sweetbreads), or the *Salzburger Bierfleisch* (beef boiled in beer)—all updated Salzburgian classics. Meals are served in the unmistakable atmosphere of a *stile Salzburg* house with four nicely decorated salons. Landing a table can be a challenge because of the many local regulars, so book in advance. Upstairs are some delightfully gemütlich guest rooms. ⊠*Salzachtal-Bundesstrasse Nord 62, A-5400 Hallein-Taxach* ☎*06245/82415–0* 📠*06245/8241572* ⚐*Reservations essential* ⊘*Closed Mon., except during summer festival* ⊟*MC, V.*

$$–$$$$ ✕**Stiftskeller St. Peter.** "St. Peter's Beer Cellar," part of a famous Benedic-
Fodor'sChoice tine abbey, is Austria's oldest restaurant, documented back to at least
★ 803, and it remains one of the most dazzling dining experiences in Salzburg. Choose between the fairly elegant, dark-wood-panel Prälatenzimmer (Prelates' Room) or one of several less-formal banqueting rooms. On summer days the dramatic gray-stone courtyard is a favorite spot for a glass of wine or beer, accompanied by morsels of fried Wiener Schnitzel. Along with other Austrian standards, you can dine on fish caught in local waters, and, of course, Salzburger Nockerl. For the full St. Peter splendor, attend a candlelight Mozart Dinner Concert (€45, plus drinks) in the abbey's beautiful Baroque Hall. ⊠*St. Peter Bezirk 4* ☎*0662/841268–0, 0662/828695–0 Mozart dinner* ⊕*www.stiftskellerstpeter.at* ⊟*AE, DC, MC, V.*

$$–$$$ ✕**Mundenhamer.** Set next to Mirabell Palace, this old-fashioned restaurant is masterminded by chef Ernst Breitschopf, who knows good old Upper Austrian dishes inside out. Specialties include Innviertler (raw ham with horseradish, dark bread, and butter); garlic soup with croutons; roast pork chop with dumplings and warm bacon-cabbage salad; and homemade spaetzle with braised white cabbage and bacon. For dessert, few can resist the Mohr im Hemd (Moor-in-a-shirt): the warm chocolate cake garnished with fruits, chocolate sauce, vanilla ice cream, and whipped cream. ⊠*Rainerstrasse 2* ☎*0662/875693* ⊟*AE, DC, MC, V* ⊘*Closed Sun.*

$$–$$$ ✕**Zum Eulenspiegel.** This inn dates back to at least 1713, and today,
★ spiffily restored, it allures with rustic wooden furniture, antique weapons, and open fireplaces. The unique setting is matched by the delicious food. Try the potato goulash with chunks of sausage and beef in a creamy paprika sauce, or the house specialty, fish stew Provençal. These are served at lunch, or all day in the bar downstairs. A final plus: the staff speaks English. ⊠*Hagenauerplatz 2* ☎*0662/843180–0* ⚐*Reservations essential* ⊟*AE, DC, MC, V* ⊘*Closed Sun., except during festival, and Jan.–mid-Mar.*

$–$$$ ✕**Café Sacher.** Red-velvet banquettes, sparkling chandeliers, and lots of gilt mark this famous gathering place, a favorite of well-heeled Salzburgers and an outpost of the celebrated Vienna landmark. It's a

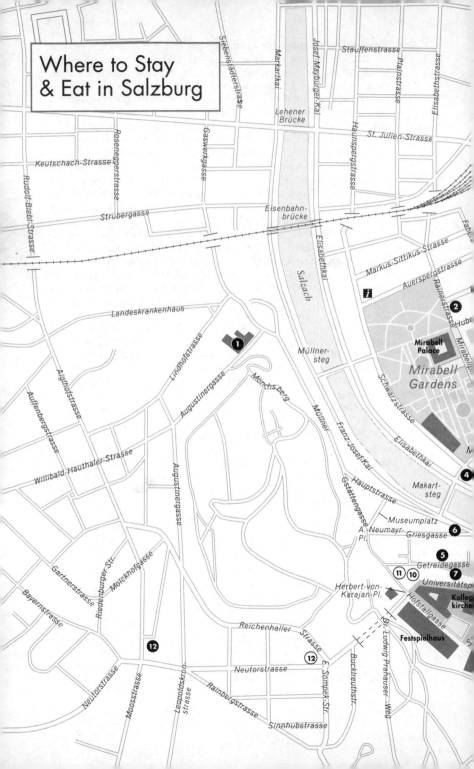

Where to Stay & Eat in Salzburg

5

perfect choice for a leisurely afternoon pastry (especially the famous chocolate Sachertorte) and coffee—and of course the coffee is second to none. Full meals are also served and they offer a no-smoking room, too. (Pastries and coffee are in the $ category.) ⊠*Schwarzstrasse 5–7* ☎*0662/889770* 🖃*AE, DC, MC, V.*

$$ ✕**Gablerbräu.** Many like to stop here for a fast bite, but you should ponder the historic vibes, too. In this old inn Richard Mayr—a star of Vienna's State Opera House—was born. He later became one of the organizers of the Salzburg music festival. After studying the parlor of Mayr's parents—a dark, neo-Gothic interior from the end of the 19th century—head for a table and settle down to "hot breads and cold beer": a selection of beers from different provinces along with a large variety of sandwiches. There is also a self-service salad buffet. Other menu items are northern Italian, including polenta croquets with ratatouille and Gorgonzola cream sauce, and linguine with zucchini in tomato sauce. ⊠*Linzergasse 9* ☎*0662/88965* 🖃*AE, DC, MC, V.*

$$ ✕**K&K am Waagplatz.** This old house was once the domicile of the Freysauff family, who counted among their close friends Leopold Mozart, the composer's father. Its cellar, the downstairs section of the restaurant, is still called the Freysauff (but don't be misled by the name, which translates as "free drinks"). The restaurant is particularly pleasant, with white-linen tablecloths, candles, and flowers, and windows opening onto the street. Menu selections consist of locally caught fish, delicious chicken-breast medallions, lentil salad with strips of goose breast, and traditional Austrian dishes, including game in season. ⊠*Waagplatz 2* ☎*0662/842156* 🖃*AE, DC, MC, V.*

$$ ✕**Kuglhof.** In Maxglan, a famous Austrian "farmer's village" tucked
★ behind the Mönchsberg and next to the Stiegl Brewery (best, therefore, reached by taxi), Alexander Hawranek perfects Old Austrian specialties by giving them a nouvelle touch. The setting is your archetypal black-shuttered, begonia-bedecked Salzburgian farmhouse, cozily set with a tile oven, mounted antlers, embroidered curtains, and tons of *gemütlichkeit*. The signature dish *Beuschl* (calf's lights) with dumplings, available in season, and the best bet for dessert is the *Apfelschmarrn*, sliced pancake with apples. In summer opt for a table in the shady garden. ⊠*Kuglhofstrasse 13* ☎*0662/832626* ⊕*www.kuglhof. at* 🖃*AE, DC, MC, V* ⊘*Closed Mon. and Tues.*

$–$$ ✕**Café Tomaselli.** This inn opened its doors in 1705 as an example of
Fodor's Choice a new-fangled "Wiener Kaffeehaus" (Vienna coffeehouse). It was an
★ immediate hit, popular with, among others, Mozart's beloved Constanze, who lived just next door. The Tomasellis set up shop here in 1753, became noted as "chocolatmachers," and are still running the place. Feast on the famous "Tomaselliums Café" (mocca, Mozart liqueur, and whipped cream) and the large selection of excellent cakes, tarts, and strudels. Inside, the decor is marble, wood, and 18th-century portraits. In the summer, however, the best seats are on the terrace and at the pretty "Tomaselli-Kiosk" on the square. ⊠*Alter Markt 9* ☎*0662/844488–0* ⊕*www.tomaselli.at* 🖃*No credit cards.*

$–$$ ✕**Fabrizi Espresso.** Named after its house's former Italian owner, this is a top spot for tasting Marzemino, the red wine Don Giovanni drinks in Mozart's opera. But there are plenty of other goodies here: some of the best Italian coffees in the city; outstanding Austrian *Apfel-oder Topfenstrudel* (apple or cheese pie) and the best Salzburger Nockerl; various salads; and a fine wiener schnitzel. ⊠ *Getreidegasse 21* ☎ *0662/845914* 🖃 *No credit cards.*

$ ✕ **Wilder Mann.** "After a certain time all men become wild." So goes a famous Salzburg saying, perhaps coined after someone drank too much of the local "liquid bread"— Stiegl beer. In fact, when this inn opened its doors in 1884 it became one of the most important burgher houses in the Altstadt. Today it offers the true time-stained ambience of an old Salzburg *Gasthaus,* right down to the wooden chairs that generations of locals have sat on and the enormous plates of *Bauernschmaus* (farmer's dish), overflowing with veal, pork, sausage, cabbage, and dumplings. ⊠ *Getreidegasse 20* ☎ *0662/841787* 🖃 *No credit cards* ⊗ *Closed Sun.*

¢–$ ✕ **Augustinerbräu.** One of the largest beer cellars in Europe, the cel-
★ ebrated Augustinerbräu is at the north end of the Mönchsberg next to St. Augustine's church. You can even bring your own food—a relic of the tradition that forbade breweries from serving meals in order to protect the status of restaurants. Pick up a stone jug of strong, frothy Augustiner beer and sit in the gardens or at a dark-wood table in one of the large refectory halls. Shops in the huge monastery complex sell a vast array of salads, breads, and pastries, as well as sausage and spit-roasted chicken. ⊠ *Augustinergasse 4* ☎ *0662/431246* 🖃 *No credit cards* ⊗ *Weekdays 3–11, weekends 2:30–11.*

WHERE TO STAY

Salzburg is not a tiny town, and location is important. It is best to be near the historic city center; it's about a mile from the railway station to historic Zentrum (center), right around the main bridge of the Staatsbrücke. The Old City has a wide assortment of hotels and pensions, but there are few bargains. Also note that many hotels in this area have to be accessed on foot, as cars are not permitted on many streets. If you have a car, you may opt for a hotel or converted castle on the outskirts of the city.

If you're looking for something really cheap (less than €50 for a double), clean, and comfortable, stay in a private home (though the good ones are all a little way from downtown). The tourist information offices

---

ON THE MENU

Many restaurants favor the *neue Küche*—a lighter version of the somewhat heavy traditional specialties of Austrian cooking, but with more substance than nouvelle cuisine. Salzburgers also have a wonderful way with fish—often a fresh catch from the nearby lakes of the Salzkammergut. Favorite fish dishes are usually *gebraten* (fried). The only truly indigenous Salzburg dish is *Salzburger Nockerln,* a snowy meringue of sweetened whisked egg whites with a little bit of flour and sugar.

5

don't list private rooms; try calling Eveline Truhlar of **Bob's Special Tours** (☎*0662/849511–0*), who runs a private-accommodations service.

If you're planning to come at festival time (July and August), you must book as early as possible; try to reserve at least two months in advance. Prices soar over their already high levels.

Room rates include taxes and service charges. Many hotels include a breakfast in the room rate—check when booking—but the more expensive often do not. A property that provides breakfast and dinner daily is known as *halb pension,* and one that serves three meals a day is *voll pension.* If you don't have a reservation, go to one of the tourist information offices or the accommodations service (*Zimmernachweis*) on the main platform of the railway station.

WHAT IT COSTS IN EUROS					
	¢	$	$$	$$$	$$$$
FOR 2 PEOPLE	under €80	€80–€120	€120–€170	€170–€270	over €270

Prices are for a standard double room in high season, including taxes and service.

$$$$
★ ⊞ **Altstadt Radisson SAS.** Venerable is the word to describe this outpost of the Radisson group: after its founding in 1372 it was a brewery for centuries, then became one of the city's first inns, and has been a luxury hotel since 1992. The exterior is an Old City charmer, done up in buff pink, white trim, sash windows, and iron lanterns. Inside there's been major renovation, but historic stone arches and antiques adorning many rooms maintain the traditional ambience. On one side, rooms overlook the river; on the other, upper rooms sneak a peek at the fortress. Despite smaller windows and original beamed ceilings, rooms are light and spacious. The elegant Symphonie Restaurant is done in royal-blue and gold hues, ashimmer under Rococo chandeliers. Added bonuses are the central yet quiet location and generous buffet breakfast. ⊠*Judengasse 15/Rudolfskai 28, A-5020* ☎*0662/848571–0* 🖷*0662/848–5716* ⊕*www.austria-trend.at/ass* ⬅*42 rooms, 20 suites* ⚲*In-hotel: restaurant, bar* ⊟*AE, DC, MC, V* ⍾*BP.*

$$$$
Fodor'sChoice
★ ⊞ **Goldener Hirsch.** The "Golden Stag" has long been the place to experience patrician pampering in Salzburg. The location is tops, just down the street from Mozart's birthplace and steps from the Festspielhaus. Inside it's delightfully rustic, with woodwork, peasant-luxe furniture, medieval statues, and some of the lowest ceilings in town. The hotel is made up of four town houses, connected in a welter of staircases and elevators, and some rooms have snug dimensions. There are two restaurants—the regal dining room and its smaller bistro-brother, "s'Herzl"—and the bar is probably the world's most beautifully decorated *Bauernstil* room. Long run by Count Johannes Walderdorff, the hotel is now part of the Starwood hotel chain, and some high-rollers complain it's not what it used to be. . . but what is? ⊠*Getreidegasse 37, A-5020* ☎*0662/8084–0* 🖷*0662/848511–845* ⊕*www.goldener-hirsch.com* ⬅*64 rooms, 5 suites* ⚲*In-room: refrigerator. In-hotel: 2 restaurants, bar, parking (fee), Internet* ⊟*AE, DC, MC, V.*

$$$ 🏨**Blaue Gans.** "The Blue Goose" has always been a popular option—
its location on the main shopping drag of Getreidegasse, within sight
of the Festival theaters, Mozart's Birthplace, and the Pferdeschwemme
fountain, is tops. It has a 400-year-old pedigree and still retains its
ancient wood beams, winding corridors, and low archways. But today
this is an "art hotel," the first in Salzburg. The avant-garde works of
local artists Erich Shobesberger, Christian Ecker, and Waldemar Kufner
adorn the walls. Upstairs, the guest rooms are spacious and have con-
temporary furnishings, whitewashed walls with cheeky framed posters
and cheerful curtains; a few have skylights. The popular restaurant has
lively contemporary art on the walls and nouvelle Austrian delights on
the dishes. ⊠*Getreidegasse 43, A-5020* 🕿🕿*0662/842491-0* ⊕*www.
blauegans.at* 🛏*40 rooms* 🛁*In-room: refrigerator, no a/c (some). In-
hotel: restaurant, bar, parking (fee), Internet, minibar* ☰*AE, DC, MC,
V* 🍽*BP.*

$$-$$$ 🏨**Auersperg.** Would you like to start your mornings with a stroll by a
pool flowered with water lilies? You'll find this green oasis beside the
two buildings that comprise the Auersperg, built in 1892 by the noted
Italian architect Ceconi. The lobby welcomes you with Biedermeier
antiques, while upstairs, the soigné guest rooms contain mostly mod-
ern pieces accented with classic ornaments. A rich breakfast buffet and
the use of the roof sauna and a steam bath are included. Outside the
door, and you're five minutes from the historic section. A big plus: just
around the corner is a treasured restaurant/beer garden, Die Weisse.
⊠*Auerspergstrasse 61, A-5020* 🕿*0662/88944* 🖷*0662/889-4455*
⊕*www.auersperg.at* 🛏*51 rooms* 🛁*In-room: no a/c. In-hotel: park-
ing (no fee), Internet* ☰*AE, DC, MC, V* 🍽*BP.*

$$-$$$ 🏨**Elefant.** An old-time favorite, this hotel was once graced by the real
Maria von Trapp. But we mean really old: the 700-year-old house
began life as an inn that hosted the likes of Maximilian II, who was
accompanied by an Indian elephant named Soliman; that's why guests
are welcomed by the sight of an elephant sculpture in the lobby. Most
of the decor is less exotic—in fact, much of the local color has dis-
appeared since the Elephant was rounded up by Best Western. Some
rooms are alluring, with pale yellow striped wallpaper, blue accents,
and antique-style furniture, but others are much more generic. For
real history, repair to the hotel's "Ratsherrenkeller," one of Salzburg's
most famous wine cellars in the 17th century. Today it's the restaurant
Bruno, which serves alluring candlelight dinners. ⊠*Sigmund-Haffner-
Gasse 4, A-5020* 🕿*0662/843397* 🖷*0662/840109-28* ⊕*www.elefant.
at* 🛏*31 rooms* 🛁*In-room: refrigerator. In-hotel: restaurant, parking
(fee), Internet* ☰*AE, DC, MC, V* 🍽*BP.*

$$ 🏨**Neutor.** A two-minute walk from the Old City and next to the historic tunnel that plows through the Mönchsberg, this modern but
classy option, run by the Schwärzler hotel group, is divided between
two buildings on opposite sides of the street. The decor is bright and
shiny—a real blessing on a gray, rainy day—and all rooms are equipped
with modern technology. Children ages six and under are free; ages
7-12 get a 50% reduction for the third bed in the parent's room. There
are a few parking spaces behind the hotel, but if they are occupied you

will have to pay to park either along the street or in a garage. ⊠*Neutorstrasse 8, A-5020* ☎*0662/844154–0* 🖷*0662/84415416* ⊕*www.schwaerzler-hotels.com* ⇘*89 rooms* ♿*In-room: no a/c. In-hotel: restaurant, bar* ▤*AE, DC, MC, V* ❚❘❘*BP.*

$$ ⚏ **Stadtkrug.** Snuggled under the monument-studded Kapuzinerberg and a two-minute walk from the bridge leading to the center of the Altstadt, the Stadtkrug (dated 1353) hits an idyllic, romantic, and quiet vibe, thanks to its mountainside setting. A traditional wrought-iron sign greets you, the lobby tinkles with chandeliers, and the main-floor restaurant is your archetypal, white, classic, vaulted Salzburg sanctorum. Upstairs you find a charming atmosphere, even if some of the rustically furnished rooms are tiny. Head up to the roof to enjoy a restaurant that is terraced into the mountainside and set with statues, potted begonias, echoes of Italy, and lovely views. ⊠*Linzergasse 20, A-5020* ☎*0662/873545–0* 🖷*0662/87353454* ⊕*www.stadtkrug.at* ⇘*34 rooms* ♿*In-room: no a/c. In-hotel: 2 restaurants* ▤*AE, DC, MC, V* ❚❘❘*BP.*

$$ ⚏ **Weisse Taube.** In the heart of the pedestrian area of the Altstadt, the centuries-old "White Dove" is around the corner from Mozartplatz, the Residenz, and a block from the cathedral. Comfortably renovated into a hotel—now family-run for four generations—this 14th-century burgher's house has been traditionally restored, but some time-burnished touches remain: uneven floors, ancient stone archways, and wood-beam ceilings. Guest rooms are simply furnished, with dark-wood accents. Several no-smoking rooms are available, and the main section of the breakfast room is also no-smoking. The staff is most friendly. ⊠*Kaigasse 9, A-5020* ☎*0662/842404* 🖷*0662/841783* ⊕*www.weissetaube.at* ⇘*33 rooms* ♿*In-room: no a/c. In-hotel: bar, parking (fee), no-smoking rooms, Internet* ▤*AE, DC, MC, V* ⊘*Closed 2 wks in Jan.* ❚❘❘*BP.*

$$ ⚏ **Wolf-Dietrich.** Two houses opposite each other: the Altstadt and the
★ Residenz. Guest rooms in this small, family-owned hotel across the river from the Altstadt are elegantly decorated (some with Laura Ashley fabrics—two "romantic" apartments are designed like stage settings for Mozart's *The Magic Flute*) and have extra amenities, such as attractive sitting areas. Those in the back look out over the looming Gaisberg and the cemetery of St. Sebastian. The staff is warm and helpful. ⊠*Wolf-Dietrich-Strasse 7, A-5020* ☎*0662/871275* 🖷*0662/882320* ⊕*www.salzburg-hotel.at* ⇘*32 rooms* ♿*In-room: no a/c, dial-up. In-hotel: restaurant, pool, parking (fee), no-smoking rooms* ▤*AE, DC, MC, V* ❚❘❘*BP.*

$ ⚏ **Bergland.** A 10-minute walk from the train station, this cheerful, pleasant, family-owned pension offers modern, comfortable rooms with breakfast included in the price. The sitting room includes an English library. ⊠*Rupertgasse 15, A-5020* ☎*0662/872318* 🖷*0662/872318–8* ⊕*www.berglandhotel.at* ⇘*17 rooms* ♿*In-room: no a/c. In-hotel: parking (no fee), no-smoking rooms* ▤*AE, DC, MC, V* ⊘*Closed Nov.–Christmas* ❚❘❘*BP.*

$ ⚏ **Cordial Theaterhotel.** Music lovers will enjoy studying the myriad production posters and photographs of famous artists that festoon the lobby here. Part of a classy chain, this is a modern option, with comfy guest rooms. The location is about a 10-minute walk from the city center, as are the auditoriums on both sides of the Salzach River. ✉ *Schallmooser Hauptstrasse 13, A-5020* ☎ *0662/881681–0* 🖷 *0662/88168692* ⊕ *www.cordial.at* ❧ *58 rooms, 10 apartments* ⊘ *In-room: no a/c. In-hotel: restaurant, bar* ⊟ *AE, DC, MC, V* ⵏ◎⎸ *BP.*

$ 🖭 **Turnerwirt.** In the former farmer's village of Gnigl, part of Salzburg's outskirts, this is a quaint complex of buildings. The most charming is the small "Villa," an adorable mansion fitted out with begonia-hung windows, red storybook roof, and fairy-tale turret. Out front is the massive Gasthaus, with a classic design that looks straight out of an Albrecht Dürer engraving. Both offer a friendly family-owned atmosphere, and guest rooms are decorated in a traditional and pleasing style. The largest suites have three and four bedrooms. To get to Salzburg's center city, hop on the No. 4 bus for a 10-minute ride. By car, the Turnerwirt can be reached from Salzburg by taking the motorway and exiting after 2 mi (1 km) at Salzburg Nord or Wallersee. ✉ *Linzer Bundesstrasse 54, A-5020* ☎ *0662/640630* 🖷 *0662/6406–3077* ⊕ *www.turnerwirt.at* ❧ *62 rooms* ⊘ *In-room: no a/c. In-hotel, parking, no elevator* ⊟ *AE, DC, MC, V* ⵏ◎⎸ *BP.*

THE ARTS

Before you arrive in Salzburg, do some advance research to determine the city's music schedule for the time you will be there, and book reservations; if you'll be attending the summer Salzburg Festival, this is a must. After you arrive in the city, any office of the Salzburg Tourist Office and most hotel concierge desks can provide you with schedules for all the arts performances, and you can find listings in the daily newspaper, *Salzburger Nachrichten.*

THE SALZBURG MUSIC FESTIVAL

The biggest event on the calendar—as it has been since it was first organized by composer Richard Strauss, producer Max Reinhardt, and playwright Hugo von Hofmannsthal in 1920—is the world-famous **Salzburger Festspiele** (✉ *Hofstallgasse 1, A-5020 Salzburg* ☎ *0662/8045–500 for summer festival, 0662/8045–361 for Easter festival* 🖷 *0662/8045–555 for summer festival, 0662/8045–790 for Easter festival* ⊕ *www.salzburgfestival.at*). The main summer festival is usually scheduled for the last week of July through the end of August. In addition, there are two other major affiliated events: the Easter Festival (early April), and the Pentecost Baroque Festival (late May).

The most star-studded performances, featuring the top opera stars and conductors, have tickets ranging from €22 to €340; first-night attendees still pull out all the stops—summer furs, Dior dresses, and white ties stud the more expensive sections of the theaters. Other performances can run from €8 to €190, with still smaller prices for events outside the main festival halls, the **Grosses Festspielhaus** (Great Festival Hall) and

"Oh, the Hills Are Alive . . ."

Few Salzburgers would publicly admit it, but *The Sound of Music,* Hollywood's interpretation of the trials and joys of the local Trapp family, has become their city's most eminent emissary when it comes to international promotion. The year after the movie's release, international tourism to Salzburg jumped 20%.

Perhaps the most important *Sound* spin-offs are the tours offered by several companies *(for a number of them, see Tour Options in Salzburg Essentials, below).* These four-hour rides have the advantage of giving a very concise tour of the city. The buses generally leave from Mirabellplatz; lumber by the "Do-Re-Mi" staircase at the edge of the beautifully manicured Mirabell Gardens; pass by the hardly visible Aigen train station, where in reality the Trapps caught the escape train; and then head south to Schloss Anif. This 16th-century water castle, which had a cameo appearance in the opening scenes of the film, is now in private hands and not open to the public.

First official stop for a leg-stretcher is at the gazebo in the manicured park of Schloss Hellbrunn at the southern end of the city. Originally built in the gardens of Leopoldskron Palace, it was brought out here to give the chance for taking pictures. This is where Liesl von Trapp sings "I Am Sixteen Going on Seventeen"

and where Maria and the Baron woo and coo "Something Good." The bus then drives by other private palaces with limited visiting rights, Schloss Frohnburg and Schloss Leopoldskron, with its magical water-gate terrace, adorned with rearing horse sculptures and "site" of so many memorable scenes in the movie. The bus continues on to Nonnberg Convent at the foot of the daunting Hohensalzburg fortress, then leaves the city limits for the luscious landscape of the Salzkammergut. You get a chance for a meditative walk along the shore of the Wolfgangsee in St. Gilgen before the bus heads for the pretty town of Mondsee, where, in the movie, Maria and Georg von Trapp were married at the twin-turreted Michaelerkirche.

Tour guides are well trained and often have a sense of humor, with which they gently debunk myths about the movie. Did you know that Switzerland was "moved" 160 km (100 mi) eastward so the family could hike over the mountains to freedom (while singing "Climb Every Mountain")?

For something different, try the **Sternbräu Dinner Theater** (✉ *Griesgasse 23* ☎ *0662/826617*). Their dinner show features songs from the movie, as well as traditional folksongs from Salzburg and a medley of Austrian operettas. The cost of the dinner show is €43; without dinner it's €31.

the **Haus für Mozart** (House for Mozart), located shoulder to shoulder on the grand promenade of Hofstallgasse. The halls are modern constructions—the Grosses Haus was built in 1960 with 2,200 seats—but are actually "prehistoric," being dug out of the bedrock of the Mönchsberg mountain. There are also concerts and operas performed at many other theaters in the city. You can catch Mozart concertos in the 18th-century splendor of two magnificent state rooms the composer himself once conducted in: the Rittersaal of the Residenz and the Marble Hall of the Mirabell Palace. Delightful Mozart productions are offered by the Salzburger Marionetten Theater. In addition, many important concerts are offered in the two auditoriums of the Mozarteum.

■ TIP➜ Note that you *must* order your tickets as early as possible, therefore make your decisions as soon as the program comes out (usually in the middle of November, though sometimes earlier). Many major performances are sold out two or three months in advance. Tickets can be purchased directly at the box office, at your hotel, or, most conveniently, at the festival Web site listed above. Next to the main tourist office is a box office where you can get tickets for Great Festival Hall concerts Monday through Friday, 8 to 6: **Salzburger Kulturvereinigung** (⊠ *Waagplatz 1A* ☎*0662/845346*). The following agencies also sell tickets: **Salzburg Ticket Service** (⊠*Mozartplatz 5* ☎*0662/840310* 🖷*0662/842476*). **Polzer** (⊠*Residenzplatz 3* ☎*0662/846500* 🖷*0662/840150*). **American Express** (⊠*Mozartplatz 5* ☎*0662/8080–0* 🖷*0662/8080–9*).

MUSIC

There is no shortage of concerts in this most musical of cities. Customarily, the Salzburg Festival headlines the Vienna Philharmonic, but other orchestras can be expected to take leading roles as well. Year-round there are also the Palace-Residenz Concerts and the Fortress Concerts, while in the summer there are Mozart Serenades in the Gothic Room at St. Blase's Church. In addition, there are the Easter Festival, the Pentecost Baroque Festival, Mozart Week (late January), and the Salzburg Cultural Days (October).

Fodor$Choice ★ The **Salzburger Schlosskonzerte** (⊠*Theatergasse 2* ☎*0662/848586* ⊕*www.salzburger.schlosskonzerte.at* 🎟*€29–€35*) presents concerts in the legendary Marmorsaal (Marble Hall) at **Mirabell Palace,** where Mozart performed.

The **Salzburger Festungskonzerte** (⊠*Fortress Hohensalzburg* ☎*0662/825858* ⊕*www.mozartfestival.at* 🎟*€31–€38*) are presented in the grand Prince's Chamber at Festung Hohensalzburg. Concerts often include works by Mozart. A special candlelight dinner and concert-ticket combo is often offered.

Organizer of the important Mozart Week held every January, the **Mozarteum** (⊠*Schwarzstrasse 26* ☎*0662/88940–21* ⊕*www.mozarteum.at*) center is open to scholars only. However, thousands flock here for its packed calendar of important concerts.

OPERA

The great opera event of the year is, of course, the **Salzburger Festspiele** (⇨*above*), which mount a full calendar of operas every year. Prices range from €5 to €600.

The season at the **Landestheater** (⊠*Schwarzstrasse 22* ☎*0662/871512–21* 🖷*0662/871512–70* ⊕*www.theater.co.at*) runs from September to

June. You can place ticket orders by telephone Monday and Saturday 10–2, Tuesday–Friday 10–5.

☾ The delightful, acclaimed **Salzburger Marionettentheater** (✉ *Schwarz-*
Fodor's Choice *strasse 24* ⊕ *www.marionetten.at* ☎ *0662/872406–0* 🖷 *0662/882141*)
★ is also devoted to opera, with a particularly renowned production of *Così fan tutte* to its credit. Performances are staged during the first week of January, during Mozart Week (late January), from May through September, and December 25 through January 7. Tickets usually range from €18 to €35. The box office is open Monday through Saturday 9–1 and two hours before the performance.

SALZBURG ESSENTIALS

TRANSPORTATION

BY AIR

Salzburg Airport, 4 km (2½ mi) west of the city center, is Austria's second-largest airport. There are direct flights from London and other European cities, but not from the United States. Americans can fly to Munich and take the 90-minute train ride to Salzburg.

Information Flughafen München (MUC) (☎ *08997500* ⊕ *www.munich-airport. de*). **Salzburg Airport (SZG)** (✉ *Innsbrucker Bundesstrasse 96* ☎ *0662/8580* ⊕ *www.salzburg-airport.com*).

GROUND If you fly to Munich, you can take the 90-minute train ride to Salz-
TRANSPORTATION burg. Alternatively, you can take a transfer bus from or to the Munich airport: contact Salzburger Mietwagenservice for details. Taxis are the easiest way to get downtown from the Salzburg airport; the ride costs around €13–€14 and takes about 20 minutes. City Bus No. 2, which makes a stop by the airport every 15 minutes, runs down to Salzburg's train station (about 20 minutes), where you can change to Bus No. 3 or 5 for the city center.

Taxis & Shuttles Salzburger Mietwagenservice (✉ *Ignaz-Harrer-Strasse 79a* ☎ *0622/8161–0* 🖷 *0622/436324*).

BY BIKE

Salzburg is developing a network of bike paths as part of its effort to reduce car traffic. You can rent a bike by the day or the week from Top Bike or VELO active. It's best to call and reserve in advance; you will need to leave your passport or a deposit.

Bike Rentals Top Bike (✉ *Rainerstrasse/Café Intertreff and Griesgasse* ☎ *06272/4656 or 0676/476–7259*). **VELO active** (✉ *Willibald-Hauthaler-Strasse 10 and Mozartplatz* ☎ *0662/4355950 or 0676/4355950*).

BY BUS

The Old City, composed of several interconnecting squares and narrow streets, is best seen on foot. An excellent bus service covers the rest of the city. A tourist map (available from tourist offices in Mozartplatz and the train station) shows all bus routes and stops; there's also a color-coded map of the public transport network, so you should have no problem getting around. Virtually all buses and trolleybuses (O-Bus) run via Mirabellplatz and/or Hanuschplatz.

Single tickets bought from the driver cost €1.80. Multiple-use tickets, available at tobacconists (*Tabak-Trafik*), ticket offices, and tourist offices, are cheaper. You can buy five single tickets for €1.60 each (not available at tourist offices), or a 24-hour ticket for €3.40.

Bus Information Salzburger Verkehrsverbund (Main ticket office) (⊠ *Schrannengasse 4* ☎ *0662/44801500*).

BY CAR
The fastest routes into Salzburg are the autobahns. From Munich it's 150 km (93 mi) on A8.

The only advantage to having a car in Salzburg is that you can get out of the city for excursions and cheaper accommodations. The Old City is a pedestrian zone (except for taxis), and the rest of the city, with its narrow, one-way streets, is a driver's nightmare. A park-and-ride system at major freeway exits is being developed, and there are several underground garages in the city. Try the Altstadt-Garagen. The entrance is at the back of the Mönchsberg hill, to the right of the main tunnel. It costs €14 for 24 hours; one hour is €2.40. Many shops and restaurants offer a reduction of €3 for a four-hour fee.

BY TAXI
There are taxi stands all over the city; for a radio cab, call the number listed below. Taxi fares start at €3. On Sunday and holidays, a special offer is the bus-taxi running between 11:30 and 1:30 at night, which has routes through the city and into the neighboring villages—the fare is €3.70. Limousines can be hired for €210 to €250 per hour (three-hour minimum) from Salzburg Panorama Tours. They also offer a private "Sound of Music" limousine tour for €280.

Taxi Information Radio Cab (☎ *0662/8111*). **Salzburg Panorama Tours** (☎ *0662/883211–0* 🖷 *0662/871628* ⊕ *www.panoramatours.com*).

BY TRAIN
You can get to Salzburg by rail from most European cities. The ÖBB, the Austrian Federal Train Service, has a Web site in English. Information is also available by phone through the Salzburg Hauptbahnhof; don't be put off by the recorded message in German—eventually, you will be put through to someone who should be able to speak English. You can buy tickets at any travel agency or at the station.

Train Information ÖBB (⊕ *www.oebb.at*)

CONTACTS & RESOURCES

TOUR OPTIONS
Because the Old City is largely a pedestrian zone, bus tours do little more than take you past the major sights. You would do better seeing the city on foot unless your time is really limited.

FIAKER/HORSE
CAB TOURS

One of the most delightful ways to tour Salzburg is by horse-drawn carriage. Most of Salzburg's Fiaker are stationed in Residenzplatz, and cost €33 (up to 4 people) for 20 minutes, €66 for 50 minutes. During the Christmas season, large, decorated horse-drawn carts take people around the Christmas markets.

Contacts **Fiaker** (☎ *0662/844772*).

SOUND OF
MUSIC TOURS

The *Sound of Music* tour—*for the complete scoop, see "Oh, the Hills are Alive" earlier in this chapter*— has been a staple of visits to Salzburg for the past 30 years, and is still a special experience. All tour operators conduct one. For a more personal approach, with smaller groups and private minivans, opt for Bob's Special Tours. The most popular tours, however, are run by Salzburg Sightseeing Tours and Salzburg Panorama. Their large excursion buses usually offer four-hour tours departing daily, which include such sights as Anif Castle, Mondsee Church, and the little summerhouse in the gardens of Hellbrunn.

WALKING
TOURS

Salzburg's official licensed guides offer a one-hour walking tour through the Old City every day at 12:15, which starts in front of the Information Mozartplatz (€8—owners of the Salzburg Card get a reduced fee).

VISITOR INFORMATION

The Salzburg City Tourist Office handles written and telephone requests for information. You can get maps, brochures, and information in person from Information Mozartplatz in the center of the Old City. The railway station also has a tourist office.

Consider purchasing the Salzburg Card (SalzburgKarten), good for 24, 48, or 72 hours at €20–€34. They allow no-charge entry to most museums and sights, use of public transport, and other discounts. Children under 15 pay half.

All the major highways into town have their own well-marked information centers. The Salzburg-Mitte center is open April–October, daily 9–7, and November–March, Monday–Saturday 11–5; the Salzburg-Süd, April–October, daily 9–7; and the Salzburg-Nord Kasern service facility is open June–mid-September, daily 9–7.

Information **Salzburg City Tourist Office** (⊠ *Auerspergstrasse 6, A-5024 Salzburg* ☎ *0662/88987-0* 🖶 *0662/88987-435* ⊕ *www.salzburginfo.at*).

Tourist Information Centers **Information Mozartplatz** (⊠ *Mozartplatz 5*). **Railway Station tourist office** (⊠ *Platform 2A* ☎ *0662/88987-330*). **Salzburg-Süd** (⊠ *Park & Ride-Parkplatz, Alpensiedlung-Süd, Alpenstrasse 67* ☎ *0662/88987-360*).

VOCABULARY

	English	German	Pronunciation
Basics			
	Yes/no	Ja/nein	yah/nine
	Please	Bitte	**bit**-uh
	Thank you (very much)	Danke (vielen Dank)	**dahn**-kuh (**fee**-lun-dahnk)
	Excuse me	Entschuldigen Sie	ent-**shool**-de-gen zee
	I'm sorry.	Es tut mir leid.	es toot meer lite
	Good day	Guten Tag	**goo**-ten tahk
	Good bye	Auf Wiedersehen	auf **vee**-der-zane
	Mr./Mrs.	Herr/Frau	hair/frau
	Miss	Fräulein	**froy**-line
Numbers			
	1	ein(s)	eint(s)
	2	zwei	tsvai
	3	drei	dry
	4	vier	fear
	5	fünf	fumph
	6	sechs	zex
	7	sieben	**zee**-ben
	8	acht	ahkt
	9	neun	noyn
	10	zehn	tsane
Days of the Week			
	Sunday	Sonntag	**zone**-tahk
	Monday	Montag	**moan**-tahk
	Tuesday	Dienstag	**deens**-tahk
	Wednesday	Mittwoch	**mit**-voah
	Thursday	Donnerstag	**doe**-ners-tahk
	Friday	Freitag	**fry**-tahk
	Saturday	Samstag/ Sonnabend	**zahm**-stakh/ **zonn**-a-bent
Useful Phrases			
	Do you speak English?	Sprechen Sie Englisch?	**shprek**-hun zee **eng**-glish?
	I don't speak German.	Ich spreche kein Deutsch.	ich **shprek**-uh kine doych

Please speak slowly.	Bitte sprechen Sie langsam.	**bit**-uh **shprek**-en-zee **lahng**-zahm
I am American/ British	Ich bin Amerikaner(in)/ Engländer(in)	ich bin a-mer-i-**kahn**-er(in)/ **eng**-glan-der(in)
My name is . . .	Ich heiße . . .	ich **hi**-suh
Where are the restrooms?	Wo ist die Toilette?	vo ist dee twah-**let**-uh
Left/right	links/rechts	links/rechts
Open/closed	offen/geschlossen	O-fen/geh-**shloss**-en
Where is . . .	Wo ist . . .	**vo** ist
the train station?	der Bahnhof?	**dare bahn-hof**
the bus stop?	die Bushaltestelle?	**dee booss-hahlt-uh-shtel-uh**
the subway station?	die U-Bahn-Station?	dee oo-bahn-**staht**-sion
the airport?	der Flugplatz?	dare **floog**-plats
the post office?	die Post?	dee **post**
the bank?	die Bank?	dee **banhk**
the police station?	die Polizeistation?	dee po-lee-tsai-**staht**-sion
the Hospital?	das Krankenhaus?	dahs **krahnk**-en-house
the telephone	das Telefon	**dahs te-le-fone**
I'd like . . .	Ich hätte gerne . . .	ich **het**-uh gairn . . .
a room	ein Zimmer	ein **tsim**-er
the key	den Schlüssel	den **shluh**-sul
a map	eine Stadtplan	I-nuh **staht**-plahn
a ticket	eine Karte	I-nuh cart-uh
How much is it?	Wieviel kostet das?	**vee-feel cost**-et dahs?
I am ill/sick	Ich bin krank	ich bin krahnk
I need . . .	Ich brauche . . .	ich **brow**-khuh
a doctor	einen Arzt	I-**nen** artst
the police	die Polizei	dee po-li-**tsai**
help	Hilfe	**hilf-uh**
Stop!	Halt!	**hahlt**
Fire!	Feuer!	**foy**-er
Look out/Caution!	Achtung!/Vorsicht!	**ahk**-tung/for-zicht

Dining Out

A bottle of . . .	eine Flasche . . .	I-nuh **flash**-uh
A cup of . . .	eine Tasse . . .	I-nuh **tahs**-uh
A glass of . . .	ein Glas . . .	ein glahss
Ashtray	der Aschenbecher	dare **Ahsh**-en-bekh-er
Bill/check	die Rechnung	dee **rekh**-nung

Do you have . . .?	Haben Sie . . .?	**hah**-ben zee
I am a vegetarian.	Ich bin Vegetarier(in)	ich bin ve-guh-**tah**-re-er
I'd like to order . . .ˇ	Ich möchte . . . bestellen	ich **mohr**-shtuh . . . buh-**shtel**-en
Menu	die Speisekarte	dee **shpie**-zeh-car-tuh
Napkin	die Serviette	dee zair-vee-**eh**-tuh

MENU GUIDE

English	German

General Dining

Side dishes	Beilagen
Extra charge	Extraaufschlag
When available	Falls verfügbar
Entrées	Hauptspeisen
(not) included	. . .(nicht) inbegriffen
Depending on the season	je nach Saison
Lunch menu	Mittagskarte
Desserts	Nachspeisen
at your choice	. . . nach Wahl
at your request	. . . nach Wunsch
Prices are . . .	Preise sind . . .
Service included	*inklusive Bedienung*
Value added tax included	*inklusive Mehrwertsteuer (Mwst.)*
Specialty of the house	Spezialität des Hauses
Soup of the day	Tagessuppe
Appetizers	Vorspeisen
Is served from . . . to . . .	Wird von . . . bis . . . serviert

Breakfast

Bread	Brot
Roll(s)	Brötchen
Eggs	Eier
Hot	heiß
Cold	kalt
Jam	Konfitüre
Milk	Milch
Orange juice	Orangensaft
Scrambled eggs	Rühreier
Bacon	Speck
Fried eggs	Spiegeleier
Lemon	Zitrone
Sugar	Zucker

Soups

Stew	Eintopf
Chicken soup	Hühnersuppe
Potato soup	Kartoffelsuppe
Liver dumpling soup	Leberknödelsuppe
Onion soup	Zwiebelsuppe

Methods of Preparation

Blue (boiled in salt and vinegar)	Blau
Baked	Gebacken
Fried	Gebraten
Steamed	Gedämpft
Grilled (broiled)	Gegrillt
Boiled	Gekocht
Sauteed	In Butter geschwenkt
Breaded	Paniert
Raw	Roh

When ordering steak, the English words "rare, medium, (well) done" are used and understood in German.

Fish and Seafood

Eel	Aal
Oysters	Austern
Trout	Forelle
Flounder	Flunder
Prawns	Garnelen
Halibut	Heilbutt
Herring	Hering
Lobster	Hummer
Scallops	Jakobsmuscheln
Cod	Kabeljau
Crab	Krabbe
Salmon	Lachs
Mackerel	Makrele
Mussels	Muscheln
Squid	Tintenfisch
Tuna	Thunfisch

Meats

Veal	Kalb(s)
Lamb	Lamm
Beef	Rind(er)
Pork	Schwein(e)

Cuts of Meat

Example: For "Lammkeule" see "Lamm" (above) + ". . . keule" (below)

breast	. . . brust
leg	. . . keule
liver	. . . leber
tenderloin	. . . lende
kidney	. . . niere
rib	. . . rippe

Meat patty	Frikadelle
Meat loaf	Hackbraten
Ham	Schinken

Game and Poultry

Duck	Ente
Pheasant	Fasan
Chicken	Hähnchen (Huhn)
Deer	Hirsch
Rabbit	Kaninchen
Venison	Reh
Pigeon	Taube
Turkey	Truthahn
Quail	Wachtel

Vegetables

Eggplant	Aubergine
Cauliflower	Blumenkohl
Beans	Bohnen
green	*grüne*
white	*weiße*
Peas	Erbsen
Cucumber	Gurke
Cabbage	Kohl
Lettuce	Kopfsalat
Asparagus, peas and carrots	Leipziger Allerlei
Corn	Mais
Carrots	Mohrrüben
Peppers	Paprika
Mushrooms	Pilze
Celery	Sellerie
Asparagus (tips)	Spargel(spitzen)
Tomatoes	Tomaten
Onions	Zwiebeln

Condiments

Vinegar	Essig
Garlic	Knoblauch
Horseradish	Meerettich
Oil	Öl
Mustard	Senf
Artificial sweetener	Süßstoff
Cinnamon	Zimt
Sugar	Zucker
Salt	Salz

Cheese

Mild	Allgäuer Käse, Altenburger (goat cheese), Appenzeller, Greyerzer, Hüttenkäse (cottage cheese), Quark, Räucherkäse (smoked cheese), Sahnekäse (creamy), Tilsiter, Ziegekäse (goat cheese).
Sharp	Handkäse, Harzer Käse, Limburger.
curd	frisch
hard	hart
mild	mild

Fruits

Apple	Apfel
Orange	Apfelsine
Apricot	Aprikose
Blueberry	Blaubeere
Strawberry	Erdbeere
Raspberry	Himbeere
Cherry	Kirsche
Grapefruit	Pampelmuse
Raisin	Rosine
Grape	Weintraube
Banana	Banane
Pear	Birne

Drinks

with/without ice	mit/ohne Eis
with/without water	mit/ohne Wasser
straight	pur
brandy	. . . geist
liqueur	. . . likör
Mulled claret	Glühwein
Caraway-flavored liquor	Kümmel
Fruit brandy	Obstler

When ordering a Martini, you have to specify "gin (vodka) and vermouth," otherwise you will be given a vermouth (Martini & Rossi).

Beer and Wine

non-alcoholic	Alkoholfrei
A dark beer	Ein Dunkles
A light beer	Ein Helles
A mug (one quart)	Eine Maß
Draught	Vom Faß
Dark, bitter, high hops content	Altbier
Strong, high alcohol content	Bockbier (Doppelbock, Märzen)

Wheat beer with yeast	Hefeweizen
Light beer, strong hops aroma	Pils(ener)
Wheat beer	Weizen(bier)
Light beer and lemonade	Radlermaß
Wines	Wein
Rosé wine	Rosëwein
Red wine	Rotwein
White wine and mineral water	Schorle
Sparkling wine	Sekt
White wine	Weißwein
dry	herb
light	leicht
sweet	süß
dry	trocken
full-bodied	vollmundig

Non-alcoholic Drinks

Coffee	Kaffee
decaffeinated	*koffeinfrei*
with cream/sugar	*mit Milch/Zucker*
black	*schwarz*
Mineral water	Mineralwasser
carbonated/non-carbonated	*mit/ohne Kohlensäure*
juice	*. . . saft*
(hot) Chocolate	(heiße) Schokolade
Tea	Tee
iced tea	*Eistee*
herb tea	*Kräutertee*
with cream/lemon	*mit Milch/Zitrone*

Munich & Bavaria Essentials

PLANNING TOOLS, EXPERT INSIGHT, GREAT CONTACTS

There are planners and there are those who, excuse the pun, fly by the seat of their pants. We happily place ourselves among the planners. Our writers and editors try to anticipate all the issues you may face before and during any journey, and then they do their research. This section is the product of their efforts. Use it to get excited about your trip to Munich & Bavaria , to inform your travel planning, or to guide you on the road should the seat of your pants start to feel threadbare.

GETTING STARTED

We're really proud of our Web site: Fodors.com is a great place to begin any journey. Scan Travel Wire for suggested itineraries, travel deals, restaurant and hotel openings, and other up-to-the-minute info. Check out Booking to research prices and book plane tickets, hotel rooms, rental cars, and vacation packages. Head to Talk for on-the-ground pointers from travelers who frequent our message boards. You can also link to loads of other travel-related resources.

▌ RESOURCES

ONLINE TRAVEL TOOLS

ALL ABOUT GERMANY

The **German National Tourist Office** (⊕*www. cometogermany.com*) is an excellent source of general information on Germany. The Internet portal **Deutschland. de** (⊕*www.deutschland.de*) has lots of information about the country's best-known sights, as well as those that are often overlooked.

Currency Conversion Google (⊕www. google.com) does currency conversion. Just type in the amount you want to convert and an explanation of how you want it converted (e.g., "14 Swiss francs in dollars"), and then voilà. **Oanda.com** (⊕www.oanda.com) also allows you to print out a handy table with the current day's conversion rates. **XE.com** (⊕www.xe.com) is a good currency conversion Web site.

Safety Transportation Security Administration (TSA ⊕www.tsa.gov).

Time Zones Timeanddate.com (⊕www. timeanddate.com/worldclock) can help you figure out the correct time anywhere.

Weather Accuweather.com (⊕www. accuweather.com) is an independent weather-forecasting service with good coverage of hurricanes. **Weather.com** (⊕www.weather.com) is the Web site for the Weather Channel.

Other Resources CIA World Factbook (⊕www.odci.gov/cia/publications/factbook/index.html) has profiles of every country in the world. It's a good source if you need some quick facts and figures.

VISITOR INFORMATION

Local tourist offices are listed in the Essentials sections of the individual chapters. Many offices keep shorter hours than normal businesses, and you can expect some to close during weekday lunch hours and as early as noon on Friday.

Contacts German National Tourist Office (☎212/661–7200 or 800/651–7010 ⊕www. cometogermany.com).

> ### WORD OF MOUTH
>
> After your trip, be sure to rate the places you visited and share your experiences and travel tips with us and other Fodorites in Travel Ratings and Talk on www.fodors.com.

▌ THINGS TO CONSIDER

GOVERNMENT ADVISORIES

▌**TIP→ Consider registering online with the State Department (https://travelregistration.state.gov/ibrs/), so the government will know to look for you should a crisis occur in the country you're visiting.**

The U.S. Department of State's Web site has more than just travel warnings and advisories. The consular information sheets issued for every country have general safety tips, entry requirements (though be sure to verify these with the country's embassy), and other useful details.

General Information & Warnings Australian Department of Foreign Affairs & Trade (⊕www.smartraveller.gov.au). **Consular Affairs Bureau of Canada** (⊕www.voyage.gc.ca). **U.K. Foreign & Commonwealth Office**

(⊕ www.fco.gov.uk/travel). **U.S. Department of State** (⊕ www.travel.state.gov).

GEAR

Pack for Munich as you would for an American city: dressy outfits for formal restaurants and nightclubs, casual clothes elsewhere. Jeans are as popular in Germany as anywhere else and are perfectly acceptable for sightseeing and informal dining. Germans rarely dress in shorts and T-shirts in public. In more expensive restaurants, German men often wear a crisp, button-down shirt or even a jacket. Women in Bavaria wear stylish outfits to restaurants and the theater; you'll even see dirndls (a traditional Bavarian dress) at special occasions.

Winters can be bitterly cold; summers are warm but with days that suddenly turn cool and rainy. In summer take a warm jacket or heavy sweater if you are visiting the Bavarian Alps, where the nights can be chilly even after hot days.

To discourage purse snatchers and pickpockets, carry a handbag with long straps that you can sling across your body bandolier style and with a zippered compartment for money and other valuables.

For stays in budget hotels, take your own soap. Many provide no soap at all or only a small bar.

SHIPPING LUGGAGE AHEAD

Imagine globetrotting with only a carry-on in tow. Shipping your luggage in advance via an air-freight service is a great way to cut down on backaches, hassles, and stress—especially if your packing list includes strollers, car-seats, etc. There are some things to be aware of, though.

First, research carry-on restrictions; if you absolutely need something that isn't practical to ship and isn't allowed in carry-ons, this strategy isn't for you. Second, plan to send your bags several days in advance to U.S. destinations and as much as two weeks in advance to some international destinations. Third, plan to spend some money: it will cost at least $100 to send a small piece of luggage, a golf bag, or a pair of skis to a domestic destination, much more to places overseas.

Some people use Federal Express to ship their bags, but this can cost even more than air-freight services. All these services insure your bag (for most, the limit is $1,000, but you should verify that amount); you can, however, purchase additional insurance for about $1 per $100 of value.

Contacts Luggage Concierge (☎800/288–9818 ⊕ www.luggageconcierge.com). **Luggage Express** (☎866/744–7224 ⊕ www.usxpluggageexpress.com). **Luggage Free** (☎800/361–6871 ⊕ www.luggagefree.com). **Sports Express** (☎800/357–4174 ⊕ www.sportsexpress.com) specializes in shipping golf clubs and other sports equipment. **Virtual Bellhop** (☎877/235–5467 ⊕ www.virtualbellhop.com).

PASSPORTS & VISAS

U.S. citizens need only a passport valid for at least four months to enter Germany for stays of up to 90 days. Border guards often don't stamp passports; if you require a stamp, you often have to request it. Children must be included in a parent's passport or have their own valid passports.

PASSPORTS

We're always surprised at how few Americans have passports—only 25% at this writing. This number is expected to grow in coming years, when it becomes impossible to reenter the United States from trips to neighboring Canada or Mexico without one. Remember this: a passport verifies both your identity and nationality—a great reason to have one.

U.S. passports are valid for 10 years. You must apply in person if you're getting a passport for the first time; if your previous passport was lost, stolen, or damaged; or if your previous passport has expired and was issued more than 15 years ago or when you were under 16. All children

PACKING 101

We realize that packing is a matter of style, but there's a lot to be said for traveling light. These tips help fight the battle of the bulging bag.

■ **Make a list.** In a recent Fodor's survey, 29% of respondents said they make lists (and often pack) a week before a trip. You can use your list to pack and to repack at the end of your trip. It can also serve as record of the contents of your suitcase—in case it disappears in transit.

■ **Think it through.** What's the weather like? In some places dress may be more or less conservative than you're used to. As you create your itinerary, note outfits next to each activity.

■ **Edit your wardrobe.** Plan to wear everything twice (better yet, thrice) and to do laundry along the way. Build around one or two neutrals and an accent (e.g., black, white, and olive green).

■ **Be practical.** Put comfortable shoes atop your list. Pack lightweight, wrinkle-resistant, compact, washable items. Stack and roll clothes, so they'll wrinkle less. Unless you're on a guided tour or a cruise, select luggage you can readily carry.

■ **Check weight and size limitations.** In the United States you may be charged extra for checked bags weighing more than 50 pounds. Abroad some airlines don't allow you to check bags over 60 to 70 pounds, or they charge outrageous fees for every excess pound—or bag.

■ **Check carry-on restrictions.** Research restrictions with the TSA. Rules vary abroad, so check them with your airline if you're traveling overseas on a foreign carrier. Consider packing all but essentials (travel documents, prescription meds, wallet) in checked luggage. This leads to a "pack only what you can afford to lose" approach that might help you streamline.

■ **Rethink valuables.** On U.S. flights, airlines are liable for only about $2,800 per person for bags. On international flights, the liability limit is around $635 per bag. But items like computers, cameras, and jewelry aren't covered, and as gadgetry can go on and off the list of carry-on no-no's, you can't count on keeping things safe by keeping them close. Although comprehensive travel policies may cover luggage, the liability limit is often a pittance. Your home-owner's policy may cover you sufficiently when you travel—or not.

■ **Lock it up.** If you must pack valuables, use TSA-approved locks (about $10) that can be unlocked by all U.S. security personnel.

■ **Tag it.** Always tag your luggage; use your business address if you don't want people to know your home address. Put the same information (and a copy of your itinerary) inside your luggage, too.

■ **Report problems immediately.** If your bags—or things in them—are damaged or go astray, file a written claim with your airline *before leaving the airport.* If the airline is at fault, it may give you money for essentials until your luggage arrives. Most lost bags are found within 48 hours, so alert the airline to your whereabouts for two or three days. If your bag was opened for security reasons in the States and something is missing, file a claim with the TSA.

under 18 must appear in person to apply for or renew a passport. Both parents must accompany any child under 14 (or send a notarized statement with their permission) and provide proof of their relationship to the child.

■ TIP→ Before your trip, make two copies of your passport's data page (one for someone at home and another for you to carry separately). Or scan the page and e-mail it to someone at home and/or yourself.

There are 13 regional passport offices, as well as 7,000 passport acceptance facilities in post offices, public libraries, and other governmental offices. If you're renewing a passport, you can do so by mail. Forms are available at passport acceptance facilities and online.

The cost to apply for a new passport is $97 for adults, $82 for children under 16; renewals are $67. Allow six weeks for processing, both for first-time passports and renewals. For an expediting fee of $60 you can reduce this time to about two weeks. If your trip is less than two weeks away, you can get a passport even more rapidly by going to a passport office with the necessary documentation. Private expediters can get things done in as little as 48 hours, but charge hefty fees for their services.

VISAS

A visa is essentially formal permission to enter a country. Visas allow countries to keep track of you and other visitors—and generate revenue (from application fees). You *always* need a visa to enter a foreign country; however, many countries routinely issue tourist visas on arrival, particularly to U.S. citizens. When your passport is stamped or scanned in the immigration line, you're actually being issued a visa. Sometimes you have to stand in a separate line and pay a small fee to get your stamp before going through immigration, but you can still do this at the airport on arrival.

Getting a visa isn't always that easy. Some countries require that you arrange for one in advance of your trip. There's usually—but not always—a fee involved, and said fee may be nominal ($10 or less) or substantial ($100 or more).

If you must apply for a visa in advance, you can usually do it in person or by mail. When you apply by mail, you send your passport to a designated consulate, where your passport will be examined and the visa issued. Expediters—usually the same ones who handle expedited passport applications—can do all the work of obtaining your visa for you; however, there's always an additional cost (often more than $50 per visa).

Most visas limit you to a single trip—basically during the actual dates of your planned vacation. Other visas allow you to visit as many times as you wish for a specific period of time. Remember that requirements change, sometimes at the drop of a hat, and the burden is on you to make sure that you have the appropriate visas. Otherwise, you'll be turned away at the airport or, worse, deported after you arrive in the country. No company or travel insurer gives refunds if your travel plans are disrupted because you didn't have the correct visa.

U.S. Passport Information U.S. Department of State (☎877/487-2778 ⊕http://travel.state.gov/passport).

U.S. Passport & Visa Expediters A. Briggs Passport & Visa Expeditors (☎800/806-0581 or 202/464-3000 ⊕www.abriggs.com). **American Passport Express** (☎800/455-5166 or 603/559-9888 ⊕www.americanpassport.com). **Passport Express** (☎800/362-8196 or 401/272-4612 ⊕www.passportexpress.com). **Travel Document Systems** (☎800/874-5100 or 202/638-3800 ⊕www.traveldocs.com). **Travel the World Visas** (☎866/886-8472 or 301/495-7700 ⊕www.world-visa.com).

GENERAL REQUIREMENTS FOR GERMANY	
Passport	Must be valid for 4 months after date of arrival.
Visa	Upon entering Germany, you receive an automatic tourist visa for 90 days.
Vaccinations	None
Driving	International driver's license required; CDW is compulsory on car rentals and is included in the quoted price

SHOTS & MEDICATIONS

Germany is by and large a healthy place. There are occasional outbreaks of measles—including one in Northrhine-Westfalia—so be sure you have been vaccinated. *For more information see Health under On the Ground below.*

■ TIP→ **If you travel a lot internationally—particularly to developing nations—refer to the CDC's** *Health Information for International Travel* **(aka Traveler's Health Yellow Book). Info from it is posted on the CDC Web site (www.cdc.gov/travel/yb), or you can buy a copy from your local bookstore for $24.95.**

Health Warnings National Centers for Disease Control & Prevention (CDC ☎877/394–8747 international travelers' health line ⊕www.cdc.gov/travel). **World Health Organization** (WHO ⊕www.who.int).

TRIP INSURANCE

What kind of coverage do you honestly need? Do you even need trip insurance at all? Take a deep breath and read on.

We believe that comprehensive trip insurance is especially valuable if you're booking a very expensive or complicated trip (particularly to an isolated region) or if you're booking far in advance. Who knows what could happen six months down the road? But whether you get insurance has more to do with how comfortable you are assuming risk.

Comprehensive travel policies typically cover trip-cancellation and interruption, letting you cancel or cut your trip short because of a personal emergency, illness, or, in some cases, acts of terrorism in your destination. Such policies also cover evacuation and medical care. Some also cover trip delays because of bad weather or mechanical problems as well as lost or delayed baggage. Another type of coverage to look for is financial default—that is, when your trip is disrupted because a tour operator, airline, or cruise line goes out of business. Generally you must buy this when you book your trip or shortly thereafter, and it's only available if your operator isn't on a list of excluded companies.

If you're going abroad, consider buying medical-only coverage at the very least. Neither Medicare nor some private insurers cover medical expenses anywhere outside of the United States besides Mexico and Canada (including time aboard a cruise ship, even if it leaves from a U.S. port). Medical-only policies typically reimburse you for medical care (excluding that related to preexisting conditions) and hospitalization abroad, and provide for evacuation. You still have to pay the bills and await reimbursement from the insurer, though.

Expect comprehensive travel insurance policies to cost about 4% to 7% of the total price of your trip (it's more like 12% if you're over age 70). A medical-only policy may or may not be cheaper than a comprehensive policy. Always read the fine print of your policy to make sure that you are covered for the risks that are of most concern to you. Compare several policies to make sure you're getting the best price and coverage available.

Trip Insurance Resources

INSURANCE COMPARISON SITES		
Insure My Trip.com	800/487–4722	www.insuremytrip.com
Square Mouth.com	800/240–0369	www.quotetravelinsurance.com
COMPREHENSIVE TRAVEL INSURERS		
Access America	866/807–3982	www.accessamerica.com
CSA Travel Protection	800/873–9855	www.csatravelprotection.com
HTH Worldwide	610/254–8700 or 888/243–2358	www.hthworldwide.com
Travelex Insurance	888/457–4602	www.travelex-insurance.com
Travel Guard International	715/345–0505 or 800/826–4919	www.travelguard.com
Travel Insured International	800/243–3174	www.travelinsured.com
MEDICAL-ONLY INSURERS		
International Medical Group	800/628–4664	www.imglobal.com
International SOS	215/942–8000 or 713/521–7611	www.internationalsos.com
Wallach & Company	800/237–6615 or 504/687–3166	www.wallach.com

BOOKING YOUR TRIP

Unless your cousin is a travel agent, you're probably among the millions of people who make most of their travel arrangements online.

But have you ever wondered just what the differences are between an online travel agent (a Web site through which you make reservations instead of going directly to the airline, hotel, or car-rental company), a discounter (a firm that does a high volume of business with a hotel chain or airline and accordingly gets good prices), a wholesaler (one that makes cheap reservations in bulk and then re-sells them to people like you), and an aggregator (one that compares all the offerings so you don't have to)?

Is it truly better to book directly on an airline or hotel Web site? And when does a real live travel agent come in handy?

■ ONLINE

You really have to shop around. A travel wholesaler such as Hotels.com or Hotel-Club.net can be a source of good rates, as can discounters such as Hotwire or Priceline, particularly if you can bid for your hotel room or airfare. Indeed, such sites sometimes have deals that are unavailable elsewhere. They do, however, tend to work only with hotel chains (which makes them just plain useless for getting hotel reservations outside of major cities) or big airlines (so that often leaves out upstarts like jetBlue and some foreign carriers like Air India).

Also, with discounters and wholesalers you must generally prepay, and everything is nonrefundable. And before you fork over the dough, be sure to check the terms and conditions, so you know what a given company will do for you if there's a problem and what you'll have to deal with on your own.

■ TIP➔ To be absolutely sure everything was processed correctly, confirm reservations made through online travel agents, discounters, and wholesalers directly with your hotel before leaving home.

Booking engines like Expedia, Travelocity, and Orbitz are actually travel agents, albeit high-volume, online ones. And airline travel packagers like American Airlines Vacations and Virgin Vacations—well, they're travel agents, too. But they may still not work with all the world's hotels.

An aggregator site will search many sites and pull the best prices for airfares, hotels, and rental cars from them. Most aggregators compare the major travel-booking sites such as Expedia, Travelocity, and Orbitz; some also look at airline Web sites, though rarely the sites of smaller budget airlines. Some aggregators also compare other travel products, including complex packages—a good thing, as you can sometimes get the best overall deal by booking an air-and-hotel package.

■ WITH A TRAVEL AGENT

If you use an agent—brick-and-mortar or virtual—you'll pay a fee for the service. And know that the service you get from some online agents isn't comprehensive. For example Expedia and Travelocity don't search for prices on budget airlines like jetBlue, Southwest, or small foreign carriers. That said, some agents (online or not) *do* have access to fares that are difficult to find otherwise, and the savings can more than make up for any surcharge.

A knowledgeable brick-and-mortar travel agent can be a godsend if you're booking a cruise, a package trip that's not available to you directly, an air pass, or a complicated itinerary including several overseas flights. What's more, travel agents that specialize in a destination may

Online Booking Resources

AGGREGATORS		
Kayak	www.kayak.com	also looks at cruises and vacation packages.
Mobissimo	www.mobissimo.com	
Qixo	www.qixo.com	also compares cruises, vacation packages, and even travel insurance.
Sidestep	www.sidestep.com	also compares vacation packages and lists travel deals.
Travelgrove	www.travelgrove.com	also compares cruises and packages.
BOOKING ENGINES		
Cheap Tickets	www.cheaptickets.com	a discounter.
Expedia	www.expedia.com	a large online agency that charges a booking fee for airline tickets.
Hotwire	www.hotwire.com	a discounter.
lastminute.com	www.lastminute.com	specializes in last-minute travel; the main site is for the U.K., but it has a link to a U.S. site.
Luxury Link	www.luxurylink.com	has auctions (surprisingly good deals) as well as offers on the high-end side of travel.
Onetravel.com	www.onetravel.com	a discounter for hotels, car rentals, airfares, and packages.
Orbitz	www.orbitz.com	charges a booking fee for airline tickets, but gives a clear breakdown of fees and taxes before you book.
Priceline.com	www.priceline.com	a discounter that also allows bidding.
Travel.com	www.travel.com	allows you to compare its rates with those of other booking engines.
Travelocity	www.travelocity.com	charges a booking fee for airline tickets, but promises good problem resolution.
ONLINE ACCOMMODATIONS		
Hotelbook.com	www.hotelbook.com	focuses on independent hotels worldwide.
Hotel Club	www.hotelclub.net	good for major cities worldwide.
Hotels.com	www.hotels.com	a big Expedia-owned wholesaler that offers rooms in hotels all over the world.
Quikbook	www.quikbook.com	offers "pay when you stay" reservations that let you settle your bill at checkout, not when you book.
OTHER RESOURCES		
Bidding For Travel	www.biddingfortravel.com	a good place to figure out what you can get and for how much before you start bidding on, say, Priceline.

have exclusive access to certain deals and insider information on things such as charter flights. Agents who specialize in types of travelers (senior citizens, gays and lesbians, naturists) or types of trips (cruises, luxury travel, safaris) can also be invaluable.

■**TIP→** Remember that Expedia, Travelocity, and Orbitz are travel agents, not just booking engines. To resolve any problems with a reservation made through these companies, contact them first.

A top-notch agent planning your trip to Russia will make sure you get the correct visa application and complete it on time; the one booking your cruise may get you a cabin upgrade or arrange to have bottle of champagne chilling in your cabin when you embark. And complain about the surcharges all you like, but when things don't work out the way you'd hoped, it's nice to have an agent to put things right.

Germans travel a great deal, which is why the reputable DER agency can be found in most train stations. The nationally franchised company has packages to destinations in Germany and the rest of the world. Look for the DER logo in a yellow and blue circle. Deutsche Bahn, the German railway company, also has excellent packages.

Agent Resources American Society of Travel Agents (☎703/739–2782 ⊕www. travelsense.org).

Germany Travel Agents DER (⊕www.der. de). **Deutsche Bahn** (⊕www.bahn.de).

■ ACCOMMODATIONS

The standards of German hotels, down to the humblest inn, are very high. You can nearly always expect courteous and polite service and clean and comfortable rooms. In addition to hotels proper, the country has numerous *Gasthöfe* or *Gasthäuser* (country inns that serve food and also have rooms). At the lowest end of the scale are *Fremdenzimmer,* meaning simply "rooms," normally in private houses. Look for the sign reading ZIMMER FREI (room available) or ZU VERMIETEN (to rent) on a green background; a red

sign reading BESETZT means there are no vacancies.

If you are looking for a very down-to-earth experience, try a *Urlaub auf dem Bauernhof,* a farm that has rooms for travelers. This can be especially exciting for children. You can also opt to stay at a winery's *Winzerhof.*

CATEGORY	COST
$$$$	over €225
$$$	€176–€225
$$	€101–€175
$	€50–€100
¢	under €50

Hotel prices are for two people in a standard double room, including tax and service.

Room rates are by no means inflexible and depend very much on supply and demand. You can save money by inquiring about deals: many resort hotels offer substantial discounts in winter, for example. Likewise, many $$$$ and $$$ hotels in cities cut their prices dramatically on weekends and when business is quiet. Major events like Munich's Oktoberfest will drive prices through the ceiling.

Tourist offices will make bookings for a nominal fee, but they may have difficulty doing so after 4 PM in high season and on weekends, so don't wait until too late in the day to begin looking for your accommodations. Outside of Munich, you can try asking someone—like a mail carrier, police officer, or waiter, for example—for directions to a house renting a Fremdenzimmer or a Gasthof.

Most hotels and other lodgings require you to give your credit-card details before they will confirm your reservation. If you don't feel comfortable e-mailing this information, ask if you can fax it (some places even prefer faxes). However you book, get confirmation in writing and have a copy of it handy when you check in.

Be sure you understand the hotel's cancellation policy. Some places allow you to cancel without any kind of penalty—even if you prepaid to secure a discounted rate—if you cancel at least 24 hours in advance. Others require you to cancel a week in advance or penalize you the cost of one night. Small inns and B&Bs are most likely to require you to cancel far in advance. Most hotels allow children under a certain age to stay in their parents' room at no extra charge, but others charge for them as extra adults; find out the cutoff age for discounts.

■**TIP**→ Assume that hotels operate on the European Plan (**EP**, no meals) unless we specify that they use the Breakfast Plan (**BP**, with full breakfast), Continental Plan (**CP**, continental breakfast), Full American Plan (**FAP**, all meals), Modified American Plan (**MAP**, breakfast and dinner) or are all-inclusive (**AI**, all meals and most activities).

APARTMENT & HOUSE RENTALS

Renting an apartment is an affordable alternative to a hotel or B&B. *Ferienwohnungen,* or vacation apartments, are especially popular in more rural areas. They range from simple rooms with just the basics to luxury apartments with all the trimmings. Some even include breakfast. The best way to find an apartment is through the local tourist office or the Web site of the town or village where you would like to stay.

Contacts At Home Abroad (☎212/421–9165 ⊕www.athomeabroadinc.com). **Barclay International Group** (☎516/364–0064 or 800/845–6636 ⊕www.barclayweb.com). **Drawbridge to Europe** (☎541/482–7778 or 888/268–1148 ⊕www.drawbridgetoeurope. com). **Homes Away** (☎416/920–1873 or 800/374–6637 ⊕www.homesaway.com). **Hometours International** (☎865/690–8484 ⊕thor.he.net/~hometour). **Interhome** (☎954/791–8282 or 800/882–6864 ⊕www. interhome.us). **Suzanne B. Cohen & Associ-**

10 WAYS TO SAVE

1. Join "frequent guest" programs. You may get preferential treatment in room choice and/or upgrades in your favorite chains.

2. Call direct. You can sometimes get a better price if you call a hotel's local toll-free number (if available) rather than a central reservations number.

3. Check online. Check hotel Web sites, as not all chains are represented on all travel sites.

4. Look for specials. Always inquire about packages and corporate rates.

5. Look for price guarantees. For overseas trips, look for guaranteed rates. With your rate locked in you won't pay more, even if the price goes up in the local currency.

6. Look for weekend deals at business hotels. High-end chains catering to business travelers are often busy only on weekdays; they often drop rates on weekends.

7. Ask about taxes. Verify whether local hotel taxes are included in quoted rates. In some places taxes can add 20% or more to your bill.

8. Read the fine print. Watch for add-ons, including resort fees, energy surcharges, and "convenience" fees for such things as unlimited local phone service you won't use.

9. Know when to go. If your destination's high season is December through April and you're trying to book, say, in late April, you might save money by changing your dates by a week or two.

10. Weigh your options (we can't say this enough). Weigh transportation times and costs against the savings of staying in a hotel that's cheaper because it's out of the way.

ates (☎207/622–0743 ⊕www.villaeurope.
com). **Vacation Home Rentals Worldwide**
(☎201/767–9393 or 800/633–3284 ⊕www.
vhrww.com). **Villanet** (☎206/417–3444 or
800/964–1891 ⊕www.rentavilla.com). **Villas
& Apartments Abroad** (☎212/213–6435
or 800/433–3020 ⊕www.vaanyc.com). **Villas International** (☎415/499–9490 or
800/221–2260 ⊕www.villasintl.com). **Villas of
Distinction** (☎707/778–1800 or 800/289–
0900 ⊕www.villasofdistinction.com). **Wimco**
(☎800/449–1553 ⊕www.wimco.com).

BED & BREAKFASTS

B&Bs are popular options in Germany,
but are considered more a practical
accommodation than a destination for a
romantic getaway, replete with antiques.
For breakfast, expect some muesli, cheese,
cold cuts, jam, butter, and hard-boiled
eggs at the very least. Some B&Bs also
supply lunch baskets if you intend to go
hiking or arrange an evening meal for a
very affordable price.

Reservation Services Bed & Breakfast.com
(☎512/322–2710 or 800/462–2632 ⊕www.
bedandbreakfast.com) also sends out an online
newsletter. **Bed & Breakfast Inns Online**
(☎615/868–1946 or 800/215–7365 ⊕www.
bbonline.com). **BnB Finder.com** (☎212/432–
7693 or 888/547–8226 ⊕www.bnbfinder.com).

CASTLE-HOTELS

Staying in an historic castle, or *Schloss*,
is a great experience. The simpler ones
may lack character, but most combine
four-star luxury with antique furnishings, four-poster beds, and a baronial
atmosphere. Some offer all the facilities
of a resort. Euro-Connection can advise
you on castle-hotel packages, including
four- to six-night tours.

Contacts Euro-Connection (☎800/645–
3876 ⊕www.euro-connection.com).

FARM VACATIONS

Almost every regional tourist office has
a brochure listing farms that offer bed-
and-breakfasts, apartments, and entire
farmhouses to rent (*Ferienhöfe*). The German Agricultural Association provides

an illustrated brochure, *Urlaub auf dem
Bauernhof* (Vacation Down on the Farm),
that covers more than 2,000 inspected
and graded farms, from the Alps to the
North Sea. It costs €9.90 and is also sold
in bookstores.

**German Agricultural Association DLG
Reisedienst, Agratour** (German Agricultural
Association ☎069/247–880 ⊕www.
landtourismus.de).

HOME EXCHANGES

With a direct home exchange you stay in
someone else's home while they stay in
yours. Some outfits also deal with vacation homes, so you're not actually staying
in someone's full-time residence, just their
vacant weekend place.

Exchange Clubs Home Exchange.com
(☎800/877–8723 ⊕www.homeexchange.
com); $59.95 for a 1-year online listing.
HomeLink International (☎800/638–3841
⊕www.homelink.org); $80 yearly for Web-only
membership; $125 includes Web access and
two catalogs. **Intervac U.S.** (☎800/756–4663
⊕www.intervacus.com); $78.88 for Web-only
membership; $126 includes Web access and
a catalog.

HOSTELS

Germany's more than 600 *Jugendherber-
gen* (youth hostels) are among the most
efficient and up-to-date in Europe. The
DJH Service GmbH provides a complete
list of hostels it represents, but remember
that there are also scores of independent
hostels. Hostels must be reserved well in

advance for midsummer. Note that weekends and holidays can mean full houses and noisy nights. Either bring earplugs or choose more expensive, but quieter, accommodations.

Many hostels are affiliated with Hostelling International (HI), an umbrella group of hostel associations with some 4,500 member properties in more than 70 countries. Membership in any HI association, open to travelers of all ages, allows you to stay in HI-affiliated hostels at member rates. One-year membership is about $28 for adults; hostels charge about $10–$30 per night. Members have priority if the hostel is full; they're also eligible for discounts around the world, even on rail and bus travel in some countries.

Information DJH Service GmbH
(☎05231/74010 ⊕www.jugendherberge.de).
Hostelling International—USA (☎301/495–1240 ⊕www.hiusa.org).

HOTELS

Most hotels in Germany do not have air-conditioning, nor do they need it, given the climate and the German style of building construction that uses thick walls and recessed windows to help keep the heat out. Smaller hotels do not provide much in terms of bathroom amenities. Except in four- and five-star hotels, you won't find a washcloth. Hotels often have no-smoking rooms or even no-smoking floors, so it's always worth asking for one when you reserve. Beds in double rooms often consist of two twin mattresses placed side by side within a frame. When you arrive, if you don't like the room you're offered, ask to see another.

Among the most delightful places to stay—and eat—in Germany are the aptly named Romantik Hotels and Restaurants. The Romantik group has 98 members in Germany. All are in atmospheric and historic buildings—a condition for membership—and are run by the owners with the emphasis on excellent amenities

and service. Prices vary considerably, but in general they are a good value.

Contacts Romantik Hotels and Restaurants (☎800/650–8018, 817/678–0038 from the U.S., 069/661–2340 in Germany ⊕www.romantikhotels.com).

SPAS

Taking the waters in Germany, whether for curing the body or merely pampering it, has been popular since Roman times. Health resorts, mostly equipped for thermal or mineral water, mud, or brine treatments, are set within pleasant country areas or historic communities. The word *Bad* before or within the name of a town means it's a spa destination, where many patients reside in health clinics for two to three weeks of doctor-prescribed treatments.

Saunas, steam baths, and other hot-room facilities are often used "without textiles" in Germany—in other words, naked. Wearing a bathing suit is sometimes even prohibited in saunas, but sitting on a towel is always required (you may need to bring your own towels). The Deutsche Heilbäderverband has information in German only.

Contacts Deutsche Heilbäderverband (German Health Resort and Spa Association ☎0228/201–200 ⊕www.deutscher-heil-baederverband.de).

▌ AIRLINE TICKETS

Most domestic airline tickets are electronic; international tickets may be either electronic or paper. With an e-ticket the only thing you receive is an e-mailed receipt citing your itinerary and reservation and ticket numbers.

The greatest advantage of an e-ticket is that if you lose your receipt, you can simply print out another copy or ask the airline to do it for you at check-in. You usually pay a surcharge (up to $50) to get a paper ticket, if you can get one at all.

10 WAYS TO SAVE

1. Nonrefundable is best. If saving money is more important than flexibility, then nonrefundable tickets work. Just remember that you'll pay dearly (as much as $100) if you change your plans.

2. Comparison shop. Web sites and travel agents can have different arrangements with the airlines and offer different prices for exactly the same flights.

3. Beware those prices. Many airline Web sites—and most ads—show prices *without* taxes and surcharges. Don't buy until you know the full price.

4. Stay loyal. Stick with one or two frequent-flier programs. You'll rack up free trips faster and you'll accumulate more quickly the perks that make trips easier. On some airlines these include a special reservations number, early boarding, access to upgrades, and more roomy economy-class seating.

5. Watch those ticketing fees. Surcharges are usually added when you buy your ticket anywhere but on an airline Web site. (That includes by phone—even if you call the airline directly—and paper tickets regardless of how you book.)

6. Check early and often. Start looking for cheap fares up to a year in advance.

7. Don't work alone. Some Web sites have tracking features that will e-mail you immediately when good deals are posted.

8. Jump on the good deals. Waiting even a few minutes might mean paying more.

9. Be flexible. Look for departures on Tuesday, Wednesday, and Thursday, typically the cheapest days to travel.

10. Weigh your options. What you get can be as important as what you save. A cheaper flight might have a long layover, or it might land at a secondary airport, where your ground transportation costs might be higher.

The sole advantage of a paper ticket is that it may be easier to endorse over to another airline if your flight is canceled and the airline with which you booked can't accommodate you on another flight.

■**TIP**→ Discount air passes that let you travel economically in a country or region must often be purchased before you leave home. In some cases you can only get them through a travel agent.

The least expensive airfares to Germany are often priced for round-trip travel and usually must be purchased in advance. Airlines generally allow you to change your return date for a fee; most low-fare tickets, however, are nonrefundable. Fares between the British Isles and Germany through "no-frills" airlines such as Air Berlin, EasyJet, and Ryanair can range from €15 to €70.

▌RENTAL CARS

When you reserve a car, ask about cancellation penalties, taxes, drop-off charges (if you're planning to pick up the car in one city and leave it in another), and surcharges (for being under or over a certain age, for additional drivers, or for driving across state or country borders or beyond a specific distance from your point of rental). All these things can add substantially to your costs. Request car seats and extras such as GPS when you book.

Rates are sometimes—but not always—better if you book in advance or reserve through a rental agency's Web site. There are other reasons to book ahead, though: for popular destinations, during busy times of the year, or to ensure that you get certain types of cars (vans, SUVs, exotic sports cars).

■**TIP**→ Make sure that a confirmed reservation guarantees you a car. Agencies sometimes overbook, particularly for busy weekends and holiday periods.

If you are going to rent a car in Germany, you will need an International Driving Permit (IDP); it's available from the American Automobile Association and the National Automobile Club. These international permits are universally recognized, and having one in your wallet may save you problems with the local authorities. In Germany you usually must be 21 to rent a car. Nearly all agencies allow you to drive into Germany's neighboring countries. It's frequently possible to return the car in another West European country, but not in Poland or the Czech Republic, for example.

Rates with the major car-rental (*Mietwagen*) companies begin at about €55 per day and €300 per week for an economy car with a manual transmission and unlimited mileage. Most rentals are manual, so if you want an automatic, be sure to request one in advance. If you're traveling with children, don't forget to ask for a car seat when you reserve. The German railway system, Deutsche Bahn, offers discounts on rental cars.

Depending on what you would like to see, you may or may not need a car for all or part of your stay. Since most parts of Bavaria are connected by reliable rail service, it might be a better plan to take a train to the region you plan to visit and rent a car only for side trips to out-of-the-way destinations.

Automobile Associations U.S.: **American Automobile Association** (AAA ☎315/797–5000 ⊕www.aaa.com); most contact with the organization is through state and regional members. **National Automobile Club** (☎650/294–7000 ⊕www.thenac.com); membership is open to California residents only.

Local Agencies Europcar (☎0180/580–00 ⊕www.europcar.de). **Sixt** (☎01805/252–525 ⊕www.sixtusa.com).

Major Agencies Alamo (☎800/522–9696 ⊕www.alamo.com). **Avis** (☎800/331–1084 ⊕www.avis.com). **Budget** (☎800/472–3325 ⊕www.budget.com). **Hertz** (☎800/654–3001 ⊕www.hertz.com). **National Car Rental** (☎800/227–7368 ⊕www.nationalcar.com).

Wholesalers Auto Europe (☎888/223–5555 ⊕www.autoeurope.com). **Europe by Car** (☎212/581–3040 in New York, 800/223–1516 ⊕www.europebycar.com). **Eurovacations** (☎877/471–3876 ⊕www.eurovacations.com). **Kemwel** (☎877/820–0668 ⊕www.kemwel.com).

CAR-RENTAL INSURANCE

Everyone who rents a car wonders whether the insurance that the rental companies offer is worth the expense. No one—including us—has a simple answer. It all depends on how much regular insurance you have, how comfortable you are with risk, and whether or not money is an issue.

If you own a car, your personal auto insurance may cover a rental to some degree, though not all policies protect you abroad; always read your policy's fine print. If you don't have auto insurance, then seriously consider buying the collision- or loss-damage waiver (CDW or LDW) from the car-rental company, which eliminates your liability for damage to the car. Some credit cards offer CDW coverage, but it's usually supplemental to your own insurance and rarely covers SUVs, minivans, luxury models, and the like. If your coverage is secondary, you may still be liable for loss-of-use costs from the car-rental company. But no credit-card insurance is valid unless you use that card for *all* transactions, from reserving to paying the final bill. All companies exclude car rental in some countries, so be sure to find out about the destination to which you are traveling.

■**TIP→** Diners Club offers primary CDW coverage on all rentals reserved and paid for with the card. This means that Diners Club's company—not your own car insurance—pays in case of an accident. It *doesn't* mean your car-insurance company won't raise your rates once it discovers you had an accident.

10 WAYS TO SAVE

1. Beware of cheap rates. Those great rates aren't so great when you add in taxes, surcharges, and insurance. Such extras can double or triple the initial quote.

2. Rent weekly. Weekly rates are usually better than daily ones. Even if you only want to rent for five or six days, ask for the weekly rate; it may very well be cheaper than the daily rate for that period of time.

3. Don't forget the locals. Price local companies as well as the majors.

4. Airport rentals can cost more. Airports often add surcharges, which you can sometimes avoid by renting from an agency whose office is just off airport property.

5. Wholesalers can help. Investigate wholesalers, which don't own fleets but rent in bulk from firms that do, and which frequently offer better rates (note that you must usually pay for such rentals before leaving home).

6. Look for rate guarantees. With your rate locked in, you won't pay more, even if the price goes up in the local currency.

7. Fill up farther away. Avoid hefty refueling fees by filling the tank at a station well away from where you plan to turn in the car.

8. Pump it yourself. Don't buy the tank of gas that's in the car when you rent it unless you plan to do a lot of driving.

9. Get all your discounts. Find out whether a credit card you carry or organization or frequent-renter program to which you belong has a discount program. And confirm that such discounts really are a deal. You can often do better with special weekend or weekly rates offered by a rental agency.

10. Check out packages. Adding a car rental onto your air/hotel vacation package may be cheaper than renting a car separately.

Some countries require you to purchase CDW coverage or require car-rental companies to include it in quoted rates. Ask your rental company about issues like these in your destination. In most cases it's cheaper to add a supplemental CDW plan to your comprehensive travel-insurance policy (⇨ *Trip Insurance under Things to Consider in Getting Started, above*) than to purchase it from a rental company. That said, you don't want to pay for a supplement if you're required to buy insurance from the rental company.

■ **TIP**➔ You can decline the insurance from the rental company and purchase it through a third-party provider such as Travel Guard (www.travelguard.com)—$9 per day for $35,000 of coverage. That's sometimes just under half the price of the CDW offered by some car-rental companies.

■ VACATION PACKAGES

Packages *are not* guided excursions. Packages combine airfare, accommodations, and perhaps a rental car or other extras (theater tickets, guided excursions, boat trips, reserved entry to popular museums, transit passes), but they let you do your own thing. During busy periods packages may be your only option, as flights and rooms may be sold out otherwise.

Packages will definitely save you time. They can also save you money, particularly in peak seasons, but—and this is a really big "but"—you should price each part of the package separately to be sure. And be aware that prices advertised on Web sites and in newspapers rarely include service charges or taxes, which can up your costs by hundreds of dollars.

■ **TIP**➔ Some packages and cruises are sold only through travel agents. Don't always assume that you can get the best deal by booking everything yourself.

Each year consumers are stranded or lose their money when packagers—even large ones with excellent reputations—

go out of business. How can you protect yourself?

First, always pay with a credit card; if you have a problem, your credit-card company may help you resolve it. Second, buy trip insurance that covers default. Third, choose a company that belongs to the United States Tour Operators Association, whose members must set aside funds to cover defaults. Finally, choose a company that also participates in the Tour Operator Program of the American Society of Travel Agents (ASTA), which will act as mediator in any disputes.

You can also check on the tour operator's reputation among travelers by posting an inquiry on one of the Fodors.com forums.

Organizations American Society of Travel Agents (ASTA ☎703/739–2782 or 800/965–2782 ⊕ www.astanet.com). **United States Tour Operators Association** (USTOA ☎212/599–6599 ⊕ www.ustoa.com). ■**TIP→ Local tourism boards can provide information about lesser-known and small-niche operators that sell packages to only a few destinations.**

■ GUIDED TOURS

Guided tours are a good option when you don't want to do it all yourself. You travel along with a group (sometimes large, sometimes small), stay in prebooked hotels, eat with your fellow travelers (the cost of meals sometimes included in the price of your tour, sometimes not), and follow a schedule.

A knowledgeable guide can take you places that you might never discover on your own, and you may be pushed to see more than you would have otherwise. Tours aren't for everyone, but they can be just the thing for trips to places where making travel arrangements is difficult or time-consuming (particularly when you don't speak the language).

Whenever you book a guided tour, find out what's included and what isn't. A "land-only" tour includes all your travel (by bus, in most cases) in the destination, but not necessarily your flights to and from or even within it. Also, in most cases prices in tour brochures don't include fees and taxes. And remember that you'll be expected to tip your guide (in cash) at the end of the tour.

TRANSPORTATION

Germany's transportation infrastructure is extremely well developed, so all areas of the country are well connected to each other by road, rail, and air. The Autobahn is an efficient system of highways, although it can get crowded during holidays. In winter, you may have to contend with closed passes in the Alps. High-speed trains are perhaps the most comfortable way of traveling. Munich to Hamburg, for example, a trip of around 966 km (600 mi), takes at most six hours. Many airlines offer extremely cheap last-minute flights, but you have to be fairly flexible.

▌ BY AIR

Flying time to Munich is 2 hours from London, 8½ hours from New York, 9½ hours from Chicago, and 11½ hours from Los Angeles.

Airlines & Airports Airline and Airport Links.com (⊕www.airlineandairportlinks.com) has links to many of the world's airlines and airports.

Airline Security Issues Transportation Security Administration (⊕www.tsa.gov) has answers for almost every question that might come up.

AIRPORTS

Frankfurt is Germany's air hub, but there are a few nonstop services from North America to Munich.

Airport Information Frankfurt: **Flughafen Frankfurt Main** (FRA ☎01805/372–4636, 069/6900 from outside Germany ⊕www.frankfurt-airport.de).

Munich: **Flughafen München** (MUC ☎089/97500 ⊕www.munich-airport.de).

FLIGHTS

Lufthansa is Germany's leading carrier and has shared mileage plans and flights with Air Canada and United, among other airlines.

Germany's internal air network is excellent, with flights linking all major cities in little more than an hour. A handful of smaller airlines—Deutsche BA, Germanwings, and TUIfly—compete with low-fare flights within Germany and to other European cities. These companies are reliable, do most of their business over the Internet, and often beat the German rail fares. The earlier you book, the cheaper the fare.

Airline Contacts Air Canada (☎888/247–2262). **American Airlines** (☎800/433–7300 ⊕www.aa.com). **Continental Airlines** (☎800/523–3273 for U.S. and Mexico reservations, 800/231–0856 for international reservations ⊕www.continental.com). **Delta Airlines** (☎800/221–1212 for U.S. reservations, 800/241–4141 for international reservations ⊕www.delta.com). **Icelandair** (☎800/223–5500 ⊕www.Icelandair.com). **LTU** (☎866/266–5588 ⊕www.ltu.de). **Lufthansa** (☎800/645–3880 ⊕www.lufthansa.com). **Northwest Airlines** (☎800/225–2525 ⊕www.nwa.com). **United Airlines** (☎800/864–8331 for U.S. reservations, 800/538–2929 for international reservations ⊕www.united.com). **USAirways** (☎800/428–4322 for U.S. and Canada reservations, 800/622–1015 for international reservations ⊕www.usairways.com).

Within Germany Air Berlin (☎01805/737–800, 0870/738–8880 in the U.K. ⊕www.airberlin.com). **Deutsche BA** (☎01805/359–322 ⊕www.flydba.com). **Germanwings** (☎0900/191–9100 ⊕www.germanwings.com). **TUIfly** (☎01805/757–510 ⊕www.TUIfly.com). **Lufthansa** (☎0180/380–3803 or 0180/5838–42672 ⊕www.lufthansa.com).

▌ BY BUS

Germany has good local bus service. Deutsche Touring, a subsidiary of the Deutsche Bahn, has offices and agents countrywide and travels from Germany to other European cities. You can check

FLYING 101

Flying may not be as carefree as it once was, but there are some things you can do to make your trip smoother.

Minimize the time spent standing in line. Buy an e-ticket, check in at an electronic kiosk, or—even better—check in on your airline's Web site before leaving home. Pack light and limit carry-on items to only the essentials.

Arrive when you need to. Research your airline's policy. It's usually at least an hour before domestic flights and two to three hours before international flights. But airlines at some busy airports have more stringent requirements. Check the TSA Web site for estimated security waiting times at major airports.

Get to the gate. If you aren't at the gate at least 10 minutes before your flight is scheduled to take off (sometimes earlier), you won't be allowed to board.

Double-check your flight times. Do this especially if you reserved far in advance. Schedules change, and alerts may not reach you.

Don't go hungry. Ask whether your airline offers anything to eat; even when it does, be prepared to pay.

Get the seat you want. Often, you can pick a seat when you buy your ticket on an airline Web site. But it's not guaranteed; the airline could change the plane after you book, so double-check. You can also select a seat if you check in electronically. Avoid seats on the aisle directly across from the lavatories. Frequent fliers say those are even worse than back-row seats that don't recline.

Got kids? Get info. Ask the airline about its children's menus, activities, and fares. Sometimes infants and toddlers fly free if they sit on a parent's lap, and older children fly for half price in their own seats. Also inquire about policies involving car seats; having one may limit seating options. Also ask about seat-belt extenders for car seats. And note that you can't count on a flight attendant to produce an extender; you may have to ask for one when you board.

Check your scheduling. Don't buy a ticket if there's less than an hour between connecting flights. Although schedules are padded, if anything goes wrong you might miss your connection. If you're traveling to an important function, depart a day early.

Bring paper. Even when using an e-ticket, always carry a hard copy of your receipt; you may need it to get your boarding pass, which most airports require to get past security.

Complain at the airport. If your baggage goes astray or your flight goes awry, complain before leaving the airport. Most carriers require this.

Beware of overbooked flights. If a flight is oversold, the gate agent will usually ask for volunteers and offer some sort of compensation for taking a different flight. If you're bumped from a flight *involuntarily*, the airline must give you some kind of compensation if an alternate flight can't be found within one hour.

Know your rights. If your flight is delayed because of something within the airline's control (bad weather doesn't count), the airline must get you to your destination on the same day, even if they have to book you on another airline and in an upgraded class. Read the Contract of Carriage, which is usually buried on the airline's Web site.

Be prepared. The Boy Scout motto is especially important if you're traveling during a stormy season. To quickly adjust your plans, program a few numbers into your cell: your airline, an airport hotel or two, your destination hotel, your car service, and/or your travel agent.

its bilingual German-English Web site for schedules. It offers one-day tours along the Romantic Road. The Romantic Road route is between Würzburg (with connections to and from Frankfurt) and Füssen (with connections to and from Munich, Augsburg, and Garmisch-Partenkirchen). With a regular Deutsche Bahn rail ticket, Eurailpass, or German Rail Pass you get a 60% discount on this route. Buses, with an attendant on board, travel in each direction between April and October.

All towns of any size have local buses, which often link up with trams (streetcars) and electric railway (S-bahn) and subway (U-bahn) services. Fares sometimes vary according to distance, but a ticket usually allows you to transfer freely between the various forms of transportation. Most cities issue day tickets at special rates.

Bus Information Deutsche Touring (☎069/790–350 ⊕www.deutsche-touring.de).

∎ BY CAR

Entry formalities for motorists are few: all you need is proof of insurance, an international car-registration document, and a U.S., Canadian, Australian, or New Zealand driver's license. If you or your car is from an EU country, Norway, or Switzerland, all you need is your domestic license and proof of insurance. *All* foreign cars must have a country sticker. There are no toll roads in Germany, except for a few Alpine mountain passes.

GASOLINE

Gasoline costs are around €1.39 per liter—which is higher than in the United States. Some cars use diesel fuel, which is about €0.15 cheaper, so if you're renting a car, find out which fuel the car takes. German filling stations are highly competitive, and bargains are often available if you shop around, but *not* at autobahn filling stations. Self-service, or *SB-Tanken,* stations are cheapest. Pumps marked *Bleifrei* contain unleaded gas.

PARKING

Daytime parking in cities and small, historic towns is difficult to find. Restrictions are not always clearly marked and can be hard to understand when they are. Rental cars come with a "time wheel," which you can leave on your dashboard when parking signs indicate free, limited-time allowances. Larger parking lots have parking meters (*Parkautomaten*). After depositing enough change in a meter, you will be issued a timed ticket to display on your dashboard. Parking-meter spaces are free at night. In German garages you must pay immediately on returning to retrieve your car, not when driving out. Put the ticket you got on arrival into the machine and pay the amount displayed. Retrieve the ticket, and upon exiting the garage, insert the ticket in a slot to raise the barrier.

ROAD CONDITIONS

Roads are generally excellent. *Bundesstrasse* are two-lane highways, abbreviated "B," as in B–38. Autobahns are high-speed thruways abbreviated with "A," as in A–7. If the autobahn should be blocked for any reason, you can take an exit and follow little signs bearing a "U" followed by a number. These are official detours.

ROADSIDE EMERGENCIES

The German automobile clubs ADAC and AvD operate tow trucks on all autobahns. NOTRUF signs every 2 km (1 mi) on autobahns (and country roads) indicate emergency telephones. By picking up the phone, you'll be connected to an operator who can determine your exact location and get you the services you need. Help is free (with the exception of materials).

Emergency Services Roadside assistance (☎01802/222–222).

ROAD MAPS

The best-known road maps of Germany are put out by the automobile club ADAC, by Shell, and by the Falk Verlag. They're available at gas stations and bookstores.

RULES OF THE ROAD

In Germany, road signs give distances in kilometers. There *are* posted speed limits on autobahns, and they advise drivers to keep below 130 kph (80 mph) or 110 kph (65 mph). A sign saying *Richtgeschwindigkeit* and the speed indicates this. Speed limits on country roads vary from 70 kph to 100 kph (43 mph to 62 mph) and are usually 50 kph (30 mph) through small towns.

Don't enter a street with a signpost bearing a red circle with a white horizontal stripe—it's a one-way street. Blue EIN-BAHNSTRASSE signs indicate you're headed the correct way down a one-way street. The blood-alcohol limit for driving in Germany is very low (.05%). Note that seat belts must be worn at all times by front- *and* backseat passengers.

Note that German drivers tend to drive fast and aggressively. If you wish to drive comfortably on the autobahn, stay in the right lane. Speeds under 80 kph (50 mph) are not permitted. Though prohibited, tailgating is a favorite sport on German roads. Do not react by braking for no reason: this is equally prohibited. You may not use a hand-held mobile phone while driving.

SCENIC ROUTES

Germany has many specially designated tourist roads that serve as promotional tools for towns along their routes. The most famous is the Romantische Strasse *(Romantic Road)*, which runs from Würzburg to Füssen in the Alps, covering around 355 km (220 mi).

Among other notable touring routes are the Strasse der Kaiser und Könige (Route of Emperors and Kings), running from Frankfurt to Passau (and on to Vienna and Budapest); and the Deutsche Alpenstrasse, running the length of the country's Alpine southern border from near Berchtesgaden to Bodensee (Lake Constance).

∎ BY TRAIN

Deutsche Bahn (DB—German Rail) is a very efficient, privatized railway. Its high-speed InterCity Express (ICE), InterCity (IC), and EuroCity (EC) trains make journeys between the centers of many cities—Munich–Frankfurt, for example—faster by rail than by air. All InterCity and InterCity Express trains have restaurant cars and trolley service. RE, RB, and IRE trains are regional trains. It's also possible to sleep on the train and save a day of your trip. CityNightLine (CNL) trains serving Austria and Switzerland and Nachtzug ("night train" or NZ) long-distance trains have sleepers.

Once on your platform (*Gleis*), you can check the notice boards that give details of the layout of trains arriving on that track, showing the locations of first- and second-class cars and the restaurant car, as well as where they will stop along the platform. Large railroad stations have English-speaking staff handling information inquiries.

Fare and schedule information on the Deutsche Bahn information line connects you to a live operator; you may have to wait a few moments before someone can help you in English. The automated number is toll-free and gives schedule information. On the DB Web site, click on "English." A timetable mask will open up. To calculate the fare, enter your departure and arrival points, any town you wish to pass through, and if you have a bike.

If you would like to work out an itinerary beforehand, Deutsche Bahn has an excellent Web site in English (⊕*www.bahn.de*). It'll even tell you which type of train you'll be riding on—which could be important if you suffer from motion sickness. The ICE, the French TGV, the Swiss ICN, and the Italian Cisalpino all use "tilt technology" for a less jerky ride. One side effect, however, is that some passengers might feel queasy, especially if the track is curvy. An over-the-counter drug for motion sickness should help.

BAGGAGE

Most major train stations have luggage lockers (in four sizes). By inserting exact change into a storage unit, you release the unit's key. Prices range from €1 for a small locker to €3 for a "jumbo" one. Smaller towns' train stations may not have any storage options.

Throughout Germany, Deutsche Bahn can deliver your baggage from a private residence or hotel to another or even to one of six airports: Berlin, Frankfurt, Leipzig-Halle, Munich, Hamburg, or Hannover. You must have a valid rail ticket. Buy a *Kuriergepäck* ticket at any DB ticket counter at which time you must schedule a pickup three workdays before your flight. The service costs €14.90 for each of the first two suitcases and €15.80 for each suitcase thereafter.

DISCOUNTS

Deutsche Bahn offers many discount options with specific conditions, so do your homework on its Web site or ask about options at the counter before paying for a full-price ticket. For round-trip travel you can save 25% if you book at least three days in advance, 50% if you stay over a Saturday night and book at least three to seven days in advance. However, there's a limited number of seats sold at any of these discount prices, so book as early as possible, at least a week in advance, to get the savings. A discounted rate is called a *Sparpreis*. If you change your travel plans after booking, you will have to pay a fee. The surcharge for tickets bought on board is 10% of the ticket cost, or a minimum of €5.

The good news for families is that children under 15 travel free when accompanied by a parent or relative on normal, discounted, and some, but not all, special-fare tickets. However, you must indicate the number of children traveling with you when you purchase the ticket; to ride free,

the child (or children) must be listed on the ticket. If you have a ticket with 25% or 50% off, a *Mitfahrer-Rabatt* allows a second person to travel with you for a 50% discount (minimum of €15 for a second-class ticket). The *Schönes Wochenend Ticket* (Happy Weekend Ticket) provides unlimited travel on regional trains on Saturday or Sunday for up to five persons for €32 (€30 if purchased online or at vending machine). Groups of six or more should inquire about *Gruppen & Spar* (group) savings. In Bavaria, ask about the *Bayern-Ticket*, which lets up to five people travel from 9 AM to 3 AM for €25.

If you plan to travel by train within a day after your flight arrives, purchase a heavily discounted "Rail and Fly" ticket for DB trains at the same time you book your flight. Trains connect with 14 German airports.

FARES

A first-class seat is approximately 50% more than a second-class seat. For this premium you get a bit more legroom and the convenience of having meals delivered directly to your seat. Most people find second class entirely adequate. ICs and the later-generation ICE trains are equipped with electrical outlets for laptops and other gadgets.

Tickets purchased through Deutsche Bahn's Web site can be retrieved from station vending machines. Always check that your ticket is valid for the type of train you are planning to take, not just for the destination served. If you have the wrong type of ticket, you will have to pay the difference on the train, in cash.

The ReisePacket service is for travelers who are inexperienced, elderly, disabled, or just appreciative of extra help. It costs €11 and provides, among other things, help boarding, disembarking, and transferring on certain selected trains that serve the major cities and vacation areas. It also includes a seat reservation and a voucher for an on-board snack. Purchase the service at least one day before travel.

PASSES

If Germany is your only destination in Europe, consider purchasing a German Rail Pass, which allows 4 to 10 days of unlimited first- or second-class travel within a one-month period on any DB train, up to and including the ICE. A Twin Pass saves two people traveling together 50% off one person's fare. A Youth Pass, sold to those 12–25, is also much the same but for second-class travel only. Prices begin at $229 per person in second class. Twin Passes begin at $169 per person in second class, and Youth Passes begin at $188. Additional days may be added to either pass.

Rail 'n Drive combines train travel and car rental. For instance, two people pay $159 each for two rail-travel days and two car-rental days within a month. You can add up to three more rail days, and each additional car-rental day is $49.

Germany is one of 17 countries in which you can use Eurail Passes, which provide unlimited first-class rail travel in all participating countries for the duration of the pass. Two adults traveling together can pay either $499 each for 9 consecutive days of travel or $539 each for 10 days of travel within one month. The Youth fare is $378 for 15 consecutive days and $489 for 10 days within one month. Eurail Passes are available from most travel agents.

Eurail Passes and some of the German Rail passes must be purchased before you leave for Europe. You can purchase a German Rail pass for 5 or 10 days of travel within one month at the Frankfurt airport and at some German train stations, but the cost will be higher (a youth ticket for 5 days of travel is just under €149). When you buy your pass, consider purchasing Railpass insurance in case you lose it during your travels.

In order to comply with the strict rules about validating tickets before you begin travel, read the instructions carefully. Some tickets require that a train official validate your pass, while others require you to write in the first date of travel.

Many travelers assume that rail passes guarantee them seats on the trains they wish to ride. Not so. You need to book seats ahead even if you are using a rail pass; seat reservations are required on some European trains, particularly high-speed trains, and are a good idea during summer, national holidays, and on popular routes. If you board the train without a reserved seat, you take the chance of having to stand. You'll also need a reservation if you purchase sleeping accommodations. Reservations are free if you make them online at the Deutsche Bahn Web site or at the time of ticket purchase at a vending machine. Otherwise, seat reservations on InterRegion Express and InterCity trains cost €3, and a reservation is absolutely necessary for the ICE-Sprinter trains (€10 for second class). There are no reservations on regional trains.

Information Deutsche Bahn (German Rail ☎0800/150–7090 for automated schedule information, 11861 for 24-hr hotline €0.39 per minute, 491805/996–633 from outside Germany €0.12 per minute ⊕www.bahn. de). **Eurail** (⊕www.eurail.com). **Eurostar** (☎0870/518–6186).

ON THE GROUND

LOCAL DO'S & TABOOS

■ **Customs of the Country:** Being on time for appointments, even casual social ones, is very important. Germans are more formal in addressing each other than Americans. Always address acquaintances as Herr (Mr.) or Frau (Mrs.) plus their last name; do not call them by their first name unless invited to do so. The German language has an informal and formal pronoun for "you": formal is "*Sie*," and informal is "*du*." Even if adults are on a first-name basis with one another, they may still keep the *Sie* form between them.

■ Germans are less formal when it comes to nudity: a sign that reads FREIKÖRPER or FKK indicates a park or beach that allows nude sunbathing. If enjoying a sauna or steam bath, you will often be asked to remove all clothing.

■ **Greetings:** The standard *Guten Tag* is a way to greet people throughout the country, but in Bavaria, *Grüss Gott* (God's greetings) is standard. When you depart, say *Auf Wiedersehen* or try the Bavarian way of saying good-bye, *Pfueti*, a contraction of a phrase meaning "God protect you." "Hallo" is also used frequently, as is "Hi" among younger people. A less formal good-bye is *Tschüss* or *ciao*.

■ **Language:** Even if you speak German, you'll have trouble understanding Bavarians when they speak their dialect among themselves. Everyone can speak "high German" as well. English is spoken in most hotels, restaurants, airports, museums, and other places of interest. However, English is not widely spoken in rural areas nor by people over 50. Learning the basics before going is always a good idea, especially *bitte* (please) and *danke* (thank you). A good tip is to apologize for your poor German before asking a question in English. This makes locals feel respected and begins communication on the right foot.

▌ COMMUNICATIONS

INTERNET

Nearly all hotels have in-room data ports, but you may have to purchase, or borrow from the front desk, a cable with an end that matches German phone jacks. If you're plugging into a phone line, you'll need a local access number for a connection. Wireless Internet (called WLAN in Germany) is more and more common in high-end hotels. The service is not free, however. You must purchase blocks of time from the front desk or online using a credit card. The cost is fairly high, however, usually around €4 for 30 minutes.

There are alternatives. Some hotels have an Internet room for guests needing to check their e-mail. Otherwise, Internet cafés are common, and many bars and restaurants let you surf the Web.

Contacts Cybercafes (⊕ www.cybercafes. com) lists more than 4,000 Internet cafés worldwide.

PHONES

The good news is that you can now make a direct-dial telephone call from virtually any point on earth. The bad news? You can't always do so cheaply. Calling from a hotel is almost always the most expensive option; hotels usually add huge surcharges to all calls, particularly international ones. In some countries you can phone from call centers or even the post office. Calling cards usually keep costs to a minimum, but only if you purchase them locally. And then there are mobile phones *(⇨ below)*, which are sometimes more prevalent—particularly in the developing world—than land lines; as expensive as mobile phone calls can be, they are still usually a much cheaper option than calling from your hotel.

The country code for Germany is 49. When dialing a German number from abroad, drop the initial "0" from the local area code.

Many companies have service lines beginning with 0180. The cost of these calls averages €0.12 per minute. Numbers that begin with 0190 can cost €1.85 per minute and more.

CALLING WITHIN GERMANY

The German telephone system is very efficient, so it's unlikely you'll have to use an operator unless you're seeking information. For information in English dial 11837 for numbers within Germany and 11834 for numbers elsewhere. But first look for the number in the phone book or online (⊕*www.teleauskunft. de*), because directory assistance is costly. Calls to 11837 and 11834 cost at least €0.50, more if the call lasts more than 30 seconds.

A local call from a telephone booth costs €0.10 per minute. Dial the "0" before the area code when making a long-distance call within Germany. When dialing within a local area code, drop the "0" and the area code.

Telephone booths are not a common feature on the streets, so be prepared to walk out of your way to find one (most post offices have one). Phone booths have instructions in English as well as German. Most telephone booths in Germany are card-operated, so buy a phone card. Coin-operated phones, which take €0.10, €0.20, €0.50, €1, and €2 coins, don't make change.

CALLING OUTSIDE GERMANY

International calls can be made from any telephone booth in Germany. It costs only €0.13 per minute to call the United States, day or night, no matter how long the call lasts. Use a phone card. If you don't have a good deal with a calling card, there are many stores that offer international calls at rates well below what you will pay from a phone booth. At a hotel, rates will be at least double the regular charge.

CON OR CONCIERGE?

Good hotel concierges are invaluable—for arranging transportation, getting reservations at the hottest restaurant, and scoring tickets for a sold-out show or entrée to an exclusive nightclub. They're in the know and well connected. That said, sometimes you have to take their advice with a grain of salt.

It's not uncommon for restaurants to ply concierges with free food and drink in exchange for steering diners their way. Indeed, European concierges often receive referral *fees*. Hotel chains usually have guidelines about what their concierges can accept. The best concierges, however, are above reproach. This is particularly true of those who belong to the prestigious international society of Les Clefs d'Or.

What can you expect of a concierge? At a typical tourist-class hotel you can expect him or her to give you the basics: to show you something on a map, make a standard restaurant reservation (particularly if you don't speak the language), or help you book a tour or airport transportation. In Asia concierges perform the vital service of writing out the name or address of your destination for you to give to a cab driver.

Savvy concierges at the finest hotels and resorts can arrange for just about any good or service imaginable—and do so quickly. You should compensate them appropriately. A €10 tip is enough to show appreciation for a table at a hot restaurant. But the reward should really be much greater for tickets to that U2 concert that's been sold out for months or for those last-minute orchestra seats at the opera house.

Access Codes AT&T Direct (☎0800/225–5288). **Sprint International Access** (☎0800/888–0013). **MCI WorldPhone** (☎0800/888–8000).

CALLING CARDS

Post offices, newsstands, and exchange places sell cards with €5, €10, or €20 worth of credit to use at public pay phones. An advantage of a card: it charges only what the call costs. A €5 card with a good rate for calls to the United States, United Kingdom, and Canada is EuroExtra.

MOBILE PHONES

If you have a multiband phone (some countries use different frequencies than what's used in the United States) and your service provider uses the world-standard GSM network (as do T-Mobile, Cingular, and Verizon), you can probably use your phone abroad. Roaming fees can be steep, however: 99¢ a minute is considered reasonable. And overseas you normally pay the toll charges for incoming calls. It's almost always cheaper to send a text message than to make a call, since text messages have a very low set fee (often less than 5¢).

If you just want to make local calls, consider buying a new SIM card (note that your provider may have to unlock your phone for you to use a different SIM card) and a prepaid service plan in the destination. You'll then have a local number and can make local calls at local rates. If your trip is extensive, you could also simply buy a new cell phone in your destination, as the initial cost will be offset over time.

■**TIP**➔**If you travel internationally frequently, save one of your old mobile phones or buy a cheap one on the Internet; ask your cell phone company to unlock it for you, and take it with you as a travel phone, buying a new SIM card with pay-as-you-go service in each destination.**

Contacts Cellular Abroad (☎800/287–5072 ⊕www.cellularabroad.com) rents and sells GMS phones and sells SIM cards that work in many countries. **Mobal** (☎888/888–9162 ⊕www.mobalrental.com) rents mobiles and sells GSM phones (starting at $49) that will operate in 140 countries. Per-call rates vary throughout the world. **Planet Fone** (☎888/988–4777 ⊕www.planetfone.com) rents cell phones, but the per-minute rates are expensive.

■ CUSTOMS & DUTIES

You're always allowed to bring goods of a certain value back home without having to pay any duty or import tax. But there's a limit on the amount of tobacco and liquor you can bring back duty-free, and some countries have separate limits for perfumes; for exact figures, check with your customs department. The values of so-called "duty-free" goods are included in these amounts. When you shop abroad, save all your receipts, as customs inspectors may ask to see them as well as the items you purchased. If the total value of your goods is more than the duty-free limit, you'll have to pay a tax (most often a flat percentage) on the value of everything beyond that limit.

For anyone entering Germany from outside the EU, the following limitations apply: (1) 200 cigarettes or 100 cigarillos or 50 cigars or 250 grams of tobacco; (2) 2 liters of still table wine; (3) 1 liter of spirits over 22% volume or 2 liters of spirits under 22% volume (fortified and sparkling wines) or 2 more liters of table wine; (4) 50 grams of perfume and 250 milliliters of eau de toilette; (5) 500 grams of roasted coffee or 200 grams of instant coffee; (6) other goods to the value of €175.

If you have questions regarding customs or bringing a pet into the country, contact the Zoll-Infocenter, preferably by mail or e-mail.

Information in Germany Zoll-Infocenter (☎069/4699–7600 ⊕www.zoll.de).

U.S. Information U.S. Customs and Border Protection (🌐 www.cbp.gov).

▌ EATING OUT

Almost every street in Germany has its *Gaststätte,* a sort of combination restaurant and pub, and every village its *Gasthof,* or inn. The emphasis in either is on simple food at reasonable prices. A *Bierstube* (pub) or *Weinstube* (wine cellar) may also serve light snacks or meals.

Service can be slow, but you'll never be rushed out of your seat. Something else that may seem jarring at first: people can, and do, join other parties at a table in a casual restaurant if seating is tight. It's common courtesy to ask first, though.

BUDGET EATING TIPS

Imbiss (snack) stands can be found in almost every busy shopping street, in parking lots, train stations, and near markets. They serve *Würste* (sausages), grilled, roasted, or boiled, and rolls filled with cheese, cold meat, or fish. Many stands sell Turkish-style wraps called *Döner.* Prices range from €1.50 to €2.50 per portion. It's acceptable to bring sandwich fixings to a beer garden and order a beer there.

Butcher shops, known as *Metzgerei,* often serve warm snacks or very good sandwiches. Try *Warmer Leberkäs mit Kartoffelsalat,* a typical Bavarian specialty, which is a sort of baked meat loaf with mustard and potato salad.

Restaurants in department stores are especially recommended for appetizing and inexpensive lunches. Kaufhof, Karstadt, Wertheim, and Horton are names to note. Germany's vast selection of Turkish, Italian, Greek, Chinese, and Balkan restaurants are often inexpensive.

MEALS & MEALTIMES

Most hotels serve a buffet-style breakfast (*Frühstück*) of rolls, cheese, cold cuts, eggs, cereals, yogurt, and spreads, which is often included in the price of a room. Cafés, especially the more trendy ones, offer breakfast menus sometimes including pancakes, omelets, muesli, or even Thai rice soup. By American standards, a cup (*Tasse*) of coffee in Germany is very petite, and you don't get free refills. Order a *Pot* or *Kännchen* if you want a larger portion.

For lunch (*Mittagessen*), you can get sandwiches from most cafés and bakeries, and many fine restaurants have special lunch menus that make the gourmet experience much more affordable. Dinner (*Abendessen*) is usually accompanied by a potato or Spätzle side dish. A salad sometimes comes with the main dish.

Gaststätte normally serve hot meals from 11:30 AM to 9 PM; many places stop serving hot meals between 2 PM and 6 PM, although you can still order cold dishes. If you feel like a hot meal, look for a restaurant advertising *durchgehend geöffnet,* or look for a pizza parlor.

Once most restaurants have closed, your options are limited. Take-out pizza parlors and Turkish eateries often stay open later. Failing that, your best option is a train station or a gas station with a convenience store. Many bars serve snacks.

Unless otherwise noted, the restaurants listed in this guide are open daily for lunch and dinner.

PAYING

Credit cards are generally accepted only in moderate to expensive restaurants, so check before sitting down. You will need to ask for the bill in order to get it from the waiter, the idea being that the table is yours for the evening. Round up the bill 5% to 10% and pay the waiter directly rather than leaving any money or tip on the table.

Meals are subject to 19% tax (abbreviated as MWST on your bill) and are included in the menu prices.

For guidelines on tipping see Tipping below.

CATEGORY	COST
$$$$	over €25
$$$	€21–€25
$$	€16–€20
$	€9–€15
¢	under €9

Restaurant prices are per person for a main course at dinner.

RESERVATIONS & DRESS

Regardless of where you are, it's a good idea to make a reservation if you can. We only mention them specifically when reservations are essential (there's no other way you'll ever get a table) or when they are not accepted. For popular restaurants, book as far ahead as you can (often 30 days), and reconfirm as soon as you arrive. (Large parties should always call ahead to check the reservations policy.) We mention dress only when men are required to wear a jacket or a jacket and tie.

Note that even when Germans dress casually, their look is generally crisp and neat.

SMOKING

For such an otherwise health-conscious nation, Germans smoke a lot. When warm weather doesn't allow for open windows and terraces, bars can become uncomfortably smoky. No-smoking sections in restaurants are becoming increasingly popular, though they are seldom in separate rooms, so you may be a little inconvenienced. A smoker will find it intrusive if you request him or her to refrain.

WINES, BEER & SPIRITS

"Wines of Germany" promotes the wines of all 13 German wine regions and can supply you with information on wine-festivals and visitor-friendly wineries. It also arranges six-day guided winery tours in spring and fall in conjunction with the German Wine Academy.

WORD OF MOUTH

Was the service stellar or not up to snuff? Did the food give you shivers of delight or leave you cold? Did the prices and portions make you happy or sad? Rate restaurants and write your own reviews in Travel Ratings or start a discussion about your favorite places in Travel Talk on www.fodors. com. Your comments might even appear in our books. Yes, you, too, can be a correspondent!

Germany holds its brewers to a "purity law" that dates back to 1516. It's legal to drink beer from open containers in public, and having a beer at one's midday break is nothing to raise an eyebrow at. Bavaria is the place to try beer. While Munich's beers have achieved world fame—Löwenbräu and Paulaner, for example—beer connoisseurs will want to travel to places like Bamberg, where smaller breweries produce top-notch brews.

Wine Information German Wine Academy (☎06131/282–942 ⊕www.germanwines. de) **Wines of Germany** (☎212/994–7523 ⊕www.germanwineusa.org)

▎ ELECTRICITY

The electrical current in Germany is 220 volts, 50 cycles alternating current (AC); wall outlets take Continental-type plugs, with two round prongs.

Consider making a small investment in a universal adapter, which has several types of plugs in one lightweight, compact unit. Most laptops and mobile phone chargers are dual voltage (i.e., they operate equally well on 110 and 220 volts), so require only an adapter. These days the same is true of small appliances such as hair dryers. Always check labels and manufacturer instructions to be sure. Don't use 110-volt outlets marked FOR SHAVERS only for high-wattage appliances such as hair dryers.

Contacts **Steve Kropla's Help for World Traveler's** (⊕www.kropla.com) has Information on electrical and telephone plugs around the world. **Walkabout Travel Gear** (⊕www.walkabouttravelgear.com) has a good coverage of electricity under "adapters."

▌ EMERGENCIES

Throughout Germany call ☎110 for police, ☎112 for an ambulance or the fire department.

Foreign Embassies **Embassies** (✉Neustädtische Kirchstr. 4–5, D–10117 Berlin ✉Clayallee 170 [consular section] ☎030/83050, 030/832–9233 for American citizens ⊕www.usembassy.de).

▌ HEALTH

If you intend to do a lot of hiking, especially in the southern half of the country, be aware of the danger of ticks spreading Lyme disease. There is no vaccination against them, so prevention is important. Wear high shoes or boots, long pants, and light-color clothing. Use a good insect repellent, and check yourself for ticks after outdoor activities, especially if you've walked through high grass.

For information on travel insurance, shots and medications, and medical-assistance companies see Shots & Medications under Things to Consider in Before You Go, above.

▌ HOURS OF OPERATION

Banks are generally open weekdays from 8:30 or 9 AM to 3 or 4 PM (5 or 6 PM on Thursday), sometimes with a lunch break of about an hour at smaller branches. Some banks close by 2:30 on Friday afternoon. Banks at airports and main train stations open as early as 6:30 AM and close as late as 10:30 PM.

Most museums are open from Tuesday to Sunday 10–6. Some close for an hour or more at lunch. Many stay open until 8 PM

or later one day a week, usually Thursday. In smaller towns or in rural areas, museums may be open only on weekends or just a few hours a day.

Most pharmacies are open 9–6 weekdays and 9–1 on Saturday. Those in more prominent locations often open an hour earlier and/or close an hour later. A list of pharmacies in the vicinity that are open late or on Sunday is posted on the door under the sign *Apotheken-Bereitschaftsdienst.* When you find the pharmacy, it will have a bell you must ring.

All stores are closed on Sunday, with the exception of those in or near train stations. Larger stores are generally open from 9:30 or 10 AM to 7 or 8 PM on weekdays and close between 6 and 8 PM on Saturday. Smaller shops and some department stores in smaller towns close at 6 or 6:30 on weekdays and as early as 4 on Saturday. German shop owners take their closing times seriously. If you come in five minutes before closing, you may not be treated like royalty. Apologizing profusely and making a speedy purchase will help.

Along the autobahn and major highways as well as in larger cities, gas stations and their small convenience shops are often open late, if not around the clock.

HOLIDAYS

The following national holidays are observed in Bavaria: January 1; January 6 (Epiphany); Good Friday; Easter Monday; May 1 (Workers' Day); Ascension; Pentecost Monday; Corpus Christi; Assumption Day; October 3 (German Unity Day); November 1; December 24–26 (Christmas).

Pre-Lenten celebrations in Munich and Bavaria are known as Fasching, and are not as raucous as the Carneval celebrations in the Rhineland.

▮ MAIL

A post office in Germany (*Postamt*) is recognizable by the postal symbol, a black bugle on a yellow background. In some villages, you will find one in the local supermarket. Stamps (*Briefmarken*) can also be bought at some news agencies and souvenir shops. Post offices are generally open weekdays 8–6, Saturday 8–noon.

Airmail letters to the United States, Canada, Australia, and New Zealand cost €1.55; postcards, €1. All letters to the United Kingdom and within Europe cost €0.55; postcards, €0.45. These rates apply to standard-size envelopes. Letters take approximately 3–4 days to reach the United Kingdom, 5–7 days to the United States, and 7–10 days to Australia and New Zealand.

You can arrange to have mail (letters only) sent to you in care of any German post office; have the envelope marked "Postlagernd." This service is free, and the mail will be held for seven days. Or you can have mail sent to any American Express office in Germany. There's no charge to cardholders, holders of American Express traveler's checks, or anyone who has booked a vacation with American Express.

SHIPPING PACKAGES

Most major stores that cater to tourists will also ship your purchases home. You should check your insurance for coverage of possible damage.

The Deutsche Post has an express international service that will deliver your letter or package the next day to countries within the EU, within one to two days to the United States, and slightly longer to Australia. A letter or package to the United States weighing less than 200 grams costs €48.57. You can drop off your mail at any post office, or it can be picked up for an extra fee. Deutsche Post works in cooperation with DHL. International carriers tend to be slightly cheaper

(€35–€45 for the same letter) and provide more services.

Express Services Deutsche Post Express International (☎08105/345-2255 ⊕www.deutschepost.de). DHL (☎0800/225-5345 ⊕www.dhl.de). FedEx (☎0800/123-0800 ⊕www.fedex.com). UPS (☎0800/882-6630 ⊕www.ups.com).

▮ MONEY

Credit cards are welcomed by most businesses, so you probably won't have to use cash for payment in high-end hotels and restaurants. Many businesses on the other side of the spectrum don't accept them, however. It's a good idea to check in advance if you're staying in a budget lodging or eating in a simple country inn. When you get large bills in euros, either from an exchange service or out of an ATM, it's a good idea to break them immediately so that you have smaller bills for unexpected expenses, such as restroom attendants.

Prices throughout this guide are given for adults. Substantially reduced fees are almost always available for children, students, and senior citizens.

▮TIP→ **Banks never have every foreign currency on hand, and it may take as long as a week to order. If you're planning to exchange funds before leaving home, don't wait till the last minute.**

ATMS & BANKS

Twenty-four-hour ATMs (*Geldautomaten*) can be accessed with Plus or Cirrus credit and banking cards. Your own bank will probably charge a fee for using ATMs abroad, and some German banks exact €3–€5 fees for use of their ATMs. Nevertheless, you'll usually get a better rate of exchange via an ATM than you will at a currency-exchange office or even when changing money in a bank. And extracting funds as you need them is a safer option than carrying around a large amount of cash. Since some ATM keypads show no letters, know the numeric equivalent of your password.

■ **TIP→ PIN numbers with more than four digits are not recognized at ATMs in many countries. If yours has five or more, remember to change it before you leave.**

CREDIT CARDS

All major U.S. credit cards are accepted in Germany. The most frequently used are MasterCard and Visa. American Express is used less frequently, and Diner's Club even less. Since the credit card companies demand fairly substantial fees, some businesses will not accept credit cards for small purchases. Cheaper restaurants and lodgings often do not accept credit cards. It's always a good idea to ask beforehand.

Throughout this guide, the following abbreviations are used: **AE**, American Express; **DC**, Diners Club; **MC**, MasterCard; and **V**, Visa.

It's a good idea to inform your credit-card company before you travel, especially if you're going abroad and don't travel internationally very often. Otherwise, the credit-card company might put a hold on your card owing to unusual activity—not a good thing halfway through your trip. Record all your credit-card numbers—as well as the phone numbers to call if your cards are lost or stolen—in a safe place, so you're prepared should something go wrong. Both MasterCard and Visa have general numbers you can call (collect if you're abroad) if your card is lost, but you're better off calling the number of your issuing bank, since MasterCard and Visa usually just transfer you to your bank; your bank's number is usually printed on your card.

If you plan to use your credit card for cash advances, you'll need to apply for a PIN at least two weeks before your trip. Although it's usually cheaper (and safer) to use a credit card abroad for large purchases (so you can cancel payments or be reimbursed if there's a problem), note that some credit-card companies *and* the banks that issue them add substantial percentages to all foreign transactions, whether they're in a foreign currency or not. Check on these fees before leaving home, so there won't be any surprises when you get the bill.

■ **TIP→ Before you charge something, ask the merchant whether he or she plans to do a dynamic currency conversion (DCC). In such a transaction the credit-card *processor* (shop, restaurant, or hotel, not Visa or MasterCard) converts the currency and charges you in dollars. In most cases you'll pay the merchant a 3% fee for this service in addition to any credit-card company and issuing-bank foreign-transaction surcharges.**

Dynamic currency conversion programs are becoming increasingly widespread. Merchants who participate in them are supposed to ask whether you want to be charged in dollars or the local currency, but they don't always do so. And even if they do offer you a choice, they may well avoid mentioning the additional surcharges. The good news is that you *do* have a choice. And if this practice really gets your goat, you can avoid it entirely thanks to American Express; with its cards, DCC simply isn't an option.

Reporting Lost Cards American Express (☎800/992–3404 in U.S., 336/393–1111 collect from abroad ⊕www.americanexpress. com). **Diners Club** (☎800/234–6377 in U.S., 303/799–1504 collect from abroad ⊕www.dinersclub.com). **MasterCard** (☎800/622–7747 in U.S., 636/722–7111 collect from abroad ⊕www.mastercard.com). **Visa** (☎800/847–2911 in U.S., 410/581–9994 collect from abroad ⊕www.visa.com).

CURRENCY & EXCHANGE

Germany shares a common currency, the euro (€), with 11 other countries: Austria, Belgium, Finland, France, Greece, Ireland, Italy, Luxembourg, the Netherlands, Portugal, and Spain. The euro is divided into 100 cents. There are bills of 5, 10, 20, 50, 100, and 500 euros and

WORST-CASE SCENARIO

All your money and credit cards have just been stolen. In these days of real-time transactions, this isn't a predicament that should destroy your vacation.

First, report the theft of the credit cards. Then get any traveler's checks you were carrying replaced. This can usually be done almost immediately, provided that you kept a record of the serial numbers separate from the checks themselves.

If you bank at a large international bank like Citibank or HSBC, go to the closest branch; if you know your account number, chances are you can get a new ATM card and withdraw money right away.

Western Union (☎ 800/325–6000 ⊕ www.westernunion.com) sends money almost anywhere. Have someone back home order a transfer online, over the phone, or at one of the company's offices, which is the cheapest option.

The U.S. State Department's **Overseas Citizens Services** (☎ 202/647–5225) can wire money to any U.S. consulate or embassy abroad for a fee of $30. Just have someone back home wire money or send a money order or cashier's check to the state department, which will then disburse the funds as soon as the next working day after it receives them.

coins of €1 and €2, and 1, 2, 5, 10, 20, and 50 cents.

You should have no problem exchanging currency. The large number of banks and exchange services means that you can shop around for the best rate, if you're so inclined. But the cheapest and easiest way to go is using your ATM card.

At this writing, the exchange rate was €0.69 for a U.S. dollar.

■TIP➜ Even if a currency-exchange booth has a sign promising no commission, rest assured that there's some kind of huge, hidden fee. (Oh ... that's right. The sign didn't say no *fee*.). And as for rates, you're almost always better off getting foreign currency at an ATM or exchanging money at a bank.

TRAVELER'S CHECKS & CARDS

Some consider this the currency of the cave man, and it's true that fewer establishments accept traveler's checks these days. Nevertheless, they're a cheap and secure way to carry extra money, particularly on trips to urban areas. Both Citibank (under the Visa brand) and American Express issue traveler's checks in the United States, but Amex is better known and more widely accepted; you can also avoid hefty surcharges by cashing Amex checks at Amex offices. Whatever you do, keep track of all the serial numbers in case the checks are lost or stolen.

American Express now offers a stored-value card called a Travelers Cheque Card, which you can use wherever American Express credit cards are accepted, including ATMs. The card can carry a minimum of $300 and a maximum of $2,700, and it's a very safe way to carry your funds. Although you can get replacement funds in 24 hours if your card is lost or stolen, it doesn't really strike us as a very good deal. In addition to a high initial cost ($14.95 to set up the card, plus $5 each time you "reload"), you still have to pay a 2% fee for each purchase in a foreign currency (similar to that of any credit card). Further, each time you use the card in an ATM you pay a transaction fee of $2.50 on top of the 2% transaction fee for the conversion—add it all up and it can be considerably more than you would pay when simply using your own ATM card. Regular traveler's checks are just as secure and cost less.

Contacts American Express (☎ 888/412–6945 in U.S., 801/945–9450 collect outside of the U.S. to add value or speak to customer service ⊕ www.americanexpress.com).

▌ RESTROOMS

Public restrooms do exist, although you are not guaranteed to find one in an emergency. If you are in need, there are several options. You can enter the next café or restaurant and ask very politely to use the facilities. You can find a department store and look for the "WC" sign. Museums are also a good place to find facilities.

Train stations are increasingly turning to McClean, a privately run enterprise that demands €0.60 to €1.10 for admission to its restrooms. These facilities, staffed by attendants who clean almost constantly, sparkle. You won't find them in smaller stations, however. Their restrooms are usually adequate, however.

On the highways, the vast majority of gas stations have public restrooms, though you may have to ask for a key. We won't vouch for their cleanliness, however. You might want to wait until you see a sign for a restaurant.

It's customary to leave a €0.20–€0.30 gratuity if a restroom has an attendant.

Find a Loo The Bathroom Diaries (⊕www. thebathroomdiaries.com) is flush with unsanitized info on restrooms the world over—each one located, reviewed, and rated.

▌ SAFETY

Germany has one of the lowest crime rates in Europe. There are some areas, such as the neighborhood around train stations and the streets surrounding red-light districts, where you should keep an eye out for potential dangers. The best advice is to take the usual precautions. Secure your valuables in the hotel safe. Don't wear flashy jewelry, and keep expensive electronics out of sight when you are not using them. Carry shoulder bags or purses so that they can't be easily snatched, and never leave them hanging on the back of a chair at a café or restaurant. Avoid walking alone at night, even in relatively safe neighborhoods.

When withdrawing cash, don't use an ATM in a deserted area. Make sure that no one is looking over your shoulder when you enter your PIN code. And never use a machine that appears to have been tampred with.

▌TIP→ Distribute your cash, credit cards, IDs, and other valuables between a deep front pocket, an inside jacket or vest pocket, and a hidden money pouch. Don't reach for the money pouch once you're in public.

▌ TAXES

Most prices you see on items already include Germany's 19% value-added tax (V.A.T.) included. Some goods, such as books and antiquities, carry a 7% V.A.T. as a percentage of the purchase price. An item must cost at least €25 to qualify for a V.A.T. refund.

When making a purchase, ask for a V.A.T. refund form and find out whether the merchant gives refunds—not all stores do, nor are they required to. Have the form stamped like any customs form by customs officials when you leave the country or, if you're visiting several European Union countries, when you leave the EU. After you're through passport control, take the form to a refund-service counter for an on-the-spot refund (which is usually the quickest and easiest option), or mail it to the address on the form (or the envelope with it) after you arrive home. You receive the total refund stated on the form, but the processing time can be long, especially if you request a credit-card adjustment.

Global Refund is a Europe-wide service with 225,000 affiliated stores and more than 700 refund counters at major airports and border crossings. Its refund form, called a Tax Free Check, is the most common across the European continent.

The service issues refunds in the form of cash, check, or credit-card adjustment.

V.A.T. REFUNDS AT THE AIRPORT

If you're departing from Terminal 1 at Frankfurt Airport, where you bring your purchases to claim your tax back depends on how you've packed the goods. If the items are in your checked luggage, check in as normal, but let the ticket counter know you have to claim your tax still. They will give you your luggage back to bring to the customs office in departure hall B, Level 2. For goods you are carrying on the plane with you, go to the customs office on the way to your gate. After you pass through passport control, there is a Global Refund office.

If you're departing from Terminal 2, bring goods in luggage to be checked to the customs office in Hall D, Level 2 (opposite the Delta Airlines check-in counters). For goods you are carrying on the plane with you, see the customs office in Hall E, Level 3 (near security control).

At Munich's airport, the Terminal 2 customs area is on the same level as check-in. If your V.A.T. refund items are in your luggage, check in first, and then bring your bags to the customs office on Level 04. From here, your bags will be sent to your flight and you can go to the Global Refund counter around the corner. If your refund items are in your carry-on, go to the Global Refund office in the customs area on Level 05 south. Terminal 1 has customs areas in modules C and D, Level 04.

V.A.T. Refunds Global Refund (☎800/566-9828 ⊕www.globalrefund.com).

▌ TIME

Germany is on Central European Time, which is six hours ahead of Eastern Standard Time and nine hours ahead of Pacific Standard Time. Daylight savings time begins on the last Sunday in October and ends on the last Sunday in March.

Germans use military time (1 PM is indicated as 13:00) and write the date before the month, so October 3 will appear as 03.10.

▌ TIPPING

Tipping is done at your own discretion. Theater ushers and tour guides do not necessarily expect a tip, while waiters, bartenders, and taxi drivers do. Rounding off bills to the next highest sum is customary for bills under €10. Above that sum you should add a little more. In hotels you should tip bellhops and porters €1 per bag or service. It's also customary to leave a small tip (a euro or so per night) for the room-cleaning staff. Whether you tip the desk clerk depends on whether he or she has given you any special service.

Service charges are included in all restaurant checks (listed as *Bedienung*), as is tax (listed as *MWST*). Nonetheless, it is customary to round up the bill to the nearest euro or to leave about 5%–10%. Give it to the waitstaff as you pay the bill; don't leave it on the table, as that's considered rude. Bartenders don't expect tips, but do appreciate them. Those who bring drinks to your table do expect a small tip.

In taxis, round up the fare. The change is fine for a short journey, while a tip of about a euro is appropriate for a longer trip. This means that for a €6.40 fare, give the driver €7. For a €12.30 fare, give €13.50. Give a bit more if you have particularly cumbersome or heavy luggage.

TIPPING GUIDELINES FOR BAVARIA

Bartender	Round up the bill for small purchases. For rounds of drinks, around 10% is appropriate.
Bellhop	€1 per item.
Hotel Concierge	€3–€5 if the concierge performs a special service for you.
Hotel Doorman	€1–€2 if he helps you get a cab.
Hotel Maid	€1 per day.
Hotel Room-Service Waiter	€1 per delivery.
Taxi Driver	Round up the fare if the ride is short. For longer trips, about €1 is appropriate.
Tour Guide	€1–€2, or a bit more if the tour was especially good.
Valet Parking Attendant	€1–€2, but only when you retrieve your car.
Waiter	Round off the bill, giving 5% to 10% for very good service.
Restroom Attendant	€0.20–€0.30 is fine for most places, but about €1 is expected in high-end establishments.

INDEX

PHOTO CREDITS

NOTES

ABOUT OUR WRITERS

Uli Ehrhardt, a native German, has had a long career in the travel and tourism fields. He began as an interpreter and travel consultant in the United States and then for 20 years served as director of the State Tourist Board Bodensee–Oberschwaben (Lake Constance–Upper Swabia). He now makes his home in the city of Ulm as a tourism consultant, writer, and teacher at a state college for tourism.

Marton Radkai is a native New Yorker of Bavarian-Hungarian descent and lives in Munich. Since 1985 he has worked as a travel photographer, translator, editor, and writer for radio and print media in Germany and Austria.

Horst E. Reischenböck is an authority not only for his hometown of Salzburg but also for Austria in general. The author of two books on Salzburg's music history, he has worked for four decades as a journalist and as a personal guide for English-speaking visitors.

Kevin White is a native of California who has spent much of the last 10 years working overseas, finally settling in Munich in 1999 as a freelance translator, writer, and editor for a variety of publications and agencies.